About the Author

CAS le Hane was born in the city of Cape Town, South Africa. He has told and written stories that fascinate, intrigue and cause laughter. This book includes the story that he has not had the courage to tell.

This book would not be possible had it not been for the many years of support and encouragement given me by Alyda, my wife.

To my wonderful son and daughter, Rudi and Leila

About the front cover

Conceptualised by Rudi le Hane

The work does not reflect the reality; instead, it serves to introduce narrative by bringing together two landscapes that are thousands of kilometres apart.

CAS le Hane

THE BLUE SUITCASE

AUSTIN MACAULEY
PUBLISHERS LTD.

A CIP catalogue record for this title is available from the British Library.

ISBN 9781785542275 (Paperback)
ISBN 9781785542282 (Hardback)
ISBN 9781786129741 (E-Book)

www.austinmacauley.com

First Published (2016)
Austin Macauley Publishers Ltd.
25 Canada Square
Canary Wharf
London
E14 5LQ

Acknowledgments

Mrs Joan Cameron, Father Larry Kaufmann and Dr Elizabeth Leaver.

Author statement:

This story is a compilation and dramatization of actual events. All the characters mentioned are based on people I know.
Place names and that of individuals have been changed.

Contents

Prologue

"Ya! Boy! Sam! Stop talking to the dog!"

Pa was born with a cleft palate and as a result he spoke through his nose, not like other people whose voices are heard through their mouths. As a boy I never knew about this. Pa's must have been one of the first voices I heard, so how then was I to know that it was different? No one ever said anything about my Pa's speech defect, neither my sister, Jane nor my Ma.

"Ya!" was a term Pa used before speaking, as if to clear his nasal passages for the sound to travel through, otherwise it would be muffled and then I too had difficulty understanding what he was saying.

Maybe it was due to this, and the way people treated him, that Pa was strange. I don't really know.

"I can't understand why Pa is so naughty." That is what Ma said whenever Pa disappointed us. At first it was nothing, but later, as I grew to be a man, things started not to add up.

I tell this story as an adult. To look back is sometimes sore, so bear with me, please? Through the process of creating this work, which has been brewing in my head for more than thirty years, I realised why Ma was sometimes bitter and always at war with Pa. Maybe after reading this you will realise too, or maybe you will be cross with Ma.

Pa must have been ridiculed as a child. Children are often cruel towards one other—adults are sometimes more so—I know this from personal experience.

Jane, my older sister and I were both born at St Monica's Maternity Home in Bo-Kaap, the Malay quarter of Cape Town.

She and I were teased when we arrived at boarding school in Natal, a province on the east coast of South Africa and about one thousand five hundred kilometres away from Cape Town. We were teased because Jane's skin was too light and I was left handed. A further oddity was that at first Jane had ash blonde hair. I too had light coloured hair, but within a few years it changed. My hair became darker, which helped me blend in, albeit just a bit. I spoke with a Cape Town accent. The other children laughed at me. They said of my speaking that it sounded as if I was trying to sing. This too changed and like Jane I also became slightly more accepted.

At least we, Jane and I, could adapt but Pa's scars made him appear eccentric; or maybe he pretended?

I turned ten years old in the last quarter of 1970. It was then, and quite by chance, that I discovered my father's voice sounded different.

We were buying cakes at a shop in Tokai, an affluent suburb on the southern part of Cape Town's Peninsula. There were many customers waiting to be served that afternoon. A nearby school, Zwaanswyk High School, had already finished for the day and many of those pupils were in the shop. Most, like us, were there to buy the cheaper day-old cakes. When it was Pa's turn he ordered two banana, date and honey loaves, and with a quick turn to me he asked: "Ya! Would you care to have cinnamon buns?" After my eager nod Pa asked the shop assistant to add four buns. By her manner it was obvious that she did not understand anything Pa had said, even though he repeated the request several times. I think that she didn't want to give offence, so instead of battling to understand and have him repeat it yet again, the shop assistant followed where he pointed.

By then the younger people in the shop were sniggering. I overheard a boy exclaim to his friends: "He's a blowy," and then the same boy touched his nose in a gesture to demonstrate what he meant. "He talks through his nose," said another. The commentary was about Pa and the boys were speaking loud enough for him to hear. I felt like saying "Ssh!" but it was too late because my Pa had already heard. He chose to ignore the comments from those little boys that afternoon. In time I learned that Pa often ignored talk when it was too painful to hear.

That afternoon's realisation answered a question I carried in my child-mind: why did Pa hear certain things and not others? At times Pa pretended to be deaf because - and I worked this one out by myself - if he didn't hear then there was no need to respond. If he did not respond then people wouldn't laugh at the sound of his voice.

I suppose that was how he protected himself: if he did not hear then there was no need to feel foolish when those who had no empathy chose to laugh and mock my Pa's sound.

This is what happened in the shop that afternoon when I was almost ten. They, those schoolboys, laughed and mocked my Pa. I sensed his humiliation.

As we walked through the doorway with our cakes in a brown paper bag, all the schoolboys had smiles plastered across their faces. Those smiles were not friendly. When we were outside I heard the chorus of mockery continue. Pa too must have heard.

I carried the cake while Pa searched his pockets for the car keys. He always misplaced car keys. We drove in the blue Mini Minor Panel Van, Pa's car. He had a choice when buying the car, either the Mini, or a Renault 4—he chose the Mini.

Pa was unusually silent while driving on that afternoon. He seemed cross and drove the car very hard. Usually Pa was a cautious driver, irritatingly so, was what I always thought, but that afternoon he was firm with the steering wheel, all the while pretending that nothing was the matter.

My recollection of the day, the day I learned that my hero spoke through his nose, remains vivid. I felt sorry for Pa.

And I was embarrassed too. I was often embarrassed by Pa, but that afternoon was different. It was not Pa's fault that he was born with a defective palate. There was no need for me to be embarrassed by the clothes Pa wore, or by the way his hair was groomed. His eccentric manner and funny beard; that insatiable need to lock everything away and be secretive were also not to be embarrassed about. Neither was I embarrassed about Pa being blunt with people whom he did not like much, or that he wore odd shoes which he painted with wall paint. *I was not embarrassed because all those things can be changed, but how do we fix a broken voice?* I asked myself.

Even though it repeated in my mind, I didn't discuss what happened in the cake shop with anyone.

Pa, Samuel Arthur Levy, continued to be my hero, but why hadn't I noticed his speech defect before that fateful day in the cake shop? Yes, later I also found it odd that Pa and I have the same names. What else didn't I know?

We went to that cake shop because Pa was en route to Simon's Town. It had been a long time since I was allowed to travel along. Simon's Town, where the South African Naval Base is located, is the southernmost town on the Cape Peninsula, down at the foot of Africa.

When we got there Pa parked on the side of Main Road, right near the statue of Just Nuisance in Jubilee Square (Just Nuisance, a Great Dane, is the only dog ever to be officially enlisted in the Royal Navy). I had to sit on a bench near the statue and keep an eye on the car, which was Pa's instruction. As soon as I got out Pa locked the car and disappeared inside an art shop across the road. Through the shop window I could see glimpses of Pa and a taller man in animated discussion. There were no other people in the shop. To pass time I walked, one foot over the other, all along a line that marked the border of the square, balancing with my arms outstretched as I went along. When done, I sat on the bench as instructed until Pa returned.

"What was the meeting about, Pa?"

"Ya! It was about business." He almost barked that reply.

The drive home was better. Pa seemed less cross. It was fun driving along the sea. We passed Fish Hoek and drove on toward Kalk Bay. After Kalk Bay we passed Muizenberg. In the corner of Muizenberg Beach people rode the waves on boards that were strapped to their legs. We were so close that I could see their faces across the railway line. We crossed over Sunrise Circle, a roundabout in the road, and then headed along Prince George Drive to where we lived.

What happened in the cake shop kept repeating in my head. In a way I was pleased that my school holiday was about to end. Jane and I were to journey back to boarding school in a few days' time. Three days on the train, that was how long it took.

When we were on the train Jane sensed that I was hiding something from her. At intermittent and most unexpected times, she'd ask: "So, what happened at home Sammy; why aren't you telling me?"

In reply I would make up a story ... My wish was to discuss how I felt, yes, but it had to be with Ma. I did not want to discuss it with Jane, and I had no real reason why, or one that comes to mind—it was just a feeling. There were other questions too, which I wanted Ma to answer.

Ma was a social worker and she listened to everyone when they had problems. When I could sit down and tell her about what happened in the cake shop then it would be my turn. I wanted my own turn.

§

Then we were back at boarding school and life continued in the way that had become the norm for Jane and me. While at school, neither of us knew when next we'd be able to return home.

Almost two years passed before I saw my chance to speak with Ma like I had planned to do. It was a Friday evening. Ma and I were going to be alone after she finished work. My twelfth birthday was just four months away. Jane and I both celebrated our birthdays in October. It would be her seventeenth and my twelfth. We were always at school on our birthday.

That June evening with Ma was going to be special, I knew. My plan was to pretend that it was our birthday, even though Jane was not there to play her part. It also created the opportunity for which I had been wishing; when I could talk about what happened in the cake shop. I remembered everything as if it had happened the day before.

Jane had not travelled home with me that time because Mr van Heerden, the owner of Chubby Chicken, a butcher shop near our school, had asked her to work as his cashier for the duration of the school holidays. The usual cashier was on maternity leave. Jane was happy to work because it meant that with the money she'd earn, both of us would be able to travel home for Christmas. Although I was tall, my age disqualified me from being employed.

So, instead of spending yet another holiday with the school care giver, Mammy Cynthia and her family, at their home in Mpophomeni, Jane agreed that I could travel home alone to spend the June winter recess with Ma.

I did not enjoy having to travel home on my own. The saddest part of the journey, when I travelled alone, was when the train got closer to Cape Town Station. The highlight of the trip was to share the excitement of being close to home with Jane. That was what I missed most when travelling alone.

It was my last night at home. I wished that Ma would finish with her client, so that we could talk. My school train was scheduled to depart from Cape Town the following day, Saturday afternoon.

Ma's final client for the day took long to finish. Pa was away, working, he said; Pa was always working.

By then Pa was no longer arriving home at six in the evening, as had been his custom. No, by then he left for work, and sometimes returned three days later. That time too, when I arrived home he had been away for many days, and it took another while before he returned.

Once, I remember, the inside of his car seemed like someone had been bleeding there. Later on the same day, when I checked to confirm that it was blood I saw, the stains had been removed. It was again not my place to ask. None of us knew what work Pa did. It was a secret. He kept it a secret and whenever any of us asked he'd tell an obvious lie. I followed Pa one day, but it proved impossible on my bicycle.

Ma had a lot to say about Pa not being home. She would scold but he'd insist: "I have to work, otherwise we won't have a house for much longer." After each squabble with Ma, Pa got in his car and drove off, returning home a week later, that was his new norm. I had been home for two weeks when Pa eventually arrived back.

"Ya! Were you expelled from school? Why are you home for such a long time?"

The Friday afternoon seemed to drag. Ma's last consultation for the day went on for much longer than was expected. I dawdled in the house; looked at Pa's carpets and his paintings. There were newspaper clippings that he had accumulated. It was held together with a big paper grip. He hung the clippings on a hook behind a curtain in the lounge room.

My bags were packed for the journey back to school, and back to Jane. I continued to busy myself while waiting for Ma. Our plan was to spend the last night at home talking with each other and I would make believe it to be our birthday. I was becoming anxious to get started. It was difficult to know when Ma and I would be together next. Something could happen, as it often did.

Each year Jane and I planned to come home for Christmas, but sometimes, for unknown reasons, we would not be able to undertake the journey. Neither of us ever understood why that happened. It was no surprise then, when Jane insisted that she earn the train fare for us to travel home for the December holidays.

Ma's client must have had a serious problem that Friday evening because they took forever to finish. To kill more time I stood upstairs in Ma's room singing quietly to myself while looking down on the flooded street. It had been raining on and off for about a week. The June winter holidays were over. Cape schools had re-opened. School terms were different in each of the four provinces.

The rain fell steadily. Cape Town was wet and windy. Some say that the Cape is like a baby, either it is wet or it has wind. During my time at home the wind blew and was accompanied by what appeared to be an incessant soft rain. There were short dry spells, times when only the wind howled. That ever-present wind often reached gale force, so powerful that it would topple double-decker buses. When it wasn't raining the wind made a whistling noise and carried fine dry sand. The area where we had to live is referred to as the Cape Flats. This expanse of sandy soil stretches between two distant mountains. It is close to where the south-flowing warm water of the Indian Ocean's Agulhas current meets the north-flowing cold Benguela stream. Together they form the Cape of Storms: feared among sailors as one of the most treacherous seas in the world.

We lived on the southernmost edge of the world's second-largest continent—Africa—the continent that cradled the birth of humankind.

From Ma's room I could see when her client left the house.

Cape Town's rains are always beckoned by a wind from the north. That evening was no exception. There was a soft continuous rain that left everything wet in its wake. Wet was everywhere. The poorly maintained roads flooded easily because the Divisional Council of the Cape did not care to do a good job where people like us lived. Workers who lived where we did built the roads and maintained drainage systems in affluent suburbs. Yet our township was unkempt and became a wet wasteland when it rained.

Dams formed in open spaces on fields. With a chisel, a heavy knife, a block hammer, or a hacksaw blade, township children would cut the roof off an old broken and discarded car. There were many abandoned cars in the area where we lived. When turned upside down the car roof became a boat. With long sticks poking into the soggy soil, we children raced one another across the temporary dams. In the dry season those fields were where we played football. At night the self-same fields and its surrounds were notorious for criminal activity.

The water stood long enough for tadpoles to hatch. Catching them became another pastime. My favourite was the quicksand. It formed where water saturated the sandy parts of the field. We stomped and sank in as far as our knees. This was usually followed by a hiding from parents when they got home to find traces of mud in the house. The skin on our feet dried to form a crispy outer layer that would crack down to our flesh. The pain it caused was a second punishment.

The following year children did the same, save for those who had become too grown-up. Most of the young adults bore scars from the time when they raced car-roof boats. Scars are like painful memories; they travel along with us for the rest of our lives. We forgot about the pain, but the scars remained—left over from deep cuts. When the rowers, with their long sticks, misjudged the depth of the soggy soil they often slipped and fell. The falls were invariably onto one of the jagged metal pieces where the roof had been cut away from the old car body. Those races and accidents happened when the rain stopped and only the wind blew, usually from south to east. And that was a sure sign that dry weather was on its way.

My wait for Ma to finish continued. From behind the voile curtain in the upstairs room of our new house, a maisonette, I watched the factory workers, mainly older men. They were cycling home in the rain. There were no other means of transport from our township to where the factories were located. The rain paused that day, as if to create a corridor, so that working folk could make their way homewards. I stood there and looked down onto Fourth Avenue which had become water-logged. It resembled a canal.

On the last day of school we had watched the film, *The Wizard of Oz*. I stood in my mother's room at dusk on that rainy Friday evening, wistfully singing a song from that film, Somewhere over the Rainbow. It was the same song that had been repeating in my mind all day. I was captivated by the melody, so much that I remembered the names of the composers, Arlen and Harburg.

Somewhere over the rainbow, way up high,
There's a land that I heard of, once in a lullaby.
Somewhere over the rainbow, skies are blue,
And the dreams that you dare to dream, really do come true.
Someday I'll wish upon a star
And wake up where the clouds are far behind me,
Where troubles melt like lemon drops away above the chimney tops
That's where you'll find me.
Somewhere over the rainbow, bluebirds fly,
Birds fly over the rainbow, why then, oh why can't I?

I always got carried away by song. It was a mood-changer. While singing I watched an older man cycling past. His bike seemed a tad too big. Going home, that was what he did. He was going home with his paper-wrapped glass carafe containing four-and-a-half litres of cheap wine strapped firmly to the bicycle carrier. Suddenly, unexpectedly, the front wheel struck a brick hidden beneath the muddy street water. I stopped singing and leaned forward, in an instinctive attempt to stop the man from falling, but I was too late, I was also too far away. He fell!

Wet all over, workman's boots and all—wet through. The weathered Fedora hat he wore floated by on the currents created by his fall.

The man had no concern other than to save his weekend companion, the wine, but he was unsuccessful. He stood up from the fall, hatless. Arms by his side, drooping shoulders and head bowed, that simple man stood showing his balding crown. Sadness enveloped his figure. Bedraggled was his appearance as he continued to gaze down at the broken glass. His clothes dripped, dripped down, to join the patch of wine-coloured street water. A grown man with clothes soaking wet. He stood there mourning the wasted wine. Then he gathered his hat and shook it a few times to rid of the excess water. The empty lunchbox too was found and so were other belongings that had fallen from his tog-bag. Finally he picked up his big bike, looked down at the broken bottle one last time, and then wheeled his cycle away. Dejected, yes, that was his manner.

The rain started again. I had to wait for a pause in the downpour before running out to remove the pieces of glass. Not to do so was like setting a booby trap for others.

Jane would have done more to help that man, but Ma had only managed to save enough money for one return train ticket. Even if Jane did not have a job, just one of us could have travelled home; and it was the last time that I could travel on a cheaper child concession ticket, so it was my turn again. Up to then it was often my turn. Sometimes I thought it unfair, but Jane never complained.

Finally Ma's last consultation was over. People came to our house so she could listen to their problems. I did not understand their circumstances because the discussions were always private. That Friday's client had spent a very long time talking...

Chapter One

Early Beginnings

The mood that Friday evening was ideal for Ma and me to talk. The minute she sat on the sofa I began to tell the story of the cake shop; it bubbled out like an overflowing drain. Ma listened attentively. She always did. My account of the event included everything that happened; about how I felt, the trip to Simon's Town and what Pa did and said.

Ma asked why it took me almost two years to have that discussion with her: "Did you feel uncomfortable discussing your experience; and was it so because Jane would participate?"

That was not my reason. I was confused, sorry and embarrassed for Pa.

"I was confused." It was an ideal time to ask: "Ma, why was I never told that Pa spoke through his nose?"

Instead of responding, Ma sat back as if she remembered something very important. Perhaps it had to do with the last consultation she had, I thought, but that too was not a reason. Ma did her usual diverting tactic and reached for a cup of tea. It was a ploy, not a habit. She did not need to drink tea at that point; no, Ma had bought time and conjured up an appropriate answer. Like Pa pretended to be deaf, so Ma did a search-for-tea whenever there was need to select one answer from a range of possibilities.

Ma stood up from the sofa as she said: "I see my tea is finished. Let me make some more and then I shall explain to you."

Before, when we got to subjects where greater explanation was required, Ma would tell me that I was not old enough to understand the complete answer. I was expecting Ma to make the "not old enough to understand" speech.

To my surprise, Ma's reaction was different from what I had expected. In time all would become clear. Later, when much older, I realised that all along Ma had been searching for an opportunity to tell us children that we were not a conventional family. With hindsight it appeared as if she also sought to disclose the reasons why.

Ma returned with her pot of tea in hand. The cup, saucer, milk, sugar and teaspoon were daintily placed on a little side table tray. Maybe I was imagining, but Ma seemed a bit on edge. That too was unusual. Ma's way was always to take charge of any situation. She was irritating like that. However, when the opportunity arose to tell me I sensed that Ma was unsure about where to begin. I pretended not to notice.

Ma began nonetheless: "All that we have said and done over the years was to shape our lives around a man and his speech defect."

Looking back to that evening I think that Ma forgot to include how we shaped ourselves around Pa's secret lives, his greed, naughtiness and possible criminal activities.

"Ma, do we have to go to school so far away from home because of Pa's speech defect?"

"No, that is not the reason. But when we get to that part of the story then you will realise that it was the best decision."

Ma's response was terse. I knew then that to be quiet and listen would be better.

Ma got cross when my questions demanded revelations that she was not comfortable discussing. There appeared to be a concern about over-exposing the reality of that which had been kept secret for so long. As my understanding evolved, I learned that Ma knew of Pa's secrets; and that by not discussing, or disclosing them, she protected him.

That evening Ma went on to tell the story. Even then, as a boy-child of not quite twelve, I knew that she was hiding something. I had the urge to ask but was not sure if my timing was right. Unlike me, Jane was not interested in how we came to be. Jane had created her own peace by way of her considerable academic talents. She, Jane, always said: "Sam, you have the gift of insight…" Perhaps she was making an excuse for my lack of talent in the field of academia.

The discussion Ma and I had veered away from the family. Messages, gifts and others that I had to take back for Jane began to dominate. I expected more, but it was not forthcoming. Ma was not relaxed so she did not talk in the way I wanted.

She switched on the radio to listen to her favourite programme, *Squad Cars*.

Back then, television was something we only heard people speak about. And later the Eldorado Bioscope screened films where we saw people watching a television set in their lounge rooms. But that Friday night I just sat next to the radio with Ma. My thoughts were about how I could get her to tell more of our story. While I sat there waiting, the memory of having overheard a conversation between Ma and one of her clients washed through my mind. The client had arrived to see Ma earlier than scheduled. I had made small talk with the woman. That is probably when she formed her opinion, for thereafter I overheard her asking Ma about me. My ears pricked up as I craned to hear Ma's reply. When told, the woman commented about my ability to hold a conversation. Ma's response was: "Even though Sam is young he understands when it is okay to speak. He has an old soul, that child of mine. His questions are simple, but often they are incredibly awkward to answer."

It was interesting to hear Ma's opinion. I was in the habit of sucking my right thumb. Apart from comfort, sucking my thumb also provided me with time to think about what other people said. I formed my own opinions by comparing what different people said about the same thing. Much of my time was spent thinking through what I had overheard. So much so that a lot of it became embedded in my memory, almost like the first trip to boarding school. That trip was before my fifth birthday.

Once at school, circumstances allowed little time to be a baby. I had become part of an extended family where individual care was not always possible. Independence became a survival skill. The same applied to other children. Jane was older and had been at the 'faraway' school for a lot longer than me. I regarded her as my sister-mommy. Jane refused to discuss the time when she first went to school, but I knew that for her the same experience had been more difficult than it was for me. She had been alone, without a sister-mommy. Jane must have become strong because of that experience, but like the children who played with the car-roof boats, she bore scars.

I would sit sucking my thumb, watching Jane play with the younger children. Most of them did not have a sister-mommy. Jane knew how those children felt; I could tell by the way she treated them. Maybe Jane did not want them to feel the same pain that she experienced, being so young and yet so far away from home. She was like that, my sister. When I was teased by the other boys Jane was always there to give me comfort. I could defend myself. Sometimes it was with a left hook, which created more trouble…

To me, the radio programme, *Squad Cars*, was very boring. It would not end, and was all about policemen who drove noisy cars and spoke as if they had lead in their moustaches: it held their top lips down and they spoke funny as a result. There were sirens blaring on the radio and the policemen spoke about places that I did not know, places like Hillbrow and Brixton. Ma was engrossed. At times during the broadcast Ma seemed eager to climb into the radio. I looked at her in amazement, for Ma cautioned the characters in the story. It was shocking, because she supported the bad guys. I looked on, sucked my thumb and thought that madness was visiting our house.

The questions that I could not ask Ma were saved for Jane. Questions like: "Is Ma our tummy-mommy and who are Charles, Anne and Brenda?" These questions came from bits of information I had accumulated, but that didn't make sense. They were from conversations that I overheard; things that people said in passing. I'd formulate my own questions but there were seldom ready answers; more questions than answers.

I felt invisible when sucking my thumb. That was also when my ability to hear improved, like when Ma argued with Pa: "… and that is what I get for being saddled with pick-up children." I carried that comment in my head until it became a question, one that I could pose to Jane.

She always tried to find the right answer, but there were times when Jane also failed. "I tried to find an answer to 'that' question you've asked, but couldn't. Sorry Sammy." she'd say.

Jane was never too busy to listen. Even though I must have been an irritant she never dismissed my questions as nonsense, nor did Jane ever stop me sucking my thumb or singing. There were times when I sang the same song over and over. Mammy Cynthia, Jane and Ma must be three of the most tolerant people. They never asked me to stop, but also never appeared keen that I continue. There must have been great relief whenever I stopped singing. I can only remember one occasion when Jane asked me to sing a certain song.

Jane was head girl in her final year at school. The school custom was that the head girl and head boy make farewell speeches at a final dinner. Jane's speech was light and friendly, but there was a section in the talk that made her sound like an old woman: "… sometimes I hear older people say that we learn most when we teach one another. I have experienced it. Whenever I teach Sam then both of us learn and it prepares us for life, I think. Thank you to those teachers who helped me and pointed me in the direction to find answers for Sam's many cryptic questions…"

I sat at the junior table and whenever Jane mentioned my name in her speech the other boys kicked my feet and the ones sitting next to me stuck their elbows in my ribs—and all the while I sat there wondering whether Jane knew stuff that I didn't.

Squad Cars finally ended and Ma appeared more relaxed. She removed the teapot's lid and spooned in some brewing leaves. Some of that anxious look continued to lurk in her eyes. I had seen Ma wearing that expression on a few occasions: once when there were questions about our family; and another time when Mrs Anthony, our neighbour, asked Ma to accompany her to Pretoria Central Prison, where her child was to be hanged.

I do not know the entire story, but one night Cedric Anthony did something dreadful in the bushes next to the football field. The next day a woman was found dead there. Cedric was guilty; a judge at the Supreme Court in Cape Town said so. He was sentenced to death by hanging and the charges were rape and murder. Jane and I were home from school when Ma and Mrs Anthony left for Pretoria to be with Cedric when he was executed. When Ma greeted us she reminded Jane and me: "Tonight before you go to bed you have to pray for Cedric and for Mrs Anthony. We are going to say goodbye to Mrs Anthony's child. It is the hardest thing that any mother can do."

That was the first time I saw Ma anxious.

Ma must have realised that there'd come a time when my questions would outnumber the answers she was prepared to give.

"You know, Sammy, whenever I try to talk about our family then Jane changes the subject. She speaks about the future rather than what happened a long time ago. That is where our discussion usually ends. You are the opposite."

I smiled and put my thumb back in my mouth. It gave me comfort and I could concentrate a lot better.

Jane pretended to know less. Her obsessive focus to obtain the best grades was the way she balanced our dysfunctional family situation.

Sister St Claire, our head teacher, wrote to Ma when Jane became head girl: "Jane is an unusual pupil. She is single-minded, focused, and determined…"

Ma continued to speak that Friday evening, though the discomfort in her voice was evident. Her speech was disjointed and the sentences she constructed were clumsy. It was unusual, as if Ma wanted to say something, but did not know how. There were times that she did not make sense, but I let it go, lest I got another curt reply. Ma poured boiling water into the teapot. The tea was left to draw underneath a cosy while she stumbled along with telling the story, all the while seeking the flow in her speech and being cautious not to let slip what she did not want to discuss.

Our family was not wealthy. We managed, but only because Ma knew how to make her little money last. Her refrain: "Pa's stinginess, selfishness and thoughtless manner have taught me how to look after my money. That is how I manage to keep you children at school."

§

Samuel Arthur Levy—Pa

When Ma found better direction in our discussion she explained: "Pa first arrived in South Africa when his father, a violinist, left Lyon, a city in east-central France. Pa and his identical twin brother, Uncle Pierre, were raised by their father. Their mother died while giving birth to them. It was 1919, on the 9th of February; their birthday. The Great War had ended in November 1918. That War, or World War I as it was later called, left certain parts of Europe in ruins. There was not much work for musicians. Following the resurgence of anti-Semitic sentiments in Europe, Zaideh (Grandfather in Yiddish) Levy, a Jew, decided to follow friends who, for similar reasons, had moved with their families to different parts of the world."

"Why did Zaideh Levy decide to move to South Africa, Ma?" I interrupted, but then her reply was less measured.

"I don't know, but the boys must have been about nine or ten years old when they arrived. It was in 1928 or 1929. There's detail that I do not know. What I am aware of though is that Zaideh Levy found work in the Overberg town of Caledon, about 120 kilometres east of Cape Town city. During the day he traded and later established a general dealer shop. At night he was the resident musician at the Royal Hotel in Dorp Street. It was across the road from his shop. The house where your Zaideh lived with Pa and Uncle Pierre was attached to the shop.

After he had settled, Edith Buckley, a St Helena woman, was employed to care for the two boys. Zaideh later married Edith, who became Grandma Edith. The two had three children together, a daughter and two sons. One of the sons, Edgar, he died."

"How did Edgar die, Ma?"

13

"I don't know," and without pausing Ma continued with the story: "It is said that Grandma Edith favoured Uncle Pierre over your Pa."

"Who told you that, Ma?"

"Auntie Rachel, Pa's only sister, she told me. Zaideh was a very gentle and softly spoken man."

"Did you know Zaideh, Ma?"

"Yes, how else would I have known that he was gentle and softly spoken? I only got to know him when he was an old man. Zaideh Levy lived for music and for the business, which he had built from nothing. I cared for Zaideh when he became too old to live on his own. He died in my house. I remember the day he died. He was in bed and stared at the clock, the same one we have in the upstairs room, Zaideh's clock. I heard him softly singing a French traditional song, but I forget what it was called. One day I shall remember. Suddenly there was silence. Zaideh stopped singing. When I checked Zaideh, whose name was Alexandre Levy, he had died. That was his end, peaceful, at ninety nine years of age and with a favourite song on his lips."

"What happened to Grandma Edith when Zaideh Levy died, Ma?"

"Oh, Zaideh was very old and by then Grandma Edith had already died. Grandma Edith was paralysed by illness. They called it the St Helena illness. She died in a frail care home. Strange how life is … it was Pa who cared for his mother when she needed someone. The others, Pierre, Rachel and their brother were too busy with their own lives.

"Uncle Pierre went to university and Pa became a confectioner at a nearby bakery in Caledon. That is where he met Uncle Flippie (Phillip), the delivery vehicle driver who became the second of Pa's three best friends. I recall how the two would embrace after not having seen each other in a while. They were like lovers and at times cried with excitement when together. They'd consume a copious amount of table wine, much to the irritation of Doreen, Flippie's wife."

"Why did they cry?"

"Oh, probably because of the naughtiness they reminded each other of, or maybe it was the amount of wine they drank. Uncle Flippie was also a very gentle man …"

"But he had the biggest ears, Ma!" That was my smart retort, one that drew a clout from my Ma, but I ducked and quickly changed the subject by asking: "Who was Pa's first best friend, Ma?"

"Tom. Tom Brickles, a pianist. He and Pa were as thick as thieves, probably thicker."

"Yes, I remember that man. Pa took me to his house when I was about eight years old. He played the piano and when his wife left the room Pa threw the flowers out and poured wine in the vase while Oom (Uncle) Tom serenaded us on the piano—Que Sera, Sera (*Whatever Will Be, Will Be*)—and many others."

"Yes, that sounds like Tom … Nonetheless, Uncle Pierre excelled as an architect and Pa, who refused to continue living in his brother's shadow, decided to study electronics. Later he learned about locks but never became a locksmith. All the jobs and trades that Pa was interested in, studied and worked at, none of them required him to speak. He seemed never to be fulfilled, though.

"When his studies were completed Pa left Caledon for the big city, Cape Town. He found work as an electrician at the Athlone Power Station. There he became friends with Albert Fortune, a man who married for the first time when he was already fifty years old. Albert was Pa's third great friend. The two also drank wine together, raced pigeons and were intense about political developments in the world. In addition, Pa nurtured interests in growing hybrid plants, pottery, sculpture, and with whatever time was left, he built radio-controlled model airplanes. This too was not enough for your Pa. There was always a new interest lurking to overthrow the old. His latest new interest became the art of making hand-woven rugs. This interest was extended to include the trade in Middle Eastern artefacts. That is the man I got to know, your Pa. He is a very naughty man and later you will get to know all about his naughtiness."

Pa also had an unusual taste in interior decorating. The reasonably-sized open plan lounge and the dining area in our house were his domain: that was where he worked and entertained himself.

When I got back from boarding school and saw the new furniture, Ma explained: "Pa re-upholstered the sofa and chairs with a Kashmiri fabric that he thought would be better than the previous covers." Without saying a word he stripped the old lounge chairs, chopped, hammered and sewed. This activity went on for weeks before he was done. That was how he passed every evening until all the furniture was re-upholstered. Thereafter the mysterious work, late nights out and unexplained periods of absence began."

I remembered when Pa worked at home. His companion was a cassette-tape recording of marching bands, piano accordion music, bird calls and songs sung by young children. Pa suffered from insomnia and slept for about three or four hours per night. I never saw him asleep.

Another of Ma's refrains: "His naughtiness haunts him," - that was Ma's view. She often spoke about Pa's naughtiness, likened it to his insomnia, but never said more.

Back when Pa arrived home at a normal time he'd have dinner, work at the dining room table, read, or write letters to politicians. He read about plants, carpets, or building designs. Other times he darned an old carpet from shabby to new. It was not unusual to find Pa working at the dining room table at three in the morning, accompanied by a canary singing its lungs to a quiver from inside a Sanyo cassette tape recorder. Pa sat beneath a very bright spotlight that hung over the dining room table. His work clothes included a khaki dust coat, white shirt, grey trousers, black-rimmed reading glasses, very shiny painted shoes and a sombrero hat to soften the glare from his bright overhead light.

The way our lounge was decorated reflected his eccentricity. When I questioned why he did things in a certain way, the reply was always: "Ya! Don't do things just because others do it—do what you want."

15

The lounge room walls were almost entirely covered with hanging carpets. Other parts were covered with picture frames that featured powder-blue hessian cloth instead of pictures. Mounted on the blue cloth were carefully arranged dried leaves. Pa collected leaves of different shapes, sizes and textures. He would place the leaves underneath the floor rugs to dry before using them to create various designs on the framed hessian. Every piece, be it framed dried leaves, or oriental rugs, would have two prices. The much higher 'original' price got scratched. Next to it Pa had written the term, 'WAS'. The new price, a much smaller number, was written on the same label alongside the word 'NOW'. These labels changed regularly. So too did the carpets and artefacts to which the labels were affixed. Presumably they were sold. Beneath the carefully contrived mask of being eccentric, deaf and a bit mad, it was evident that Pa was a cunning businessman.

Copper, brass and clay pots together with wooden masks adorned the rest of the room. Everything had a price. There was a mobile aviary in the room too. That was where Pa's canaries lived. During the day the aviary hung beneath the grapevine that grew over our front veranda.

Pa grew and grafted trees to produce hybrid fruit and flowers. The fused guava and plum tree was his favourite. The grafted trees grew in big pots. He loved carnations and roses. "Ya! They are too expensive to buy. I shall merge a rose with a carnation. That is how I shall have two of my favourite flowers growing as one. A fine fern leaf framing my flower shall make for the most beautiful jewel on my jacket lapel." He always wore a flower, even on the khaki dust coat in which he worked.

Then there was the time Pa decided that the wall in our dining room where he worked needed a framed painting. He was to create the picture. It was destined to be a pine tree set on an almost even section of a mountain slope. Underneath the tree he planned to paint a picnic scene. It was to include a sweet melon, kitchen knife and a man leaning against the tree. The man would be reading a newspaper. The picture never made it to the wall. It was interrupted because Pa stopped working at home. All that remained of the painting was a book of sketches.

When Pa stopped working at home he was reading about the manufacture of clay pots, but I do not know how far he had evolved that interest.

Strange, but while Pa worked on the dining room table the place never seemed cluttered. When I asked about things that were no longer there Ma shook her head, looked at me and sipped her tea. I never knew what that look meant. Our lounge was Pa's show-room, but he never showed it to anyone while I was there.

The window in our lounge was draped in a light caramel-coloured mohair curtain which stretched from one side of the room to the other. A substantial voile curtain prevented those who were outside from looking into our township house on the Cape Flats.

§

16

Before replacing the lid and the cosy, Ma shook the last of the tea leaves from the strainer back into the teapot.

"I am not waffling, but where to begin is difficult. You have to understand the story because it is yours, as it is mine."

Quietly and with my thumb in my mouth I looked at Ma, probably trying to make sense of what she was saying. At times, being quiet was best, lest the hornet's nest be stirred.

Sometimes my impatience resulted in deviations from the story. This was not good because I never had the luxury of time with Ma. My hunger for detail kept on growing but all that our discussion achieved that night was another vague insight about how Jane and I came to be. There was more detail provided about how Ma came to be, while many questions about Jane and me remained unanswered.

Ma continued to stumble over sentences and use words of which I did not understand the meaning. Being apprehensive about which questions to ask did not help either. Silence was the better option, but Ma needed help, I thought. So I suggested: "Don't worry, Ma, we can talk another time, there will always be another time."

Saying that was like showing a red rag to a bull. Realising that I knew she was battling caused Ma to frown, probably because both of us were aware that 'next time' would not be soon.

Ma's inability to tell her own story was both intriguing and worrying. After all, Ma had been a registered professional social worker since long before I was born. How could it be that she was unable to tell her own story?

I knew that Ma had heard, responded to and participated in many difficult stories during her career. I wondered why Ma had so much difficulty talking about her story... 'our story'. Maybe I failed to understand that it is easier to solve other people's difficulties. Perhaps Ma never learned to address her own matters, only those of other people. Almost like Father Terry, Mammy Cynthia's parish priest, who buried many people, but will not be able to bury himself.

Ma continued to speak, but it felt like being in a car driven by a learner driver as we jerked along. At first she spoke fine and then all of a sudden I would stop understanding.

I was sick of hearing: "When you are older then all will make sense; do not allow life to take from you the way it has taken from me" and "No matter where we start, it is how we end that counts."

Again Ma repeated these stock responses and I had to bite my tongue—well, in my case, my thumb—because what Ma said had no context for me, other than my sense that things were not the way they 'should' have been. I did not know why.

As Ma spoke I would see and hear how she found solutions to her own problems. Respectfully I also thought about how strange it was that Ma did not heed her own advice, but instead continued to have Pa 'take from her'.

Ma spoke about Pa's speech, but said nothing that I did not already know. I was concerned about not having known, prior to the cake shop incident, that Pa had a speech defect. I wanted to know why it was never explained to me, never mentioned or referred to in any manner or form.

Instead of answering the question I had asked and expected answers to, Ma chose to use it as a pillar for a lot more. It was unexpected, but I was, like Uncle Flippie, all ears! Even in her struggle to tell a coherent story Ma showed glimpses of her gift, which was the ability to be simple. This did not surprise me, but what did was that she was being cagey. It was something that I could not put my finger on. There were many unexplained gaps in her story; those were the cagey bits. I was afraid to ask Ma the questions uppermost in my mind: 'What could be so bad; and, why can I not be told?' Those were the queries that repeated in my mind while I sucked my thumb.

As the evening wore on the talking became easier. The simplicity of Ma's manner when explaining that with which she was comfortable conjured in me an emotion similar to when I sang a sad song. Yet, her words were not sad; what stirred in me was as a result of the sincerity with which she spoke when not trying to hide something. I was nearly twelve years old after all. In my memory, whenever I was stirred by the way Ma explained pain and sorrow, she'd notice my reaction, pause and move her bottom lip up against the top. It would make her mouth droop and at the same time her extensive dimples would be accentuated. She did so that evening too, a number of times. I knew what it meant: that everything would be all right and that I should not be too upset. Then she'd smile. Ma has a smile that heals me.

§

Thelma Llewellyn (Wilson) (de la Cruz) Levy—Ma

"My own story begins, as I was told, near the port city of Aberdeen, Scotland, and also in Jamestown on the isle of St Helena. Later parts of the story will clarify how the people of Cape Town became part of who we are."

Ma was concerned that she would die and proffered this as the reason why the details of her life should be shared with Jane and me. Upon hearing about my mother's potential death I interjected with: "I do not think that you are going to die, Ma." I had a need to be convinced that Ma's death was not imminent. If Ma had to die, then Jane and I would have no one. My assurance to Ma that she would not die brought a smile to her face. That smile was different. I think it meant: "Thank you for loving me."

Ma poured her tea. I was on the carpet sucking my thumb. Lampo, Ma's pet dog, the one I spoke to when there was no one else, was on the carpet alongside me.

After a good sip of the fresh tea, Ma spoke again: "Pa's nasal voice was one of the first things I noticed when we met, twenty years ago this year. Yes, we met in 1952; it was winter, I remember."

Ma had a faraway look in her eyes when she spoke about that time. She gazed up at the ceiling as if preparing to read from a script. I asked and Ma promised to tell how they met: "Later in the story—" and I noticed how she stopped herself saying, "—you will understand better when you're older."

Again I smiled and was quiet while Ma changed the subject to Jane and me at boarding school.

That story was very familiar. I lived it and could remember details vividly. Nonetheless, Ma explained again that Jane had been at the faraway boarding school for four years before I joined her. I chose not to interrupt.

A source of amusement at school was that both Jane and I celebrated our birthdays on the same date, 8th October. Jane was born five years before me. In the beginning, October was a festive time at school. As we grew older October became marred by study and school examinations. My first birthday at school was when I turned five. The years I spent at home are vague in my memory. The only part that I can recall vividly is Ma teaching me to pray before I slept at night. I also remember visiting Charles, Ma's son from an earlier marriage.

We'd never been to church but I had to pray to Gentle Jesus every night. Many of our neighbours went to different churches on a Sunday. There were many churches that were within walking distance of our house. I would have asked why Ma did not go to church, but her reply to that kind of question was always in the form of a fob-off story.

Anyway, Ma taught me to pray for those in the family whom we did not see. Jane was also taught to pray before she left for school. Later I discovered that both of us had the same habit of praying every evening before going to bed. At boarding school too, we'd pray before sleeping—it was our norm. The other boys teased me but I was bigger than them and they knew that my left hook was well rehearsed.

At home, during the prayer ritual, Ma always sat on the chair in her bedroom while I knelt on the floor beside her. With my hands folded together up against my chest I would look up at Zaideh Levy's clock and start praying:

Gentle Jesus, meek and mild,
Look upon this little child;
Pity my simplicity,
Suffer me to come to Thee.
Bless Pa, Ma, Uncle Pierre, Auntie Rachel, Auntie Liza, Auntie Agnes,
Charles, Brenda, Anne, Jane,
All people who suffer,
The poor and those

Who did not have food to eat tonight.

Amen.

Then I'd hug Ma and get into bed. We seldom kissed and never spoke about love.

After talking about Jane and me at boarding school Ma realised that she had jumped from one subject to another and that it had caused a disconnect in her story.

"Okay, let me try again; my father was Jeffrey Llewellyn, a Welshman. I do not know why he lived in Scotland. It was there where Able Seaman Jeffrey Llewellyn was stationed for the Royal Navy. During World War I my father was a cook on a naval warship. It is said that the ship he was assigned to was moored off the island of St Helena. Most passing ships stopped there in those days, to replenish supplies. My father met my mother, Mabel, when he was on shore leave. When he left my father promised to return after the war. The war ended in November 1918. My father kept his promise and my parents got married during February of 1919. I was born in 1923, the youngest of three daughters, Agnes, Winifred and then me."

Ma paused and again she looked up at the ceiling. There was sadness in her voice when she spoke: "Pa is the only man I know who is happy and pleasant to be with when he drinks wine. My Dad drank a lot of whisky. He was horrible to us girls and to my Mommy after he had been drinking."

I do remember being at home when Pa was drinking wine. His wine was always hidden in the garage. During the course of an evening, usually a Friday, Pa would constantly disappear. On reappearing he always seemed happier. It was fun for Jane and me to be at home then.

"What happened to your Mo—?"

"I am getting there, be patient," was Ma's quick reply. I cringed for having interrupted what seemed like a sensitive matter.

Ma looked at the ceiling for a while longer before continuing. "My Mommy died from a disease, a genetic sickness that affected people who lived on isolated islands like St Helena, Tristan da Cunha and others. It had to do with children from people who shared the same bloodline—in many instances they were unaware of it."

"What was your Mommy like, Ma?"

"I was only five years old when my Mommy died. Auntie Agnes says that our Mommy was 'a delicate and quiet woman', a hardworking dressmaker. I think that she was no different to Agnes.

"After Mommy died, Dad continued to be away. He worked at sea and each trip lasted many weeks. Auntie Agnes was only twelve years old, like you, when she had to care for Auntie Winnie and me.

"When Dad came home we'd stock up with fish. We only ate vegetables and fish. It wasn't strange to live like we did because there were many child-headed households on the islands. Many men worked at sea as fishermen. Those who stayed on the shore worked in support of the fishing and the farming industries. People often died. There was not much medical care on the islands, and it was not unusual for women to die during childbirth. Many men also died of the same genetic disease my Mommy suffered from."

"Maybe one day Jane and I will meet Auntie Agnes," was my attempt at moving the story along.

"You are trying to jump ahead of the story again. You must wait. I shall tell you the whole story."

I tried hard, but sometimes the questions just popped out and then Ma would get cross. Ma was taking too long to tell me that which I wanted to know about.

"Well, a number of years after Mommy died my Dad decided that we should be adopted by his wartime friend, a Scotsman who had married a St Helena woman and moved to settle in Cape Town, South Africa—Daddy and Mommy Wilson. They had one daughter, Liza, who was five years old at the time. Mommy Wilson wanted to have more children, but she suffered from diabetes which made it dangerous for her to have more of her own—we were her remedy."

"How did you get to Cape Town then, Ma?"

"Well, St Helena is nearly two thousand miles away from Cape Town. The only way to travel was by ship. Before that trip none of us had ever left St Helena Island. I had not seen a ship that big before because all ships would moor away from the island and we only saw them in the distance. We were at sea for a long time, sailing on a big steamship from Jamestown to Cape Town."

"How long did it take you to get to Cape Town, Ma? Was it longer than three days?"

"I don't know, but it must have been about six days, it felt much longer. I remember when we arrived. It was four weeks to the day before my eighth birthday."

"Ma, then you must have arrived on 15 July. It was winter, was it raining?"

"Yes, we arrived on that date; it is stamped on our entry permit. That was also the day we met Daddy and Mommy Wilson for the first time, in 1931, but I can't remember whether or not it was raining. My recollection of the journey is faint in most instances and vivid in others. Auntie Winnie and I were little girls; she was nine years old and I was nearly eight. The sea was rough at times and both Winnie and I clung to Agnes. In stormy seas the three of us would huddle together in the cabin until the ship stopped swaying. Those rolling actions in rough seas were very scary. The wind constantly blew at gale force, stronger even, I think. Once, as we sat holding onto one another, we were flung off the bed. I think it was when a big wave struck the side of our ship. We feared so much that the experience remains etched in my mind. To this day I have not set foot in the ocean. We were sick—sea sickness. There were times on that journey when we believed that the ship would not reach Cape Town, but here I am, more than fifty years later."

"Where was your Dad, Ma? Didn't he travel to Cape Town with you?"

"That is a good question, my boy. Of all the memories, I remember this one most clearly. It is of we girls waving at our Dad. Agnes nearly fell overboard as she stretched to wave for one last time. As was usual, the big steamship was moored in deeper waters outside Jamestown Port. The port was too small for most of the big ships to enter. We watched as the little boat that brought us from the shore to the ship disappeared behind big swells on its way back to the quay … our Dad was on that boat. The big ship we travelled on began to move to even deeper waters, and then the high sea, en route to Cape Town. Agnes was sadder than Winnie and me; she must have known that it was the last time we'd see our Dad."

"Why Ma, did he drown?"

"No, no. He didn't drown. You know, Winnie was taken from us when we arrived in Cape Town. I always asked why, but never got a good answer. The answers weren't clear. One day Agnes and I were chatting while she sewed. I asked the same question again, the one about Winnie. Agnes let go of the material in her hand and took her foot off the sewing machine's pedal. I did not recognise the expression on my sister's face that day. 'Our Dad gave us away.' That was all she said and continued to sew. Agnes never had much to say about most things. I have not had a proper answer about Winnie, but I think that it is because Daddy and Mommy Wilson only wanted two more children. That is why Winnie did not come to stay with us."

"Shame … Auntie Winnie must have missed you. What was St Helena like, Ma?"

"Oh no, I can't remember. All I know is that which I've read and been told. Auntie Agnes knows more, but—I shall explain later why I don't think she will ever again speak about St Helena Island.

"It is a very poor country, was once a prison, but mainly a halfway station for passing ships. I know that the St Helena of my time existed so that Britain could take from it. Certainly this was the case when I was born. It is also said that the Portuguese founded the island in 1502, or thereabout, and that when they arrived it was uninhabited. You can read the rest of the history about slaves from Madagascar and Java who escaped and started their own families... the Japanese, the Dutch and about Napoleon who died there. It makes me cross to think that the Brits took from us and gave little in return. The taking from me has never stopped …"

Ma glanced up at the ceiling one more time.

"I am speaking to you like you are an adult, my boy. If I say something that is unclear then you must stop me; or, say if there is something that you do not understand, you hear?"

"Would I have called your Mommy, Granny, Ma; what do you think? Many of my friends call their grandmothers Ma, or Granny."

"I was five years old when my Mommy died and before that she was in bed, sick. That's all I remember. It had something to do with her bones being soft and as a result her legs became deformed, particularly after I was born. Sorry, I do not remember too much, but ..."

Ma did not finish the rest of that sentence. She was probably going to tell me that Auntie Agnes, whom I was yet to meet, would know the answer. "I have to write this story so that you can read it later when you have greater understanding."

I pulled a face at hearing Ma say that again. It was the wrong thing to have done because Ma saw and immediately climbed onto her high horse.

"You can pull your face as many times as you like, but when you are older and when Jane becomes interested then my writing will be there for all my children and for your children to read."

To nod in agreement was the best solution, so that is what I did, because my interest had moved to when their big ship docked in Cape Town.

"What happened, Ma, when you and the aunties arrived in Cape Town?"

"When we arrived, our only possession was a crumpled brown paper bag that was given to each child passenger who boarded the ship in St Helena. Each bag contained a night dress and our St Helena school tunic. By the time we got to Cape Town the brown paper bag had been opened and closed so many times that it was quite worn through. Oh, that is what I remember too, all three of us were very careful that our brown paper bag did not break. Auntie Agnes insisted so because we had to make a good first impression."

"Why did you not have plastic bags, Ma?"

"No, no, people only used plastic bags much later. I think that here in South Africa plastic bags were introduced in the 1960s, but let's not get side-tracked. When the ship arrived Agnes recognised Mommy Wilson. Agnes always told me that Mommy Wilson looked like a St Helena woman. She had dark hair, alabaster skin and brown eyes. I can't remember what she was wearing but Daddy Wilson wore a dark suit and a hat. His eyes were very blue, that's what I remember. Mommy and Daddy Wilson became our parents. Auntie Liza was a delightful child. We were instant friends.

"There were other people waiting for Winnie. She went with them and I did not say goodbye to her. Many St Helena children on the ship were introduced to their new families on that day. Most of them were sad, some cried, but Agnes and I had each other.

"We lived at Number 4, Page Street, Woodstock. From there it took fifteen minutes to walk to the centre of Cape Town city. Our school was the Holy Cross Roman Catholic School in District Six. The nuns were strict but the discipline we were taught at the St Helena Island School stood us in good stead; Agnes led by example and together we were model pupils.

"I missed Winnie. Agnes and I thought and spoke about her frequently. One moment I would be happy and the next, sad. It was always sad to wonder what Winnie was doing because we could not be truly happy without our sister."

"When did you see Auntie Winnie again, Ma?"

"You have to wait, it's in the story!"

When Ma smiled beautiful dimples appeared on either side of her face—I can't forget that.

"Agnes and I played our part in raising Liza while Mommy Wilson made dresses, suits and other garments for paying clients. We girls did everything together, particularly Liza and me; Agnes was older and before long I could not imagine life without Liza."

By telling this story Ma answered one of my questions: that Ma and Auntie Liza did not have the same natural parents. I sensed that Ma knew my thoughts. She ignored them though and instead brought her teacup closer as if to drink, when I interrupted: "You said that Auntie Agnes completed Year Eight. What did she do after that, Ma?"

"Auntie Agnes was an apprentice to Mrs Frey, a seamstress. Agnes studied dressmaking and Mrs Frey was her principal. Within four years my big sister passed a trade test. She became a qualified dressmaker. I was four years younger than her, but so proud. My 'sister-mommy', the gentle quiet one who found her passion in making clothes for all who asked—it was what she lived for."

Ma paused to have a sip of tea proper and dab her eyes.

"Why do you become sad when speaking about Auntie Agnes, Ma, did she die?"

"No, my boy, for me Auntie Agnes is not dead, although maybe I am dead for her."

Ma paused to look at the ceiling for a much longer time.

"Let me go on with the rest of the story and you'll see. I shall describe the entire saga, but I have to tell you these parts first, otherwise it will…"

Ma paused mid-sentence and I could see that she was distressed. It was not clear why, and I was bothered by the suddenness of her changed mood.

Ma settled first and then continued: "You know Boy, Agnes sewed the most beautiful frocks. Within a short time my sister was the dressmaker of choice for almost every wedding. We lived within a strong and vibrant Cape Malay community. Their ancestors were brought to Cape Town from several Indian Ocean countries and were sold as slaves.

"Their customs and religion were handed down. The traditions like dress, language and food also influenced the way we lived. It is said that the first written form of the new language that started in the Cape, a mix of several languages, was recorded using the Arabic alphabet. It came from the Islam religion. The slaves were mainly Muslim. Together with religion came customs and language that changed the face of Cape Town. I don't suppose that you will learn this at school because the history we learn is sometimes different, depending on who writes it."

"Did Auntie Agnes have her own business; did she have a factory?"

"You make me laugh! Auntie Agnes worked at home. Our house was her factory. She was very neat, particular and tidy. Wedding dates were planned around when Agnes could produce a frock. Every one of the dresses she made was different. There were days when our house was like a carnival. To fit the wedding dress, that's what brought the carnival into our home. Family members accompanied the bride. The 'Ghalaties' / Aunties came along to give advice to the dressmaker, our Agnes. During such consultations Agnes would listen and then repeat to her clients what they had said. That was how she formulated and refined her brief. People enjoyed working with Agnes because not only was she good at her job, but she was also very pleasant and patient.

"I remember an occasion like that, shortly after a young Spanish immigrant, Jesús, began to visit Agnes. He and I were in a nearby room while the wedding party spoke with Agnes. Listening to them talk about the dress had both of us agree that the crowd of people who gathered for the fitting were more excited about the dress than about the wedding."

"Jesús visited Auntie Agnes?"

"Yes, and about two years later Uncle Jesús and Auntie Agnes were married."

"So Jesus is my uncle!" I interjected, impishly. "I can't wait to tell Jane this part of the story. Does she know?" I asked these questions without removing my thumb.

Ma frowned at me. "There is no need to be silly."

She paused for a moment.

"We were all happy then, a 'real' family. We joked excitedly about grandchildren and how they would spend weekends with Mommy, Daddy, Liza and me. Jesús and Agnes were married about a year before Mommy became completely blind."

Chapter Two

Ma's First Job; Liza, Winnie and Agnes; on Being Pretty…

"Back then people got married and stayed together until one of them died. They seldom got divorced and when they did the women were looked down upon, by society, as failures."

"What about the men, those from whom the women got divorced, were they also seen as bad, Ma?"

"No. Life is not fair, particularly to women; most men went on to marry again and have new families. Those men seldom cared for their first family. You should take notice of this because I do not want you to grow up treating people, particularly your own children, in a way that you would not find acceptable. One of the lessons I've learned is, when you treat people well, and with kindness, then there is a greater chance that they will respect you in return. If you do not treat people well, then don't be surprised when their reaction toward you is negative."

I was bored by the detail and yawned. Ma noticed and reminded me that if I did not understand the beginning then the end wouldn't make sense.

"No, Ma, no, I'm fine, and very interested," I said hastily, though my eyes felt tired. As a rescue attempt from further embarrassment I changed the focus slightly, asking what sort of work people who left school after Year Eight had done.

Ma nodded before answering: "When young people finished, or had to leave school, most found work as machinists in factories. There were many clothing factories within walking distance from where we lived. Boys were encouraged to learn trades and others found jobs at sea as fishermen, or on the buses as conductors. To find a job was not easy. People accepted whatever was available."

"Did people not start their own businesses?"

"No, people like those who lived in our street did not start businesses. We were employees, workers. Our parents told us to finish school and find good jobs, not to start businesses. We were not encouraged to become business

26

owners. And none of us took the initiative. Today most continue to be employees. Often children worked in the same business as their parents.

Auntie Agnes had her own business, and before becoming ill Mommy was also a business owner. On occasion both Mommy, in her day, and Agnes in hers, did contract work for factories, operatic companies, churches, but mainly for couples who got married. They made their price, bought the material, did the work and got paid; yet they never thought of themselves as business owners. It is because they did not have a vision beyond making dresses and suits for those who requested and agreed to their price. Both Mommy and Agnes never thought about expanding, hiring premises or employing people. It was like that. We believed that only other people owned businesses and we were meant to be workers."

"So, Ma, when did you go to university, and which one did you attend?"

"See, you are running ahead of the story again. Only a small number of people from our community finished school in Year Twelve and, of them, an even smaller number furthered their studies at a university or a college. I left school at the end of Year Eight, but I finished Year Twelve on my own, at night, after work and on Saturday mornings."

The indigenous rooibos tea Ma brewed and occasionally poured was by then a deep red colour. She sipped at it with such appetite that I too was tempted to have some. I poured myself a cup and whilst there I stole a moment to check what it was that Ma stared at, longingly, on the ceiling. There was nothing!

Ma continued talking while holding her teacup and as I reclaimed my seat next to Lampo.

"The expectation was that children should earn money and contribute to the family. It was also the reason why I left school when I did. Liza was almost nine years old when Mommy Wilson was diagnosed with the beginning stage of diabetic eye disease. After the diagnosis the deterioration of her sight was rapid. Less than two years after being diagnosed Mommy was completely blind. Those who thought they knew said that it was a throwback from the 'Island Disease'. I've done some reading about the disease on St Helena and it's not true that Mommy Wilson's illness and subsequent blindness had anything to do with the genetic disease from which my maternal mother died."

"How old was Auntie Liza when Mommy Wilson went blind?"

"Not yet eleven, no, can't be; yes, she was not yet eleven when Mommy became completely blind, I think."

"Shame Ma … what year were you in at school when Mommy Wilson went blind; how did you cope?"

"We managed. There was nothing else to do, but to continue. Some days Auntie Agnes brought her machine and worked in our lounge room; by doing so she was a companion to our Mommy during the day. Other days Mommy waited for Mrs Abrahams, our neighbour, who would visit and help her get by. I was in Year Eight at school. We had planned for it to be my last year of formal schooling and I was determined to complete it.

"While the others could sew, or cook like chefs, I enjoyed reading and learning.

"About six months after Mommy went blind, tragedy struck our family again. It was probably the pressure and added responsibility of change at home that became too much for Daddy Wilson. He was illiterate and relied on Mommy to read and interpret many of his private matters. Being a proud man, Daddy never asked any of us children for help; I doubt whether he ever asked anyone other than Mommy. Daddy was stranded when Mommy became ill and particularly when she went blind. In September of that year, 1936, Daddy suffered a stroke while at work and that same morning, while in hospital, he had a fatal heart attack."

"Wow! Ma, where were you when Daddy Wilson died? What did you do when you heard; —who told you?"

"I was at school when the head teacher called me to her office. That's how I learned of Daddy's death ... the head teacher told me. No, I can't remember anything else, other than that I did not believe it ... I wanted the head teacher to tell me that it was not true, but she didn't. That morning I had packed Daddy's lunch, a serving of the previous evening's cabbage and lamb stew that I had saved for him to take to work. Dad and I spoke that morning while he drank coffee. Daddy always left at 5:30am. I walked with him to our front gate and we hugged. That was the last time I saw Daddy alive.

"Liza and I left for school at 7:15am. First we took the house key to Mrs Abrahams, next door, and then Liza and I walked to school, that was our routine."

"Where did Daddy Wilson work, Ma, and what did he do?"

"Daddy was a baker, at Duens Bakery. He had worked there since that business started, back in the early 1920s, I suppose. We never thought about the possibility of Daddy dying ... we never saw the signs. He was slim and seemed healthy, a clean-living family oriented man. It was a huge shock when Daddy died. He was only forty-five years old. Apart from a small pension at work Daddy had made no other financial arrangements for when he died."

"Where did Uncle Jesús and Auntie Agnes live, Ma; and how old were you when Daddy Wilson died?"

"Oh, after they were married Jesús and Agnes rented a semi-detached house on the slope of Devil's Peak, in University Estate. We could walk to their house from ours; not too often, because the steep slope made the one mile feel like ten. Good exercise, but not for us. We walked, or used the bus service, whenever we had to go anywhere.

"I was almost fourteen years old when Daddy died. Uncle Jesús stepped in to help with the funeral arrangements. He was also an immigrant and did not have many friends in Cape Town. At first we were a happy family, but that was not to last ..."

"You said that Uncle Jesús came from Spain ... what work did he do?"

"Uncle Jesús was a shipbuilder. He arrived in Cape Town to do repair work on ships that had suffered storm damage around Cape Point. He met Auntie Agnes during that time and stayed because he wanted her to be his wife. Jesús was a gentleman and came from Cádiz in Spain, also a port city, like Cape Town. At first his English was not good, but it improved quickly."

"If his English was so poor, Ma, how did he manage to arrange Daddy Wilson's funeral?"

"He got help from friends. They arranged a beautiful funeral. Daddy was buried out of St Mark's Anglican Church in District Six."

Ma glanced up at the ceiling again, briefly this time, before reaching for another cup of tea.

Maybe it was time to change the subject, I thought, because when Ma spoke about Auntie Agnes and Uncle Jesús then it felt as if something very bad had happened … I decided not to ask … Ma would explain when she was ready.

"When Daddy died Ma, who looked after you?"

"After Daddy's death Liza and Mommy became my responsibility. There was no alternative. We stayed on in the Woodstock house. Our only income was the shillings Mommy received as a widow's pension from Duens Bakery, but by the end of that year the money was no longer enough."

"Did you stop going to school then, Ma?"

"No, I finished formal school that year, at the end of Year Eight. To tide us over I found a part time job at José's fruit and vegetable shop in Main Road, Salt River. It was a convenient job because I could walk there; it was about five minutes from where we lived. The owner was Jesús's friend. Each day I worked from three in the afternoon until seven in the evening. On Saturdays the working hours were from seven in the morning until seven at night. Shops were always closed on Sundays back then. Sometimes, particularly during the summer months, there were wilted vegetables that I could take home. Those vegetables were cooked in stews with potatoes and either fish, meat or dried lentils. Someday I shall teach you to make split pea and barley soup. When not working at José's I searched for a full-time job.

"By the end of 1939 the world was at war for the second time. South African politicians were wrestling among themselves about whether to participate on the side of the Brits or to remain neutral.

"The war campaign then spread across Europe and North Africa. There were no jobs. Food was scarce as the world was focused on supporting the war effort. It was my third year at José's shop and despite intensifying the search for a full-time job there was nothing … instead, factories were closing down as the demand for manufactured goods decreased and more men were sent to fight, or support the fighting in North Africa, Abyssinia and Italy. There was a big military presence in Cape Town, mainly because of the essential sea route. 1940 was the beginning of the toughest years for the three of us living in the Woodstock house."

"How did you look for a job, Ma?"

"I looked in the daily newspaper. Sometimes, when there was no money to buy a paper I'd wait for the public library to make their copy available. One day I found an advert calling on all would-be factory workers to be at a certain factory gate on the following Monday morning; there were five vacancies for experienced machinists. '… be there by seven o' clock sharp' read an extract from that advert.

"It was a perfume factory. Such was my determination to find work that I was at the given address by six o' clock on that Monday morning. I had no experience and was barely 16 years old. On arrival and to my surprise, a sizeable crowd had already gathered … most had spent the night there in the hope that they would be at the front of the queue. The factories that had not closed were producing uniforms and other essentials needed for the war effort in Europe and elsewhere. I could not understand the role of a perfume manufacturer during those trying times, but the prospect of having a full-time job was all that mattered. Many people were unemployed. Food was available in rations. We were battling … not only for money with which to buy food, but finding essentials to buy was also near impossible at times.

"By seven o'clock that Monday morning about four hundred people had gathered in front of the factory gate. From where I stood only the top part of the surrounding fence was visible. All the people there were hoping to be one of the five chosen for the available vacancies.

"Shortly after seven a very important looking short man appeared. He wore a dark pin-striped wide-leg suit, white and black Crocket & Jones shoes and a wide brim black hat. I watched as he walked down the stairs from the factory entrance to near where the crowd had assembled. The biggest cigar hung from his mouth … he bit into it like a lollipop while climbing a stepladder in an effort to get onto a wooden crate—the makeshift rostrum. That scary man held a clipboard in his left hand, I could see. Once on top of the box he released the cigar, put the side of his hand to his forehead and surveyed all the unemployed who had gathered before him. After a further puff on his substantial cigar and while the pall of smoke lingered, he let out a booming scream from atop that makeshift podium behind the fence: 'You, you!' he screamed. '… with the hair – Indian Doris Day!' The scene was depressing and had I not been so desperate it would have made for a comedy skit. 'Yes you!' He continued to scream and point: 'You! Step forward!'

I wondered who the little man was calling. When I turned to look the others said that it was me. He was calling me. It was me he was referring to like that!

I involuntarily walked to the factory gate. There was a big security man who let me and the others in. I felt humiliated by the little man's manner and realised then that no matter what your status, money cannot buy class. It was the first time in my life that someone had screamed at me like that … like in the Frankenstein films that Liza and I saw at the Bijou Bioscope. I would have walked the other way. It was possible, but that day I needed a job more than the worry of having my dignity fidgeted with. I remember squeezing past the other hopefuls and the effect of their remarks. What they said was not unlike what the boys did to Pa in the cake shop you spoke of earlier."

"Why, Ma; why did they pass comments; did you also have a funny voice?" Ma knew that I was just teasing.

"No, my voice was always the same. But when people compete and depending on the level of their desperation, jealousy can get the better of them. That is when they become very unkind. We had to be tolerant. Jobs were hard to come by during the war years. Everybody needed to support their families, so I could understand why they thought that their comments were justified."

"How did you feel, Ma? Were you happy, to have a job, I mean; or were you unhappy because of what the people said?"

"I was embarrassed. My dignity had been affected by being screamed at like that. Yes, I was happy for having a job, but I was disappointed by the comments; more so because some of the people who commented were people I knew. Strange how it is, but what is said cannot be unsaid. Also, people often can't undo what they do to one another.

I continued to suffer long after the little man screamed at me. Manie Steyn was his name, a Jew from Milnerton. I am sure, had he screamed a little louder that morning his pencil moustache would have been flung off his face! Nonetheless, getting a job meant that I was able to earn a better living for my family."

"How old were you then, Ma; and Auntie Liza?"

"Seventeen, yes, I must have just turned seventeen. That was when and how I got the job at the perfume factory. Liza would have been thirteen years old; she was in Year Eight and planning to leave school at the end of that year. Already there was a young bus conductor who visited Liza on Sunday afternoons. Mommy and I teased her whenever Herbert visited. Herbert Kuhn was a very dapper man. With each visit he brought gifts for all of us. The best gift was reserved for Liza."

"What was Auntie Liza like as a child, Ma? Was she happy?"

"Oh, Liza was a lot of fun. She was very likeable and had a naughty sense of humour. For instance, after I had told her about Manie Steyn she mimicked him for months … some nights we laughed until our tummies hurt at Liza's antics. She was a very pretty child, but that was, by the by, because she had much more than a pretty face. Liza was our entertainment and she lifted our spirits whenever times were tough. We celebrated Liza's comic ways during those times; you see, Boy, it helped us to forget about life for a while; especially when we did not have money or food for dinner. We often gave our bit of food to Mommy so that she would not worry about whether there was enough for all to eat. On such evenings Liza and I would sleep after each of us had a cup of boiling water; that is how we know what it feels like to sleep on an empty stomach. It is also one of the reasons why Liza and I are such good friends—because we experienced hard times together. We were friends, sisters too, all these years, but above all we love each other very dearly."

After that episode of the story Ma did it again, she put her bottom lip up against the top, making her mouth droop. I was moved ... and Ma gave me one of those healing smiles.

"On Liza's sixteenth birthday she and Herbert married. He was then 19 years old. Agnes made the wedding dress and I was the maid of honour. Jesús walked Liza up the aisle to the altar in St Mary the Virgin, an Anglican Church in Woodstock.

We were beautiful then; Liza is beautiful now. After their marriage Liza and Herbert shared the house with Mommy and me. Since Daddy died it was reassuring to have a man in the house. It did not last long though. Herbert was earnestly saving to buy his own house. About a year later, almost to the day, Herbert and Liza moved to make their own home in Athlone. Mommy and I remained in the Woodstock house."

"When did you see Auntie Winnie again, Ma; I mean, after she was taken from you and Auntie Agnes, on the day when you arrived in Cape Town?" I asked in a clumsy way because again it may not have been the right time for that question.

"Yes, yes ... it was wonderful to see her again," Ma said hurriedly, placing her cup back in its saucer, "it was shortly after Liza and Herbert married. You are going ahead of the story, but not by too much. It was one of those experiences that shall stay with me forever; let me tell you."

Lampo did her tipple-dance, which usually meant that she needed to go outside for a wee. I opened the front door and stood there waiting. Waiting for Lampo to finish always felt like waiting too long. Ma continued when Lampo and I were back on the carpet.

"Someone whom she met on the bus had told Agnes that our sister, Winnie, did not go to school after we arrived in South Africa. Upon hearing that I became more determined than ever to find her. It took me a long time, but eventually I found out what had happened to Winnie.

"It was a Saturday morning. I was en route to do the weekly shopping in town. Wellington Fruit Growers, in Darling Street, across the road from the Grand Parade, is where we bought our cheese, cold meats and nuts. Mommy liked nuts. While walking into the city, on Darling Street, I noticed a woman carrying a baby. She was among many who were crossing the Grand Parade that Saturday morning. Her face seemed familiar. I slowed down until she also reached the sidewalk. The baby was wrapped in a powder-blue shawl. She must have been speaking to him because I heard her voice—it was the same as Agnes' and mine. Without thinking I put my hand on her shoulder. Winnie turned her head to look. 'Goodness gracious!' I said. 'It's me, Thelma.'

"Within a moment the three of us were in a tight embrace. We cried. Passers-by must have thought we had hurt one another, or the baby. 'Hello ... how is Agnes?' Where have you been ... we missed you! 'I missed you too; you are my life. I am so happy; I can't think straight.' 'Who is the baby, what is his name; how old is he?' 'How are you? Where do you live? I missed you so!' We spoke at the same time and then hugged; cried too ... but it was a happy cry. It felt like just one minute had passed even though we must have been there for much longer.

"The baby almost fell and people stood by, perhaps in case we fell down too. Many guessed what was happening, so they didn't interfere. By then I had not seen Winnie in twelve years. There we were, two young women, standing on the Grand Parade trying to salvage time that had been lost forever. In order to move forward we had to make peace with the past. It is impossible to recover the past and there is no way to fix it either. We had to make peace with our past and embrace the future. Winnie was married and holding her baby. The little wall around one of the two palm trees on the Parade became our seat. No other people mattered. We spoke, hugged, cried and laughed some more.

Auntie Winnie had arranged to meet Dan, her husband, under that tree.

Dan Begg was an Indian-looking man, a traffic policeman. I met him for the first time that Saturday morning, under the north palm tree on the Grand Parade. Winnie and I spoke and tried to cram all our lost years into one morning. Afterwards neither of us could remember the detail. She had never ceased searching for Agnes and me. From that day onwards Winnie and I were real sisters again."

"Wow! That's a nice story, Ma. I shall put it in my book someday. But why did Auntie Winnie not go to school?"

"Her adoptive family was very poor and she had to find a job when one of the parents suffered a sudden death. Winnie was in Year Five when her adoptive father died… I'm sorry, but I don't know the rest of that story."

"So Auntie Winnie did go to school?"

"She did, but not for long. That did not make her less kind, less of a person, or less of a sister. Being educated is not about how long you go to school … no, education is about your ability to think and behave in a manner that is not humiliating, but uplifting. Education is only successful if it improves the way you behave. Back then it was the norm for girls to finish school after completing Year Eight and not Year Five."

"What did Auntie Winnie do when she left school, Ma?"

"Oh yes, Auntie Winnie worked in a dairy until she got married."

"You took Jane and me to Auntie Winnie's house many times. She lived in Bishop Lavis. It is in a township like where we live. There was a big police station near her house, right?"

"Yes, that's right, you remember," Ma smiled that smile although I was not in need of any healing just then … yet it was comforting to see her deep dimples again.

"I remember Auntie Winnie's peanut butter sandwiches on white bread. She always gave us that to eat when we visited. We enjoyed it, me more than Jane. To this day I always think of Auntie Winnie when we eat peanut butter sandwiches. I liked to visit with Auntie Winnie because she was not concerned about what we looked like. Eppie, or Edward as he was sometimes called, would shout at me for sucking my thumb. Was he the baby that Auntie Win had wrapped in the shawl when you became sisters again, Ma?"

Ma's bottom lip went up against her top lip as she nodded; I think it was because she enjoyed me saying: 'when you became sisters again, you and Auntie Win'.

"I could see that you and Auntie Winnie are sisters; you look alike and you sound the same too, Ma, although Auntie Winnie has a very light complexion, light hair, blue eyes … but she's also gentle and calm. Auntie Winnie has many children; all of them are much older than Jane and me. I remember when we first went there: Millie, Magdalene and Caroline would be in the kitchen doing something for their mother. It was a small council house. There were newspapers lining the bottom of Auntie Winnie's kitchen cupboards. Various patterns had been cut into those papers. I had not seen something like that before and was fascinated."

"You remember a lot, Sammy. That is why I like to talk with you. You listen, and notice everything."

I smiled and was … well, I was a bit embarrassed. When sucking my thumb the things I noticed were often that for which non-thumb-suckers were too busy. In order to move on I asked: "Did Auntie Winnie stop working at the dairy when she got married, Ma?"

"I don't know, probably when Eppie was born, her first son."

"Did you work at the perfume factory for a long time, Ma?"

"Yes, working there was fun. I had to give up the job in the vegetable shop though. Those were hard times and people had to look after the little they had. My decision to leave the fruit and vegetable job was not easy. Mommy needed me at home in the evenings, to cook, clean and bathe her, but more importantly, so that she could have a companion. Each evening Mommy would show me and talk about her knitting, which kept her occupied during the long lonely hours of each day. Job shortages increased as the war intensified. Many of the men in our area were sent to serve as drivers and labourers in World War II."

"Why not as soldiers, Ma, why were the men who lived in your area not soldiers? It was a war. Why were they drivers and labourers and not soldiers?"

"Well, they were soldiers, but their roles were to support those who fought. Men from our community were not allowed to fight using guns. That is a very important question because it relates to the South Africa we know today, in 1972. It had to do with the classification of people. Those with dark skins, like mine, were not allowed to take up arms against people with a lighter complexion, like those who came from Europe."

"Even during the war, Ma?"

"During the war too, yes and I have the books … if you are interested then you can read about it. Nonetheless, even more people were becoming unemployed during that time. It was about 1940. There was little to no demand for perfume during the war years. The factory I worked in was losing business due to a decreasing demand. I became very anxious. Finding another job would have been almost impossible.

People on the streets of our neighbourhood continued to comment and pass remarks about why I was chosen for the job in the perfume factory. There were others who had more experience, but they chose me instead. Sometimes the world chooses you because of what you look like and it is not always right because your ability may not be the best suited for the available job. I listened when people commented. They'd say many things, but the one that comes to mind is, '… the only reason this one got that job is because she has straight hair and is pretty'. Occasionally they said similar things within earshot. It was meant to make me feel bad. Until then, 'pretty' was a term family and friends used only when describing Winnie, Agnes and Liza. My sisters are very pretty… but suddenly I was called pretty too."

"Why did you think that you were not pretty Ma?"

"You see, my boy, I grew up in a world where the colour of your skin determined whether you were pretty or not. It also determined what you could and could not do. Winnie, Agnes and Liza are light-skinned. I must be more like my mother's people—they were islanders and were dark-skinned.

"I read about the workers on St Helena Island. They worked the fields and the authors describe them as having 'Bronze skins that glistened in the early afternoon sun'. I am of those people, but it did not mean that my work is limited to fields. After all, I am a person first, like any other person. The colour of my skin, my hair, the shape of my nose and lips is what I look like. But before that I am a person, like everyone else. I aspired to become a social worker. It was an achievement that came true through persistent hard work. Nothing worthwhile comes without a struggle and some sacrifice. Sometimes we have to do things that are difficult, but nothing is impossible."

I enjoyed Ma most when she spoke like that. To describe exactly how I felt is very difficult. All I recall is that it was an experience to behold when Ma spoke like that—in addition she knew how to spell the words that I did not understand, and it became homework if I repeated incorrectly.

"How did you feel, being the only one in your family with a dark skin, Ma?"

"You don't miss that which you do not know. I did not think about it… what could I do? You see, when you are a man of average height people seldom refer to how tall or short you are. But be short or tall, then people remind you, as though you could forget. In my case not a day went by without someone reminding me of how dark my skin was. To be self-conscious about it was not going to contribute to realising my dreams. My skin is very pretty. Look at it?" Ma put her arm in front of me to examine, as if I had not noticed that her skin was dark.

"When I apply Oil of Olay to my face it nourishes my skin. After a few applications my face becomes soft, clear and smooth. I could not understand why it bothered the others so much. When I looked in the mirror my skin seemed very pretty."

"What did you do when the others teased you, Ma?"

"Yes, maybe some of them were only teasing … but the constant reminding about my dark skin did not bother me; nor was I upset by the fun they had at my expense. It was the unspoken suggestion that I was the lesser sister, the ugly one, and the one that was not clever like Agnes, all because of my dark complexion. Those were the comments that hurt. Yes, when I was younger those comments made me very sad. I can remember asking Gentle Jesus why it had to be me who got the dark skin, but after a while I refused to have those comments hurt me … because … my skin is pretty. When I was outside, where the African sun lived, there was seldom a time when my skin hurt. Not like my sisters, they had to apply lotions and potions, wear hats and behave as if melting was imminent. The entire society, even the country, possibly the world too, everyone seemed obsessed with skin colour."

I tried to think and feel the way Ma must have felt and it was sad; so without much ado my next question followed: "Did you ever wish to have a light skin, Ma?"

"There's nothing wrong with my skin. Other people decided that there was something wrong, probably because someone had told them that dark skins are ugly. I made a lot of mistakes in my life. But one of the things I did right was not to allow negative comments to make me less of a person.

"Perhaps Pa's mistake was to allow the comments about his speech defect to determine who he became.

"You know, people believe that tall is better than short; that thin is better than fat and that blonde hair is prettier than brown hair. People can't help themselves; they discriminate against one another at the slightest opportunity, which is how they've been conditioned.

I realised during the late 1930s that the comments made about my dark skin were not always said in jest. By then the media had begun to differentiate between people who were light-skinned and those who were dark. Those who were light were encouraged to believe that they were better than those who were dark; most believed it without question, and the joke was always on me, because I was dark-skinned."

"Sorry to ask again Ma, but what did you do?"

"There was not much that I could do! I only knew South Africa then, but I think that in other parts of the world it was the same; people who had dark skins were automatically second and third class citizens.

In the mid to late 1940s laws were introduced that made it legal to discriminate against people based on their skin colour. Those with light appearances were, according to the law, the best people. It began then and steadily became worse; we were judged, classed and placed into categories determined by complexion, hair texture, thickness of lips and by the shape of our noses. Those who had tight curly hair, broad noses and thick lips, in addition to being dark-skinned, became third class citizens. Light-skinned people were encouraged by the media, the laws and the norms to believe that they were

36

superior and every indication was in place to make dark-skinned people feel inferior. I refused to be inferior. There was nothing much that I could do about it!"

"But you had to do something, Ma; what did you do? What are you doing now, in 1972, when those rules continue to be applied? Do you accept it; are you a second class person, Ma?"

"In South Africa, to discriminate against people because of external features became the cornerstone of our law; and it, the law, always determines how we live. Laws are like rules; they determine how we live too. I am forced to accept it, Boy. Sorry if I disappoint you, but I also want to have peace in my lifetime you know."

My memory is one where I wished that I too had a healing smile to offer my Ma—like those she gave me. At the same time I was cross because my Ma accepted being a second class citizen; I was also angry because it was stupid of my Ma to do nothing but accept stuff that was wrong and unfair. To apply different norms as determined by the colour of the person's skin did not only apply to Ma. No, it applied to all people in South Africa. We do that to one another without care for what it feels like, or for whether it is the right thing to do.

That look of helplessness had returned to Ma's eyes. I felt sad. Ma gathered herself to continue with the explanation.

"According to the law in South Africa I continue to be a second class person and as a woman I am treated as less of a person than a man. Technically it makes me a third class person. This is not the reason I want you to know the entire story, our story ... as you grow older you will begin to see, experience and learn what it feels like to be lessened."

"Do Jane and I also experience the effect of that word, discrimination?"

"Yes, everyone does and most of the time we are not aware. The sad part is that we have become accustomed to receiving and giving discrimination—it has become the way we are. We can stop but only if we understand what it is; there's no other way."

"Ma, how did you react when you were discriminated against?" I asked.

"Nobody told me about it. I learned the hard way. It affected me badly. Instead of seeing it behind every tree I developed a subconscious need to prove myself equal to others.

Whenever I dressed in one of the frocks that Agnes sewed, people commented about my beauty. It made me love Agnes more. She was responsible for me feeling like a person, feeling that I belonged. To be pretty is a responsibility though. The whole of you has to be pretty before you can own that accolade. I know that you won't understand what I mean, but promise that you will remember?"

"I shall remember, Ma; that being pretty is a responsibility; that being pretty only applies if the person's behaviour is also pretty ... yes?"

"There, you understand it better than I thought ..."

Ma paused to look at the ceiling. When she looked back at me I could see tears welling in her eyes. I did not know why. Ma sipped more tea and dabbed her nose before explaining: "It was good to hear people say that I was pretty. I think that all people need to hear something good. The comment about my beauty was always welcome, but Agnes, Winnie and later Liza, they were always the most beautiful."

"I think that you are beautiful too, Ma. Did Mommy Wilson discriminate against you like Grandma Edith did against Pa?"

"Thank you for saying that I am pretty. No, Mommy Wilson treated me like she did Agnes and Liza; Mommy got on with life and there was no time for discrimination. Mommy, Agnes and I came from St Helena to live in Cape Town. Other people recognised it on our accents when we spoke. They referred to us as 'Saints'—though some St Helenians were anything but saintly! We worked hard. It is not unusual for foreigners to work hard. Little is known about the immigrants from Saint Helena who arrived in South Africa, or those who went to live and work in England and other countries. Perhaps it is because we were workers, a peaceful people, not entrepreneurs… that must be the reason why so little is known about us."

Chapter Three

James de la Cruz, Mrs Freeman and the Harpist

"Ma, you were married to Anne, Charles and Brenda's father; where did you meet, and when did you stop being married?"

"Yes, I was married to someone else. It was long before I met and married your Pa. I met James de la Cruz at the perfume factory. We were employed on the same day; he was one of the five people chosen by Manie Steyn."

Ma began to speak in that selective way again—short and stubby. It felt as if her sentences were incomplete. There was obviously detail that she did not want to share, so I decided to listen without interrupting.

"We were friends for a long time before I invited James to meet my family. It was a Sunday afternoon when he visited for the first time. My sisters, Agnes and Liza were there when James joined us for afternoon tea.

Mommy asked many questions after James had left. Most important for her was what he looked like. I explained, although I felt uncomfortable about Mommy's motive. Liza on occasion, and Agnes too, had their chances to describe him to Mommy.

Winnie would have understood how I felt had she lived with us. She was always my 'thought rescue blanket'. In other words, I thought 'what would Winnie say?' whenever life got tough and when I needed someone to support me.

Mommy spoke a lot about James after he visited us. She said many negative things, probably as a result of what the others had told her. I got the impression that Mommy did not want me to have a partner. Once, and out of the blue, Mommy asked me: 'Thelma, when James puts the comb through his hair, does it hurt?' I was offended by her question. That question served to identify and class anyone who did not fit the European mould. Mommy's question implied that James was not like us and that he was not welcome. I chose not to reply."

"What did Mommy Wilson say when you did not respond, Ma?"

"Oh, after his first visit James was not allowed to come to our house. My mother said so. Thereafter, James and I met secretly on street corners, in bus shelters and at work."

"How did the people at work behave towards you?"

"The jealousy at work continued. Colleagues were of the opinion that I got the job because of favouritism. After all, it was their family members and friends who had more experience and yet were not appointed. 'Doris Day and the ugly prince' was what others called James and me."

"When did you marry, Ma?"

"You are in a hurry again. When James was eventually allowed to visit, that was when we got married … because when I was out meeting James then Mommy was alone. My mother's diabetic condition made her very frail. She needed full-time care. The neighbours helped when I was at work, but it was not enough and Mommy insisted that she not be placed in a care facility.

"Anne, Charles and Brenda were born while James and I lived with my mommy in her Woodstock home. When Brenda was born I told James that we had to find a place of our own with our three children and Mommy.

"The country was changing rapidly by then. Woodstock was becoming more and more industrialised. Shops and factories appeared where previously there were houses, parks and open fields. Many people were encouraged to live in the suburbs. Townships were created to house ordinary working people.

"Athlone was the collective name given to a section of the Cape Flats that was reserved for people who were neither light nor very dark-skinned. The greater Athlone area was further divided into separate sections where professional people, tradesmen and workers lived. Skin colour is the big differentiator in South Africa.

"People from District Six and Woodstock were encouraged to live in Athlone. It was in keeping with the new South African policy of separate development. District Six was left to deteriorate until it was a slum. After all the residents had moved, many by force, the state declared District Six an exclusive residential area for light-skinned people.

"The last dark-skinned people were moved out by force, despite their protests. It was all part of a bigger plan, which was to aggregate and accommodate people with similar physical appearances in the same predetermined areas. The government had decided that people who looked more or less the same and who shared a 'common culture' should live together. The same policy was applied throughout the country."

As Ma explained, I wondered how she knew all those things.

"I suggested to James that if we rented a house in Alicedale, a suburb of Athlone, then my mother could live with us. By then my mommy was fond of James; his tight curly light brown hair no longer mattered. She could not see anyway. James spent time talking with her about things that my Mommy was interested in. You will find that there are attractive characteristics about most every person.

"Alicedale was close to where Liza and Herbert lived. I thought it a good idea for the family to live closer."

"When did you move to Athlone, Ma?"

"We never did. James was not interested in moving. Women cannot take leading decisions without the consent of their husbands. That is how the law is—now in 1972. The law takes more notice of the husband than it does of the wife. I think this is so because it's mainly men who make the rules.

"Life carried on, as it does, and we continued to live in Woodstock.

"World War II ended on 15 August 1945. It was my twenty-second birthday on that day. Jobs remained scarce. More than sixty million people died in that war. Afterwards large parts of Europe had to be reconstructed.

"Meanwhile the South African authorities continued to expand their separate development laws. All citizens had to be identified by specific group labels. It was a divide and rule social and economic system."

"Could people choose which group to belong to, Ma?"

"Well, by 1950 South Africa had a Population Registration Act. People who needed to be part of another group could apply to the Electoral Officer for reclassification."

"What does it mean to be reclassified?"

"Well, if people met certain criteria, then they could have themselves registered under a different label. That was referred to as reclassification."

"But why did people need to be reclassified?"

"You must understand, Boy, the new system did not allow people from different groups to live together, get married and have children. Both had to belong to the same group. So, one of the two had to take a test, or apply for re-labelling. Reclassified and re-labelled is the same thing. Those who passed the test were reclassified. People with different skin colours who continued to live together were arrested. They were charged and imprisoned for contravening the Immorality Act.

"Those people, who are labelled 'native' are forced to live in far off areas— 'homelands,' a kind of reserve. When so-called natives migrate to Cape Town they have to have properly endorsed passbooks. When the endorsements in the passbooks expire then the individual has to return to the 'homeland'. Failure to go back results in arrest and repatriation."

"What does repatriation mean, Ma?"

"In this case it means that the police arrest people and take them back to where they came from, the 'homelands'."

As the years progressed the laws became more limiting, prescriptive and brutal. It was 20 June 1972 when Ma and I had that discussion. South Africa was a police state and its citizens were controlled by a politicised police force. The South African Police Force supervised the application of all discrimination laws.

During that discussion I remember asking: "With the reclassification of people, what labels did they use, Ma?"

Ma's reply then was: "There were many labels. Some changed over time. At first the labels were: European, Indian, Mixed and Native. Every group was allocated separate privileges. The Europeans had the most beneficial privileges; followed by the 'mixed' and Indian groups. Those who are labelled 'native' get the worst treatment under the discrimination laws. This group, the 'natives', as a collective, are the majority group in the country.

"Well, all people who did not fit into an obvious category formed part of the 'mixed' group. I was labelled 'mixed'. In time the government decided to change this label, but I'll explain that later."

"Was it really only about skin colour?"

"Yes, and it continues to be about skin colour. Back when it started, cultural practices, religion and language played a part too. But primarily the institutionalised discrimination was about skin colour.

"So obsessed were people about their complexion that many who were dark-skinned applied harmful bleaching creams in order to have lighter skins. The media and the laws in the country created an environment that lured dark-skinned people into thinking that they were inadequate and ugly. That is why dark people applied bleaching ointment to their skins.

"The same was done to tight curly hair. Instead of grooming the hair to a healthy and beautiful natural shine, people who had tight curly hair relaxed it by using various chemicals. Some of the chemicals were harmful. Often the result of hair relaxing treatments was stiff straight hair that appeared very dry and sometimes even hard. People generally see in others that which is better than what they have naturally, but it is just perception. Watch that you don't also fall into that media trap.

"The law continues to reinforce that people with light skins are superior to those who are dark. The laws and the media are so successful that despite the risk of contracting skin cancer, dark-skinned people continue to apply bleaching creams.

"Meanwhile, people who have lighter skins are almost oblivious to the trappings of superiority. Certain so-called 'natives' sought to become members of the 'mixed' group. Those who were part of that mixed group sought, if they could, to become part of the European group. It was not unusual for those in the 'mixed' group, who looked European, to take what was called 'The Pencil Test'. If the person passed the test they were reclassified and joined the European group—terms and conditions applied though. It was not very different to the way animals were graded.

"In time the entire South African society was affected by the segregation laws. Today every group has its own schools and universities. Post offices and shops developed separate entrances for people with different classifications. Churches, buses and train carriages, bioscopes and other entertainment centres are also geared to accommodate the different groups separately. The best beaches at the seaside are reserved for light-skinned people. Rocky beaches and those with a dangerous backwash current are where the left over folk swim. Eventually everything became as you now experience it, in 1972. Since 1948 many more measures were introduced to reserve the best parts of the country for exclusive use by those who were initially labelled European."

"Do you know people who were reclassified, Ma?"

"Yes, when the Population Registration Act was accepted as law, Agnes, my sister, took the test—'The Pencil Test'. Agnes wished to be reclassified because her husband, Jesús, was European. According to the law either one of them would have had to be reclassified. Agnes took advantage of her light skin, her European features and the gentle curl in her auburn hair. Their daughter, Linda, was two years old at the time. If Agnes failed the reclassification test then she would have broken the law by continuing to live with Jesús and Linda. Agnes would then have been arrested and put in jail. You will learn about those laws someday—the Mixed Marriages Act of 1949 and the Immorality Act of 1950."

When Ma said this I repeated the words 'Immorality Act' because I thought that the other one was simple enough to understand. Later I learned that the Mixed Marriages Act first became law in South Africa back in 1927 and that it had been amended in 1949. This, for me, raised a number of questions about both my parents and my grandparents.

Ma seemed concerned that I did not understand everything that she discussed. After all, I was just twelve years old. Ma insisted that she speak with me as if I could understand everything. "You have to understand these things otherwise the conditions in this country will consume you like it does so many of us. Do you understand what I am explaining to you, Sammy-boy?"

"Yes Ma. I understand. Don't forget that you, Pa and all the people who come to our house when Jane and I are home, you always talk about these things. That is how I learned to understand, and also to use some of those words. But every time there are new words, where do you learn them?"

Ma briefly checked the ceiling, shook her head slightly, ignored my question and then continued: "When the pencil was put in Agnes's hair by the Electoral Officer it fell out without resistance. That is how Agnes was reclassified."

"What happened after that, Ma?"

"The Population Registration Act also changed group labels. The new classification changed how my sister related to me. After her reclassification Agnes no longer visited our Woodstock home. When Liza and I walked to her house she would pretend to not be at home. There was never a response when we knocked. Yet, when Liza went there by herself Agnes welcomed her. I concluded that it was because Liza too was light and had fair hair.

"I think Agnes was afraid that the neighbours and her new European friends would see her and my likeness. When we were younger, without fail, people would say that I was the dark version of my older sister. Agnes feared being branded a 'half-breed'. That is how I lost my sister-mommy. It was when that pencil fell out of her hair. I was saddened beyond measure. Because her skin was light and a pencil fell from her hair, that is why I lost my sister-mommy. Twenty-two years later and the pain remains the same, fresh, like it happened yesterday. The taking from me never stops..."

Tears spilled from Ma's eyes this time. I stood up from the carpet and put my arm with its spit-wet thumb around her neck. My body had grown since my last visit. I could no longer sit on Ma's lap without hurting her. Instead I sat next to her and said: "Don't worry, Ma, someday all people will be the same in South Africa."

Ma poured more tea, dabbed her eyes, blew her nose and peeped at the ceiling once more before resuming her story.

"I also hope that someday we will all be the same in South Africa. The reality is that people do to others that which was done to them. I know that we will come to our senses. But will we have learned that it is wrong to inflict this pain on one another?

"I am afraid that when that time comes then we will not yet have learned our lesson and then we'll do much the same as now to one another.

"You see my boy, when the government makes a law they do not do enough to check with the people if it is acceptable. Separating people by way of the law causes a lot of misery and unhappiness. That is why I think that it will not continue forever. Nothing that is bad goes on forever. The laws will have to be replaced. Hopefully the new laws will not find reasons why some of us are to be advantaged above others."

"Pa says that we will get a democratic government after this. What is a democratic government, Ma?"

"That is why I am afraid. I am afraid that the experience of ordinary people will be the same even though the government will refer to itself as democratic."

"Yes, but what is 'democratic', Ma?"

"You see, you are being impatient again. I am trying to explain to you! Where was I? None of us, yes, none of us was born selfish and greedy. When we get power to act, that is when we change. That is when we become selfish and greedy. We enact what we saw others do when they had the power to act. When you are older then read a book by a man who uses the name, George Orwell. The book is called *Animal Farm*. Read that book carefully and then you'll begin to understand what I mean. People do what they see others do. You will realise that people copy the behaviour of those who had power before them. Maybe to be greedy, selfish and arrogant is a human trait; perhaps it is not something that people copy from one another, I don't know."

"Can I get that book to read on the train tomorrow, Ma, while I travel to school?"

"Yes, but then we have to leave earlier. You can wait at the station while I run up to buy a copy at Cranford's Bookshop in Long Street. I have a few books that should be exchanged too. My plan was to go next week, when alone again... but we can go tomorrow."

"But Ma, when the 'police force government' is replaced then we will get a democracy. That is what Pa says. What is a democracy? You have not told me yet."

"Democracy is supposed to mean that if the majority of the citizens make the same decision it will be applied by the government. The word comes from the Greek language and means 'the rule of the people'. At school you will learn that democracy is a form of government that allows all citizens to participate equally. According to my understanding of the term, democracy is wonderful in theory. It makes sense, but in reality it is often impractical, particularly here in Africa. Our rules do not apply to everyone equally. If you grease someone's palm, or have the right friends, then any wrong can become right. Perhaps this is what happens elsewhere in the world too, I do not know."

"What does 'grease someone's palm' mean, Ma?" She smiled before answering: "To grease a palm is an idiomatic expression which means that you can pay someone in authority to ignore the wrong that you do, or, you can pay and in return receive special favours. Others refer to it as corruption, or bribery. We need to talk more about what system we use instead of democracy. You and I will talk about that when you have accumulated enough knowledge with which to think.

"How did we get to speak about politics, I wonder? I want to tell you the story of our lives, not discuss the politics. Yet, the politics here in South Africa determines how and where we live."

"I learned a lot from what you said, Ma. We do not get to speak about the politics in South Africa at school. All that I know is what you and Pa discuss and what you have told me. But we were talking about Auntie Agnes; when next did you talk with her, Ma?"

"No. I have not seen Auntie Agnes since she was reclassified. Apparently there's a section in the Population Registration Act about successful reclassifications being reversed if it is found that the person has dark-skinned siblings. I think that may be the reason why Auntie Agnes refuses to have anything to do with me."

"Did you not try to see her, or to speak with Auntie Agnes, Ma?"

"Yes, many times. I'll tell you as the story progresses, but I did not have much time to worry about my sister; not with three young children, a husband and a blind mother to care for!"

Ma had become cross, I could see, but she soon calmed herself. I settled back on the floor with Lampo so that Ma would continue with the story, our story.

"Yes," Ma liked to say 'yes' before speaking. Maybe it was a habit she learned from Pa, even though he said 'Ya!' for different reasons. After a quick sip of tea Ma continued: "It was a Thursday, about five thirty in the evening. I arrived home an hour earlier than usual. Those aluminium pots, Hart Pots, were dancing on our Dover coal cooker. It was winter, 21 June 1951—the kitchen, and later the entire little terrace house was warm and cosy. I was making tomato and spaghetti food, pot-food. It's a winter favourite in most every Cape home. I used companion herbs: thyme, sweet basil, a bit of clove and some bay leaves."

"I want to learn how to cook that stew."

"Oh, I thought that you knew? You stood next to me while I cooked it a few nights ago. That is why I sent you to Dick's Butchery, remember?"

"Yes."

"Well, you need stewing lamb, spaghetti, tomatoes, an onion, salt and just a touch of sugar. Because I worked during the day pot-roasted meat and fish were cooked on a Sundays and frozen for use during the week. That Thursday James took the portion of cooked stewing lamb out of the communal freezer. In the evening, when I arrived home, Anne would have heated the meat and with extracted meat-oil she braised the onions to a golden brown colour. I added a section of garlic and some herbs. The six tomatoes were already blanched in boiling water to remove the skin. They were added to the meat with some salt and a touch of sugar to address bitterness from the tomatoes.

"There, my pots were ready to dance for eight to ten minutes while I checked on Mommy. James had only to cook the spaghetti.

"When you start to cook then watch out for the garlic. It can make your hands smell for days. Try this: after working with garlic rub your hand on metal, any metal. The kitchen tap is a good metal. You'll find that it absorbs the smell and your hands will be fine thereafter. Mrs Abrahams, our neighbour, 'Auntie Girlie', she taught me that remedy. Sorry, I have no advice for the aromatic miasma that will surround you after having eaten raw garlic. Eat parsley, which is said to help. However, cooked garlic will not leave you breathing like a dragon. No matter what others say, that smell on your breath is anti-social.

"So, when my pots were dancing I went off to check on Mommy. In passing I warned the others that dinner was almost ready. By implication they knew to eat while I was with Mommy. It is most infuriating when the meal is served and people are not ready to eat. Spaghetti! James had again forgotten to cook the spaghetti that night, so I was back in the kitchen. I asked James to watch and ensure that it did not become too soft. For this dish the spaghetti only needs five minutes in boiling water. Then, when it is added to the tomatoes and meat the other flavours will infuse. Let it simmer for about ten minutes before serving."

"When we next spend time at Mammy Cynthia's home then I shall ask her to let me cook there. Does Jane know how to cook this meal, Ma?"

"Yes, I taught her a long time ago."

I could not help wondering what else Ma taught Jane—told Jane—that she had not (yet) shared with me.

"Well, that evening, when I got to Mommy, her room had a strange feel to it. I greeted her in my usual happy way. I did so to lift her spirits a bit. Unlike the other days, that evening Mommy only moved her hand to acknowledge me. She lay on the bed. Other evenings Mommy asked me to lift her for greater comfort. Whilst doing so I would tell her about my day at work and share bits of news. I always tried to do so in the most animated way.

46

"That night was different. The bed-bath utensils were in place. When the inner plate of the Dover cooker was removed then the old cast iron water pot got direct heat. Within minutes boiling water for Mommy's bed-bath was ready.

"I encouraged James and the children to eat before I took the bath water through to Mommy's room. Yes, they knew not to wait for me, particularly when I was talking to Mommy. That evening Mommy seemed keen to have me closer. In an almost-whisper voice she asked about the colour of my dress. I sensed that Mommy was not really interested, but merely needed me to speak. 'It is a light green, Mommy. Agnes sewed it last December; the dress that has little black roses all over the fabric.' Mommy did not remember. It was unusual because she had a special interest in designs, colour and fabric. I continued to explain: '...you will know, Mommy; it has a round, almost boat-shaped neck and snug sleeves onto my elbows. I wear it with a narrow black belt; black shoes; and a matching handbag. From my waist the dress opens into a pleated flair with the skirt down to my knees. You know, Mommy; remember the time I asked to use your black clutch bag? Well, that dress was very pretty when worn with those Mary Jane black patent leather heeled sandals that I saved to buy. I have to dress down when going to work. I can't walk that long distance on those heels. My work shoes are nice, comfortable too.' Mommy mouthed what I thought was, 'That is a pretty dress.'

"Her speech took so much effort that evening. I spoke loudly, with enthusiasm and a lot of detail, so that Mommy did not have to talk much. Perhaps that was a mistake, maybe she should have spoken. When we're wrapped up in concern, too busy with care and worry, then we forget to let people be. Mommy went quiet; that too was unusual. I was a motor-mouth and failed when I should have attended to her distant presence. Other times Mommy was visibly anxious to speak; on occasion she'd finish my sentences so that it could be her turn, but that evening was different.

"My hand was up against the top part of her back. Washing the top of Mommy's back was the easiest, followed by her lower ... then suddenly that evening I was unable to hold her up by myself, let alone with one hand while the other washed.

Realising the moment I let go of the washcloth. With both hands I gently lowered Mommy and laid her down in the bed. Knowing what had happened I managed only to stand back in shock. Maybe I said out loud: 'Here is the woman who loved me before we met; who took me to her home to be her daughter and companion to the end.' Mommy died that evening and I had no words, no feeling, nothing. The taking never stops, that's how it is."

Ma's left hand was over her mouth. Tears streamed from underneath her bi-focal spectacles as she relived the moment when Mommy Wilson died.

"It was hard, my boy. Mommy and I had our differences. At the end though she was my true friend, and I knew that she cared and loved me like only a mother can. There is a special bond between people who struggle together and those who end the day hungry; they grow even closer because of that experience."

"I am sorry, Ma."

That was all I could think of to say. Sometimes I felt in the way and useless, because I could not contribute properly to most things.

"When I got home at night Mommy was always eager to hear about my day. Mommy always had a need to hear everything in detail. My talking to her at night allowed Mommy to see the world. During the day I would write notes to myself. That is how I remembered to tell Mommy everything in the evenings when she bathed. Each day I looked forward to my time with Mommy. That evening though, that evening was the last ..."

"What happened next, Ma? Did your mommy really die that night?"

"Well, I sat down on the chair, the one beside the bed. I sat there and thought back to my seventh year. In my mind's eye there was a black school tunic, bare feet and my night dress in the worn brown paper bag. My sisters and I were equally afraid and nervous when we walked down that ship's gangway on arriving in Cape Town. I continued to replay the event that resulted in Mommy Wilson becoming my mother. Agnes and Winnie were there and Agnes spoke for all three of us. I remember, Agnes had a book in which she sketched, and she too had a nightie in her own brown paper bag. That was all we had when Mommy Wilson became our mother.

"The people of Cape Town spoke a different language. Later I learned that they pronounced words differently to us. 'Sounds like singing when these people speak,' Agnes frequently remarked. Mommy and Daddy Wilson were our new parents. That, I suppose, was reassuring. My Dad sent us here with a promise that he would visit. He never did. I sat beside Mommy and looked at her while continuing to replay in my mind that which had made us a family. Mommy was a St Helena woman and I wanted to do for her what I could not do for my own mother.

"I've told you this before, but it was what played over in my mind whilst sitting next to Mommy at the hour of her death."

"Yes, Ma, you said most of this earlier, but this time I have a better understanding."

I remember fighting against the emotion in my voice at the time. I was more interested in what happened afterwards. Ma insisted on talking, so I didn't change the subject with what could have been an insensitive question.

"Mommy Wilson and my mother were friends when they both lived on the island. This is another reason why we came to live with the Wilsons; they were the closest we could get to experiencing family." Ma paused to look at the ceiling before she proceeded to tell more: "Mommy's death made me an orphan again. Then I was an adult orphan.

"About an hour went by with me thinking and possibly talking to myself. By then James had fed the children and after Anne had done the dishes all of them went to bed. Without opening the door James came to enquire: 'Are you nearly done?' Without pausing for an answer James said: 'The children are in bed, waiting to say goodnight to you.'

"I told James to come inside. After he recovered from shock we decided on the next steps: to inform the police, hospital and the rest of our small family. I went to the room to greet the children, so that they could sleep. James was not being very helpful.

"We did not have ready access to telephones back then. The following morning I sent telegrams to those family members and friends who were not easily contactable. Liza, Herbert and I; we made all the funeral arrangements. A special letter was written to Agnes. The walk up the hill to University Estate was strenuous, but it was my duty that mattered more. As usual, my knocking at their front door went unanswered. Before leaving I placed the letter underneath a brass door knocker.

"Mommy Wilson was buried in the Wolraad Woltemade Cemetery near Goodwood; in the section reserved for people whom the government labelled as 'mixed'."

"Wow! They discriminate against people when they are dead too?"

"Yes, every population group has its own facilities. It includes where you get buried. I think that the reason for this is not only to keep the dead apart, but also to ensure that those who visit the graves do so, in keeping with the law."

"Did you see Auntie Agnes at Mommy's funeral Ma?"

"No, Agnes, Jesús and Linda did not attend Mommy's funeral and I don't know why. I did my duty to inform her that the woman who had given of herself so that we could have, had died."

"Did you dislike Auntie Agnes because of what she did to you, Ma?"

"Auntie Agnes is my sister …"

Ma looked up at the ceiling again. It felt different. I was anxious that Ma would become upset. Maybe I should not have asked that question, was a brief thought.

"Was your life very different after your mommy died, Ma?" I asked quickly, so as to make Ma forget about my earlier dumb question.

"At first I missed Mommy, but to look after a blind, frail woman who increasingly needed more care was difficult. My ambition was to finish school and to study about people so that I could work for them."

"Did you continue to live in your mommy's house, Ma?"

"You mean, James and me with the children? Well, yes, we continued to live in Woodstock. I was exhausted. Having looked after Mommy for all those years, since Agnes and Liza got married and having had no leave, not even maternity leave, had taken its toll. I was tired. And James was no longer the man I had married. He was not interested in being a father to our children. Every morning I was up early. At four, that was when my day started. James refused to help. He would take his lunch and go to work leaving me to take the older children to school and Brenda to a day-care mother. Fortunately the school was within walking distance and very soon Anne and Charles were able to walk there without me. The day-care facility was conveniently situated on my route to work."

"Was the war over by then, Ma?"

"Yes, by then the war was long past."

"And you Ma, did you continue to work at the perfume factory?"

"I continued to work there. It was nine years later and there were many efforts afoot to reconstruct Europe after the war. Perfume products continued to be luxury items and there was less need for them. Our sales volumes were low and many contracts were cancelled.

"The same man who hired me more than ten years earlier, Manie Steyn, he arranged and then spoke at a staff meeting. By then Mr Steyn had lost the arrogant manner and had become quite the gentleman. You see how people can change? Mr Steyn explained to the staff why business was bad; he provided reasons; and then concluded with a plan to save as many jobs as was possible, but: 'Despite these attempts,' he warned '… there are those of you who are going to be retrenched. The business is not making enough money to pay all salaries.' It was the first time I heard of retrenchment."

"What did you do, Ma?"

"Not having a job was the worst that could happen to me. I had three children at school, and an un-cooperative husband. Then I was in the second year of completing Year Twelve via a correspondence course. Weeks later the first wave of retrenchments began 'To avert foreclosure,' said Mr Steyn."

The night was dragging on and I was becoming tired. There was a lot more that I wanted to know about and to ask.

"What is that, what is foreclosure, Ma?"

"Foreclosure happens when a business can no longer pay its debts. James was among the first to be retrenched. Thereafter he stayed home and drank wine all day. So much that I was not able to leave the children in his care. Fortunately all three were at school during the day and Anne was able to care for the others without her father's help.

"It was not unusual to return home and find James asleep on the lounge floor with empty bottles beside him. Music blaring from the wireless could be heard from the front gate and the children would be behind a closed door in what was once Mommy's room. When I got home Anne would report on what had happened; she'd say: 'Mamma, Pappa had visitors and when the two men left he shouted at us to go to the room and stay there until you got home. I asked him to turn the volume down but he shouted in response, saying that it was his radio and that he could make it as loud as he wanted.'

"I worried about the children and also about our neighbours, many of whom were Muslim. It was disrespectful of James to appear drunk in the street when the religious views of our neighbours opposed the drinking of wine and other alcoholic beverages. When James drank, his entire personality changed. It was as if the wine drank him. On Fridays he went off with friends and often only returned on a Monday. When I got home on a Monday night James would be there. Every week he had a different excuse. His favourite was that he visited with family in Worcester and got a lift with cousins on a Monday morning. I tried to speak with James but he refused to respond. It was clear that he preferred to spend weekends in Worcester instead of at home with the children and me. He was not making any effort to find work. All he did was dress up and drink wine with friends who were also unemployed. My talking to James only made matters worse. Clearly, our marriage was over.

"I had to think of the future, particularly for my three children. I trained them to become more self-sufficient. It allowed me to complete Year Twelve and start work on ultimately achieving a university qualification.

"When James and I divorced he moved to live in Worcester. It was about two hours by car from Cape Town. The children became entirely my responsibility. James did not have a job and had no income. When he had work there was no contribution either. The result was that I reared my children alone. It remains more trouble than it is worth for a woman to fight in court over financial support from a man for his own children, particularly if the man is unemployed."

"How did you manage to work, look after three children and study, Ma?"

"Well, my lessons were posted to me. I did the homework when the children went to bed and submitted assignments by posting it ahead of the due date. It took me two years to complete Year Twelve and obtain my final high school certificate. I studied and completed three subjects each year.

"At first it was difficult, but after I had developed and settled into a routine the schoolwork became easier. My first goal was to rent a house in Alicedale, Athlone, and then to study, so that I could have a career. When Daddy Wilson died and Liza and I lived alone with Mommy, a social worker from the Child Welfare Department regularly visited us. Mrs Hennesey checked that we were doing well. That social worker left a big impression on me. She was gentle and kind. Whenever Mrs Hennesey visited she always first listened to Mommy before talking with Liza and me. She always kept her word. We looked forward to her visits. I wanted to be like Mrs Hennesey. That is why I studied Social Work, Sociology, Social Anthropology and English."

"What about the segregation laws Ma, did it make it more difficult to study?"

"No. I realised that if you set your mind to do something then it could be done. I found a way. It was to make a selection, develop a routine and be consistent.

"Though we were denied access to good libraries and other needed facilities, I forged ahead regardless. Most people forgot and younger people did not realise that they were living restricted lives. Life carried on. Being restricted had become normal in our world. For me it was different, probably because I had the early experience of a life where we were free to be people. Let's not forget that people lost loved ones due to the divide and rule policies in South Africa; I lost a sister.

"But I persisted with the studies. That was how I would give my children a better chance to live out their dreams."

"It must have been very difficult, Ma, but I suppose that for me it will be the same, if not more difficult. When the segregation laws are replaced then there will probably be other problems. It sounds as if nothing was easy."

"Oh, it was very difficult, particularly the schoolwork. I didn't know any other person who studied the same subjects as me. For that reason sharing and learning from others was not possible. Teachers at nearby schools could have helped, but I was at work and in the evenings there were other responsibilities that needed my attention. During the week I recorded all the questions that were not clear, or that were not sufficiently discussed in my study guides. On a Saturday morning I went for help to the Cape Town City Library. The library was inside the City Hall and across from the Grand Parade.

"I would leave home early. Anne, who was about eleven or twelve years old, would take charge of Charles and Brenda. I first shopped for food and other essentials before visiting the library for about two hours. The library was reserved, but not for me. I thought that it was okay because my intention was only to page through a few reference books. Most of what I needed to learn more about was contained in encyclopaedias.

"To my surprise, instead of being chased away, I got a lot of help from many of the library employees. That was how I became a regular at the Cape Town City Library on Saturday mornings. In time it became part of my routine. The friendlier I became with the librarians, the more they took an interest in my progress. Eventually they were like my own faculty of teachers. In order to stay within the law I would be taken through to a back room, away from the eyes of other library users. Once there the librarians showed me the material they had set aside for when I visited."

"Did you do well, Ma, like Jane, or better?"

"No, I do not think that it is right for us to compare with each other. You have to do the best that you can and make yourself proud. When you are proud of yourself then only let others be proud of you. Watch out for being fooled by your own achievements, because being at the bottom is never far off.

"When the results were released that year, the head librarian wrote a congratulatory letter. All the library workers and my 'faculty of teachers' signed the letter. A few wrote little messages for me, while others signed their names alongside hand-drawn sketches of their smiling faces and one even drew a bunch of flowers. That letter is never very far and is re-read whenever I feel down and need motivation to continue. After all, the flowers in the drawing never wilt.

"My letter was given me at a special function, one that was held in my honour. I asked to meet all the people who had helped me. My intention was to thank them, but when I arrived, Mrs Freeman, the Head Librarian, had asked the library staff to assemble. She made a short speech and presented me with the signed letter. Mr Leslie McDonald, Manager of the Cape Town Symphony Orchestra, who shared the building with the public library, he and Mrs Freeman had arranged for a harpist to play. It was the most beautiful sound. The harpist was there to play for me, imagine that!"

"How did you feel, Ma?" I remember not removing my thumb when asking. That was how I controlled myself whenever emotions threatened to spill. I did not know, then, why the need to cry—I know now. It was a celebratory need, an after-the-fact celebration of how people can make one another whole by being kind.

"When I asked Mrs Freeman why the harpist was there, she said that he had come to play for me. You see, Boy, not all people accepted what being divided made us do to ourselves and others. Before that I had only read about the harp and had never seen it played, or heard its sound. It is a most beautiful instrument, my favourite. I was never honoured like that before, but I now know what it feels like, and that is why I like to honour others."

Chapter Four

Broken Finger

Lampo stirred, got up, turned round a few times, settled, yawned, and was instantly asleep. Ma consulted the ceiling: for her cues, probably. I shifted about in search of greater comfort. Those carpets can become quite hard to sit on.

"You know Sammy; to receive recognition is second only to giving recognition. Both are blessings, different blessings. My academic success inspired me with confidence to study again. In 1954 I registered with the University of South Africa. It is also a distance learning institute. My field of study was geared to equip me with skills so that I could help people who struggled with life. The course was not defined, but the subjects were. I wanted to learn to understand how people thought. My interest was also to discover how people experienced pain. It is so easy for us to inflict pain on one another. Most times it is mindless pain, probably born from our selfishness, greed and arrogance. I was interested in learning how best to manage the pain that we receive."

"Were you not interested in learning how to stop people from inflicting pain on one another, Ma?"

"That is an important point, one that I've wrestled with for a long time. My short answer is yes. I was interested in preventing the pain we cause one another. It is a concern that continues to bother me and I do not have a solution to your question. My goal was always to teach people how they could manage and live with their pain. Pain is real and all people suffer pain at some or other stage of their lives.

"I did not want to be closed up in an office. To be out there, working and showing was how I wanted to add value to people's lives. I was also interested in how people lived, formed groups, why some became superior and others inferior.

"Soon after I registered to study, my routine became as intense as it was the previous years. The mornings at home with the children were a jamboree of instructions, reprimands and cautions.

"My children were always welcome in our neighbour's home. Mr and Mrs Abrahams were both older and retired. Their children were married and were independent. Charles, Brenda and Anne became their adopted grandchildren and they were my trusted older friends. I often looked to them for guidance. When the children arrived home from school Mrs Abrahams, or Auntie Girlie as she was affectionately known, watched over them until I returned from work. We were like a family. They were of the Muslim faith and we were Christian by default."

"Don't forget Ma, I know Mr Abrahams and Auntie Girlie too. You took Jane and me to visit them a few times. That was when you showed me the house you lived in, the Woodstock house."

"Yes, I remember. The Abrahams family never would accept payment in return for offering me their support and friendship. Instead, we exchanged gifts on special days, like Labarang (Eid). I used those occasions to express our gratitude. Each child would create a gift and we'd have a small ceremony to give thanks when handing it over."

"You were working in the factory while completing Year Twelve, hey Ma? When you were done, did you look for a better job?"

"There were no jobs. For us the routine continued: evenings consisted of cooking and bathing and when the children were asleep I did academic work until midnight. The economy was poor. Food and jobs remained in short supply and the perfume industry was not doing well at all. In order to save jobs we worked fewer hours and took cuts in wages. Yet, those cautionary steps were not enough to save the business.

"On a particular Monday there was an air of gloom when we arrived for work because on the previous Friday the business had lost its last big contract. All of us knew what that meant, hence the gloom. Mr Steyn was seen nervously pacing about his office. The cigar and other apparel had long since gone. At 10:00am that morning the remaining twenty-three employees were summoned for a meeting. We were there to hear the inevitable breaking news. I had no other source of income. My children were a priority and they had to eat. The breaking news: 'Foreclosure is the only alternative.' All employees were retrenched with immediate effect. Every one of us received an envelope containing a small severance amount and a letter detailing the drastic decision to render all workers unemployed. I was not interested in the detail. The shock of being unemployed was of much greater impact."

"What did you do not to go hungry, Ma; where did you find food to feed Anne, Charles and Brenda when your money ran out?"

"Well, after the last money was used we had nothing. I had three children and no means with which to feed them. Anne had one more year of school to complete. I considered finding her a job to augment our income. In theory that was possible, but reality told a different story. Experienced workers were also unable to find jobs. It was much more difficult for young school leavers to find work. The only way to prevent starvation was for me to find another job. I had already sold some of my mommy's antique furniture by then. The price each piece fetched was not good. No one had money.

"I searched for a job at every opportunity. When all leads and possibilities were exhausted I'd settle down to work on an assignment until the next newspaper was available on the streets. Despite the tension and stress of being unemployed, I soldiered on with my studies. The rest of the time was spent reading, caring for my children, writing and revising. What made it more difficult was that other factories faced similar circumstances. This resulted in secure jobs being even harder to come by. Many people from the surrounding factories had already been retrenched when the perfume factory closed. Those people were also out on the streets searching for work. The number of unemployed increased every time a factory ran into trouble and had to retrench workers.

"The only work I could get was to do ironing and cleaning of houses on one morning and two afternoons per week. My jobs were up on the mountain slopes in University Estate, where Agnes lived. That is how I became a domestic worker. I cleaned dishes, made beds, scrubbed floors, toilets, ironed clothes and addressed my bosses as *madam* and *master*. It was all in a day's work. With my small wage I ensured that the children had food, were clean and could go to school. I could walk to work and ate only when very hungry. That is how I saved money to pay fees and buy food while searching for a better job. One of my employers lived next door to Agnes; actually, they were in the other half of the two semi-detached houses. I hid my identity by wearing a full scarf, like a Muslim woman does. When my madam asked why I had a Christian name and dressed like a Muslim my response was to lie, because I had to protect my sister."

"That's very funny, Ma, but why did you have to hide your identity for Auntie Agnes, when she did not want to have anything to do with you, why?"

"I knew that Agnes could get into trouble if people found out that she was my sister and I wanted to avoid that at all cost." Ma had responded to my question very quickly and then tried to change the subject somewhat.

"Well, one day when I got home there was a message from the perfume factory. The message was a request for me to return to work.

"Upon arrival the next morning I found nine ex-colleagues who had also been invited to return. Mr Steyn explained that he had to comply with contractual obligations. Again I did not understand the detail. It had to do with an order that he had to deliver and failure to comply would result in legal problems.

"All that mattered to me was the opportunity to work and earn money. Through managing my time and negotiating with Mr Steyn I was able to do the factory work as well as the three domestic jobs.

"After a while the long hours of work took its toll; physical strain set in and to make matters worse I had two academic assignments due within days of each other. There was no time to rest. I must have slept an average of three hours per night during that time. At seven in the morning I was at my machine in the factory. On one such morning, as I was sitting down in front of the spinning machine, something happened. Within an instant my machine, clothes and everything around me were covered in blood. The top segment of my right index finger had been cut and when I looked, it was dangling on a thread of remaining skin. For a short while pandemonium reigned. First aid boxes were brought out and bandages applied. Mr Steyn rushed me to Groote Schuur Hospital, the casualty section, the one reserved for people like me.

"My finger healed. Most things heal in time. Look!" as Ma said that, she showed me her finger. The top end of her right index finger was angled as if to point around a corner.

I had always wondered what was wrong with her finger, but never had the courage to ask. "A boy in my class at school is double-jointed and he can bend all the tips of his fingers like that."

"The injury came as a big shock, but the inconvenience was much greater."

"How did you do your jobs with a sore finger, Ma?"

"It was done with great difficulty. I needed both hands for all the tasks. After being stitched back my finger was placed in a splint and bound with several bandages—my entire hand was put in a plaster cast. The cast went up to my forearm. Doctors at the hospital said that my finger would heal over six weeks.

"The factory closed for good after the contract was complied with. I was then only a casual employee and there was no paid sick leave. Mr Steyn must have felt sorry for me because he gave me a small payment, an honorarium, that's what he called the few shillings I got. It was a struggle to continue, but I had to work. It was probably because of the constant strain during the healing process that my finger grew back like this, all askew. We survived and that is most important. The people I worked for were most understanding and accommodating.

"So then, I was a charwoman; 'Indian Doris Day, the charwoman' is probably what my old factory colleagues said, when they heard the story. Due to my sore finger I could not do the usual char duties. Instead I became the baby-sitter for surrounding neighbours' domestic workers who had agreed to do my chores and in exchange I cared for the children they were looking after. During that six week period when I cared for neighbouring children, Linda, Agnes's daughter, was part of the group I looked after. No-one knew."

Ma was on a roll, but it was my turn to use the bathroom. It was already after nine that Friday night. Tiredness was beginning to creep up on me, but I thought it important to have Ma tell as much as she wanted. Ma carried on after she also used the bathroom and made fresh tea.

"There were times when I used another route to work, a shorter route. The children delayed me some mornings. Charles would not shine his shoes, or Brenda lost her ribbons. On those mornings the shorter route would take me past Agnes's house. The sun shone and I could see a big green fern plant in her lounge room. On occasion I saw Agnes standing behind the net curtain. She must have been unaware that passers-by could see into the room when rays from the sun filtered through her voile curtain. I knew that my sister would have spoken to me if she could; it must have been equally sore for her to see me and not be able to talk. She was burning to ask about my hand; there was no doubt in my mind about that. Agnes was my sister-mommy after all."

"Didn't you wave at her, Ma? Surely the people would not have seen had you just waved at her?"

"No, I looked at her and walked past pretending not to see. Meanwhile I saw my sister standing in her comfortable lounge looking out at me. I was just passing by en route to clean her neighbour's house. I told you, Agnes was afraid that people would notice our likeness. She would be in trouble should one of them complain to the authorities."

"Did you, Ma, dislike her for not waving?"

Ma consulted the ceiling, like she did before, and gave the same reply: "Agnes is my sister."

"Agnes's fear that the neighbours would see our resemblance kept her from asking what had happened to my hand. That pencil, the one that dropped from her hair during the test, had brought this pain. It was also the reason why she failed to join the rest of our small family when we buried the mother who accepted us when our father gave us away.

"Of course, Agnes could have spoken to me!" Ma suddenly remonstrated with a burst of what seemed like anger. "Jesús too must bear some of the blame for her behaviour. I think he should have told Agnes that to stay away from Mommy's funeral because dark-skinned people were to attend was wrong— there are times when the law is not right. Perhaps Jesús was afraid that Agnes would have to leave him if people found out. Or maybe he was afraid that the two of them would argue. The truth about family and responsibility was the way it was and no amount of pretence would change that. I don't know … but I do know that her reaction and behaviour were not right!"

"What is it about family and having responsibility, Ma?"

"Well, if all else fails then you will always have your family. For that reason you cannot turn your back on those who were once part of your household. It is not the way to live your life. You have a responsibility to do the best you can and to make yourself proud. The other responsibility is toward those who are nearest and dearest to you, your family. You see, when I met Jesús on the street years later and we had an opportunity to speak, he told me, in that old broken English way of his, he said: 'People who convert to new religion are very worse than the one who are born like that.' I knew what he was saying. It is a stupid excuse. I told him so. We were talking about my sister, not some delinquent who found religion and became obsessive. I hope that he understood what I meant, went home to tell Agnes and hopefully the two of them took what I had said from whence it came."

"Did Auntie Agnes contact you after that, Ma?"

"No!" and Ma looked at that ceiling again.

"Do you miss Auntie Agnes?"

"She's my sister!" was the quick reply.

The way Ma said that brought a lump to my throat, but my thumb, it could stall tears. But Ma noticed and gave me a healing smile before continuing with her story.

"I went back to my domestic job after having the finger cast removed. The doctor warned that I should be careful when using my hand, as the finger had not completely healed. I was very pleased to do my own work again. The debt of gratitude could never sufficiently be repaid to those women, Louise, Margie and Josephine, the charwomen who did my work during the difficult time when my finger was in a cast.

"One evening, as I walked from work, I saw a young girl running towards me. It was Anne. She ran up the sidewalk on Main Road with an envelope in her hand. I recognised it as being a telegram. 'Must be good news, why else is the child so happy?' was what I thought. The telegram informed that I had to attend a meeting at Valkenberg Psychiatric Hospital. I had applied for a job there, but tried hard not to become excited because by then I had been let down too many times.

"The meeting, which was actually an interview, took place two days later. I wore my best dress. Even though the position was for a general worker and cleaner I had to make the best impression.

"It took three days after the interview before I received a further telegram, this time to inform me that I had got the job. I was happier than can be described, but the children were the happiest. Maybe the taking has stopped, I thought. Friends jokingly referred to my new place of work as a madhouse. They'd say: 'Beware, madness is contagious.' The cleaning work—well cleaning is cleaning, but the environment I worked in was very interesting. Whilst mopping and cleaning around the patients I encountered many instances where the discussions were similar to the descriptions in my textbooks. When doctors and other medical professionals discussed various conditions I recorded the topics in a little notebook. Later I'd find an opportunity to read more about what they were discussing.

"Every morning I got onto a bus from Main Road to Observatory. From there I walked, crossed the railway tracks and on toward where the Liesbeeck River flowed past. Before I could cross the river bridge there was a wetland that also had to be negotiated. My work day, like in the factory, started at 7:00am every weekday morning. During winter months it was dark and often rained in the morning when I walked to work. On such rainy days I'd walk around the wetland to the front entrance of the hospital. It was a longer walk, but I had a good raincoat, waterproof boots and a see-through umbrella that covered my head and shoulders. There were few street lights in those parts back then.

"Anne assumed more responsibilities in our household, Charles too, and so did Brenda as she became a young teenager. Our lives were coming together and the children were a great help. I went out to earn and Anne was sister-mommy to her siblings. Like Agnes before her; Anne took care of our house before and after school.

"It was an interesting time—exciting. We lived for the future. I had three years to go before obtaining a bachelor's degree. It was exciting to learn about people. The manual work I did was neither empty, nor was it aimless or without purpose. Time passed quickly. Within what felt like no time at all, I had been working at the hospital for two years.

"It was a rainy morning when I decided to walk along the road instead of across the wetland. There had been a consistent soft rain all night. The roads and fields were wet. I liked to be early. At six that morning, is when I walked down Station Road, alongside Hartleyvale Stadium. As I approached the stop street where Station and Liesbeeck Roads crossed, I heard a screech, followed by the sound of metal scraping against a hard surface. Where the lonely streetlight was, a dog darted with its tail between its legs, clearly running away from something that had just happened. The rest of the area was dark, pitch dark. The only other lights were from a few passing cars. There were not many cars on the streets in those years.

"Without a second thought I turned and rushed in the direction from which the dog was running. To see if I could help, that was my objective. There was a man lying in the road. He had been riding a scooter and seemed to have been riding in from the south, from the Athlone side. It was clear that the scooter had slipped and that he had fallen. 'Swerved for a dog,' is more or less what I think he said. I could see that the road was wet. That is how I met your Pa."

I was very keen to hear the rest of the story, but Ma was tired and I was hiding my yawns, not because of boredom, but because tiredness was taking its toll. It had been an eventful evening and both Ma and I needed to sleep.

The next day, Saturday, was another big day. Ma suggested that we go to bed and continue with our discussion in the morning. "I can write the rest and post it to you and Jane."

"No, I do not want to read it, Ma. I want you to tell me the story." It felt better, more real, when Ma spoke. But to agree with Ma's suggestion, which was that she write the rest of the story, was a safer option. My last comment before saying goodnight was: "Thanks for sharing your story, Ma …"

To which Ma responded: "Why do I get the sense that there is a 'but' at the end of that 'thank you'?"

Over time I grew to realise that Ma is an 'incurable' listener. She often heard much more than was said. This time was no exception.

"Well, we were supposed to speak about Pa's voice … and you said almost nothing about it, Ma."

"My boy, in order for you to understand your Pa it is important that you know the background. That's why I decided to start at the beginning."

Ma sounded a bit irritated and I didn't want to go to bed with her being cross with me, so I sat down to listen some more.

"The sound of your Pa's voice was the first I noticed about him. Remember, it was early morning and dark. He was lying in the street. It had been raining and everything was wet. That motorcycle helmet and a leather jacket that closed up around his neck made hearing him more difficult. Pa struggled to tell me what had happened, or perhaps it was me who could not understand what he was saying. It was the first time that I heard him speak. I could hear that Pa had a cleft palate. Other people I knew had the same affliction. His was worse. We never discussed it because people who suffer from that condition are usually very sensitive about their disability."

"Remember Pa's sister, Auntie Rachel?" I nodded to affirm.

"Well, when he introduced me to her, and after she knew me, Rachel confirmed that Pa was very touchy about his speech defect. Little did I know how it would impact on the way he conducts his life, and how those who live with him are affected. It was about then when I decided to discuss his cleft palate only if he spoke about it first. But Pa has never raised the subject and as a result we have not had that discussion."

"Is Pa cross about his speech, Ma?"

"I have only seen Pa angry once. With all the teasing that he must have endured Pa has learned to pretend that he is not cross, when in fact he is seething with anger. You will find that people who hide their anger become cross with those who are closest to them first. They become cross with others too—often when least expected."

"I saw, Ma. Pa seemed cross when we left the cake shop that afternoon. He drove faster than usual … was it because he was trying to hide his anger?"

"I see, you do not understand entirely, but you will in time, don't worry. You must remember your Pa has heard many unfriendly comments about his voice. People have probably passed remarks about Pa's voice for as long as he was able to speak. He taught himself how to hide his hurt, his anger and the embarrassment he felt. I am sure that, as a child, Pa suffered a lot of teasing from other children. That has to be one of the reasons for his eccentric behaviour. Instead of feeling worthless and like an outcast, Pa developed an ability to be mean and vengeful, even to people who never wronged him.

"In my studies I learned why so many young men here on the Cape Flats join gangs. One of the reasons is because they feel worthless. In order to gain acceptance, become worthy and experience belonging, young men join others who have the same social needs. That is how gangs are formed. By joining, young men found their purpose. They became worthy that way, and invincible too. Crime in our township has always been cruel.

"Pa did not join or form a gang. Instead he became a loner."

"When did you see Pa cross, Ma?"

I interrupted deliberately. Maybe because I was not ready to hear what Pa was capable of, or what he had done in the past. It was a strange reaction by me because the purpose of telling Ma about what happened in the cake shop was so that I could learn more about Pa and his speech defect. Yet when Ma was about to discuss its consequences in greater detail I was not ready. Ma's intuition was always alert: even then when she must have been very tired, Ma immediately saw my dilemma and without skipping a beat she went on to discuss something else instead. I regret not allowing Ma to continue. The details and extent of Pa's actions against people who had wronged him remains a secret.

By then it was after ten and way past my bedtime. Both Ma and I seemed more awake than we had been an hour earlier.

"If you felt sad about what those children were doing to Pa in the cake shop, can you imagine what he was feeling while being humiliated in front of his boy?

"It is no different to the laws here in South Africa. Often I find that the laws we have to live by are implemented without proper consideration. Look at the effect many of the laws have on different groups. If the laws were properly considered then they would not have been as punitive to the majority of people in this beautiful country we live in.

"The South African Government is like the children in that cake shop. Look how the children mocked Pa, all because of his disability. They did not think of the effect their taunts would have. People with disabilities cannot help having the condition they live with. Sometimes we have no empathy for disability. When disabled people have had enough taunts thrown at them then it is not surprising that they react in a manner we find harsh, cruel and spiteful.

"Pa suffered a lot of rejection because of his speech and it must, in some way, have shaped the way he is. The way Pa behaves and conducts his life is not normal. When he has had wine, then the stories are often amusing. That is so, but then there are those actions which are not right, particularly concerning his family. Do not think that I am making excuses for the way Pa is, do you understand me, Sammy?"

I understood what Ma was saying, but maybe not completely. I said yes, but my intention was to ask Jane for a more detailed explanation.

When I got to bed that night sleep came only after tossing, turning and remembering everything that Ma had said.

The following morning, as Ma was getting ready to see a client, I had one further question. My question related to the previous night's discussion: "What can I do to help Pa, Ma?"

Ma looked at me and smiled before explaining: "Pa is not the kind of man that you can help. Over the years he has not only become set in his ways, but also stubborn beyond measure. Pa has created a world around himself. That world fits how he is … never the other way round."

"Tell me about the time when you saw Pa angry, Ma?"

"Oh! Boy." Ma looked at me and shook her head from side to side. "It was a very long time ago. We had been married for about five years then. That Saturday morning Pa was up way before the sun. First he made breakfast. It always consisted of cheese, tomato and lettuce on rye bread and a mug of sweet milky coffee. When he was done making the sandwich and while waiting for the milk to boil Pa would, with the knife and fork, drum and whistle the tune, *Onward Christian Soldiers*. It was a tune the marching band from the Anglican Church played on Sunday mornings. Pa would rather die than go to church, but he could never get enough of a marching band. When he heard the band approach his deafness was always miraculously cured. He'd be out in the street recording the sound like a reporter trying to capture a street interview on tape."

"What would you do while Pa did all of that, Ma?"

"No, I never got involved in his madness, no!" Ma sighed, glanced at the ceiling and then continued: "Well, on that Saturday morning, after having had breakfast, I heard Pa fidget with his bunch of keys and then he said: 'Ya! Thelma, I am going to see my brother now.' Next, I heard the car as he drove off. Both brothers had similar mannerisms and habits; they'd visit each other without prior announcement and at any time of the day or night.

"About an hour later Pa stormed back into the house. Both his hands were covered in blood and he was shaking with anger. I had never before seen that man in such a state.

'Did you see Pierre?' I asked him.

'Ya! No!' was his quick and limited reply.

"Shortly afterwards Uncle Pierre arrived. He too was shaking with anger. On seeing me, Pierre asked for his brother: 'There's been a big misunderstanding, Thelma,' he said.

"I pointed to the bathroom where Pa was treating his bleeding hands with an antiseptic which he had diluted in warm water. Uncle Pierre and Pa walked out and sat in the yard. They sat there speaking in animated French for a long time."

"But what happened, Ma? Why was Pa bleeding, and why were both Uncle Pierre and Pa so angry; did they fight with each other?"

"No, you never fight with your brother, it is not allowed. Family is all that you have. Listen to me Boy: when all else fails then family is the only thing you have—it is there for longer than your life.

"Neither of them would tell me what happened, but when Uncle Pierre left, he asked me to walk out with him. When we reached his car, Pierre told me: 'Thelma, my brother (they always referred to each other like that) had a disagreement with, Esmé,' (Pierre's wife) ..."

"I remember, Ma that is the Auntie with the shrill voice, like the woman who always sang ahead of the choir at the church, that one? Surely Pa did not fight with the Auntie?"

"No, but he did smash the front of their house."

"Why?"

"Apparently, when Pa arrived Uncle Pierre was not home. Pa then asked Auntie Esmé if he could wait a while. Esmé refused and told Pa to go away. They argued. Pa said that it was his brother's house and that he would wait with or without her permission. Esmé responded by mocking his speech. Pa lost his temper and with his bare hands he smashed the house."

"Wow! Did he really?"

"Yes, and for many years after the incident we only saw Esmé on the rarest of occasions. At such gatherings the tension between Pa and her would be evident and Uncle Pierre would be around his brother like a broody hen. It was obvious who the favourite in that relationship was!"

"Was Uncle Pierre cross with Pa for breaking his house?"

"Uncle Pierre and Pa are twin brothers. Long after the fight, when Pierre came to drink his whisky at my house, he said that he and Esmé nearly got divorced because of how she treated his brother.

"Well, to answer your question, that was the one and only time that I saw your Pa angry."

At that moment Ma's client arrived. She stood up from the chair: "Let me talk with this lady. When I am done then we can continue, or I shall write to you as promised."

"Okay Ma, but don't forget to tell me what happened after Pa fell off the scooter!"

Ma nodded as she walked away to work: "Okay, I shall remember."

While Ma spoke with her client I dragged the blue suitcase to the front door. There were not many things packed that belonged to me. I often complained about having to carry so much for Jane, but then Ma would remind me of my duty, which was to take part of our home so that Jane could share in the experience.

Years later I would become aware of Ma's concern for *fairness,* but also that she frequently lost track of what was *right.* In time Ma and I would discuss the difference between right and fair. Ma would say: "It is right that I wait up until Pa gets home."

"But it is not fair, Ma," was my response, "is it fair that you wait up given that so often Pa does not come home?"

Ma's approach was more philosophical than practical and Jane was less diplomatic than me when she addressed Ma on that subject: "You are not being logical Ma," was the crux of what Jane would say. I agreed with Jane because Ma often took decisions that led her to do without while others enjoyed whatever she had given them.

I remember a time when Jane won a scholarship at school. At the end of that year and after all expenses had been paid she had some money left over. When we were travelling home that December Jane used the leftover money to buy Ma's Christmas present—a duffle coat. Jane's intention was that Ma could use the coat during the cold wet winters of the Cape.

It so happened that I was home during the following winter holidays (June). Ma had been working on a farm in Stellenbosch for several years by then, probably for as long as I was alive. It was cold, wet and windy there during winter. The surrounding mountains were covered in snow.

I accompanied Ma when she did 'home visits'. While Ma worked I played with the children who were about my age.

On one of those days we visited a family who lived in a single room that had been constructed from wood and iron. It had been raining a lot the previous evening. Their room had flooded. It was early morning when we arrived. Three young children were sitting on the bed, which the father had raised with stones so that the blankets could remain dry. Their kitchen utensils were floating in floodwater in their one room home.

As we were leaving Ma took off her duffle coat and gave it to the woman.

"Why did you do that, Ma?" I asked.

"Oh shame, those people have nothing. I have a coat, two jerseys and an umbrella. Now that woman has a coat and I am left with two jerseys and an umbrella."

Ma had found that it was too expensive to bring both of us home whenever the school term ended. The unspoken understanding was that I, being the younger sibling, would return to Cape Town for the longer mid-year school break. Since turning sixteen Jane always had holiday jobs. Sometimes she had three to choose from. Jane was often spoilt for choice. The money she earned was used to buy train tickets so that we could go home together for the Christmas holidays. When there was no money for our train fare we'd spend school holidays either with the nuns at school, or with Mammy Cynthia at her home in Mpophomeni. When Jane worked I stayed at school. It was very unpleasant to be at school by myself.

It was during one of those school holidays when I was 'home alone' at school that Mr Thompson, the physical training teacher, introduced me to surfing. The sea was nearly one hundred kilometres away. As my interest in surfing exploded into an obsession, Boet Sam, the school's driver, assisted by fitting swivel wheels to an old locker door. That became my make-believe 'surfboard' during the times when I could not get to the ocean. I would ride my locker-door-on-wheels in the school quad from early morning until it became too dark to see. That quad was my imaginary beach and it was always high tide there. Most important was that the quad beach was not reserved. Anyone who could surf was allowed, particularly those who did so better than me, they were most welcome because that was how I would learn. Many hours were spent there executing the most complicated surf moves with all the other better surfers in attendance… albeit in my head.

To spend school holidays in Mpophomeni, at Mammy Cynthia's house, was my and Jane's favourite. Waking up at school on a Christmas morning was no fun. It rates as one of my worst experiences—that and getting a comfort dummy from Pa as a Christmas present.

Mammy Cynthia lived with Khokho, her mother-in law. Khokho is the Zulu name for great-grandmother. Well, Khokho Mbala cared for Precious and Thami, Mammy Cynthia's grandchildren. Being there was like being at home. Precious was the same age as Jane, and Thami was two or three years older than me; I was never sure of Thami's age. He was shorter than me and when I was little, age was measured by height: like in, 'he was a big boy' and 'no, but the other boy was bigger'. Girls never mattered because—they wasted time, first when they were younger by playing with dolls and later, with cooking food and baking cakes.

But Khokho always told us interesting things about Zulu culture and about how the Zulu nation formed after having gradually moved from the far eastern parts of Africa to eventually settle in that province, Natal. I found Khokho's explanation of how they came to live in Mpophomeni very interesting too. A big dam was built in the area where they had lived, Khokho explained: "The Midmar Dam was going to be built and we had to move. It was about 1963 when the authorities decided that the area where we were living had to become a dam. After taking the decision they set out to clear a big area of land. It was close to where our original houses were. When these houses were built, here in Mpophomeni, that was when we moved to this one. My son, Sipho, was one of the workers who built the dam. That is another reason why we got this house. When Cynthia and Sipho married they stayed with me. Both their children were born in my house. When we moved, I came to stay with them—that's often how life is."

"Where is Baba Sipho now, Khokho?" Jane was sometimes interested in detail and other times not. Baba Sipho was obviously gone. Maybe he was like Pa, always working.

"Oh no, Jani," Khokho always referred to Jane as Jani, "Sipho died at work when they were building the dam wall—just above where the spray is. That is what they told me. We don't know what really happened. Some say that he slipped and fell; others they say that he was not wearing the safety equipment and fell while trying to stop a bucket hanging on a chain from a crane, or something like that. As his mother I want to believe that Sipho died at work, that's all. My heart remains very sore, but what can I do? We were sad for a long time, but you know, those who are dead are alive in our heads."

When Khokho told this tragic story I removed my thumb, and simultaneously Jane and I said: "Sorry, Khokho."

Strange, but after that discussion with Khokho and when Jane and I were alone, she said to me: "So, Sammy-boy, when you are dead someday, you will not really be dead because you will live in my head." It was strange to me because without saying it, I had been thinking the same about Jane.

We learned many valuable lessons during those years. Through her gentle manner, Mammy Cynthia taught us to *be* sorry and not only to *say* sorry. She also taught us not to litter. We had to respect everyone. Older people were identified for special respect, irrespective of whom or what he or she might be.

All the while, Mammy Cynthia was teaching us to have empathy. When older I realised just how blessed Jane and I were to have had such gentle and graceful people like Khokho and Mammy Cynthia as our role models.

In South Africa the school calendar begins in January and ends at the beginning of December. Almost every year Jane and I were able to travel home by train, but as we grew older Ma did not have enough money. I refused to go home at Christmas time without Jane.

We have many fond memories of the bus journey from Ixopo to Pietermaritzburg, and then from there to Mpophomeni. The weeks we spent being part of Mammy Cynthia's household would remain a valuable part of our lives.

Chapter Five

Ma's Letter from Stellenbosch

When Jane worked part-time we would put her earnings together with what Ma had saved. That was how we were both able to travel home for Christmas. There were even years that we had enough money to buy presents for Mammy Cynthia, Khokho, Ma, Thami and Precious.

Our school year always began in late January, so the December holiday was the longest time that we spent at home. It was a joyous time. Ma prepared over the entire year for that December day when we would arrive. Part of her preparing for the Christmas holiday season included the purchase of a 'hamper'; a lay-by of clothes; school shoes; and whatever else we needed. For twelve months she would pay regular monthly instalments until everything was paid for. The 'hamper' contained our favourite luxuries and clothes were routinely delivered during the first week of December, ahead of our return from school.

The otherwise dull atmosphere at home was transformed when we arrived. This was particularly so when Jane was home. From early in the morning until late in the evening Jane and I would vie for Ma to listen and hear our respective versions of the same story. Motor-mouth Jane always beat me in the race to talk. I let her, because there was always my thumb, a song to sing and a new one to learn. Joyful memories of those years shall also stay with me forever.

No matter how poor we were it was our tradition to have roast turkey, or at least a grilled Cornish hen for Christmas. The neighbourhood was such that those who did not have, received from those who had. The gift of food was always concealed when taken to the neighbour who did not have, and whilst wrapping it, Ma would say: "Next year it could be our turn." Or she'd say: "There go I but for the grace of God."

Muslim people also joined the celebration. At the end of a month of fasting from sunrise to sunset the Muslim community celebrated Labarang, also referred to as Eid Mubarak, and then too there would be a communal celebration.

Food was important, but so were the clothes and new shoes. Clothes and shoes were wrapped and placed beneath the decorated tree in our lounge room. Together as a family we opened our gifts on Christmas morning. The lay-by clothes were Ma's not-so-much-of-a-surprise Christmas gifts to us.

This lay-by tradition began one year when Jane, then about thirteen years old, announced that Ma should no longer buy toys as gifts—that clothes and school apparel would be better. I sometimes wished that she would speak for herself, but to argue with a motor-mouth remained last on my list. It was always better to suck my thumb, or sing a song.

Sadness enveloped our home as it became just a house. This happened whenever we began to prepare for the school trip. I always packed the blue suitcase. During the trip, it had become my job to haul the case on and off whatever rack was designated to hold luggage. The sadness at home became pervasive. Lampo also felt it; she took up position at the front door and refused to move, wag her tail, or look after Ma's slippers, as was her norm.

"Look Boy, she can sense that you are leaving us again."

It was interesting to observe how Lampo would have a very deliberate change of manner when Jane and I began the preparation for school. Jane too would go quiet as we converted the home to its former state. No matter how many times we had to say goodbye, leaving Ma remained one of the most unpleasant things. Pa was working—he was always working. Ma took us on the bus whenever we went to the 'school train'. The train always departed from Cape Town Station. Our school was a three day train ride away.

Ma has told me how she mourned whenever we left: for weeks afterwards her life was filled with remorse for having sent us to the faraway school. It was her conviction that education was the best possible investment in our futures that got Ma through those trying times. She would insist: "Education is only successful if it changes the way you behave" and "...society fools itself by judging those who are educated based on the academic qualification they hold. Look at the Prime Minister, Mr Vorster. He is a qualified lawyer. The Vorster family are large, they were very poor, but he earned two degrees from of the best universities. However, look at the laws he helped to create, defends and supports. Would you expect such behaviour from an educated person?"

Ma was fierce in her opposition to the laws in South Africa that sought to discriminate against people based on the shade of their skins. She was equally opposed to anyone and anything that contributed to Auntie Agnes being estranged from the family. I knew better than to interrupt or seek clarity when Ma spoke out about the South African Government and its policies. She was venomous in her opposition. Asking her to explain further anything that involved the South African state could last an entire holiday. Ma's explanations were very detailed and factual. The extent of her knowledge was astounding. After every information session Ma found books that Jane and I would have to read. She made a lot of effort to find the books. That is one of the reasons why we were obliged to read them. Just as well too because the next time that we were home Ma would have a verbal comprehension test ready on each of the books. Ma never recommended that we read books that she had not read. Being home at times resembled school.

Only when I insisted did Ma describe the pain she felt when we left for school, followed by how she coped: "It is a dull pain when you two are away and I am alone. I only get to feel better long after you've left. The front page of my diary, where the calendar is, becomes my favourite page. That's where I measure when we will all be together again. In the beginning the return date is a long way off, but I turn it into a goal—that return date becomes *my goal* and I get there, one day at a time. Whenever life becomes unpleasant I remind myself how short the time is before you and Jane will be home. This is what pushes me to continue."

It was disappointing whenever we could not make the journey to Cape Town, our home. Jane and I had each other, Mammy Cynthia and her family. Ma had Pa, but by then he was always working, or as she put it: "…All he did when home was rattle around in silence."

There was a time when Ma spent two consecutive Christmas holidays at home by herself. She did not have enough money for both our train fares. We worried about Ma that time, or maybe it was just our longing to be home.

I asked her what it felt like to be alone over Christmas. Her reply was different: "Perhaps time is a great healer; but I am never completely healed. So much has been taken from me … and with my children at a faraway school, it feels as if I am encouraging the taking."

Ma worked for the Department of Social Welfare. Her job was with farm workers and families who suffered the ravages of alcohol abuse. "People's behaviour changes when they drink too much wine," she'd say.

Many became addicted to alcohol and that, together with the impact it had on their families, was what Ma tried to remedy. Husbands and wives who fought with each other in the home; babies born to parents who were addicted to alcohol; and child abuse, all formed part of Ma's daily tasks. Meanwhile, farmers continued the age-old practice of rewarding workers with cheap bottom barrel wine as part of their weekly wages. Farm owners were to a large extent a law unto themselves, and workers were dependent on the farmer for their livelihoods.

Ma described her work experience as: "Traumatising—because the drinkers, the children and the troubles I see, are imprinted on my memory. I live with it Boy, every moment."

When referring to her life, Ma often made cryptic comments, such as: "I did not have time to think about my own life and, without my realising it, the situation at home was deteriorating at a rate that I never could imagine."

Ma was only allowed to work with people who were, like her, categorised as 'mixed'. Her clients worked on fruit farms in the area that stretched from Paarl through Klapmuts to Stellenbosch. These towns are situated about sixty kilometres from Cape Town city. It is where most of South Africa's grapes are grown. Pears, plums, guavas and strawberries were among the other produce farmed, but grapes were the most popular crop.

Every opportunity she had, Ma would identify an example of how unfair the laws in South Africa were. For instance, she was prevented from working with farm owners. In the work she did this became her main concern because Ma regarded the farmer, who was part of the *superior* group, as the catalyst in that nucleus of alcohol abuse. She was never, in all her time in that job, allowed to work with farmers. Ma likened the situation with the South Africans who fought in the Second World War: "Only Europeans or those who labelled themselves like that were allowed to participate in active combat. During the war South Africans, those who were referred to as European, came from families that arrived back on African soil about two hundred and fifty years earlier."

Ma's use of the phrase 'back on African soil' puzzled me. Despite knowing that a major lecture was to follow, I asked: "Why do you say that the Europeans arrived back on African soil, Ma?"

"Well," she started. Ma poured tea and then only was set to continue. "If humanity began in Africa, then all humans are African. Some moved to faraway places and thousands of years later, their children returned to Africa. Because of circumstances like climate, diet and more, the people who came back here no longer looked like Africans. But they originated from here, all humans do. Europeans were originally Africans who moved to Europe. That is why I say they returned to Africa ..."

How the farms came to be and how they were worked has always fascinated me. So much that I did more than was required when a school task was set to examine the history of farming in the Cape. This pleased my teacher. She thought that I was finally to follow Jane's academic example. My burst of enthusiasm was unfortunately short-lived, but the experience I had whilst doing that research was more than enlightening.

I found that some farm owners were descendants from the Dutch and English who, in earlier centuries, had colonised and settled in the Cape. However, other farmers were from a third or fourth generation of largely Calvinist French Protestants. The Huguenots had been persecuted in France for their Protestant religious practices, so they emigrated to the Cape.

The law in South Africa did not allow people, other than those referred to as Europeans, to own farms in the area where Ma's clients lived and worked. It is also true that, at the beginning of the farming cycle in that region, indigenous people did not have the expertise needed to become profitable farmers.

The common spoken language was Afrikaans. It is a language similar to Dutch and Flemish. In the Cape this young language was influenced by many older and more established tongues. As a result, there exists a multitude of Afrikaans dialects that continuously evolve.

Ma's clients shared a close ancestral connection with the Khoi. The Khoi are the indigenous people of Southern Africa. Khoi is a collective name used in reference to several indigenous tribes who were the first known human beings to live across Southern and South West Africa. As is the case with most indigenous groups, the Khoi too were allegedly robbed of the land on which they lived. They were ambushed, abused and killed. Those who remained were forced onto reserves. According to popular belief, it was the European settlers who robbed the Khoi people. Less is said about the onslaught on the Khoi by greater numbers of African tribes that moved south on the east side of the continent.

Those tribes did not only fight with one another as they moved south, but in order to occupy and take over the land they killed the Khoi people.

All that remain of the original Khoi families are rock paintings. Southern Africa was their ancestral home. The land was annexed and others now claim it as theirs. The remaining Khoi people have been urbanised, and the few original families are found on reserves. These simple hunter-gatherer and subsistence farming communities were virtually exterminated. The perpetrators were other African tribes and those who returned after living in Europe for thousands of years. Those two groups of people, Africans and Europeans as a collective, were responsible for the Khoi genocide in Southern Africa.

Many Khoi became slaves and bore children with Europeans and other Africans. The Khoi were assimilated into the definition, 'mixed'—the same as Ma and her clients.

Ma did the same work for close on ten years. Every week day night she returned to a state allocated rural cottage. That is where she lived from Monday to Friday, every week.

The cottage was in a temporary section designated by the state to house a social worker whose job it was to assist the mixed group in the area. Ma lived there by herself. There, she would write down all that occupied her thoughts while cycling between farms in her quest to bring relief to the afflicted of 'her group'. Ma's worst days were when she visited families where mothers drank excessive amounts of wine and, as a result, their children suffered. There were times when Ma was emotionally bereft and in a constant state of exhaustion. It was the consequence of both the dysfunction within her own family unit coupled with the strenuous nature of her work.

The pain derived from her work, the eccentric nature of her husband, her migrant worker lifestyle and the longing to be with all her children amounted to Ma's heavy burden: added to this was that Ma often stressed about her clients, their children and her lack of money. During such times the patch of eczema at the bottom of her right leg would flare.

When home I'd often sit with my thumb in my mouth and listen to Ma think aloud: "Sometimes I feel like a wall plug. People plug in and take what they need, then without any care or consideration for me, they move on. When do I ever get a chance to plug in and take that which I need? When will the taking from me ever stop?"

Ma often mumbled thoughts like these when settling down to spend private time—always with a cup of tea. See, I became invisible when my thumb was in my mouth. Ma never knew that I was listening when she thought aloud.

Occasionally I accompanied Ma to her rural cottage. It was interesting to observe how happy she was to introduce Jane or me to her clients. Ma's clients were farm workers. Many of them had no front teeth.

"I like to introduce you to my friends and their children here on the farms because you make yourself proud, and that is why I am proud of you too," was what Ma said before introducing me to people

72

Ma was obviously speaking in reference to Jane. She, Jane, achieved at school and I was just average. But average was not good enough, that was the given impression.

I enjoyed it when Ma showed me where she sat in her cottage when writing to us. Despite not saying anything then, I felt it important to have the picture in my mind of Ma sitting at the table when she wrote those complicated letters to Jane and me.

While we were away at school, no matter how tired Ma was, every evening she'd sit at the dining room table, light a candle and write a letter. When we received it, there were candle wax stains on the paper. In the body of one letter Ma explained that the long midnight chime stirred her awake. She'd been asleep at the Cape Provincial Administration table, supposedly writing. Ma wrote about clutching her pen and cold tea when she awoke during the clock's chime.

The University of South Africa (UNISA) writing pad upon which her head rested when overcome by tiredness sometimes became wet. However, relentless in her determination, the next night Ma tried again, until finally she had composed a most compelling weekly letter for Jane and me. We lived for that letter even though it took me several days to understand everything Ma had written.

Ma's first letter arrived two weeks after our Friday chat. I had read *Animal Farm* on the train journey back to school. The book made very little sense to me then—not like when I read it years later and could relate. When I asked why Ma took so long to write after we had been home; her initial response was very complicated.

"It's like when your child dies: the memories, pain and the eternal question, 'Why?' live inside you. That is, to a certain extent, how I feel about you children being away. I know that it is best for you. My life is no environment for learning. Children need routine, discipline and healthy role models to emulate. I cannot provide that given the circumstance of my work. It hurts me to see you go; that is why I take a while to settle and write."

Every time when the postman delivered mail to the principal's office there would be an impromptu assembly. Sister St Claire would climb onto the rostrum and read names as she drew envelopes from the postbag. When the last letter had been handed to its recipient Sister would end the gathering with: "Oh well, those who did not receive today, maybe tomorrow; that's all for now. God bless you."

Our response was always in unison: "Thank you very much for our letters and may God bless you too Sister St Claire." We thought that Sister St Claire had the most beautiful Irish accent; but when we waited and there was no letter, her accent was terrible! There was no better feeling than to receive that letter every week. Jane was usually not excitable, but she also could not contain her joy when we received mail. We'd run off to a corner, Jane and I; she'd read Ma's letter aloud while I stood by sucking my thumb. Once I understood what Ma had written, the words would sketch pictures in my mind. Sometimes, when Jane read, it was as if I could hear Ma's voice speaking those words. When done, Jane always kissed the letter, gave it to me and then ran away in her Bata Toughee school shoes. She ran to be with those who had not received news from home on that day.

There was always a turn for every child at school to receive a letter and when she or he did, somebody else would be sad. No one ran to comfort Jane when we did not receive. The same with Ma, no one ever ran to give her comfort, but she was always there for all who had a need. Perhaps it was so because Jane and I had each other and because Ma had us.

We wrote to Ma once a week. When I was younger Jane wrote for both of us; and before Jane could write her own letters, Mammy Cynthia wrote on her behalf. Mammy Cynthia struggled, but the English teacher taught her to read and write before we arrived at school. That is how Jane, along with the other older children, also had something to send home on the days that all school letters were taken to the post office. Mammy Cynthia told me that she could not write well, yet, she taught us and we've not done too badly.

Ma wrote one letter and the first half was always addressed to Jane, followed by one just for me. Our return letter was sent on a Tuesday morning, addressed to Ma at a poste restante address, Klapmuts Post Office. Ma collected her letter on a Friday morning. There was no mail delivery service where Ma lived and post boxes were reserved for other people. This was also because she was not a permanent resident of the area.

Ma's Friday morning routine, she told me, included a cycle ride to Klapmuts Post Office. Once there, she used a chain to lock her bicycle to a pole before collecting her mail. The counter clerk knew Ma and always had her letter ready for collection. No questions were asked. They exchanged knowing smiles, that's all. Ma took her letter, mailed the new one and went about the rest of her business.

The new letter had to arrive at school on a Tuesday morning, failing which we would be very disappointed. In order to avoid our being disappointed Ma had to comply with the mail clearance time, which was displayed on the post box door.

I had told Jane all that Ma discussed with me on that last Friday evening. By then it felt okay to speak about Pa's nasally speech. Jane did not seem surprised. I think that Jane was aware of a lot more than she shared with me.

Ma's letter, which we received two Tuesdays after I had returned to school, contained two instructions:

1.   *This letter is for both of you, and;*
2.   *When you reply, ask the questions for which you want answers and I shall post more detail with the next letter.*

Ma's letter always started with the date:
18 July 1972

74

My Dear Children

Each time you leave, something inside me goes to sleep. It does not die, no, it sleeps and I do not feel whole until you return. The encouraging thought is that soon you will be making your way back home. It will be summer then and I shall have applied to enjoy my accumulated annual leave when you are here.

When you arrive then I become alive. This time, Jane, when you also come home, that is when I shall be complete. From now until December is not a long time, and then we will be together one more time.

You must work hard. You already know that. Make yourself proud and all others will be proud of you too; only if they want to be, but it all starts with you. Remember, they can colonise your body but they can't imprison your mind, unless you allow them.

I have been thinking about how best to continue telling our story. Sam, you would have told Jane about our discussion? I shall send the rest when it is written. It will be uncomfortable to write though. That is why my preference is for us to sit and talk about it rather. On the other hand, when written, our story will be recorded by the people who lived it.

My preference will always be to sit across from you and answer your questions. Okay, let me write the story in parts so that you can develop the best possible understanding and re-read that which may not be clear. Keep the letters in a safe place. When you have children, then they too can read about the experiences we've had.

Jane knows most of the story that I have explained to you, so I shall continue where Sam and my discussion ended:

§

Remember, I was a cleaner at the psychiatric hospital? Well, one day, while working, I received a message that someone had arrived to meet me and that the person was waiting at the head cleaner's office. I had a visitor, said the messenger.

A tall man stood waiting outside when I got to the office. He wore a black sleeveless cardigan, beret and had a short-trimmed but full beard. He wore a patterned shirt with its sleeves turned up to above his elbows. His trousers and workman shoes were like those worn by most workmen of the time. I failed to recognise him at first, that is, until he greeted me: "Ya! Hello, Thelma." I recognised that nasal voice. It was the man, the one who had the accident on the scooter, but by then I had forgotten his name. My dress was a cleaner's overall and I looked anything but presentable. It was embarrassing.

My response was without pause for breath: "Hello how is your leg; sorry for the way I look; you should have warned me of your visit; how did you find me?"

He did not answer all my questions.

"Ya! My name is Samuel Levy ..." I heard that voice again.

By then the others, my colleagues, had gathered to take in the look of this dapper man who was visiting me at work.

"I came to thank you for helping me. Sorry for taking so long to get here, but I was recovering."

I waved my hand to interject, but he continued: "My leg was in a cast. I had to wait for it to heal before making the trip to thank you."

He sounded hesitant, as if not an English speaker, or unsure of what to say.

"Ya! I work at the Athlone Power Station." He pointed in the direction of an open field with only a few small red face brick buildings. It was way before the two big cooling towers were constructed.

"Ya! I am an electrician there," he pointed again, as if I had not seen the first time. "My plan was always to come here and thank you when this leg healed," he said while pointing to the sore leg.

My bashful temperament got the better of me again as I stood there filled with a combination of wonder and embarrassment.

"Ya! What time do you knock off, and can I give you a lift home?"

Without thinking, I agreed: "Yes, I finish at five." He did not allow me to complete the sentence.

"Ya! That's fine; I'll be at the gate, just on five o'clock."

Then he turned to start his scooter and rode away without waving. I stood listening to the scooter until it merged with other sounds of the day. When he left the teasing started, and I could not get my colleagues and the head cleaner to stop. For the rest of that afternoon I tried to focus on my work. I tried hard to ignore the buzz of teasing chatter that flurried among the others about my visitor. After all, my children and the life that we were making was my primary concern. What would they think if I arrived home with a man, travelling on the back of his scooter? What would the neighbours think?

I decided that Samuel and I would have to postpone our meeting, but contacting him was a problem. Many questions occupied my mind while the teasing continued. I am sure that my work was not up to its usual standard that afternoon. There were no complaints though.

Gosh! When I opened my bag there was the reminder note. My assignment had to be mailed the following day. Suddenly getting home became more urgent. Samuel would have to understand, I thought.

Time flew by. Soon queues were forming at the clock-machine. This device recorded when we reported for and went off duty. Our wages were determined by what that clock printed onto attendance cards. Of course, we worked each day. However, the number of hours actually worked were used to calculate what we earned.

As I came through the workers' exit Samuel was there, waiting. He wore a helmet on his head and held one in his hand for me. I felt nervous. It was to be my first time on a scooter and I was not sure where to hold on. Samuel might think me forward if I held on to his waist ... but to hold onto the seat might land me in the street. These were some of the thoughts that raced through my mind as I struggled to fasten the helmet.

He wore a leather jacket; I wore my coat, the one that protected me against the morning cold. After I had given him my address he placed my bag between his feet and we were off, supposedly in the direction of my house. The easy route was via Main Road in the direction of the city and right onto Page Street. My house was number four. I screamed directions, but to no avail. Samuel went in the opposite direction. My scream might as well have been to myself: 'Turn right!' I shouted, and he turned left. This man had no sense of direction. That was another of his characteristics.

I took the opportunity, when we got to a stop street, to give further direction. That is what got me home, but it would have been quicker to walk.

We stood outside my house, talking. Samuel kept the scooter motor idling. Children and their parents came out to investigate the unusual sound. I explained to Samuel about my three children, my academic responsibilities and suggested that we should have tea at another time. We agreed to meet on the following Friday afternoon. Both of us and the children were home early on Friday afternoons.

Samuel insisted that he bring me home every weekday evening. That is how I got to know more about him. He learned about me too during that time. Samuel was also divorced and had three children, all boys. His ex-wife lived together with her boys in Worcester. This was your Pa.

Soon he was fetching me in the morning and taking me to work. In the evening he would be parked across the road when I left work. My children were doing well at school. Pa spent most evenings sitting in the lounge reading the Cape Argus newspaper. I studied, or did assignments, while the children did their homework or prepared for bed.

Pa did maintenance around the house. Ours was an old house. In a quiet way he seemed to get along with my children. Light-heartedly Pa said that he wished to convert our Dover coal-burning cooker into an electric stove. He's always had an off-beat sense of humour.

Charles was the first of my children to say that Pa favoured the girls. I noticed that Pa did not care much for him. This was a concern, because I love Charles. He is my son, my first boy. I had been a single mother for a while then. It was difficult to raise three children on my own. It was particularly tough for Charles to live in a house with three women.

Pa left for his home at about eight o'clock every evening. He lived with Auntie Rachel, his sister, out Athlone way.

Anne finished school and became a dressmaker like her Aunt Agnes. Soon she too was as popular with people who needed garments for weddings and special occasions. Anne became very good and sought after. She had much practice making our clothes.

One day, and without warning, Pa asked me to marry him. 'No,' I replied. I had planned never to marry again. He insisted and would not accept that I did not want to marry again. My children were most important to me and we had a plan which did not include Pa. My academic programme, that I had started years earlier, was nearing completion. The dream of having our own home was no longer out of reach and there was no room for a man in our lives.

The superintendent of the psychiatric hospital offered me an internship, but only if I successfully completed a bachelor's qualification in social work. Like an apprentice, I would learn to apply the techniques and other information that were contained in my course material. After receiving the proposal I began to feel pride in my academic achievements. The letter explained that for twelve months after graduating I would be employed as a junior intern social worker in the hospital section reserved for people of the 'mixed' group. I had been a cleaner in that same section for almost seven years by then. The excitement about the opportunity encouraged me to work even harder—and I did.

Pa kept insisting that I marry him. My answer was a consistent 'no' and remained so until the day when he said that if I did not marry him, he'd kill me. I had a strange feeling about Pa's threat at the time, but it soon passed. I knew that it was not said in jest.

Yet, I liked Pa a lot by then. He was an interesting man—knowledgeable beyond the common folk. You know, I have not heard Pa use a swear word, ever. These were important attributes and seemed to overshadow the negative. Pa was of sober habits, a hard worker and a very handsome man. Those were the positive thoughts that bubbled in my mind. Perhaps it was only because I deliberately suppressed the negative.

There are many things that he never discussed: what he remembered of France is one, his speech defect another, and having been born a Jew... there are others too and as I got to know him the list grew—it continues to grow. I learned that Pa avoided discussing anything that he found hurtful, or was uncomfortable with.

Pa had all but lost his faith by the time I met him. He was an agnostic, or that is what I thought; religion and faith were subjects that Pa also refused to discuss.

Zaideh Levy had successfully applied for reclassification from being European to 'mixed'. He did so because Grandma Levy had curly hair and would have failed the pencil test. New government laws ensured that people with a similar heritage, or those who did not fit in, were grouped together under the label 'mixed'.

When the Population Registration Act became law, it introduced new labels for all the groups. From then on, those who previously had been referred to as 'mixed' were re-labelled 'coloured'. The term 'coloured' denotes a person of mixed heritage—like a mongrel. I hate that label. Remember this: you can never be non-racist if you use racist terms to describe people.

The term, 'native', was a label used to describe all tribes that moved south on the African continent. In reality, the Khoi people are the only people who are native to this region. The label, 'native', was replaced by the term, 'bantu'; and 'white' replaced the term 'European'. To this day, I refuse to use any of these terms because continuing to do so serves only to legitimise one group oppressing another—we are people, and that is enough.

The renaming and re-labelling of the groups was a fiasco of note. Descendants of Europeans who settled in the Cape had been given access to the best facilities. The laws ensured that they became and remained the superior group.

It is not right that people get to use certain facilities simply because they have light skins, while others are not allowed to because their skins are dark. There will come a day when this madness will end. That time will bring with it a new responsibility for you and others of your generation. You will have to ensure that new leaders do not do what they have learned from the experience of living like we do now. That is the reason why the two of you should read _Animal Farm_.

You should ensure that there is no job reservation and that people will be free to attain that which is their potential to achieve; they should apply for and be appointed against jobs that match their ability and not as determined by the colour of their skins. The only way that we are going to build a successful country after this madness heals is through using the best talented and skilled people where they are most suited. The colour of their skins must not matter more than the value that they represent.

I write this to you, my children, because it is important that you understand. You must identify with the pain that has been inflicted on all the people of this beautiful country. You have to ensure that no group of persons inflict the same pain when this despicable era of oppression is overthrown.

Pa and I were married in 1954. He worked hard and did not wait for me to ask for our own house. The Woodstock house was no longer home to me. The environment had changed for the worse.

Pa was never a man of many words. He was not interested in anything that required of him to speak. Pa bought a block of land on the south peninsula shortly after we were married. Every evening he would rush home to have dinner and afterwards go to do some building work on the land. When the outbuildings had been built, we moved there. Brenda changed schools to live with us. Anne, then already a young woman, remained in the Woodstock house so that she could be near her clients—that was what she said.

The building process was fraught with peculiarities. In time I realised that Pa was the strangest man. He became stingy beyond measure and sought the least expensive route with whatever he did. I recall a day when our cooker broke and he could no longer repair it. He used a clothes iron and converted it into a hotplate for me to cook on until we had saved enough money to buy a new cooker. On another occasion, when our refrigerator broke, he made a wire cage and hung it in a tree to keep the milk and meat cool.

The funniest of his strangeness was also the most embarrassing. For instance, one day Pa arrived home with the ugliest little dog. The dog, Ellie, grew into a vicious beast. Her role was to guard the building material when we were at work. Ellie was lovable in her own way, but did not tolerate anyone other than the three people she knew.

Our neighbour was not happy with Pa doing building work at night. It was the bright light that irritated her most of all.

I was home one day when the building inspector arrived. It was a Wednesday, a rare day to be at home but the eczema on my leg was bad that week. When the inspector saw the dog he stood at the front gate and instead of entering he yelled: 'Hello! Hello ...!' until I responded.

"Good morning Ma'am," he said, "... the man who lives here; he's a bit deaf and somewhat mad?" indicating the madness with a circular movement of his index finger alongside his head. I was amused but confirmed that he, the inspector, was at the right house. When I told Pa the story that evening he looked at me and cleared his throat as if to speak, but must have cancelled the thought.

Well, the building inspector was there to check that Pa was complying with building regulations.

As he opened the gate, Ellie ran out. The inspector almost wet himself. Ellie was down 11th Road in a flash. I tore behind her like a confused wind—all the while shouting, 'Ellie! Ellie! Ellie!' When my aching leg got the better of me I began to hobble.

Next, and without warning, the complaining neighbour appeared in the street. She wore no clothes, just a towel wrapped around her head—I saw that her towel wrap had hooked on and remained at the front gate. She responded to my calls and was there to assist.

I had forgotten that our neighbour was called Ellie too. She was responding to what must have sounded like a desperate cry for help.

The building inspector was in a state of shock. So bad that I had to feed him sugar water. He calmed down, but to this day I don't know if he was shocked at seeing the big dog or the bigger naked woman.

After collecting her gown, Ellie, the neighbour, insisted that I explain the reason for yelling with such panic in my voice. The building inspector got into the municipality owned utility vehicle that he had arrived in and drove off. I never saw him again.

When Pa arrived home that evening I told him to change the dog's name.

He cleared his throat, like he does, and laughed, as if from the bottom of his belly: "Ya! That dog is too stupid, but the woman is very clever; maybe we must change her name!" was his reply.

I seldom saw Pa laugh. Almost as if to augment his strangeness, Pa's sense of humour was at times at least equally bizarre.

Charles, who was interested in becoming a bricklayer, had asked to live with his father, James. Pa and Charles never could agree and no amount of my bickering served to improve their relationship.

Brenda graduated from high school the same year that I obtained an academic degree in social work. There was trouble with her. It was the same trouble we had with Anne about four or five years earlier. Brenda then moved to stay with Anne in the old Woodstock house.

The internship at the mental hospital was interesting, but I found it difficult to work with people who continued to see me as their cleaner. My former and new colleagues were not being supportive. I likened it to when people changed their names. You know, when a Christian girl marries a Muslim boy, then often times she converts to Islam and both her surname and first name change. To lessen the impact the new first name is usually matched with her original Christian name and she is accepted. When I moved from being a cleaner to a social worker there was no such acceptance. I moved from cleaning the office, to occupying it, leaving my former colleagues to do the cleaning.

Perhaps the transition I made was a problem for my old peers at the hospital, or maybe I am seeking excuses for their behaviour.

After discussing my thoughts with Pa we decided that, to avoid further trouble, it would be best if I found another job. It is often better to be quiet. When people argue, fuss and fight, then to respond is not always the most value-adding reaction. It is what is said when we argue that counts the most. The things that are said in anger are remembered for a very long time.

§

World War II had ended much more than a decade earlier, yet the world remained focused on reconstructing Europe. Most of the ravages of the war were in Europe. South Africa was experiencing a social reconstruction. It was not entirely different to the German objective, which was to create a superior group that could ultimately dominate the world.

I submitted applications for every opportunity that was advertised. In the process more than fifty regret letters arrived. Most of the positions were reserved for the superior group. I was too dark. That was what disqualified me from suitability for most of the advertised positions for which I was qualified. It was very disappointing when those with less experience and lower qualifications were appointed to the positions for which I had applied. It seems that human beings will never become accustomed to rejection; I never did.

With each application I visualised doing the job, and after every rejection letter was received it took me several days to recover. I consciously did not allow the rejection to deter me from thinking about the value that could have been brought to those clients. All I wanted was half a chance to prove myself capable. My positive thoughts were the stimulus driving me to continue searching for the right job. Every time, the application deadline dawned, passed and was followed by yet another regret letter. All the regret letters were the same and every one of them had an equally devastating effect on me. My resolve was not to allow the rejection to tamper with my confidence. I remained committed to working for the betterment of people, no matter who they were.

As my frustration increased, so Pa and I continued to argue. He was selfish and I suspected that he was doing other bad things too. Pa and I had endless fights because he refused to support his three boys. At Christmas time particularly, Pa did not give his children money for food, buy them gifts or provide any other form of pleasure. Pa continued to ignore my constant bickering. If the truth be told, then it was me who bought gifts for those children, because your Pa was much too stingy. Now you know why, on occasion, I did not have money to bring you home for Christmas. It broke my heart, but I could not live with myself knowing that three young boys had to sit with their mother and have nothing to eat while their father had so much.

It was some time during 1958 when I was offered the job on the farms. My tools included a lady's twenty-eight inch, three-speed BSA bicycle and my house was the state owned worker's cottage.

Pa and I discussed that position in great detail before I accepted it. Part of the offer was that I'd live in Stellenbosch from Mondays and return home every Friday evening. I accepted the job when Pa agreed.

At first, Jane, you came with me when I went to work. Of the farm workers cared for you while I saw clients. The year after your fifth birthday is when I sent you to boarding school. That school was recommended by a colleague who, years earlier, was in a similar position. At the time it was the best that I could do to ensure that you attended a good school.

Pa continued to live in his own world, as he does. He spent every free moment building the house—it was never ending. Building work, reading newspapers and listening to news on the radio were all he did, or that is what I thought. We seldom had conversations and rarely visited our friends.

I enjoy dancing, but Pa never had rhythm. It is an uncanny experience to watch him dance. His movements are spastic—too bad when my feet got in the way! There might be truth in his being hard of hearing. Recently I read an article in a medical journal where the writer discussed and concluded that there is a greater chance of hearing loss with people who have cleft palates.

When we visited with Auntie Rachel, then Pa spoke out loud and non-stop. I enjoyed those outings. He'd have some wine. Rachel, with her gentle manner, like Zaideh Levy, was a very pleasant woman. It was when visiting Rachel that I got a chance to hear what Pa was thinking and what was going on in his life.

Anne and Brenda continued to live together in the Woodstock house. It pleased me—but my preference was that we live together in one house and as one family. Anne too did not care much for Pa. She never said why, but that was the real reason why Anne lived away from him. On the face of it he treated my children well, but maybe his behaviour changed when I was not home.

My job was intense and at times it was dreadfully sad. The problems on those farms will continue for as long as alcohol formed part of the wages paid to employees. I read too many medical reports about the effect of alcohol on *families and innocent children. Wine-farm workers, their families and unborn children are the most severely affected by this practice. Many families are ruined because of the abuse that occurs when parents are addicted to alcohol. It is tragic to see and have to live with.*

The farmers saw me as unnecessary; and when I met with my clients, their workers, it was seen as a colossal inconvenience. The result was that I could not talk the farmers out of feeding the wage earners wine as part of their weekly stipend. I could also not enlist the farmers' support in correcting whatever social problems festered on different farms from time to time. There were times when my job felt as if I were scooping water from a sinking boat with that red enamel coffee mug I kept in the kitchen—there was no end to it.

On Friday afternoons I parked my bicycle in the station storeroom for the weekend. Two trains later, followed by a three kilometre walk, I would be home. There I'd spend two days in near silence before making the trip back to my alcohol-plagued nest. That became my routine.

I shall send the second half of the story when next I write. Tell me how you are and share your news, please?

As usual, I am counting the days until we can be together. There are not many to go.

I love you
Mamma

Chapter Six

Klapmuts

"I am not interested in politics or politicians. My interest is in fairness ..." That was Ma's standard reply whenever Jane accused her of being fanatical about the social construct of South Africa.

"There is no fairness in South Africa and I am bitter about it—I shall keep talking to whoever wants to hear my views. It happened before as well, but the laws have been unfriendly to the majority of South Africans ever since the official birth of institutionalised discrimination in 1948. It is not right and if we do not discuss it, then what is unfair will become fair in people's minds."

Ma bought both the English and Afrikaans newspapers on a Sunday and read a section of each every night. That was how she kept abreast with social and political developments in her own country and the world. From time to time, Ma found articles that she thought were of interest to Jane and me. On those occasions she'd include the article in her weekly letter.

I continued to listen and hear whenever we were home and Ma spoke to herself. Sometimes I would write down what she said, such as: "... all that is happening in this country cannot possibly end with it becoming a happy place" and "...theories are good only if the people that they apply to are happy ... where will it end?" She said other things too, but I did not write them down at the time, however, every time that Ma thought aloud it would conclude with: "... where will it end?"

In previous letters, Ma explained that dormitory towns were places where workers lived. It fascinated me because, at school, the junior pupils slept in dormitories. Ma felt that the more information she gave the better we would understand.

"Dormitory towns are situated close to industrial areas, but far from business centres. Workers live close to where their labour is needed, which is usually far from the cities. The cities are the preserve of the privileged group. The dormitory areas are called townships, locations and native yards. Public transport there is basic and most workers leave home before sunrise and return after sunset."

Then there were the migrant workers:

"They are men and women who leave their families in the rural areas to find work in the industrial centres, or in the mines. It is not unusual for children, who are reared mainly by grandmothers, to see one, or both parents for only two or maybe three weeks per year—usually when the parents return home for Christmas."

Once Ma got started it was difficult to get her to stop. Ma wrote as much as she spoke, but when we were at school it was always refreshing to get letters from home. The way Ma explained in her letters made me understand many things very clearly. Often I'd listen to other children talk and then it would become clear that they did not understand the social issues like Jane and I did. For instance, in the letter where Ma explained the Job Reservation Policy:

"To make sure that people from the privileged group were placed in the more senior jobs, the state introduced the Job Reservation Policy. At that time the United States of America developed a similar policy. They labelled it Affirmative Action. The American policy was geared to create equal opportunities for previously marginalised minority groups. In South Africa the Job Reservation Policy affirmed a minority group. That minority group already had access to all the privileges and they had the power to act.

"A policy that favours one group of people over another on the basis of anything other than competitive ability is unfair.

"This country will never grow if people who lead development are not chosen on merit.

"If leaders are appointed using any other criteria then there will be an increase in unemployment because businesses will fail. Also remember that those who have know-how should teach others because without the practical knowledge a big business will become small, close down and result in increased unemployment. You know, Boy, people cannot teach one another experience, no, it has to be earned, and—'The Fish Rots From Its Head' and if the bus has an unqualified driver then it will collide."

In Ma's letters she usually concluded her oft-repeated speech about the evils of job reservation with: *"Even the disabled are able. They are able because of ability, not because of disability. Why is it that we fail to see past a person's disability when all of us have ability?"*

That was my Ma's war cry when persons with disabilities were treated badly. Back then it was acceptable to refer to disabled people as 'cripples' or 'crippled people', another term that Ma detested. *"Just because people cannot use their limbs, or see, does not mean that they are stupid,"* she would write.

Jane was a very diligent letter writer. I wrote too, but my new locker-door-on-wheels that Boet Sam made required lots of practice! I had homework and had to study for tests and examinations—there was always something that came up when it was time to write to my Ma, 'the revolutionary'. The excitement of receiving letters from home continued to be the highlight of my time spent at school—that, and the weekends when we went surfing.

I wrote my first unassisted letter on my ninth birthday. It was a proud moment, I had made myself proud.

As I grew older my letter writing skills improved. Jane continued to interpret for me whenever Ma wrote because her letters, to me, were very complicated. At one stage, Ma began to write about a certain Mr Verwoerd and then about a Mr Vorster. In my child's mind I thought that these men were two of Ma's clients who caused trouble when they drank too much wine—that is, until Jane showed me the newspaper articles. Those two were respectively the founder and leader of the people who made all the rules by which we lived in South Africa.

Jane slapped me behind my head when I shared my thoughts about Mr Verwoerd and Mr Vorster. I could not be blamed much, for Ma's letters often featured characters that drank too much wine, who were mad, tragic or workers who embarrassed her with their overt racism. I guessed that these two were no different. Another letter explained her views about racism. I understood, but only once Jane explained what Ma had written:

"We will never think of people as equal if we always identify one another by the colour of our skins" and *"racism is only one form of discrimination. In order to fight bad discrimination we must be able to identify it. That is the only way that we will know when it is good and when it is bad to discriminate—yes, through understanding what it is and how it affects others. Most people are racist. They practise negative discrimination without realising. Racism is a form of discrimination that is not only practised by light-skinned individuals in South Africa. Racism is probably the most widely applied form of negative discrimination in the world."*

Ma refused to write what she referred to as 'baby letters'. When I complained, she'd say: *"You will never learn to think if I write stupid letters."*

§

Jane often remained at school when I went home. Upon returning she would extract what I thought were the most minute and insignificant pieces of information about my visit to our home. I had to tell what we did, ate, who visited, about people I saw and what Lampo did. The last trip home resulted in exactly that, an almost extortion of everything that happened since I left.

Jane immediately begun to write based on what I had reported about the trip to Cape Town, and did so with even greater enthusiasm after she had read *Animal Farm*. News from Ma arrived before Jane could finish her latest letter and well before I could add to it. Some of Jane's letters were the longest that I have ever read. I remain surprised that her writing fingers did not need surgery after those big letters were written. It was upsetting because she never left anything for me to write. Jane was not only a motor-mouth, but also a motor-writer.

86

When Jane returned from comforting those who had not received letters, the two of us sat in our corner to discuss the content of Ma's latest letter. That had become our norm too.

I was a small number of weeks away from being thirteen and Jane was headed for seventeen. Yet, I needed her to explain some of the inclusions in the letter we received. Ma wrote about many things in her letters. Jane pretended not to know about the stories concerning our family. It was her behaviour in such instances that confirmed for me that Jane knew more than she was prepared to share. After our discussion Jane returned to her room. Once there she must have begun another exhaustive response to Ma's letter:

[I only got to read the following letter many years later]

21 August 1972

Dear Mamma

Thank you, Ma, for your letter. You are writing to us as adults and, as always, I enjoy that. Thank you. How is Lampo? I miss her, give her a hug and say that it is from me.

The last holiday job I did was not pleasant. At least I earned enough money to pay for our train tickets in December. This is my last trip home from school. I am so looking forward to it. Because there is no need for a return ticket I used the left over money as a deposit for Sam's new fees. The fees were increased again. Soon we will not be able to keep Sam at this school. For now though, half of next year is paid for. The other money I paid over to the University of Cape Town as a registration fee. In fact, I asked Mammy Cynthia for a small loan because the closing date for registration at the Medical School was before I was paid. Don't worry, Ma, I have returned her money, together with a thank you gift.

The career guidance people asked me to register at the University of Natal's Medical School. I did not have enough money for the registration fee, but my study permit application was turned down, on the basis that I am a Capetonian and should apply for a permit to study at the University of Cape Town instead. There was no cost when I applied for the permit to study at a reserved university. That is the reason why I submitted it way ahead of time. You know, hey Mamma; I need a permit to study at UCT because it is reserved for the privileged group. I find it funny, but the reality is very sad. You know what I mean. We'll wait and see what happens, okay? You must not worry. The career guidance advisor recommended that, if I was not accepted to study medicine at UCT, then I could always become a dentist by studying at the University of the Western Cape (UWC). I am told that UWC is reserved for people of the 'mixed' group. I have never thought of becoming a dentist, but the career guidance adviser seems to think that it is a good idea. There will then be no need for a permit if I study at that University.

It is my dream to study and then work in Cape Town. I hear many people say that Cape Town is the most beautiful city in the world. If anything, I would like to experience its beauty all year round and not only during December and early January when we are home from school.

There was a section on the application form that had to be completed if I needed accommodation. It is a good idea to live on campus, I think. Then I shall not be a burden to you. Not being in the way is uppermost in my mind. You have been a wonderful mother to thumb-sucking Sam and me. You have sacrificed so much to have us come this far. Someday, I shall thank you properly.

Will I need a permit to stay in the university residence too? Do you know, Ma? A permit to study there is like having a passbook.

Sister St Claire used my midyear academic results to apply for a bursary from the South African Medical and Dental Council. She applied to the Catholic Church too, but given that we are not Catholic I am not too hopeful about it being granted. If I am accepted at the medical school and obtain a bursary, then all my studies shall be paid for. This is on condition that my academic results remain consistently good. With a bursary I will be guaranteed a job when done studying. It will be a year-for-year bursary. I'll have to work at a state hospital for five years. That's fair, I think. It's a stunning opportunity hey, Mamma? At the end I shall be able to take care of you, like you take care of us. Oh Mamma, there is nothing like a good dream, hey?

Sister St Claire often makes reference to a thing that she has read, or heard. It has to do with dreams. Something about: 'If you cannot dream it, then you will never be it.' You have probably heard this before. Am I quoting it correctly? 'Hard work;' Sister St Claire's opinion is that hard work will get me there. I live in hope and keep on trying my best. I do not want to let myself down. As you said, I must make myself proud.

My immediate plan is to work on the Head Girl Project during the September break. Mr van Heerden of Chubby Chicken wants me to work every Friday afternoon and also Saturdays until one o'clock. I shall skip that one, because he wants me to work during the only time there is to concentrate on the Head Girl Project.

You see Ma, it is a school tradition that all head pupils write their story. Having looked at the other stories, the writing has to be about when I arrived, my memories and how the school contributed to my life.

My writing will be about that first journey I made here; and also about when Sam joined me. Sam's and my experiences are intertwined. At the moment, my persuasive skills are being put to the test. I am trying to convince Sam to write his own version of our story. Sam has a locker door that has wheels attached to it and I have to compete with a 'wheely door' for his attention. Who knows whether my efforts to persuade Sam shall be successful, and whether he will write for inclusion in my project? I hope that the locker-door-on-wheels will not be the winner in the contest for my brother's time.

Will you proof read the report for me when done, Mamma? I shall post it early on a Saturday morning; the second Saturday in September. It will arrive on the following Wednesday.

More importantly Mamma, if Sam does write, then will you help me make the two pieces read as one, can you do that for me?

All head pupils who have siblings at the school must include them in their story. I can't begin to imagine what Sam remembers, so yes, I am excited to see what he'll produce—if anything.

About your letter, Mamma: it sounds very sad. I am sorry.

You always told me how you felt when Pa failed you in his promises to take us to Cape Town Station on the days when we left for school. When you next saw him, then he'd say 'Sorry'. In my mind's eye I can see how mad you were with him. I see you point that crooked finger and say: "Sorry, you say! Sorry is not medicine," followed by: "You are a heartless man!"

Well, it is the truth about Pa; that much I've realised. In this instance I am sorry, because the story in your letter makes me think back to many unpleasant occurrences. I am sorry, Mamma, sorry also because I cannot think of anything better to say, but sorry—yet to be sorry is so empty!

Most of what you write is not new to me. To read your writing like this, Mamma, creates a lump in my throat; and it is not right that children who are far from home should feel like I do about their parents. When reading it to Sam I had to pause a few times in order to keep my composure. You know what he's like when comes the time to be sad; and when that big mouth is overcome by the emotion of the moment. So, I try my best not to be sad in front of him. This time he sat there with his thumb. In silence he listened while I battled, and then his face became wet. Before I could make my usual correction Sam had already made up his mind: "It feels as if we do not belong anywhere, Jane." I ignored that and kept composure. But my face was wet and there continued to be a lump in my throat. It's true Mamma, Sammy and I do not belong—why is it only us?

All the time though, I feel very happy, proud and excited to have you as my Mamma. You are an inspiration to the people you work with, but not nearly as much as you are a role model to me. Sam agrees. He often says how good you are to us. He says so particularly after developing an understanding of all that you write. This afternoon, when I explained the parts in your letter that he did not understand, Sam thought for a long while before responding: "Wow! Ma is so far away, but her teaching is as if she's right here, speaking through you."

We live a very isolated and protected life here at this almost farm school. The distance makes us appreciate you more. You must know that we realise and appreciate how hard you try for us.

I see that your political views have intensified. Sam studied the French Revolution at school and now he says that you are a revolutionary. My understanding of the political situation in South Africa is different when compared with other pupils in my standard. But it is best if I keep my opinions to myself. The laws we have and those that are created must be fair to all. 'Those who make rules should first check if they will be happy to have the laws applied to them.' I agree. Does the same not apply to many other things that have an impact on people? There is a better way to say this, but you understand what I mean, hey Mamma? The rules that we live by are unfair.

My big fear, like yours, is that when the situation is corrected the new government will repeat the same, or continue similar practices using different labels. Sometimes I get a chance to listen to the news. From what I hear it seems like politicians never acknowledge when they are wrong.

My last few months at school are going to be exciting. I am nervous, and also a bit sad. I know no other life than to be at boarding school, an institution where my role was infinitely defined as baby Sam's big sister. Being Sam's big sister was a dress-rehearsal for becoming Head Girl and big sister to many girls and boys. I shall miss them, Mamma, like you cannot possibly imagine.

My head is filled with thoughts about Sam at this time. I worry about how he will cope without my being here. The two boys who are his surfing companions finish school with me, so he will have no friends to share interests with. Maybe he will be fine. From next year onwards Sam will receive two letters every week: one from you and another from me. No doubt that the others will envy him. By the way, we've kept every letter that you wrote over the years. I have fourteen years of letters neatly stacked. They live in a very special place—the blue suitcase. Next year Sam can reply on Saturday evenings, when he and perhaps others are down at Scottburgh Beach.

Last week, when I collected the parcel you sent with Sam he was with the physical education teacher, Mr Thompson.

Oh! Thank you for the dress Mamma; it matches my new shoes—the ones that were in the Ackermans' lay-by, do you remember? I think that when Anne made this dress, she had those shoes in mind. The dress's belt is almost exactly like the strap on those shoes. Tell her?

We will arrive on 8 December, at three o'clock, in the afternoon—no prizes for guessing what I shall be wearing! Pa will probably be working, so don't bother asking him to fetch us. Ask Anne and Brenda to come along and let it be a surprise for Sam, okay?

Mr Thompson told me that Sam has potential to become a very good surfer. He says that Sam is a 'goofy foot' surfer. I don't know what that means. The Thompsons live in the South Coast town of Scottburgh. Someday I shall take you there, Mamma. It is very different from the Cape. The vegetation is sub-tropical and the weather is warm. June and July, when it is not too hot, are ideal holiday times on the South Coast.

Every second weekend, Mr Thompson takes three boys surfing. Sam has become obsessed with the sea and surfboards, much more than with thumb-sucking. Maybe surfing is the distraction that will stop him from sitting in a corner with his thumb in his mouth, pretending to be invisible. Sam must have told you about the surfing when he was home? He tells me that if his board were just a bit longer, then he'd suck his thumb whilst surfing! Imagine that? Maybe this is the reason why Mr Thompson thinks that our Sam is goofy! One of the workers at school has put wheels on an old locker door, and riding this door up and down in the play area is what Sam does whenever he has free time.

Reading your last letter also reminded me of the week we spent in Stellenbosch. You were working and left me with two women. Their memory of me was better than mine of them. Maybe I was too young when we first met. But they told the strangest stories about me. Meggie and Mettie is what their names were. Why do they have such odd names, and where were their front teeth? Maybe I should become a dentist, work in Cape Town and make it the false tooth capital of the world.

These two spent the better part of my visit discussing what I was like as a little girl. They spoke in Afrikaans and some of the words I could understand, but most others could have been Greek. Of the words they used most were familiar, but the way Meggie and Mettie enunciated was different. They spoke fast, so quick that all I could hear was—'Blonde hair, blue eyes, la, la, la, la'—like a song. That was the sound of their discussion. Both nodded in agreement, and laughed out loud.

They held hands while talking, and I was their subject; such warm, humble people.

While talking, one or the other would touch me. It did not make me feel uncomfortable; no, it was more of a loving, caring set of gestures. They introduced me to most every other person who dared walk by. A man driving a huge tractor pulling a big bath shaped trailer filled with harvested grapes had to stop, switch off the noisy machine and clamber down from up there—all because the two women insisted that he meet and greet me. They were excited, him too; as he held his hat while shaking my hand. He smelled of tobacco, that man, I remember. Again they spoke in Afrikaans. They were three then; discussing me, that was my sense. The tractor driver, he also remembered back to when I was little. To me it felt as if I belonged. Those are my people, I could feel it.

Afterwards, Meggie told me that her name is Margaret and that Mettie is Michele. How goofy is that! Oh, and I was introduced as Jani. Khokho Mbala of Mpophomeni also calls me Jani.

Having to explain parts of your letter to Sam gave me a better understanding of what you wrote. What is it that you always say? 'We learn most when we teach.' Well, explaining to Sam was an opportunity for me to read between the lines in places. Yes, Klapmuts and that bicycle you rode; I tried to ride it a few times and have a scar as proof!

The veld flowers of early spring, the long-stemmed purple heather, and daisies, like a carpet of yellow-and-black flowers—and those with white petals and a black centre, yes! They covered the entire veld, the daisies did—right up yonder to the foot upon which the Hottentots-Holland and Boland Mountains live. The mountains here around the area of our school are not the same.

Remember the time when I was there with you during winter, Ma? It was a very long time ago. There were arum lilies, my favourite, 'pig's ears', is what

Meggie called them. Remember, you warned that it was illegal to pick those that grew close to the road.

Oh well. You know Mamma, when others tell stories of the past, then it depresses me. It always feels better to reminisce about what I want to remember. No matter; this time I am more than excited to read what Goofy Sam remembers about our arriving at school! I so hope that he does write—it will make me very proud.

Towards the end of last year, we were each given a theme with which to write an essay. Mine was to describe an experience of the place which is most vivid in my mind. My worry is that I am not as observant as Sam. Nonetheless, I took this task to heart and after many days of introspection a plan of how to start the project emerged.

It was a Saturday morning and I had permission to go to the town library. In its reference collection there is a set of encyclopaedias similar to the one we have at home, the <u>Consolidated Encyclopaedia</u>. It is easier for me to find information in books with which I am familiar. My membership of the library goes back to when I was in Standard One. The only other letter I received was from the library. I remember that excitement as if it happened yesterday. The letter contained my borrowing dockets and a document that explained the public library rules. There were different days reserved for each group of people that lived in the area. I could pick three books and keep them for two weeks.

Well, there I was, on a Saturday morning, in the library, paging away. Later, just like your experience at the Cape Town City Library, that librarian also came to help me. Together we paged some more, she showed me how to use catalogue cards so that I could find the needed books. It's simple if you know how. You will not believe it, Mamma, but I found information about Klapmuts! This was to be the setting for my essay; the place of which I have the most vivid recollection.

Did you know that the name Klapmuts is derived from a style of men's hats that were popular in the 18th century? That is because the mountain there is shaped like a Klapmuts hat. I bet you did not know that, Mamma? But you know everything—a reality that is so frustrating at times! I shall not be surprised if you know this too. Anyway, I gathered all the information in the library that Saturday morning and then I sat down to write the entire piece. Happy memories, sad ones too; those that disappointed and continue to disappoint, they were all there, included in my essay.

With sadness I wrote about Spotty, our Staffie. Remember Mamma, the one that you adopted, whose family moved to Australia? It was cruel, the way she was run over. That man could have stopped. It remains vivid in my mind, how he drove the truck so slowly, but yet there was no attempt to swerve or apply brakes. He just ran over our dog as if she was an empty box. Sometimes I dream of her barking and then, in my mind's eye, she, with her sturdy Staffie body, chases after butterflies.

The librarian and I spoke. She told me about her Tamil religion. Since all those years ago, when my class first visited the library, that is how long she's been the librarian. Her hair was black with a small white patch in the front. She looked like you, but now her hair is completely grey and she's gained weight.

Over the years, the librarian watched me grow tall, like I saw her go grey. Whenever I went to the library, there was always a lingering feeling of being watched. On checking, I would find her, the librarian, staring at me. A frown would surround the Tamil marking on her forehead. We regularly smiled at each other back then, but never spoke. It was the one Saturday in the month that the 'mixed' group could use the library. That was when I arrived, Saturday morning. The library was quiet. There were probably only two other users in the entire facility. The librarian seized the moment to feed her longstanding curiosity.

We were lugging books from the Reference Section to the reading table when she asked: "From which place you are?" I told her. "Why you have joined that school?"

I knew why she was asking but would not give more information. Instead, I smiled and shrugged my shoulders. Skin-colour and hair are a national obsession among the different groups who live in South Africa.

I could not help myself when writing the essay. It felt important to include the experience you and I had in Klapmuts, Mamma. That experience remains vivid in my mind.

Remember, we went to the little shop next door to Klapmuts Post Office? You sent me in to buy a small packet of your favourite, Tastic Rice. While I was in the shop you popped your head in to remind me about onions, do you remember?

That was when the shop-keeper, Mrs Akkerman, spoke to you in a berating tone. She spoke in Afrikaans, I think, but it did not sound the same as when Meggie and Mettie spoke. Her dialect was different. The words she used were loud, guttural and very clear, but I did not know what Mrs Akkerman was saying. It sounded as if she was scolding you. Your demeanour was one of agreement—and then you went out, around the back to further the discussion through a mesh-covered window. All the while I was allowed to shop freely, but with your money. You know what Mamma? I think about that experience very often, more now than I did when younger. These days it makes me sadder because I understand better. It is not right, hey Mamma?

That day is alive in my mind—I was on the back carrier of your bicycle holding the onions and the rice while you cycled. That was the day I so wanted to give you my skin, so you too could be free to shop where you like, with your own money.

I wrote all of that in the library, until my essay was complete and until the story was told in a way that best reflected what the experience felt like. Remember, you cannot teach people experience, but you can tell them what it feels, or felt like?

Sometimes I think that people would not be ugly to one another if they knew what it felt like to be on the receiving end of ugliness.

93

Some weeks later I had a very upsetting experience. Sister St Claire, our Head Teacher, called me to her office. When I got there, Ms Beatrice du Pont, the English Teacher, she was seated there too. I could see that Ms du Pont had been crying. My immediate thought was that something dreadful had happened at home. When Sister St Claire told me to sit, without first responding to my greeting, I was convinced that something bad had happened. Something had happened—I just knew. Sister St Claire would not have summoned me without good reason and neither would Ms du Pont have been crying if it were not serious. Ms du Pont is my register teacher, Ma.

I continued to look at the two women and saw their sadness. Without a word being spoken a sob rose from deep beneath my chest. It was difficult to control. Ms du Pont offered me one of the wipes from a box she held on her lap. I took and dabbed my nose and eyes. It is not easy being this far from home; and knowing that we are a dysfunctional or non-conventional family does not help either.

When I think about our family, then my thoughts also reflect on your counselling others and how they revere the advice and guidance you provide—but what about your own family, Mamma?

Well, there I sat, sobbing, and Sister St Claire was feeding me sugar water with a big tablespoon. I imagine that was what you did for that building inspector, after he saw the naked woman.

"To reduce the atmosphere of pain," Sister told Ms du Pont, while continuing to feed me and her from two big spoons, "... in my hometown, Derrinturn, Ireland, my mother gave children sugar water when they experienced shock." Her speaking like that confirmed my suspicion that something horrible had happened. Then no amount of sugar in any water could contain my tears and fears.

Ms du Pont spoke first, as I tried to get a hold of myself: "It is about your mother in the shop." She dabbed her eyes, took a shuddering deep breath, blew her nose and then said: "All I want to do is say that I am sorry. I want you to tell your Mamma that I am sorry ..."

She spoke through the tears and at times her voice had different lilts, but she continued until done: "I shall never meet your Mamma, but I want you to tell her that I am sorry. She will not come to our school, your mother has never been, and I shall never go there, but please tell her that I am sorry. I am sorry that she suffered such humiliation and that it was at the hand of someone whom she will pick up should that person, Mrs Akkerman, fall."

I felt very relieved after hearing the reason for the meeting. Not having to leave school like you did Mamma, because of a death in the family, like you had to do after Daddy Wilson's sudden death, was some relief.

These two women are powerful and it was not because of their positions at school. No, they are powerful because they understand the meaning of wrong. Wrong has to do with what something feels like, whether it is unfair, or unjustified.

We sat there and looked at one another for a while. There was no more need to cry, or to talk. I know Sister St Claire to be my mother too, just like Mammy Cynthia. I felt comfortable to speak, and I did so that day. I was speaking to the women who had brought my learning to where it is now. They taught me to think and I used that opportunity to thank them: 'The men who created the divisive laws in South Africa created a better life for some and a worse life for others. It was not fair and it is also my hope that they will someday realise, or be forced to realise, that their laws are wrong and that they cause untold misery. My Mamma is afraid—that the men who make the laws will someday be replaced by others who will do the same, under a different label. My Mamma talks when she thinks that Sammy and I can't hear. What she said the last time I listened makes me wonder about how we are going to stop the wrong of tomorrow from happening once the wrongs of today are no more?'

It was not easy for me to say that to my teachers, Mamma. Maybe someone else was speaking through me? I am committed to never causing pain; you know. I shall make a point of speaking to Mrs Akkerman. She will understand, because Mrs Akkerman is a person too. So, one day when I can speak in Afrikaans, like you, Mamma, then I shall go to that shop and respectfully ask Mrs Akkerman for a meeting.

I was called to the head teacher's office so that Ms du Pont could tell me that she was sorry. She had asked Sister St Claire to strengthen her apology by being present—probably because to say sorry is so empty.

My walk back to the classroom was filled with pride. I felt proud to have you as my Mamma. The unfairness with which we treat one another in South Africa is not right. I hope that this will someday be a wonderful country. I wish that we will have laws that allow all people to have access to the same opportunities. These opportunities should be determined by ability only, otherwise we will not fulfil our potential. I look forward to the day when there will be no reference to which group people belong.

Thank you for allowing me to grow my understanding through being exposed to your experiences, Mamma.

My final examination is on 26 November. Mr Thompson asked me to help with administration work at a surfing competition where Sam will be participating. I can't wait to see what goofy-footing is all about. Mr Thompson explained that goofy-foot surfing is similar to being left-handed. It is when surfers instinctively place their right foot before their left as they stand up on a moving surfboard. He went on to say that it is usual for right-handed people to put their left foot forward when they are pushed. Did you know that? Apparently, when Sam rides a wave and when the thrust begins to propel the board, then he instinctively places his right foot forward, hence he is 'goofy-footed'—I have to see this!

The competition finishes on 3rd December and on that evening we leave for home. First we'll travel to Pietermaritzburg by bus, so that I can greet Mammy Cynthia, Khokho and the rest of the family in Mpophomeni. We'll stay the night and board the Cape Town bound train the following afternoon.

Okay Mamma, remember to help make my Head Girl Report and Sam's writing read as one. If you have a chance, then please encourage Sam to write for me? I shall send the writing to you soon. Goofy Sam can write his own letter this time.

I love you
Jane

Jane sent that letter to Ma without including one from me. I was cross after discovering that, but it was better to be quiet and do my own writing. However, after writing two paragraphs of my letter to Ma the attraction of the locker-door-on-wheels seemed greater. It felt strange to be writing by myself, but it gave me a feel for what it would be like when Jane was no longer at school. We usually wrote and sent letters together, both to save on cost and, so that our letters read more like a conversation, with each of us commenting on what the other had written. Given that Jane had changed the routine, I suspected she had written stuff that was not for my eyes. It was okay, because there were times when they wrote about girl things.

With Jane leaving school, and all the changes, my curiosity about what she had written to Ma was more intense than at other times. For days I continued to wonder what it was that Jane did not want me to see. Asking Ma to tell me would not have been fair. Instead, I read and re-read Ma's last letter to see if there were clues, but it was to no avail. Strange how small things cause bother when one is apprehensive and a bit insecure.

Chapter Seven

Report from the Head Girl

There were eight weeks remaining before the school syllabus was complete. Jane was anxious about examinations and other tasks that befell her. Slight relief came in the form of an official letter containing Jane's permit to study at the University of Cape Town, her university of choice. Her earlier application had been refused because similar courses were offered at universities that were dedicated to educating students classified as 'mixed'. Yet, when Jane's permit was granted she became very happy. The reality was that separate development continued to dog our everyday lives. We had begun to feel that it was normal to be denied and we became happy when our requests to be 'permitted' were granted. I was a little boy then, just thirteen years old, but I knew that we had become accustomed to living in isolation from the other peoples who made up our country.

Ma plodded along with her job. Increasingly, her letters reflected that her work was not achieving its objective. I remember a letter where Ma described her work. It was probably because she wanted us to understand, or, perhaps Ma just needed to talk: *"... it continues to feel as if I am dishing water out of a boat with that red mug in my kitchen; and sometimes even worse, the boat is leaking and I am dishing with a sieve in an attempt to stop it from sinking."*

After nearly ten years of working away from home for four days in every week, Ma had begun to think about finding another job. By then her free time was filled by those two Sunday newspapers she bought every week, reading journals and writing letters to us at boarding school. Her interests were fuelled by what she read. Ma analysed each story and had an opinion about most things. Those opinions featured prominently in her weekly letters, as did further comment about the work she did: *"I have to do this work better all the time. This job is never done. It would be unfair to my successor if she or he has to start at the beginning when I leave. When will we ever make a difference if we start at the beginning every time?*

I recently read a wonderful book. It describes the building of a cathedral, which starts with a plan. When the plan is drawn and accepted then the building work begins. The work is meticulous and the craft of construction intricate. Often it takes more than one lifetime to complete the entire body of work on a big cathedral. Successors follow the original craftsmen and continue with the work. Eventually, and after many generations of meticulous work, the cathedral is completed.

I think that if we do a job, it has to be done so that our successors are able to build on what we have done."

It became evident that Ma's interest had shifted from telling us about our lives and how Jane and I had come to be. Yes, she had become more interested in world matters. Newspapers, journals and her little transistor radio had become constant companions. At the top of her list was the Vietnam War, which she opposed as if her own children were fighting abroad. Ma had lived through the impacts of two previous wars. That was why it had become natural for her to follow events as they unfolded in the South East Asian countries, Vietnam, Laos and Cambodia. While many other women read *Woman's Weekly, Readers' Digest* or *Mills & Boon*, Ma bought an additional subscription to an American journal about the Vietnam War. Whenever she had read the latest edition or article which detailed what had happened in South East Asia, Ma's subsequent letters would be filled with the trauma suffered and senselessness of combat. Her letters discussed 'the shame', as she termed it: *"... Grown men decided to send young adults and boys to their deaths, fighting about something of which they had little to no balanced understanding ..."* is an extract taken from a letter Ma wrote during that time.

Military occupation of the Middle East was another of Ma's interests, but nothing occupied more of her time and writing than developments in South Africa:

"By 1967 the South African government had made it compulsory for young privileged and ruling class men to be conscripted into the national defence forces. They had to defend the national borders against 'communists'. These young conscripts were forced into dangerous situations and told that they were fighting 'communism'. Many young men were killed, maimed and scarred. Everything is geared to defend the practice of discrimination in South Africa. Nothing good can come of it ... but once a child is dead then he will be gone forever, no matter the colour of his skin!" she'd write and Jane would explain to me until I too understood what Ma was trying to teach us.

It did not matter that inside the borders of South Africa oppression was more real than the unknown threat of a theory. Ma was never interested in communism, capitalism or socialism. In the letters that Jane interpreted for me, Ma explained that no absolute was good, and that there were hundreds of different theories over which people went to war. She held definite thoughts about most things and sometimes it was difficult to have a conversation with her, because Ma's mind was already made up about almost every social issue we tried to discuss.

I understood after Jane explained Ma's views. Sometimes Jane had to explain the same thing several times before I knew what Ma tried to communicate. Maybe I was not bright enough, not like Jane who understood after just one reading. For instance, when Ma wrote about her views on war:

"Wars are always fought by children—mainly young men between the ages of nineteen and twenty-five. How can we ever have a peace which is real if we kill one another's children?"

There was a time when I suggested to Ma that she write articles for publication in our newspapers. The suggestion was probably a mistake. Following that comment Ma's letters became like history lessons. She discussed media and freedom of the press. Her explanations included that news in South Africa was subject to strict censorship standards. Ma was at pains to explain why it was futile to write about the debates that should be featured in the South African media:

"Because the threat of censorship looms large, newspaper editors are afraid that their papers will be banned if they publish anything that overtly criticises the state. The contravention of any government regulation can land the editor in jail and the newspaper will be closed down."

And:

"An important lesson that I have learned is that you cannot disagree, via the print media, with people who buy their ink by the barrel."

Toward the end of her stay in Stellenbosch, Ma was obsessed with a need to leave a legacy of success. Her relationship with Pa was marred by strife and her feelings about social developments in the world around her were at an all-time low. It was at about that time when even her meals became bland. Everything she ate was steamed. Fish and pork were 'off the menu', because they affected her bad leg.

When we were home from school Ma prepared steamed chicken and meat. On Sundays we had roast chicken, potatoes, beetroot and garden peas, followed by sago, her speciality sweet.

Life at school continued as it always did. Jane was preparing to sit for her final examinations. Two boys and I, together with our coach, Mr Thompson, spent every weekend at the beach, surfing. It was a Friday: Mr Thompson was driving; all four of the surfboards that were tied to the van's roof-racks were flung off by a gush of wind. They crashed onto the hard tarred road surface. The board that best suited my weight, height, and which I always used, was the most damaged. The spine, although intact, was protruding among shattered fibre-glass ends. After examining the broken board, Mr Thompson looked up at me, smiled and then gestured with his hand: "There, Champ, fix it and it's yours." That is how I acquired what became my first and only surfboard. Throughout my life I have only owned one surfboard—that one.

I think that Mr Thompson didn't know any of our names; we were all 'Champ' to him. It didn't matter. I was excited to get my own surfboard (even a broken one). I couldn't remember ever being more excited than the day Mr Thompson gave me a broken surfboard. Before then I had only dreamed of having my own board. To me it was like owning the most expensive car that money could buy. Before then I often saw boys at the beach who had their own surfboards. Well, there I was, about to become one of them.

Earlier that year, Thami, Mammy Cynthia's grandson, had found work with a shipbuilder. When Mammy told him about the broken board Thami excitedly offered to repair it. Jane, Mammy Cynthia and Thami each contributed to the purchase of fibreglass cloth, resin, hardener and water paper. Thami got advice from work about how to do the repair and how to use the material that we had bought. I begged Jane that we visit Mammy Cynthia at her home in Mpophomeni over the following weekend: "You can study there. Khokho will silence the noisy ones, I shall ask her." Jane was always unable to concentrate when people made a noise near where she was studying.

We travelled by bus to Mammy Cynthia's that Friday evening—as for me, I was clutching the broken surfboard and couldn't have cared less about what the other commuters thought. Although the driver was not happy about my board he allowed me to travel; probably because he recognised us. Jane with her almost white hair and me, we were known because of our different look.

After hours of pasting, sanding, rubbing and weighing, Thami and I had fixed my board. It was better than new. It took us the entire weekend, but it was worth it. At the end Thami beamed with satisfaction—it was his craftsmanship that made my board come alive again.

By then Khokho had realised how important the board was to me. Khokho, who was then older than eighty years, measured my board and within a few hours produced a surfboard cover and sling strap: "There Sammy; I used an old blanket so that your board could have a new cover."

Khokho enjoyed language. She liked words that rhymed. It was one of her many talents, I think. Carrying my board in its new casing felt like when I wore new shoes.

It took a further few weeks after the repair before I got an opportunity to test my patched board in the surf.

Jane pestered me until I wrote and informed Ma about my new interest. I delayed because Ma was not keen on anything that had to do with the sea. I remembered about her sea experience, but the stories about my interest in surfing were, according to Jane, important to share with Ma. Jane frequently told me that my letters were not half as exciting as they could be. I tried nonetheless, but left the important bits for my sister to write—she did anyway.

In a further letter Ma tried to continue with our story. The tone of that letter led Jane to suspect that Ma was no longer working in Stellenbosch. Whenever Jane asked, Ma would ignore the question. Yet, the way Ma wrote suggested that she was always at home and that Pa was working. But Pa was always working. We never knew about Ma's job because, in most instances she would be home during our school holiday visits. Letters from home continued, as always, to get Jane and me buzzing like bees at a pollen fest.

Sometimes the contents were not in keeping with our enthusiasm:

1 November 1972

While I was working in Stellenbosch Pa had found a family to rent the main house. Our agreement was that we would live in the outbuilding, a two bedroom unit attached to the house. It was there where Pa, Brenda and I lived while he was building. When I went to work in Stellenbosch, Brenda had already moved to share the Woodstock house with Anne. I woke up early one morning and knew that my time in that job had expired. I had worked in Stellenbosch for nearly ten years; it was enough, and time to move on. Change is permanent: you will know what I mean by this in time.

The next Friday evening I told Pa of my plan to change jobs. I had had enough of living and working on farms in Stellenbosch and its surrounds. At first Pa nodded, as if in agreement, but I sensed reluctance after asking that notice be served on those who lived in the main house. Pa tried to sidestep my request. I insisted. Eventually he said: 'Ya! We can't afford the cost of maintenance on one salary.' I instinctively knew that there was more to the story. Whatever it was, I refused to live in the outbuilding at my own house.

Instead of agreeing that the tenants be given notice to vacate our house, Pa began to look for another place. I thought it odd, out of character, but that's what he did.

While hanging washing and making small talk with the tenant, I learned that they had bought the house from Pa years earlier! Mrs Fredericks explained that a condition of sale was that Pa lived there until I was no longer a 'migrant worker'.

I was angry beyond measure and knew that one day, when our country was fixed, then we would have to revise the laws so that it could protect women in marriage. Imagine, in 1972, husbands can sell the family home without their wives' consent; but wives cannot buy or sell the family house without the consent of their husbands. It is not fair.

To add insult to injury, the new owners told me that they had bought the house in 1969: three years previously!

I found it difficult to accept that Pa had sold our house without including me in the decision. Each time you children asked I deliberately avoided the question. There was no point in arguing about done deeds. What Pa did with the proceeds is also a mystery, just like his reasons for selling.

Pa 'scoured' property supplements in various newspaper for a suitable development on the Cape Flats. That was how we got to our current house.

The demand for housing where we live is high. The people defined by this government as 'bantu', previously 'natives', are not allowed to own property close to the city; they can only own land in what is referred to as 'the homelands', a type of reservation with its own quasi government. The 'mixed' group are allowed to own property in designated areas and townships on the Cape Flats. Property prices in places where we live are higher than in areas reserved for the privileged group. It's all to do with supply and demand.

I told Anne, Brenda and Charles about my decision to stop working in Stellenbosch. They know about the old house and why we have a new house too. Charles had the most questions when I informed him. I'm sure you would have had too, if I told you at the time. I was embarrassed, even with my children, because I had been duped by your Pa. Yes, because Pa had made a fool of me. I worked my fingers to the bone so that he could pay for services and beautify the place. Never did I think that the house was no longer ours. No wonder that what I paid for never materialised."

Jane had finished her part of the Head Girl Report. I felt guilty for not having done my bit, particularly when asked to read and comment on what she had written.

With practice, my ability to express views and ideas in writing had shown steady improvement. From time to time, Mr Thompson left our school to do his compulsory military training. He was conscripted into the South African Army at regular intervals and upon returning he would have a boy haircut. We, the 'surfer boys', would then be subjected to the screams of military-like commands.

"C'mon Champs, this surfing platoon will become the best in the world, but you have to prrrrac-tise!"

This was followed by: "You can be good at anything if you prrrrac-tise, rrreg-u-larrrly!"

I did not believe a word of that piffle. Nonetheless, he continued with attempts to drum motivation into us when we arrived at Scottburgh beach, after an hour-long drive from Ixopo. My reaction, albeit in my head, was not unusual because I was mired in a 'phase' of being sceptical about most things. Mr Thompson's ranting was just military poppycock, I thought. If it were true, then I would be at least as good at mathematics as Jane, but no amount of 'prrrrac-tice' got me anywhere close to being okay, let alone good.

§

After reading Jane's Head Girl Report I had less than a fair idea of what my contribution could be. She affixed a pencil note to the report. It read: "Once done, Goofy Sam, then I want to send the whole thing to Mamma. Write your experience so that it will be easy for her to join the two together."

Jane's Head Girl Report explained about when I joined the school. That, I thought, was a good place to start; I could easily fill in the missing parts so that it could fit in with Jane's conclusion. There was pressure for me to write, even though I had not committed to doing so. As usual, Jane had said everything that had to be said.

Ma was very excited about the project; her role meant further involvement with the school. She had never visited us at school. In fact, Ma never knew what we looked like when we wore our school uniforms. Her only contact was the letters she received from the accountant and our quarterly progress reports. The school letters were always addressed to Pa, and that is where they remained. Ma would enquire with the fees office why she had not received a statement of our accounts. The answer frequently resulted in her having to credit the school via Barclays Bank: all so that the total fees and arrears for the two of us were settled in full before the commencement of our final examinations. There was a time when Ma had to forego seventy percent of her salary so that we could be paid up. Examination results would be withheld if school fees were not settled in full. Fortunately we were always saved from that embarrassment.

Over the years the prices of everything had increased. The cost of having two children at a private school had long ago outpaced any adjustments to Ma's salary. I recall four occasions when Ma did not have enough money for us to buy train tickets for the homeward journey, but our fees were always paid. After Jane's sixteenth birthday she regularly worked at Chubby Chicken; and without this income we would have had to stay at school more frequently, particularly after Ma stopped working in Stellenbosch. Our classmates holidayed with their parents while we stayed with the nuns. Mammy Cynthia took us to be with her family during those lonely holidays when we could not make the journey home; otherwise we would have had to stay at an empty school with the older nuns as our only companions.

Pa, well, where was Pa? In case you want to know, that was a question Jane and I asked each other too. Pa was working—he was always working, but he never had any money for us. When we asked for money, Pa's response was to recite a list of payments for which he was responsible. His list excluded Jane and me. I felt that we did not belong. There was a time though, when Pa gave me five cents to make a photocopy of a document I needed. He reached for the money and gave it to me, just like that. For about two weeks thereafter I could not stop reminding Jane of the money that Pa gave me, all in an attempt to convince myself that Pa was not stingy.

Over the Christmas periods, when we were unable to travel home, Ma would be home alone. Pa, he was working—always working. I remember a letter we received from Ma before school re-opened. It was during a time when we were unable to travel home for Christmas. We laughed after reading her letter, but later I felt disappointment because of my reaction. That was the time when Auntie Liza had seen Pa camping near a popular holiday destination. He had told Ma of a big and very urgent 'job' that had to get done.

Well, so there I was, having received Jane's Head Girl Report, or at least, what she had written. I was to read and then write my contribution:

Head Girl's Report 1975 (Extract –first draft)

My name is Jane Elizabeth Levy. I arrived by train from Cape Town at St Mary's Roman Catholic School, Ixopo. It was in January of 1963. Due to the nature of my Mamma's work, she did not live in one place for long enough and my Pa was frequently away, working, that was what he always said. I could not attend a local school. After seeking guidance from friends and colleagues, my

Mamma agreed that it would be better if I attended a boarding school. A short number of years later my brother, Sam, joined me.

My Mamma does not regret sending us to this faraway school, but each time we leave home the sadness gets worse. Yet, there was never a thought about attending another school. This school and the many things that I have been taught here are all that I know. There is a foundation in my mind, taught here at this school, and with which I think and reason.

- *Each time I fix a bed after sleeping in it, I shall think about being taught to do so properly at this school;*
- *When we eat at the table, I shall remember what the best manners are, which I have been taught at this school;*
- *When I speak, it is in order to be understood, but in a tone that I have acquired at this school;*
- *I conduct myself in a respectful manner, in order that I may demonstrate respect for others, a respect that has been taught me at this school;*
- *I share myself; and*
- *I have good friends here, because I have learned to be a good friend first.*

These are only a small number of values that I learned while attending this school. You may gloss over while reading my report, but do remember that the greatest learnings are embedded in the small things. It is the small things that make my foundation; and it is these small things that matter most.

I wish to mention Mammy Cynthia: I name Mammy Cynthia in this Report because she is my hero. Mammy Cynthia is my 'Mamma at school'. She teaches me to be humble because that is the example she sets. I remember Mammy Cynthia fetching me in Cape Town. I was sad to leave home but excited to go to school. We travelled together. Days later we reached the school. During that journey Mammy Cynthia, in her gentle way, explained and told me what being at school was like, and she was right.

On the train I'd wake up in the morning and ask Mammy if she thought that Ma was sad when we left. I remembered that Ma seemed sad when we left Cape Town Station. That was why I hugged her and said that Mammy Cynthia was going to take good care of me. Mammy did and continues to take good care of me.

When we left Cape Town, Mammy was also sad. Her sadness was because of my Mamma's hurt at seeing me leave. Though it took me a while, I know now why Mammy was also sad then.

That day, once I was seated in the train and before we departed, Mammy Cynthia went to speak to my Mamma. I could not hear what they were saying. During the journey I asked, and Mammy's reply was: 'Jane, I told your Mamma that you would be all right.'

Mammy Cynthia was right again, I continue to be all right.

The journey from Cape Town to Ixopo took us through tunnels and over mountains. It was a long trip. I thought about how my Mamma lifted me up onto the train and gave me to Mammy Cynthia. Mammy took me by the hand. Since then she has taken me by the hand many times, and every time I felt the same comfort. Mammy Cynthia has healing hands and she has frequently comforted me.

That first day on the train, after Mammy had packed the blue suitcase away, we walked down the narrow passage to our compartment. She had my birth certificate and other papers too, so all was fine.

Mammy Cynthia told me stories about her children and grandchildren. We ate sausage rolls and pies that Pa had prepared. There was soup in a flask and Mammy went out of the compartment and returned with boiling water, with which she made tea. My favourite story was about the hyena. I love that story. During the trip Mammy Cynthia had to repeat it many times.

Someday I hope to tell my children the story: 'It is about a hyena of which certain people were very afraid. Others were not scared and continued with their chores without any fear when the hyena was near. Those who had smeared fat on their bodies were the ones that the hyena would chase, catch and eat. They were the bad people.'

While telling the story, Mammy Cynthia enacted the scenes. I hid behind a cabin pillow, my make-believe tree.

The lesson in the story is that, if you do what is right then there is no need to fear. It took many years before I understood. One day, when I was describing my understanding of the hyena story to Mammy, her eyes began to glisten. With both her hands on my shoulders, she held me at arm's length, and let out her gentle signature giggle. Mammy Cynthia's ample bosoms 'always jiggled when she giggled'. That is what Khokho, Mammy's mother-in law, told me to watch out for!

The hyena story, as I later discovered, also refers to those who:

- Think they can get away without having prepared well enough;
- Who have done something wrong; and
- Who have something to hide.

These people are the only ones who have reason to live in fear.

We arrived at what must have been Pietermaritzburg Station. I could not read, remember. We boarded a bus for Ixopo, in the direction of the Transkei—a homeland for Xhosas—was what Mammy Cynthia told me. Mammy always tells me that the Xhosa Nation is the second biggest group in Southern Africa, second in size to the Zulu Nation. But back then I did not understand what was meant by the term 'homeland'. The bus dropped us at the top of a dirt road. I continued to ask many questions as we walked the (what I later learned) almost five kilometres to school.

Apparently there's a prison in Lusikisiki, on the Flagstaff road through Kokstad. It would take about three hours to drive there in a slow car from our school. My knowledge about Lusikisiki is extensive, even though I have never been. The Jefferson children at our school, they were from Lusikisiki. This was not the only reason that I was interested; for when pupils thought that they could get away with not preparing for examinations, Sister St Clare threatened them with a stint in the Lusikisiki Prison. The prison was described to be like the hyena that captured those pupils who had something to hide due to not having prepared well enough for examinations. I wonder whether Mammy Cynthia had shared the hyena story with Sister St Claire.

Together we have walked that dusty road so many times; the road from where the bus drops us to the school. Today I know the flavour of that mud. Sometimes my coughing did not keep pace with the amount of dust created when a passing car or sugar-cane truck made the sky turn orange. Strange, but I shall miss that. Mammy Cynthia wore the blue suitcase on her head like a hat and one of the many questions I asked was 'How do you do that, Mammy?' She never answered, just giggled as we continued the walk; and as for me, I held onto her dress and babbled on about anything that came to mind.

As tradition has it, the siblings of head pupils are also required to comment about how they came to be at the school. I asked Sam to write a story for inclusion in my Head Girl Report. [He has not given me his contribution at the time of writing so I have written my own recollection of when Sam first joined.]

Sam was born in October, about a year before I left for school. Two years went by before we were together again, but at four years and three months, Sam travelled to school with me. He spent the first two years in play-school. Sam was not yet old enough for regular school. It was at play-school where Sam developed an interest in drawing and music. It was also there, at play school, where the teachers discouraged him from writing with his left hand. Sam is left-handed. At school, teachers encourage all pupils to write with their right hands; to this day I think that the practice is wrong. However, in Sam's case it served to discourage him from a thumb-sucking habit.

I was nearly nine years old when he and I arrived here together, also with Mammy Cynthia. Sam was there and it was his first time. I held onto the left of Mammy Cynthia's dress while Sam clutched the right side—better for sucking his thumb! That first day when Sam was with us, a policeman at the bus shelter seemed cross with Mammy when they spoke. I did not understand what was being said, because he spoke too fast. Mammy stopped, put her hand on the suitcase, which was on her head, and waited until the policeman stopped screaming at her. Speaking in Zulu, her reply was firm, and then we walked on without any further interference.

When we were well on our way, I asked why the policeman was cross, but in the middle of my question a big truck drove by, probably one transporting sugar-cane to the mills. The amount of orange dust its wheels created formed the usual mud in my mouth. After a splutter and with Mammy Cynthia wiping my face and beating my back while balancing the case, I repeated the question: "Why was the policeman so cross, Mammy?"

We were walking again. Mammy giggled before she explained about the policeman: "We are different, Jane. You have light hair and blue eyes. 'Children like you should not be travelling with someone who looks like me,' that is what the policeman was shouting about. You two look as if you should not be walking with me."

I did not realise then that we were different. Today though, I know that we are not different. People are not born to discriminate—they learn from their parents and from those with whom they associate. They also learn to discriminate by applying the rules that are used to govern South Africa. Mammy Cynthia is a wonderful woman and it is through her influence that I've developed the ability to be Head Girl.

When we arrived at school Mammy showed us where to stay. The little ones always stayed with her, particularly those who were away from home for the first time. Most were not as young as Sam and did not have to travel as far, so Mammy Cynthia took special care of him. I too was invited to spend the first few nights with them in Mammy's room.

In the beginning we shared what then seemed like a big dormitory, the O'Brien Hall. Mammy was always there. One day Sam asked her: "When do you go to your children, Mammy Cynthia?"

The giggle first, and then came her reply: "You are my children too, and I have two grandchildren at home who stay with their Khokho. We will go to my house when you have settled, just like Jane does."

Mammy Cynthia has spent more time with me than my own mother. I love both my Mammas for different reasons and I wish to dedicate this report to them.

Mamma Thelma Levy—for her commitment and dedication to Sam and me, and for the lessons we receive in the mail each week; and Mammy Cynthia Mbala—for her embrace and love when Sam and I felt that we did not belong.

I remember a Sunday evening when Mammy returned from her home, and on passing my room, she stopped to say hello. At least that was what I thought, but during her weekend away, Mammy had realised that these were to be my last weeks at school. Upon entering my room she again put her hands on my shoulders, held me at arm's length, but did not let me go.

"I have come to wish you well for the examinations. Only afterwards will we say goodbye. Before then I want you to know that I love you, because you are like a flower. I watched you grow. Now I love you because, like an arum lily, you are blooming."

I have been at this school for thirteen years and my memory of each teacher is different. Every one of them has touched me and their touch enriched us all—Sister St Claire in particular.

I remember becoming part of this school community. I was the child who came from far away, who was not always able to make the journey home during school breaks. When I was younger, holidays were spent with other families or my teachers and occasionally classmates invited me to stay at their homes.

Thank you to all. Thank you for the rich experiences—they live in my heart and shall continue to shape who I become."

At first, when Jane asked me to write something for her Report, I feigned disinterest: "I can't remember everything," I said nonchalantly. "My first trip with you when we came to school, that's all I remember."

The look on Jane's face when I replied remains frozen in my mind. That look inspired me to do my best. *Jane is my Best Friend* was the title that no-one would ever see. I carried Jane's version of her report in my bag for several days before reading it. All the while I thought not only about what to write, but also about what an honour it was to contribute for my sister, the head girl. In many ways Jane was much more than my big sister at school.

Jane's writing made me want to write what I remembered. I began immediately. About two hours later I went looking for Mammy Cynthia, but she was not in her quarters. I placed a prepared note beneath her door. It read:

6 September 1975

Dear Mammy Cynthia
Please see me when you get this note? I want you to help me with something.
Sam

I was sitting and reading Jane's writing when Mammy climbed the stairs. Her breathing was heavy. I recognised her footsteps as she walked up the corridor toward my carrel. It was during the short September holiday when the others had gone to their homes. I was sitting on my bed when Mammy knocked, shifted my sliding door and then stepped inside.

"What's wrong Sammy? What happened?" she asked.

On seeing Mammy, I leapt off the bed and asked her to sit instead. I started by reading my writing out loud to her. Afterwards I explained the context of what I had written. Mammy Cynthia was an attentive listener and sat quietly until I had finished. She giggled before telling me what was in her memory.

The writing took a long time but it did not feel right. My wrestle was to remember back to a time when it felt as if the world was perfect. Other people who were there probably did not experience, or see, what I saw. To ask for their views was not a good idea. Mammy Cynthia tried, but we only met when I first left for school—she did not know enough.

Chapter Eight

Mr Bonds and the Meuleman racing pigeon

I continued to struggle with my part of Jane's report. Each time I wrote something it seemed more complicated; my words would not flow to fit in with what she had written. The story about how I arrived at school had to do with the ever-changing circumstances at home. I turned four years old in October of 1964, and we left for school in mid-January of the following year, 1965. I felt my contribution to Jane's Head Girl Report should start when we, Mammy Cynthia, Jane and I boarded the 'school train' for the first time. I needed Mammy's assistance to refresh my memory. I knew that she would help, but only if it were possible.

Some things were clearer in my memory. I could have asked Jane, but then my contribution would not have been a gift to her. It was my chance to make her proud; Jane always made me proud and this was my opportunity. The contribution that I decided upon was to start with our first trip to school, about being at school and also about what the experience felt like. Preparing to write for Jane was a process that included having to think back and recall the experiences I had had between the ages of four and about eight. The rest was easier to remember. Thinking back to that time felt like trying to remember when I did not have a brain. I decided too that recalling the time would better enable me to write meaningfully about when Mammy Cynthia first fetched us for the long trip to school.

§

There were no other children at our house when I was little. I'd play by myself or sit quietly, sucking my thumb. I remember Saturday afternoons when Ma had visitors. Pa never had many visitors. The women arrived to see Ma; their husbands became Pa's visitors.

The men's group was more interesting and I would eavesdrop on their conversations. I can't remember anything the group of women discussed. Whenever I was home from school the men's stories and debates became more entertaining and informative. It was much more interesting than playing with a brick, pushing it with my left hand over freshly toiled soil in a make-believe game of building roads.

Both my parents were older than forty when I was born. Jane was at school and both Ma and Pa's other children seldom visited us; they were older too, so it was unlikely that I would play my make-believe road building game with Brenda or Charles. I knew they were my brother and sister, yet our only contact was when I remembered them during evening prayers before being put to bed. Charles was just a name that Ma told me about. I had not been introduced to Pa's three boys—Cedrick, Leonard and Stephen. My experience of childhood was that of an only child. Lonely, that's how it was, but I didn't know that my situation had a label.

Pa was preoccupied with the world that he had created for himself. One of his hobbies was building fibreglass model aircraft and fitting remote control units to every one of them.

It was a time during which three American space projects were successively launched: Mercury, Gemini and Apollo. I found it interesting to listen to the men who gathered in our yard on a Saturday afternoon. They discussed the space missions. At dusk, all would gaze at the moon in wonder. It was not the only time that those men turned their eyes to the sky.

On each trip home from school I'd find that Pa had developed a new hobby. On one such occasion I found that he had become passionate about pigeon racing. He had joined a pigeon enthusiasts' club. Other pigeon fanciers had become his friends. Many of the pigeon racers lived in the informal settlement near our house. Some of their pigeon lofts were smarter than the houses in which they lived. On race days, Saturdays, the usual men and their wives arrived. The space missions were forgotten, replaced by a focus on welcoming pigeons that competed in what they referred to as Federation races. Later, two men, whom I had not previously met, also arrived. They too were pigeon racers and were welcomed by the group under the tree in our backyard. The women were in the house and the men were outside under the tree. That's how it was.

I marvelled at the men as they balanced on wooden tree stumps underneath our Port Jackson tree. Between talking to one another their eyes constantly turned to the sky. They were anticipating the first racing pigeon to drop from a passing flock. As a seven-year-old I wanted to be there every Saturday when birds arrived from places with strange names, like Philippolis, De Aar, Laingsburg and Beaufort West!

That Saturday, like every Saturday, Ma had a pot of split pea soup simmering in our kitchen. The men were more concerned about their 'maxis'. It was hidden underneath a box in an out-of-sight spot between the low branches of our Port Jackson tree. 'Maxis' was the term those yardmen used when referring to their six-bottle glass carafe of cheap wine. They drank that wine amidst heated political discussions while waiting for the first pigeon to arrive.

Soup was served. Afterwards every man there got a cup of tea to drink. Savoury cream cracker biscuits dressed with cheese and tomato were passed around.

A less enthusiastic set of tea drinkers was hard to imagine. The yardmen received their tea because they were being polite.

My little sitting stump was in a corner behind where Pa and the rest of the men were seated. Sucking my thumb and being invisible, that's what I did—while trying to make sense of the discussion. Pa sat, watched and listened, almost like me, but at times he'd chuckle. Occasionally the men would defer to him for an opinion. That was the only time Pa spoke. All of them fell silent when Pa spoke.

Mr Bonds had big bulging eyes that looked as though they could fall out of his head at any time. He was one of the men who gathered to welcome the racing pigeons. Mr Bonds was definitely not a tea drinker. It was noticeable in the way he held the cup, as if it were an unpleasant duty. He had lots to say. Mr Bonds dominated the conversation. To drink tea was definitely not his thing.

On several occasions, one or of the women in the kitchen yelled: "Bondsie! All we hear is your voice! Please give the other men a chance!"

Mr Bonds dismissed their comments. He did the same with the other yardmen who ventured an opinion. Afterwards Pa said to me that Mr Bonds knew nothing about the things he insisted on discussing. However, he hollered forth while clutching onto his saucer. It was about then when a fly, affected by the steam from his cup, fell into the tea. The other men had finished theirs by then. Mr Bonds, without a pause in his speech, tossed the tea out, and in the process almost struck Ellie, Pa's dog, then asleep in front of her kennel. He was emphatic in refusing offers to refill the cup with tea. In fact, Mr Bonds seemed relieved when the empty cup and saucer were returned to the serving tray.

As the afternoon wore on the yardmen worked their way through all the eats. When all were finished Pa rubbed his hands together. The sound was like fine sandpaper on wood. The responses from the yardmen implied that Pa rubbing his hands together signalled that something more exciting was to happen.

That rubbing of hands, I discovered, was a signal for the mighty 'maxis' to be unveiled. There was just one glass, poised over the neck of the fat bottle. Every drinker had to wait his turn as the concealed exercise was executed. Enough was poured and quickly gulped—all so that the conversation could get into the 'right' gear—and so that the next yardman could swallow his wine allocation. Yes, they never drank, those men only swallowed.

Afterwards, when I reminded Pa of what was said during discussion between the yardmen he would say: "Ya! When those men drink wine, solutions to things they don't know anything about are suddenly realised."

Mr Bonds was at the forefront, according to Pa. It was clear that he was much better at drinking wine than tea! Pa listened attentively to whoever spoke. More often than not it was Mr Bonds. I noticed how Pa sat back on his stump chair, shook his head from side to side and laughed heartily at what had been said. The speaker was always rewarded with another gulp of wine from the solitary glass. It was obvious, even to me, that Mr Bonds presented himself as the most knowledgeable; and that was why he got the most wine rewards.

During one of his many monologues and with a fourth full glass in hand, Mr Bonds was determined to complete his point, despite being reminded to 'drink up!' Pleas from the other thirsty yardmen for him to shut up and drink fell on deaf ears. Where I sat and looked in it seemed as if the wine was about to spill from Mr Bonds' glass. He didn't care. Instead he relentlessly continued talking. The wine glass swayed from side to side as he spoke and gestured. The other yardmen, who had substantial thirsts, were persistent in their encouragement for Mr Bonds to 'drink-up', but to no avail.

Another fly fell. This time it fell into Mr Bonds' wine.

I could hear the silence that followed. The kitchen-women peered to check why Bonds had suddenly gone quiet. Yes, he had stopped talking and was holding the glass, first to one side and then at another angle. His manner changed to that of inspector as he examined the fluttering blue-green fly in his wine. Mr Bonds was probably weighing up his options.

The thought of having to wait an entire round to get another swig was perhaps too daunting. Without warning, Mr Bonds plunged his outstretched index finger and thumb into the glass. He grabbed that fluttering fly. First he sucked it and then he chucked the crumpled bit to one side. A fast glug from the solitary glass was how the situation concluded.

Mr Bonds then shook the glass with its open end toward the ground; probably to ensure that it was empty. He wiped his mouth and then rubbed the back of his hand before saying something in Afrikaans while passing the glass back to Pa, the pourer. The other men laughed—so much that some lost balance and fell back with their legs a flutter in the air.

I realised that Pa and his friends were equally peculiar. This must have been one of the reasons why Jane and I could not live at home.

Intermittently Pa would leap to his feet and aim his binoculars at the sky. He looked above the distant mountains and moved from left to right, scanning for signs of racing pigeons. In less than five minutes a tiny speck in the sky would grow into a huge flock. It was early evening and the yardmen became excited when a pigeon dived down from a very high and fast-flying flock.

Pa whispered: "Meuleman."

The favoured racing pigeon began its descent for the trap door of Pa's loft. The yardmen were on their feet, all of them silently pointing to the sky. Their movements were in slow motion, so as not to distract the Meuleman in its descent for home. In that moment it seemed as if the men had not been drinking so much wine. They were excited. I was too. With glistening eyes the yardmen continued to point up into the sky.

The rest of the birds were racing to their respective lofts. That sound, their sound, bird music—Pa seemed to live for that moment, his eyes were fixed on that Meuleman pigeon. With his free hand he gestured to the yardmen to return to their stumps beneath our Port Jackson tree.

Preparations had been made inside the loft for the returning bird, which Pa bred for speed. Quick, onto the trap-landing and then into the loft; that is how he had been trained. Pa put the binoculars aside and tore ahead, followed by a legion of yardmen. All of them squashed into the loft. There was no room for me. But I could hear the racing- pigeon-clock turn as the arrival time was being recorded.

Other pigeons arrived later. They did not cause as much excitement, certainly not more than the 'maxis' did. The race was not yet over but the yardmen drank in celebration of an anticipated win. Those men would drink in celebration of sunrise, sunset, and just about anything else.

After sunset Pa took his clock to the clubhouse. The winner was decided there. Wives called out that the visit was over. Their husbands were not as fresh as they were earlier that afternoon. When the guests left the two remaining visiting pigeon enthusiasts also aimed their way to our front gate.

Pa arrived home later that evening. By then three of the women had returned to our house. All seemed unhappy. Ma told me that the men had been drinking on the sly beneath the Port Jackson tree. I already knew that. Three of them fought with their wives and children when they got home. Ma was cross. She scolded Pa: "It's you Samuel! You poured the wine into these men! Look now what you have caused!"

I enjoyed it when Pa drank wine because then he was pleasant and funny. Mr Bonds' eyes grew bigger and he could not stop talking. I was afraid of Mr Bonds.

Early the next morning, Sunday morning, there was a faint knock on the front room window. I awoke to hear Pa speak in a hushed tone: "Ya! Bondsie, what's the matter?"

"… for a head-ache drink, Pa?" came the reply.

The younger yardmen also addressed my parents as Pa and Ma. Their wives did too. But there was no fooling Ma. At her insistence Mr Bonds was given a cup of brewed coffee instead of more wine. He drank it under duress and was probably wishing for a fly! Seemingly Mr Bonds was neither a tea nor a coffee drinker! When done, Ma sent the younger man home: "Go now Boy, spend Sunday with your family and fix the wrong you did to them last night," she said. Then the bickering between Ma and Pa continued; so much that I longed to go back to school.

The two Sunday mornings that I was home on that visit were spent at Victor Verster Prison. I sat in the car, an Austin, while my parents visited Charles.

Charles's story, as I remember it, was that he was living with his father, James, and working on a building site in Worcester. On a particular Saturday afternoon he, Charles, went to a beer hall. After consuming copious amounts of liquor, Charles, in an inebriated state, got into an argument and a fight ensued. Ma explained to Jane and me that, according to the court record, the other party drew a knife. During the scuffle tables, chairs and glass were broken. Then the lights were turned out. Afterwards, it seemed that the man who had drawn the knife had fallen; he died and a knife wound was deemed to be the cause of his death.

Charles, my brother, whom I knew only by name from the evening prayers, was arrested, tried and imprisoned. At the time of my birth Charles was already in jail. Jane too, she remembered Charles like I did. Ma was informed once he began to serve a ten-year jail sentence.

Pa never had anything good to say about Charles. Yet for thirty minutes every Sunday morning Pa's Austin was parked alongside buses, cars and taxis that brought visitors to the section where Non-European felons were held. On occasion and when home from school, I would sit in the car sucking my thumb and practise being invisible, while Ma and Pa visited with Charles.

I asked many questions when my parents returned from the visit with Charles. After that I'd listen very attentively to their discussion because that was how I learned about what happened behind the high, grey-blue walls of the prison, where children were not allowed to enter. Charles was learning a trade while in prison—that was what Ma hoped for; and after his release he would work as a bricklayer. Ma said that learning a trade was one of the good things that came from having to spend time in prison.

It was early morning in the winter of 1967. I was home from school. Jane was dancing in a ballet that toured to a place outside the greater Cape Town area, so she was not at home. Our bedroom door was always ajar. I awoke that morning and saw our single bar electric heater glowing in the lounge room. The clock in our kitchen ticked as it usually did. Everything was the same, yet it felt different. I got out of bed and went into the lounge. There was a man sitting—on the small sofa. He was talking to Ma. He called her Mamma, like Jane. His hair had been shaven and he wore a khaki jacket and matching trousers, like the men at the reformatory where Ma sometimes held meetings. He looked like Ma, even had her dimples.

"Come Boy, come and meet Charles."

He was thirty years old. Charles had a gentle manner, was kind, softly spoken and instantly likeable. Later I learned that he could make toys. Charles built me a rocking horse from a sheet of wood that he had found. After he had painted the rocking horse blue it felt almost real. I loved that horse, more so when it was raining! Charles could run fast and was strong, almost like Pa. When Jane met Charles she also liked him. Soon our time together was up and we were off to school again.

Charles settled, found a job and later moved on to continue living his life. He and Pa, as in the past, did not see eye to eye. Years later we met again but by then Charles had consumed too much wine and behaved like a mad person. He too did not drink the wine—you could say the wine drank him.

Mr Bonds became an incurable alcoholic and died at the age of thirty nine.

§

114

Going to boarding school was how it always was ... "You won't miss what you don't know," was what Ma said whenever I wondered about leaving for school from home and returning in the afternoon.

Memorabilia boards were mounted at the back of the school hall. These were plaques that bore the names of all previous head pupils and those who had distinguished themselves by achievement. The following year Jane Levy's name was to appear on those boards. I imagined what it would be like having my sister's name form part of that exclusive list. My caution was not to let pride for Jane show. It was not 'festive' to be proud of your big sister!

Re-reading my notes about what I remembered, and Jane's writing, created a readiness to write my piece for inclusion in the Head Girl's Report of 1975. Jane inspired me with confidence, but while writing and making mistakes, I learned quickly that more paper would fit into the waste paper basket if it were not crumpled. The waste paper basket filled up several times, but I persisted. When my attempt felt right I asked Ms du Pont, the English teacher, to check and later re-check my writing. Without her guidance I would not have been able to achieve much and, in the process, I learned a lot. It took three days, very late nights and several overflowing waste paper baskets before I saw something that was good enough for my Jane. It had to be perfect.

But by then we were running out of time and Jane had begun to pester me with: "How far are you, Goofy Sam? I have to send the report to Mamma as promised, so let me know if you are not able, or not willing, to write your piece?"

This she repeated whenever our paths crossed on the school premises. The other boys tried teasing me, but by then most of them had intimate knowledge of my left uppercut! My responses to Jane were nonchalant but not entirely dismissive. I'd go back to the carrel and re-read what I had already written. Meanwhile the due date was looming closer. At dinner, and before the seniors were seated, I gave the foolscap pages to Jane. "I did my best," I mumbled.

Jane took the papers and looked at them briefly. Realising what they were, she smiled. To me her smiling then was confirmation that I had not let her down. I felt good. My carefully cultivated slouch as I walked away was meant to imply that nothing significant had happened. Peer pressure required of me to be 'festive'. That meant no writing, especially what appeared to be a letter to my sister.

When the formality of the senior Sunday dinner was done, Jane reneged on her ceremonial role of wishing the others a good evening and encouraging them for the week ahead. Instead, my Jane dashed out to her room. Maybe she was eager to read what I had written ...

Title: How I came to be at school with Jane Levy—my sister
By Samuel Levy
21 September 1975

My first trip to school with Jane was at the age of four years and three months. The excitement about wearing a peak cap and playing with other boys made it difficult for me to sleep during the nights before our journey began.

The thought of spending such a long time in a train was the best, and the wait for that day to arrive was long and painful. I would have counted the sleeps, but that would not have been possible. At first there would have been more sleeps than I had fingers. The excitement before the last sleep was too big for the memory to fit into my head.

Mammy Cynthia and the nuns at school were going to teach me to read and write. Afterwards I would be able to tell what time it was on the clock in our kitchen. I would be able to read time, any time. People who were going to teach me were already there; they were waiting.

This was a fact because I sat quietly each day, sucking my thumb, maintaining my invisibility, while Ma and Jane told stories about what school was like. All the while I'd become more excited.

Their stories were not all true. I discovered that much later, but they are forgiven. However, my wonder about what else Ma and Jane said that was not true persisted.

The day of our departure finally dawned.

Ma, Jane and I were on the bus.

The blue suitcase was heavy. The bus driver got up from his seat to help when he saw that our luggage was too heavy for Ma and Jane to manage on their own. I sucked my thumb. Pa was working—Pa was always working.

There were other people on the bus too. The fat lady who lived in the same street, Mrs Sprague, she was on that bus. Most of the people were glaring at us. Perhaps because I sucked my thumb; or maybe it was because Jane could not stop talking to Ma. Jane was always speaking. There were many bus stops; people got off and more got on. The new ones also stared at us, almost as if we did not belong there. When the bus stopped and the driver switched the engine off, there was a shudder followed by an announcement for all to leave. We had come to the end of the first journey. We then boarded a train to Cape Town Station. Once there we walked across to a platform from where the Pietermaritzburg train departed.

Mammy Cynthia was there. She sat outside on the station platform, next to the school train. I had met her before, when Ma brought Jane. It had become my turn. Mammy had fetched Jane many times, but that was the first time she fetched me too. I was not concerned because I knew Mammy Cynthia from stories Jane had told me. The hyena story, I was looking forward to Mammy telling me that story. The bags were heavy, but not for Mammy Cynthia. I tried to help but they were too heavy for me so I was 'forced to suck my thumb instead!' Jane also tried to help, but she could not stop herself from talking— always talking.

Jane had many books. I had a colouring-in book, a thick pencil, wax crayons, and clay. The clay was in strips. It looked like pencils, coloured

116

pencils. Ma said that I would use it at school. The smell of that clay is embedded in my memory.

We were finally going to school. Jane said that she would be in Standard Two; I was going to play-school and then only to big school.

It was exciting to be nearly five years old, 'a big boy', that was what people said

I sat on the little bunk bed in our cabin while Ma, Mammy Cynthia and Jane were talking at the window. My thoughts were with our paraplegic aunts and how sad they seemed when we passed by their house en route to catch the first bus of our long journey. Five disabled women who shared a house were outside on the veranda, waving. It felt as if they did not mean to wave. Auntie Dotty said: "I am waiting for you Sammy, for the school holidays." The other Aunties, Martha, Leah, Joan and Margaret, they were all there too, sitting in their wheelchairs waving as we passed.

The train compartment walls were covered in little drawings, little springboks, and the writing over them read 'South African Railways'. I know what was written there because Jane had told me. While the others were talking at the cabin window I was remembering more of the journey from our house to the school train. I wanted to get to school and learn to tell the time, read by myself and not always have to ask Jane, or Ma. That was what repeated in my mind. It was time for school and we were going away for a long time. I measured myself against the upright mirror in our bedroom and left a mark there just before we departed. Next time I'd be taller; that was what everyone said. I'd also speak like Jane; that was also what they said. All I wanted was to tell the time by looking at the clock, the one that hung on the kitchen wall, Zaideh Levy's clock.

Pa used the kitchen clock so that he knew when the news, boxing and rugby were broadcast on the radio set we had in our lounge room. There were times when Pa and I woke up early in the early morning. It would be dark outside, but that was when the 'big fights' were broadcast on the radio. The fighters were either Cassius Clay, George Foreman, Joe Frazier and others whose names I do not remember. That was where I heard the term 'left uppercut' being used. Who was going to get up and listen with Pa when I was at school; and what about the rugby matches? Although I did not understand what was going on Pa always woke me to sit and listen with him. Frequently I would fall asleep just as the commentator began to describe the scenes in either New Zealand for rugby, or the United States of America for boxing.

'Never mind,' was one of Ma's favourite sayings; so I too thought, 'never mind'. I was looking forward to being with boys who would also be nearly five years old. They were already at school, waiting, so that we could play together. I was very excited.

The sound of whistles filled the tunnel space and the train wheels made a screechy noise. There were banging sounds, I remember. The train was tugged once and then it began to move. We were going to the school, Mammy Cynthia, Jane and I. Ma held Jane's hand and walked alongside the slow moving train on the station platform. With her other hand Ma wiped her face. Earlier I was sad; but when the train moved my sadness was overwhelming. I could smell Ma's Oil of Olay on my face. My Ma used that face cream and I got my share when she hugged me tightly. It was a familiar fragrance and became my reminder of my Ma. I did not want Mammy Cynthia to wipe my face.

"Look after Sammy, Mammy, look after Sammy, look ..."

Those were the last words I heard Ma speak before the train's noise drowned her voice. It was my turn to lean out. I shouted at the top of my voice: "Don't cry Ma! When I come back; next week when I come back, then I will read and tell the time on the big clock in the kitchen!" But I don't think our Ma heard me.

Jane and I leaned out together while Mammy Cynthia held onto us. Mammy Cynthia has continued to hold onto us ever since. Ma stood there, a lone figure, waving from the platform, and then it became dark in the tunnel as the train left for Pietermaritzburg. We were on our way.

Jane put her arms around me: 'Don't cry Sammy, we'll be fine.'

I felt better. Whenever Jane put her arms around me, then I felt better. We were off to school, Jane was heading for nine and I was nearly five.

A while later the train conductor barged into our cabin to check if we had valid tickets. As he looked up and noticed Jane and me sitting with Mammy, he questioned why the two of us were in the same cabin with Mammy. He insisted that Jane and I leave immediately. We were to sit in a different train carriage. Mammy had to stay on her own. She objected. Jane said that he had more authority and I could see that he was much bigger than Mammy. Fortunately Mammy had my birth certificate, but we had none of Jane's official documents. After inspecting my birth and registration details the conductor agreed to me sitting with Mammy, but he was adamant that Jane leave us for another cabin in a different part of the train. Mammy Cynthia continued to try and reason with the very officious train conductor. She addressed him as 'Boss' and folded her hands like I do before saying the evening prayer. Mammy begged that conductor to leave Jane with us.

I held onto Jane's hand and she held onto mine. The train conductor was stronger. He pulled Jane into the passage and despite her cries and Mammy's pleas the conductor insisted that Jane sit in another carriage. Before closing the cabin door he told Mammy that we could see Jane through her new cabin window when the train stopped. "This child must travel with other people who look like her and not with 'Non-Europeans', what if something happens to her; and you, Girl, you are an old woman. You should know the law, shouldn't you?" The conductor's big blue eyes glared at Mammy—he was very cross. He spoke to Mammy and pointed his finger so close to her face that it nearly touched her nose.

Mammy held me until my tears stopped and all the while she was telling me that where Jane was the beds were bigger, softer and nicer than where we were.

"Why did that man call you 'Girl' Mammy?

"It was because he did not know my name. They are like that to us."
Mammy and I hugged—she kissed me on my forehead and giggled.

The train stopped a few times. Every time Mammy and I would run along the platform to find Jane and spend as much time as possible talking with her through the cabin window. It was true, Jane's cabin even had a different colour to ours; it was blue and ours was grey.

Three days later, in the morning, we arrived at Pietermaritzburg Station. I remember that because every time thereafter we travelled the same route and on a similar train. After that trip we made sure to each have our birth certificate on hand whenever we made the journey to Cape Town. For many years that was our routine. There were some men who had a lot to say to Mammy Cynthia. She laughed and joked with them. Their language had a slightly different ring to the way people in Cape Town spoke. I did not understand what they were saying to one another, but before I could ask, Jane told me that Mammy Cynthia was speaking in Zulu.

One of the men loaded the blue suitcase onto a trolley. His trolley had a strange shape, I remember. It looked like the frame of a bed but in the middle it bent upwards on both sides above the two centre wheels. Mammy Cynthia and the man continued to talk, like old friends do. He pushed the trolley to the bus. Jane held my left hand and I followed behind with my thumb seemingly glued to mouth. We greeted that man after he packed our case in the hold of the bus. Although we never saw him again, Mammy Cynthia was very happy to speak with that man. I've not seen Mammy Cynthia that happy when speaking to any other man since.

From Pietermaritzburg, we rode on the bus to near where Jane spotted our school buildings. They were atop a distant hill. It was at the end of what seemed like a long orange road. When we got off the bus I also saw, for the first time, how Mammy Cynthia lifted the heavy suitcase without much effort. She carefully placed it on her head. I knew then that if anyone came out of the surrounding sugar-cane fields and was quarrelsome then Mammy could protect us. Mammy was strong, almost like Pa.

Jane walked on Mammy's left side. The sides of the blue suitcase hung over Mammy Cynthia's shoulders. To suck my thumb and walk alongside them became difficult on that long road. Sometimes I trailed behind and they'd stop for me to catch up. Jane spoke all the time, because that was what Jane did and continues to do. They spoke about school and I was interested. The few trees around and other plants, even the colour of the road, were all different from what it was like in Cape Town.

That walk took a long time.

We arrived in the early afternoon. It was a Tuesday. I was hungry and very thirsty. That must be the reason why I remember it so vividly. The school seemed different from what I had imagined. A big disappointment: there were no children waiting to play with me.

As she unpacked the blue suitcase Mammy Cynthia explained that the other boys and girls would arrive during the following week. Mammy then bathed both Jane and me. We ate, and that night we slept in Mammy's room, in her bed.

"You've got a picture of Elvis, Mammy! Anne and Brenda also like him," was Jane's remark after she inspected Mammy's room. Jane was always quick to spot pictures.

Mammy Cynthia giggled in response to Jane's observation and shook her hips before saying: "Yes, don't tell the others, but I like Elvis." The other pictures in her room, she explained, were of Baba Sipho Mbala, her late husband, two of her children and two grandchildren who were both Jane's friends.

All that mattered to me was to be at school with my big sister. Even then I was very proud of Jane: 'because she makes herself proud,' that is what our Ma taught me—and I did not care about much else.

My task was to write about how I came to be at school with Jane. Perhaps I have not included everything. I was after all not quite fourteen years old at the time of writing, but it was my best. Only my best was good enough for Jane. My sister and I are also 'Old Friends'.

After reading my writing Jane agreed to write a concluding paragraph and then send all to Ma, so that she could knit it together as one.

"... and because that is what my brother thinks of me I am happy; sad too, because these are the last few months that we will be together. The same counts for all my friends and fellow pupils. I shall treasure the memory of those who have touched my life, Sister St Claire, Mammy Cynthia, Ms du Pont, other teachers, my friends and those who seldom are recognised: Sis Grace, Sis Thandi, Sis Ntombe and Boet Sam. Thank you for watching over me, I shall miss you."

So, Jane had found my writing acceptable and I too was happy. She mailed the report to Ma as promised.

Chapter Nine

Anne and Brenda

Ma responded after reading the Head Girl's Report. She suggested that a few changes be made. However, Ma refused to tamper with its style and content.

After amendments were added, Jane handed the report to Sister St Claire for her blessing. Thereafter it was placed, together with all other reports, in the school archive. The tradition dates back to the first class that graduated, back in 1922. All those reports are in a collection that together is the recorded history of our school. The following year Jane's report was first in the collection for the new seniors to read. The seniors always enjoyed reading reports written by those whom they knew, liked and respected. Initiation was never part of our experience there—rites of passage were. Only those who graduated had access to the head pupil reports; this was their rite of passage; and senior pupils had controlled access to past reports during their last two years of school.

Prior to Jane writing her own report, Sister St Claire had allowed complete access to all previous similar works. The purpose was to garner insight about the structure and to ensure compliance with an established content format. Ensuring access to past reports was also a way of teaching Jane how tradition forms part of life.

The Campbell Report had attracted Jane's attention most of all. Mrs Bonita Campbell, a fellow social worker, had introduced Ma and our family to the school. Times were different then. People were increasingly becoming aware of social changes in the country. Groups of South Africans responded to the inhibiting laws by striving to give their children access to education. In the cities socially inspired slogans appeared on public walls. I recall some of them:

- No Normal Sport in an Abnormal Society!
- Freedom Now; Education Later!
- Down with Gutter Education!
- Freedom in our Lifetime!
- Release all Political Prisoners!

It was intriguing to see the slogans painted on random walls, inside train carriages, on the sides of public buses and on walls in the townships where we lived. The suddenness of it all was what I found most fascinating—exhilarating too. Suddenly it was not only my Ma who held an opposing view, but many others seemed to agree with her.

The South African currency is named the 'rand'. Many years ago I cashed a postal order and received a few one rand notes; on one of the notes someone had written: 'Do not conflate multi-racialism with non-racialism'. That statement became one of the more important principals of my life. I want to be non-racist and it is not possible if people are constantly labelled.

There is no need to categorise people by the shade of their skins, and surely people have the right to define for themselves what label, if any, is most appropriate for them to wear; or by which to be defined? People have the right to embrace a label of their choice; food, clothing, cars too, but why do we need to define ourselves based on the colour of our skins? If we have to wear a label then why can it not be one that stems from the language we speak, the religion we embrace, where in the world we live, or something more meaningful than the skin tone with which we were born? Skin colour is the cause of much pain in South Africa and elsewhere. Draconian as it may be, there should be an active campaign to rid the media and the legislation of defining and categorising people as determined by the colour of their skin.

Having spent most, if not all of our formative years in an institution, a boarding school, both Jane and I were oblivious to many of the social developments that were welling up in our country.

All I wanted to do was surf and listen to some of Mr Thompson's music; that was how I spent most of the weekends during my last three years at school. ZZ Top was Mr Thompson's favourite band; I began to like them too. Those blokes had beards that would scare the biggest sharks and it probably hid several dangerous insects too. Surfing was not a recognised sport in those days but to me it was everything; that and riding my locker-door-on-wheels—save for when school examinations were looming and preparation slowly replaced all other activities.

Final examinations were the most important event on the school calendar. Silence was the order of each day at school then. All pupils were required to prepare and do their academic best. It was probably the only time that I tried.

"It matters not how well you surf if you cannot do mathematics." This was the refrain from Mr Harris when I showed no interest in his subject. Mr Harris was an excellent teacher, so they said. I did not think so. His tall, corpulent, bald-headed presence was impressive in the mathematics classroom, but he would probably cause the longest broad surfboard to sink. So, I wondered, how was mathematics related to surfing? How was everything else at school so 'important'? All I wanted to do was surf. I was at peace with those who could do mathematics, but they were not at peace with me!

One day when I arrived in the classroom, someone had written on the writing board: "Sam is dumb at mathematics!" How sad. Imagine if I had responded: "Whatever-your-name-is can't surf." The reality of mathematics being more important than surfing depends on what your passion is.

Constant comparison with Jane became the bane of my life at school. No one ever asked whether Jane could surf, but everyone asked if my mathematics was as good as hers.

We prepared for the trip back to Cape Town when the examination season was over. It had become an exciting tradition, the going home trip. The journey would start like any other but this time would be different. It was to be Jane's last journey. I did my bit to make it special by arranging the music we'd listen to on the train. The Doobie Brothers topped my list that year, and Mr Thompson had introduced me to Chicago, Billy Joel, the Commodores, Earth Wind and Fire, The Crusaders, several other jazz musicians and of course, 'the best!' - ZZ Top. The other surfers listened to The Doors, Janis Joplin, The Rolling Stones, Jimmy Hendrix and a crowd called Deep Purple who sang a song about 'Smoke on the Water and Fire in the Skies'! It all grew on me, but not as much as Queen did after the many hours spent driving up and down to the coast in Mr Thompson's VW camper van. One day, out of the blue, he said to me: "Someday you'll be the world champion—you have to ring me then, okay?"

I laughed silently, and thought it a 'festive' idea; but I had doubts that it could become real.

Jane and I planned to travel home via Mammy Cynthia's house in Mpophomeni. The excitement was palpable and both of us had difficulty sleeping during those last nights. We were excited to be going home but I think that Jane was sad to leave. She was more controlled but we were always equally excited to arrive in Cape Town, particularly when we did so together. We bought enough batteries and a cheap set of headphones, so that we didn't cause a disturbance when listening to our music while travelling on the train. Sometimes I wished that others who used the trains were as considerate.

After the examinations had run their course, Jane and I held a 'travel meeting'. We spoke extensively about who was going to be first to see the mountain. The first sight of Table Mountain is a sight to behold; whenever we missed our home, images of that mountain flashed through our minds. It is the most beautiful mountain in the world, Table Mountain—Jane's mountain—my mountain! No wonder that our 'travel' meeting was an argument about the 'reward' due to the one who would be first to spot the mountain.

Before our trips I'd wake up early and rush to Jane's room, so that together we could listen to the weather report. I did so this time too. Arriving in Cape Town was not the same when the weather was dull, so it was always worth knowing beforehand what the skies would be like when we rounded that last bend and our mountain became visible. Departures left sad memories, but arrivals were always happy occasions; it was also what we lived for, arriving back home.

We had a few days in hand to collect all that was needed for the trip, greet our school friends and, for Jane, to bid farewell to her favourite teachers.

I was ready for what was to be my final surfing competition of that year. Jane had agreed to do administrative work on the beach in preparation for the event. Both of us moved in with Mr Thompson. He, two brothers and their parents lived in a big house in Scottburgh. We stayed for the duration of the competition, which was organised from their garage. I was on the beach, surfing, from morning until night to prepare for that event. Entrants arrived from Australia, the United States of America, and New Zealand. There were surfers from Cape Town and from all along the coast. I remember seeing a lone entry from Newquay in England. The English surfer was first to arrive. He had 'cold feet', so said the others, but the warm waters of the Indian Ocean soon changed that.

The competition was held over three days. Heats were tight and the waves slight. "It is the average wave that shows off the best skill" was what Mr Thompson screamed at me whenever I referred to poor surfing conditions. I was apprehensive about participating because, despite my having surfed in many competitions, never before had there been such wide international representation as in that line-up.

Competing surfers included those who had been profiled in global surfing magazines. I read about them in Mr Thompson's car while he drove from school to the coast and shared ZZ Top with all who could hear. Competing against those athletes was daunting, but I had learned that 'knowing your stuff' was merely a confidence booster. The best surfers in the world, by a long shot, came from the United States, Hawaii, Australia and South Africa. Most of them were there. I was fourteen years old and even my patchy surfboard seemed nervous!

In the end I placed fourth in that competition. After three days in the surf the English surfer, with his newly-found warm feet, was declared the overall winner. Being placed fourth was not good enough. With silence and a tinge of disappointed, that was how I reacted after receiving a little runner-up trophy. My score was ahead of all other South African competitors, but more work had to be done because I did not 'know my stuff' well enough.

The police were at the bottom step of the makeshift podium. When I stepped down with my trophy a giant man put his hand behind my neck and led me off the beach to a waiting police van. That policeman was a Captain van Deventer. The brass name tag pinned to his chest was where I read his name. He scolded me. I could hear, by the way he pronounced certain words and constructed sentences, that the Captain was Afrikaans-speaking. In a stern voice he asked and then warned: "Why are you surfing on this beach? Don't you know that it is reserved? You are asking for trouble—do not let me see you surf here again." Mr Thompson, my coach, spoke at length to the policeman, but Captain van Deventer insisted: "Misterrr, this beach, this beach!" He pointed to the ground when he said that. "This beach! His type arre not belonging on this beach! Do you understand me Misterr?" The Captain was referring to me not belonging on the beach at Scottburgh.

I had spent all my nervous energy on the competition and had nothing left for this giant man who spoke as if his teeth ached. There was nothing else to do but wait to hear my fate. I did not care what the fate was. After all, my sorrow was that I did not do well enough in the competition. The Captain and Mr

Thompson spoke for a while before he, the Captain, declared: "Let this be a warning to you, go now and don't let me catch you playing here again!"

By then a crowd had gathered. Only Jane and Mr Thompson had stepped forward in my defence. Jane tried to assist Mr Thompson while he spoke to the tallest policeman in the world. Captain van Deventer, with the back of his hand, fluttered his fingers in a motion to indicate that Jane should move away.

I felt a bit lonely; somewhat let down too. It was because the people who gathered round were entertained by our surfing, but my darker skin was more of a concern than the entertainment that I provided. I did not belong, that much was evident.

The organisers were fined and warned that if they continued to ignore the beach restrictions, then future permits to hold competitions would be withdrawn or withheld.

Feeling somewhat disappointed and humiliated too, Jane and I bade our farewell greetings to all those who were involved in the surfabout.

Our homeward journey began after the competition and the humiliating fiasco. I carried the blue suitcase and the surfboard. We were on our way. Bus drivers were a bit unfriendly toward my surfboard. Others too; they found my board to be in the way and an inconvenience on public transport.

In the months that followed the English surfer featured in several other South African surfing competitions and on *Sportsview*, a television programme. Save for a few obscure surf-offs my requests for invitations to compete were almost always refused, or ignored. My routine continued. I was always ready for any competition that agreed to have me in its line-up. To many organisers it did not matter that I was competition ready. No, only the law that stopped me from surfing on reserved beaches was important to competition organisers. To them, the law was more important than my ability to surf. Laws should enable, not prevent ability from coming to fruition. Despite the disappointment, my resolve was to continue. 'Practise and learn your stuff,' became my personal motto. I continued regardless because surfing was my thing and sometimes, with great reluctance, my requests for invitations to participate were accepted. I became accustomed to being chased off reserved beaches. At times I knew the policemen who chased me. But despite that I never got used to being ignored and rejected by competition organisers. This even though I understood that the beach was reserved for use by others who were not of 'my type'! The tall policeman said so, after all.

Other surfers whispered among themselves that, in addition to having a brown skin, I had developed a thick skin. I wished that were true. The police in that region of our country were known for being heavy-handed with people who transgressed.

There were no beaches designated for me to use, save for the bits of surf on the outskirts of the Scottburgh main beach. No permission signboards were posted there, and I assumed that the rocky section was unreserved. Reaching the waves involved walking across an expanse of rock that was only exposed during low tide. It was useful to learn that the folk who lived nearby picked oysters, mussels and periwinkles from those rocks. Much later, that was how I dealt with occasional hunger pangs.

There was many a time when pride prevented me from asking for food when I had no money, other than the rand note which I refused to use, the one with the writing: 'Do not conflate multi-racialism with non-racialism'.

An oyster picker once asked me why my surf waves were between rocks and not on the main beach where the others caught theirs. After I had told him and using slightly different English his reply was not completely unexpected: "It's called the Indian Ocean, but we Indians are not allowed to swim in it … how that is fair?" He sounded like a man that I should have introduced to Ma. Anyway, I shrugged, smiled and got on with learning my stuff before the tide rushed in again.

In order to find suitable waves I had to go between 200 and 300 metres off-shore, or away from the beach. It was far out, but I got used to it. I was often the only person in the dark 'swells' of warm Indian Ocean water. Those swells are probably the best for surfing.

After the incident following that competition of December 1975 I resolved to use beaches where government regulations were not contravened. There were important and exciting prospects to look forward to; and there was no benefit in moping about the persecution that was meted out for my contravention.

That trip to Cape Town marked the end of two years since Jane was last at home. We were both equally excited when the journey began that December (1975). Jane was excited about seeing Ma, the rest of our family and Lampo. I had told her various things that happened and that were new. Jane was keen to see if I had been exaggerating.

Monday, 3rd December, after the surfing competition, in the evening, was when we got on the bus to Pietermaritzburg. It was a hot humid December night. Jane had already said her goodbyes by then. Again, she was sad to leave, but excited to go. As the bus departed Jane opened the window, leaned out and waved. She waved at no-one in particular. From Pietermaritzburg we planned to board another bus for the trip to Mpophomeni. That was where Mammy Cynthia lived.

"For just one last time; one last visit." Jane repeated this to me several times while we were travelling on that bus from Scottburgh to Pietermaritzburg. I knew that it was very important for Jane to greet Mammy Cynthia, Khokho, Ma Khumalo, other elders and the children with whom we had spent so many happy holidays over the years. Going there always felt like going home because we belonged.

The bus was dirty and Jane could not stop tucking her dress beneath her legs to lessen direct contact with the grimy blue velvet seat covers. We were both thankful that the journey would only last an hour and thirty minutes. Other commuters were again glaring at us; the bus was congested; my surfboard was in the way and I was hungry. There was animated discussion in Zulu about the light-skinned girl on the bus travelling with an Indian boy: "What is the world coming to?" That is what an old man who sat across from us said. He was

126

transfixed and when he spoke it was evident why: "If it was us on 'their' bus then we would have been thrown off and arrested at the first stop."

The bus stopped at Pietermaritzburg train station. I stood aside with the suitcase and surfboard while Jane sought the easiest way to Mpophomeni. Mammy Cynthia was expecting us to arrive at about nine o'clock that night. Jane could speak fluent Zulu, so I always left the communication bits to her. Changes had been made to the station since the last time we travelled through. There were many more people too; even though it was already eight o'clock at night the place was abuzz with commuters. Jane was away for about ten minutes while I watched over our stuff. On her return she told me that it was best to travel by bus to the city hall. Once there, apparently we could find onward public transport to Mpophomeni.

Unbeknown to us, Mammy Cynthia had asked Father Terry, her parish priest from the Catholic Church, if he could fetch us from the Pietermaritzburg City Hall. When the station bus arrived there Father Terry and Mammy Cynthia were waiting. Following the exchange of excited greetings and after securing all our belongings in Father Terry's white Toyota Corolla, we drove to Mpophomeni.

People always seemed very happy to see us whenever we arrived at Mammy Cynthia's house. I remember the welcoming fragrance of home-cooked food when the front gate opened. That time, the lounge had been decorated with Christmas trimmings.

Displayed on the dining room table, where we had enjoyed many meals, was a framed pencil sketch that I had drawn for Mammy Cynthia on the occasion of her birthday some years earlier. The picture was of Mammy carrying the blue suitcase on her head, with Jane and me by her side. It was a scene of us walking the orange road from the bus stop to our school on the hill. We felt at home with Mammy Cynthia's family; they had become our family. That night all of us sat together at the same dining room table. Father Terry blessed the meal and those who had prepared it. He always prayed that we would have a safe onward journey to our home in Cape Town. We ate traditional food that evening, and we spoke of long ago. I felt sad, but perhaps not as sad as Jane.

We had nothing to give, because we seldom had something, other than each other and Jane's way with words. I noticed that Jane had excused herself from the busy table.

A few moments later, Precious, who was seated alongside Jane, whispered that I should go to the bedroom.

Once there, Jane explained: "Sammy-boy, we should offer a song of thanks. It has to demonstrate what this family has meant to us over the years." Jane was at times wiser than herself. That was one such occasion.

"That Gershwin song you do so well is the best. Remember, from the songbook I got you for Christmas?" This was the first time that Jane asked me to sing. The song was from the musical, *Oh, Kay!* And it was a piece that I had learned to sing.

Although we agreed, I questioned whether the lyrics were appropriate. "That song was about two people, with one encouraging the other, to 'get on with it' so that they could be together." Jane agreed about the song not being entirely fitting: "But the piece can be interpreted differently as well. I shall explain the intended meaning before you sing."

Even though the entire family was gathered in the room, Jane addressed Khokho and Mammy Cynthia directly. Jane's insights, ability to speak and her strengths were often deeper and greater than I could understand. Even though I was already able to think, Jane continued to astound me. Maybe it had something to do with mathematics!

Before Jane could speak, inquisitive Khokho asked: "Where did you two go...?" Jane interrupted: "Sorry Khokho, but as this is the last time that both Sammy and I shall be here in your house as school children, we thought of leaving you with something to remember us by. I asked Sammy to sing, but first, let me explain the song to you. It comes from a very famous musical, written in the late 1920s. Sam sings it really well. I want you to listen to the story. Maybe it is not the best song for now, but it is the best that Sam can do, so I thought it fine. The melody is for you, Khokho, and for you Mammy Cynthia. It is for all the times we spent together and when you looked out for us. You will forever live in our hearts."

The silence in that room was filled with anticipation. Jane turned to me and after imagining the musical interlude I sang, 'Someone to Watch Over Me'.

I noticed while singing that Father Terry knew the piece, and shortly thereafter Khokho wiped her eyes and yes, Mammy Cynthia too recognised the song. They were sad, I could see, but Jane had warned me: "Khokho and Mammy will become sad while you sing, but concentrate on the singing and you'll be okay. In fact, you'll be better than okay." I did as directed.

Never before had I sung like that—like on that Friday night in Mpophomeni, for Khokho and Mammy Cynthia.

There's a-somebody I'm longing to see
I hope that she turns out to be
Someone to watch over me
I'm a little lamb who's lost in a wood
I know I could always be good
To one who'll watch over me...

When I had finished Khokho and Ma Khumalo ululated. Mammy Cynthia stood up from her chair and hugged Jane. I overheard Jane say: "Thank you for watching over us."

After the familiar giggle I too got a hug and that kiss on my forehead. By then I had to bow to get my kiss—not like years ago, when Mammy Cynthia had to go down on her haunches for me to hang with my little arms around her neck so that she could kiss me on my forehead.

We sat up at the table again and allowed for our memories of long ago to rest. The future, dreams and aspirations, and when Mammy Cynthia planned to retire from working at the school, that was what we spoke about for the rest of the evening.

Mammy's retirement was planned for May 1976.It was to coincide with when she celebrated her 65th birthday.

As Father Terry left he promised to take us to the railway station the following evening in time for the Cape Town bound train.

Days earlier, Jane received confirmation that she had earned a place at the University of Cape Town's Medical School. The confirmation included notice of an approved bursary and funding for her to live in the medical residence. Jane brimmed with enthusiastic determination. She would live her dream. Again I was proud of my sister.

Before going to bed, I saw Jane writing in her daily diary. I dared not sneak a peek, but that night she volunteered to read out loud:

03 December 1975

Sammy sang beautifully tonight. It may be the end of his treble voice, but he sang most beautifully. It is the last time I'd do this trip as a scholar. A bit sad, but all our departures are sad. Up to now, my life can be defined by sad departures, but also by happy arrivals. We are heading to Cape Town tomorrow, home, just Sammy and me, one last time, for me at least; sad to leave, but excited to go. The year has been successful and Goofy Sam has the littlest trophy to show for it!

After Jane read to me it was my turn to giggle. We said our evening prayers and then I turned my back on Jane's feet. She always got to sleep on the headboard side of the single bed we shared in Mammy Cynthia's tiny, but very happy home.

The three-day train ride from Pietermaritzburg to Cape Town started on the evening of 4th December. Jane got many farewell gifts and a special one from Mammy, on behalf of the Mbala family. We had to greet all the neighbours and other old friends before leaving with Father Terry. Jane loved old women so, in addition to our mates, the last walkabout was so that we could greet the various Gogos (grandmothers) we had come to know over the years. I was to see them soon, but that did not deter Jane from dragging me along.

Khokho Mbala had spent many months making a beadwork for Ma. It was intricate and included the colours green, black, red and white. Khokho explained that in Zulu culture, those colours, when applied in various complementary designs, represented love, happiness and domestic bliss. "Like with most things," she cautioned, "there's a positive and a negative meaning."

Khokho stressed that Jane should tell our Ma about each pattern and how every one had an equal and opposite meaning. Khokho insisted that her meaning was only intended to communicate the positive: "Tell your Mamma, Jani, when you give her my gift, tell her that my patterns are intended only to communicate good wishes?" Khokho's final request was for Jane to hand the gift to Ma on Christmas morning, with love from the entire Mbala family.

Ma Khumalo lived four houses down on the same street as Mammy Cynthia. When we drove by with Father Terry on that Saturday afternoon Ma Khumalo was outside in the street, waving with both hands and blowing kisses. Mr Khumalo stood expressionless in the doorway, leaning on his stick. One of Ma Khumalo's daughters, Beauty, Jane's friend, had earlier brought us a parcel containing food for the journey. I remember it was a roast chicken, potatoes and creamed spinach.

Ma Khumalo had been another of our mothers. When Mammy Cynthia had work to do during school holidays, Jane and I spent days and some nights with the Khumalo family. Ma Khumalo lived with her three daughters and her husband. Their house was the same size as Mammy Cynthia's. There always seemed to be room for two more; for us. The girls were all about the same age and they were good friends. I did not enjoy staying there, because Jane and the others did girl stuff: first with dolls and then with hair, nails, funny looking clothes and food. Mr Khumalo was a night-watchman at BTR Sarmcol, a rubber manufacturing factory near Howick. During the day we had to be quiet while he slept. In the afternoon, when Mr Khumalo awoke, that's when he and I played. The only game Mr Khumalo knew was to teach me stick-fighting. I had to learn 'stick-fighting techniques'. As with mathematics, I was never any good at stick-fighting. Mr Khumalo would laugh at me and say: "If there were a war Sammy, then you would die at the start. You cannot defend yourself if you close your eyes when preparing to strike the enemy with your stick!"

I have very fond memories of Mr Khumalo: his chuckle, his hat, the suit jacket he wore and his stick with a knob at one end; he loved that stick, it was always by his side.

While Father Terry drove us to Pietermaritzburg Station, Jane reminisced about Ma Khumalo having asked what it felt like to be in Cape Town: "Whenever I told stories about the mountains, the people, the sea and the wind, Ma Khumalo asked for more. One day, when I can afford it, Ma Khumalo will travel to the Cape as my guest. I shall show her that all the stories we've told are true. She will see that my Table Mountain is the most beautiful in the world. Ma Khumalo will find that the people in Cape Town are warm and she'll realise that it is the discrimination laws that result in different groups thinking about one as superior and the other as inferior."

Father Terry stood on the platform until the train departed. It felt good that we could wave to someone, a real person—that was why, when there was no one to wave at, Jane usually opened the window and pretended that people were there, for us. "It makes the journey whole," was what she said when I asked.

We were very hungry. As the train settled into its usual routine, Jane unpacked the food Ma Khumalo prepared. I remember how she wondered aloud: "Why is it that people who have so little give so much?"

I had no immediate reply to Jane's observation, other than to agree silently Perhaps it is because they give so much that they have so little.

Mammy Cynthia and Khokho had both prepared different meals for us. We left Pietermaritzburg with enough food for a train ride across the continent, not merely to Cape Town. There was enough to share with others too, which was what we occasionally did. Someone often joined us in the cabin during the trip, particularly after the train stopped at big stations like Bloemfontein.

Leaving Mammy Cynthia was almost as sad as it had been to leave Ma at the Cape Town Station. Mammy Cynthia had Khokho, Thami and Precious to be with her, whereas it felt as if Ma only had us—and we were often leaving.

After eating the prepared food on the jerky train we opened our gifts. The first was a framed photograph of Jane with Mammy. The attached card from Mammy Cynthia read: "Thank you for making my life complete." The picture was from Mammy Cynthia's 64th birthday party. It was a surprise party arranged by the cleaning and maintenance staff at school. The frame was similar to the one that held the picture of Elvis, on Mammy Cynthia's dressing table. I remembered that birthday: Jane, the girls in her class, together with the cleaning women and Boet Sam, everyone had his and her part to read from a prepared speech. I was perched high up in the tree under which the celebration occurred that lunch-time. The speech was titled: "Mammy Cynthia is an ordinary woman who has an extraordinary heart." When I think back, listening to that speech from up in the tree is the happiest memory I have of having been at boarding school.

The other gifts were to live under our Christmas tree until it was time for them to be opened.

The rest of the journey was long and uneventful, save for the music. Jane too had a collection of music that she wished to share. Her favourite was 'Kung Fu Fighting'. It was the strangest song—probably one that Mr Khumalo would have enjoyed a lot more than me!

Paul McCartney, his group, Wings, with an album entitled 'Band on the Run' together with Fleetwood Mac were additional pieces that Jane played for me. Back then almost every song I heard became my favourite!

Finally it was the dawn of day three. Our train snaked through the Hex River Valley. It is an area set in a geographic basin surrounded by blue-rock mountains and grapevines. December means summer in the Southern Hemisphere. The long, hot days there brought a fragrance, one that filled the air with a sweet perfume. It all stemmed from the fruit of those vines. That time the acrid smell of train battled to overtake the sweet aroma of ripening grapes. The next town was De Doorns, a siding en route to the city of Worcester. We never liked the Worcester stop; it was always a tad too long; so close to Cape Town and yet so far. The train only paused there but it was a stop that felt like an eternity.

The view of vines in berry with the mountain as backdrop continued when the train left Worcester Station. "It is a sight to behold," said Jane, "grapevines have a rich green colour and their beauty can make one's heart sing." I had no time for that. In my mind, we were already arriving at Cape Town Station.

In addition to securing the best spot for the first sighting of our mountain, Jane and I always tried to guess what dress Ma would be wearing. Jane was almost always right. They had an arrangement; probably wrote about it in those letters that Jane did not share with me. Many years later I discovered the reason why Jane was better at guessing the colour of Ma's dress.

It was when I set my mind on joining a cadet programme after graduating from school. I was intent on becoming a navigator at sea, with the merchant marines.

At the time, Safmarine, the then South African owned merchant marine company, had begun to expand its fleet. The vessels were painted a brilliant white and appeared graceful and impressive whenever they sailed out to sea. I often saw those vessels sail by in the distance while bobbing on my surfboard in the dark water off Scottburgh Beach. It was while surfing that I decided on working aboard a sea-going vessel. Engineering was not for me, and cleaning decks, like the boys who lived in our street at home, was also not part of my aspiration. Navigation, yes I enthused about becoming a navigator at sea.

Qualification for the cadet programme included having to pass an extensive eye test. I failed and instead of joining the cadet programme, I was issued with an official certificate declaring:

Certificate

TO WHOM IT MAY BE OF CONCERN

It is herewith confirmed that Samuel A. Levy is red and green colour blind.

Yours faithfully

_____

Port Captain

In time I became the owner of three certificates: a birth certificate, a school-leaving certificate and a colour blind certificate. Whenever people learn that I am certified as colour blind, they identify green or red items and ask me: "What colour is this?" Well, I am technically colour blind to the colours green and red, just like about 75% of male human beings. This does not mean that we are not able to differentiate those two colours; it means that we take a bit longer to identify the colours when shown them in rapid succession. This is because the sight of one colour lingers when the next is already being shown.

Jane might have been guessing better than me about Ma's dress colour, but I remain convinced that they conspired.

After crossing the expanse of vineyards beyond Worcester Station the train began a gentle ascent. It meandered through Bain's Kloof, which is an almost natural tear in the Du Toitskloof Mountain range. The grape-infused fragrance, tinged with iron oxide from the train wheels as they rolled over and screeched against the irregular tracks, further defined the experience. Nonetheless, our focus was trained on who would be first to spot our mountain, Table Mountain. The train veered to the right and then to the left as it wove along the tight track up against the mountain, en route to the next town, Wellington.

Festive cheer filled my head as Jane reached to hold my hand. We were nearly home.

The train continued its slow crawl along what seemed like the narrowest of railway-line and sharpest train track bends in the world. Then, finally, it squeaked and crept around what we knew was the last long bend. It was a clear day on the other side of that mountain, the Boland Mountain. Jane and I saw our mountain in the distance at the same time. Our hearts were ululating with pride, joy, happiness and we knew that the God of Life is bigger than any imagination ever will be. Wellington and the beautiful Paarl Valley, Klapmuts, Kraaifontein, Bellville and Ysterplaat, were among the stations that our train rushed through before arriving, tired, at Cape Town Station.

All the while I continued to crane my neck, and point out anything and everything that I thought Jane would not see. Her response was to act surprised and then she'd smile knowingly. I was a big boy then, but the little one continued to live in my soul. Jane had travelled that route many more times than me, but every time she too became euphoric as the journey drew to a close. The magnitude of Table Mountain that embraced the city of our birth was finally real for us to feel again. Jane excused herself to change into a special dress. She and Ma conspired, I just knew.

Usually Ma took us to have a burger when we got off the train. There was one restaurant with a section where people with darker skins were able to sit and enjoy a meal together; that is where we usually went after the longest train ride. Ma always had to speak with the manager, so that Jane would not be harassed while we ate. By the time the train stopped I was more than ready for that burger. Jane craned her neck and stretched to see Ma on the station platform. Ma always stood near where the second class carriages stopped. Just like when we were little, Jane sat back again and we briefly clutched each other's hands while the train blew its last exhausted sigh. By then I had moved the blue suitcase from its shelf and placed it at the carriage door. Now, the long journey seemed worthwhile. Everything was perfect: the train was on time; the weather was fantastic; Jane wore a pretty dress; and I was hungry for a burger.

We rushed. I also checked to see where Ma was. While we were searching, Mr Abrahams stepped forward. Jane recognised him as Ma's neighbour from a long time ago. He wore a white traditional fez.

"Mr Abra-hams!"

I didn't know that Jane could scream that loudly. Most people turned back to look at the girl with the different sound, a posh boarding school accent, which often drew attention. Mr Abrahams smiled gently as he stepped towards us. He moved our suitcase and in the process cleared the doorway for other passengers to alight. I collected the rest: bags, gifts and other things that Jane was taking home. Once all had been moved onto the platform, we paused to greet Mr Abrahams.

"But where is Mamma, Mr Abra-hams?"

He looked at Jane, but did not reply. Jane asked again, louder, in case the older man did not hear.

"Mr Abra-hams, please tell me where my Mamma is?"

There was a quiver in his voice when he spoke. It was then that I too got the sense that something was wrong.

"Let us get to my car and then I'll explain."

Jane and I rushed with our bags to Mr Abrahams' car. He moved slowly. It was only when we were packed and seated that Mr Abrahams began to explain:

"Last night your Mamma visited with Anne and Brenda. They spent the evening preparing for your arrival. We could smell that they were frying *samoosas* and *koesiesters* (a doughnut made from potatoes, flour and spices). Earlier Anne had collected the mince curry from our house."

When we arrived home Ma always had traditional food for us to eat.

"It looks as if after cleaning up, your mamma, Anne and Brenda went to bed. The gas cooker must have been placed atop the coal or electric stove. Maybe something went wrong; or the coal stove was too hot; or something to that effect. We will find out exactly what happened when the police report is produced."

"But what happened, Mr Abra-hams?!" Both Jane and I spoke at the same time. Mr Abrahams repeated: "The little gas stove was placed atop the electric cooker, I think; and for some reason the cooker-plate was not switched off, or something like that...

"In the middle of the night, last night, there was a very loud explosion ..."

"Is Mamma okay, Mr Abra-hams?"

Jane was crying by then. I tried to pacify her.

"Your Mamma will be okay ..."

Mr Abrahams spoke too slowly so Jane interrupted: "What about Anne and Brenda, Mr Abra-hams?"

He turned and reached for both our hands. Mr Abrahams' hands were soft and gentle. I clung to his left hand, for hope, but the demeanour of his expression was one of despair. Mr Abrahams struggled when he said: "Thelma is at Groote Schuur Hospital; she was treated and is going to be fine. Ambulances and the fire brigade came to the house minutes after the explosion. All three were taken to the hospital.

"Sorry, I am so sorry, but Anne and Brenda died: their burns were too bad. I am very sorry to have to share this bad news with you."

Mr Abrahams sat back in the driver's seat. He seemed spent. We wrestled with trying to understand what had happened. Jane asked all the questions. I felt numb.

"Please take us to Mamma, Mr Abra-hams?"

"I am going to take you to my daughters, Soraya and Amina. Auntie Girlie is also waiting there. They are all waiting for you. You will stay at home while I go to the hospital. Maybe your Mamma comes home with me. I shall try to bring her back."

Jane and I did not speak while Mr Abrahams drove down Main Road to Page Street in Woodstock.

The sadness, the shock and the suddenness of it all; the unanswered questions and the emotion of the news, all was overwhelming.

Strange, but my memory of that afternoon is no longer as vivid; we were distraught, that much I do recall. We needed to be with Ma.

Pa was working—he was always working. Sometimes he came home on a Saturday or Sunday night, but we never knew when and no-one knew where he worked, so we could not contact him.

That weekend Pa arrived home on the Sunday night. It was then when a neighbours told him of the tragedy. Pa drove to fetch us from the Abrahams home later that evening. As Pa stepped in by the front door the mood in that terrace house changed from sad to tense. Mr Abrahams invited Pa to a bedroom. They spoke in private for a long time. All the while, Ma was being taken care of by Auntie Girlie and her older daughters, Soraya and Amina. I did not feel that we should have left. Our home was just a house. Ma was nursing several physical injuries, but none could have been greater than the trauma of having lost two children.

Soraya and Amina came to our house so that they could be with Ma. Mr Abrahams offered to make most of the funeral arrangements. Pa said that he did not know to which church Brenda and Anne belonged. Mr Abrahams was of the Muslim faith and unfamiliar with Christian burial traditions. "All of us feel the pain—the loss is the same. I shall do what I must," is what I heard him tell Pa.

Jane called to inform Mammy Cynthia of the tragedy and within hours Father Terry had telephoned the priest at a nearby Catholic church to ask for help. The funeral arrangements were completed within two days. All who attended the ceremony were people whom we regarded as dear.

Uncle Herbert, Auntie Liza's husband, offered a special eulogy for Anne and Brenda. Pa's old friend, from when he was an electrician, Albie Fortune, offered a special thank you to Father Terry, in absentia, and to Father Michael who officiated. Pa's other friend, Tom Brickles, joined the church organist on a piano. There was no singing, but the sound of song was memorable. Tannie *(Auntie in Afrikaans)* Sarie, Tom Brickles' wife, dressed the church with the most beautiful proteas, arum lilies and orange pincushion-like flowers.

Jane read a thank you and condolence messages from Mammy Cynthia, the Mbala family and other sympathisers from Mpophomeni that Mrs Khumalo had dictated in a telephone conversation. I was tasked to read the notice thanking Mr Abrahams, Auntie Girlie, Soraya and Amina; I did that albeit while stuttering through the written sentences. All I can recall of the reading is the splendid traditional Muslim wear that the Abrahams family wore on the day. Also, that Mr Abrahams, sitting in the middle section of the church, adjusted his fez in acknowledgement and acceptance of our thank you offering. It felt as if the collective pain made all of us belong to one another and to those who could not be present.

Ma's refrain throughout the ordeal was: "The taking never stops..."

Years later all that Ma could recall was: "Pa bought the most beautiful white coffins, in which my daughters were buried."

That tragic event changed Ma's life completely and forever.

On occasion and after the burials I would overhear Ma talking to herself: "Is it tomorrow yet?" she'd say, "Or is it just the end of time; excuse me while I kiss the sky." When I asked, Ma said that these words often appeared among Brenda's papers and in her notebooks. "I do not know what it means, but someday I shall be reunited with my children, then I shall kiss them," she said.

136

Chapter Ten

Agnes and Linda

It was Christmas Eve, our first without Anne and Brenda. Jane and I decided that it was best to do as we had done in previous years. We dragged the cypress tree into the lounge and wrapped Christmas paper around the pot. From the box that contained old trimmings we decorated the lounge. Our house began to resemble Mammy Cynthia's home. We should have done so twelve days before Christmas, as in the English carol, which bears a similar name. That year was different. The sounds and decorations associated with festive cheer were in place, but the atmosphere was different.

I had been practising with the Anglican Church Choir for the Midnight Christmas Service. It was always interesting, not only because of the singing and the new clothes that congregants wore for Christmas, but also because a midnight service always attracted a few amusing characters. It was as if those men were there deliberately to embarrass their families—probably as reward for insisting that they come to church. After all, every risk has its own reward. The men, who had been drinking before the service, as if by design, were always positioned among the other congregants. That is how fate is. Those men would either pass silly comments, or deliver splendid descanted snores at the most inopportune times during the liturgy. I vividly recall a particular year when a drinker-man slept during the sermon. He awoke when Father Reddy requested the congregation to stand. In a loud sleepy voice the man yelled: "Why?!" I was usually tickled way beyond restraint when such incidents occurred. So much that I was unable to sing. The choir master would scowl at me. Thereafter all would be forgotten, until in the middle of a verse when the scene replayed in my mind and I would not be able to contain laughter. Ma's response when I told her was: "You will outgrow finding it funny when people are silly after drinking too much." This has not yet happened; perhaps it never will. I think that true maturity is only attained at the point of death. Prior to that maturity evolves with every new experience, save for those who refuse to learn. Something funny causes me to laugh and that which is sad causes me to cry. It is time for men to cry when they feel pain, perhaps that will help them be less ugly.

Ma very seldom went to church. Pa too, he only went when someone he knew died. After the funeral Pa would go to work, because he was always working.

While I sang in the choir that night, Jane and Ma prepared a meal for our Christmas celebration. Pa was going to be home too, but would have to leave before midday. I had to sing with the choir at the Christmas Morning Service, and again in the evening. For the rest of the day we were set, among other activities, to sit together at the dining room table, have lunch, exchange gifts and relax with one another.

Pa arrived in the early hours of that Christmas morning. He was tired and concerned about 'work' that had to be completed by Christmas afternoon.

Ma and Pa argued—they always argued. It was unpleasant. Jane retreated to her bedroom on such occasions; that night too.

Christmas Day was okay. The discussion never turned to Anne and Brenda but it was obvious that they were on our minds. Jane and I had an unspoken pact to make the home atmosphere as pleasant as possible.

We had tried, ever since returning from school, to call Charles, so that he could be informed of the tragedy. It was to no avail.

Days before Christmas Jane and I tried to reach Charles one last time, but again our attempts were flouted. We walked from one telephone booth to another until we found one that was in working order. It was almost five kilometres away from where we lived. We could have used the home telephone but Ma would have overheard the conversation and the surprise would have been spoiled.

Jane pleaded with whoever answered the phone at the various numbers she dialled. None was successful because Charles did not respond. It was clear that he did not receive our various messages. Every day we called, but our attempts yielded nothing more than telephonic promises made by people we did not know. A visit from Charles on Christmas day would have been the most special gift for Ma, but it was not to be.

Jane hid the sweetmeats that she had bought. They were the treats that both Ma and Charles relished.

Well, we were unable to locate Charles in time so Jane and I wrapped the sweetmeats and placed them underneath the cypress, our Christmas tree in the big wrapped pot. The Christmas card for Ma in 1975 read:

"To Dearest Mamma, you deserve some sweetness on this day, from Anne, Charles, Brenda, Jane, Sammy and Pa—Merry Christmas."

The gifts brought some cheer and we were all happy, but it was a short-lived sort of happiness. The sweetmeats were only half our gift to Ma. Charles seemingly never received our messages. Ma was not to know that. Pa left before lunch and we were back to being three. That was how things were.

It was summer and the wind blew all the time. The sand it carried was irritating. Doors and windows had to be kept closed, but the fine sand got in somehow. Our windows were not like those in Europe which seal to keep the harsher weather out. In Africa the sun can shine like there is going to be no tomorrow; no wind; no snow; and no sand. This becomes wishful thinking when the wind howls on the Cape Flats! On such windswept days it was best to remain indoors.

I planned my next trip to Muizenberg and visualised riding the best waves. There was a problem though: I was not allowed out on my own when Jane was home; instead, and for the rest of the time, we read old newspapers and magazines. I could not get enough of paging through an old picture book of Norma Jean. Jane was irritated by me that day. "Sammy, why can't you read and keep the contents to yourself, like a normal person; why must you always share what you've read?" was how she responded when I tried to give of my enthusiasm about what I had read. Even if she had read the article I'd share it with her, because that was also how things were! Some of the stories were just too good to keep to myself, like when Elvis asked President Nixon for an FBI badge. The President, it was reported, commented about Elvis' clothes: "You dress kinda strange, don't you?" To which, it is said, Elvis replied: "You have your show to run, Sir, and I have mine." According to Jane I was a natural at broadcasting any news!

After Christmas, the next big day was New Year. My future was going to be different without Jane. The apprehension was made worse when I overheard her speak to Ma: "Sam has a darkness of mind when unsettled." I didn't know what she meant and to ask for clarification would have resulted in hard words because I was not supposed to be listening. Maybe they were not talking about me. We were all a bit sensitive then.

Jane later disclosed to me that she was worried about how I would respond when the reality of being alone at school set in. She went on to explain that I spoke about my feelings with ease. Apparently I came across as being independent and self-sufficient; and older than my 15 years. The reality was very different. Sometimes that little boy, me, was forced to play the role of someone much older. My way of coping was to talk to myself. It was also the reason why I took to surfing, which was the one activity where there was no help, just an opportunity to do the impossible.

Ma was never comfortable with my going to the beach. She consistently refused to watch me surf. Her fear came from long ago; from the experience on that ship with our Aunties, Agnes and Winnie, when they sailed from St Helena to Cape Town on stormy seas. Ma feared that it would upset her when a big wave crashed into me. Her fear was also that I might develop a problem when riding the back waves, and that she would have to watch me being eaten up by the sea.

"What about the sharks? Is the water not too cold? Why can't you ride a bicycle, or play football like other boys your age? Why must it always be in the water?" That was Ma's standard response whenever I dared to mention the sea.

In reply, without realising it, I taunted Ma: "Someday I want to be a professional surfer, Ma; and it will not happen if I play football."

On hearing about my wish to make a career from surfing, I swear, Ma went grey with anger: "Do you know anyone who is a professional surfer; and what kind of job is that? You must finish school, do a trade, or go to university. You can always surf, but that is not how you are going to earn a living and raise a normal family. When you are back at school, then stop going to the beach with Mr Thompson! Focus on improving your grades. Leave the surfing for when you are older; am I making myself clear?"

I thought that my reply was reasonable:

"You know, Ma, when I went to school, the teacher said that I must not write with my left hand, so I learned to write with my right hand. The same teacher encouraged me to use my right hand because that, she said, would stop me from sucking my thumb. That I had to be more like other children was also something teachers said when they prevented me from using my natural hand, the left one. Never was I asked about my preference. 'Perhaps children are not allowed to exercise choice', was what I thought.

"In the beginning, writing with my right hand was like having to walk on my hands.

"When I did not enjoy playing football the other boys thought that there was something wrong with me. To please them I learned to play. I like to watch, but have never enjoyed playing.

"Swimming is my favourite sport and it has been so ever since that first day when Pa took me to the stony beach near Somerset Strand. It was before he worked all the time. We spent time together then. We walked out onto that old wooden jetty. I asked so many questions and today those answers clutter my memory; useless information, most of it.

"In a rock pool at that place, Strand, in Somerset West, that's where I learned to swim. While the grown-ups were picking periwinkles, mussels and other sea urchins, for a meal, I taught myself to swim in that rock pool.

"The other boys could swim on the sandy beach: 'You are not allowed,' that was all the grown-ups said. Eventually I understood why, but back then all I wanted was to be in the water where the other boys swam. Only the paper boat I made was allowed to float from my rock pool for a swim on that reserved beach with the other boys.

"No matter though, that rock pool was nice to swim in just the same. Not better than the Steenbras Dam pool, no, that pool was the best. It had fresh water and my eyes never burned after swimming there. The many hours spent in rock pools and dams, immersed in water, have left me with wonderful memories of being happy. The pool at Steenbras Dam was only two feet deep, but swimming there was better than in the rock pool at Strand, a reserved beach.

"Remember Ma, the big metal bath and how we warmed cold water by placing it out in the sun? It was my very own big swimming pool, filled with warm water. Those are some of my fondest memories; and now, look! Now you want to stop me from swimming!

"Playing the piano, my only other interest, music, is also out—because Pa did not want to buy a piano.

"I was introduced to surfing by Mr Thompson. Warm water, strong swells and the sound the board makes when pushed by a wave are much better than sucking my thumb. I *like* to surf, Ma."

Listening without interrupting was what defined Ma. She did so with everyone.

"My boy, I am afraid that something will happen to you when out there where the water is rough and you are alone. If surfing is your preferred sport then you should continue with it, but I worry that something will happen when you are out in that deep water. That's all."

I sensed that Jane was tired of talking about my swimming and surfing. After all, she had tolerated the same conversation with me for the longest time. Ma moved the conversation on to Pa—she did so frequently.

We had seen Pa for two days after the burials and then he announced that there was work to be done. Pa left. It was a week before Christmas and as stated, Pa returned home in the middle of the night on that Christmas morning. He left again on Christmas Day, but not before Jane had one of her customary 'goes' at him. Her comments were telling, and because Jane never spoke ill of others I was all ears to hear what she had to say to Pa.

"You spent more time at home when Sam and I were little, Pa. Then, you worked in the garden, fixed carpets on the dining room table and you had time to joke with us. These days you are never at home…"

Jane's comments were sufficient fodder for Pa to feign being cross. As usual, he used make-believe anger as an excuse to leave. About midday Pa left. It was before we could share the Christmas meal together. We next saw Pa during the following December holidays, 1976.

When Pa rushed out he left Ma, Jane and me to eat Christmas lunch on our own. I remember the sound of Pa's car fading into the distance as he drove further away on that Christmas Day. Pa left in a huff, pretending to be consumed by anger at Jane's temerity to question his work. I sensed Ma's disappointment and Jane seemed furious. Given what had happened that Christmas Day the honesty of my question to Ma could, perhaps, have been more subtle:

"When Pa and you are at home together Ma, then, for as long as I can remember, you two argue. It is as though you don't like each other. Sometimes I think that Jane and I are the cause of it—are we, Ma?

"Look what happens when Jane and I are home; look how it is. Why can't we also be like other families, together at Christmas time? We have enough sadness! Soon I shall have to go back to that school, alone this time! Christmas should not have been …"

Ma sat, looked and listened as I spoke like a big boy. Her reply was not immediate, but that expression was back. It was a look that I recognised. Ma wore that look when she had something on her mind. It was usually something that she wished to share with us, but would not. Instead, we sat and passed platters of different dishes to one another. Then, after a long pause, Ma spoke again:

"It's easy for you children to talk. You do not have to go through what I have had to endure. The reality is that this situation with Pa began before you were born. When you were away at school Pa began to leave home early and return late at night. This went on for a while. Thereafter he stayed away one night, then two nights, and these days he is only a visitor here, perhaps twice per month, if that.

"Before the tragedy, Anne told me that Pa visited them frequently. He would not come home, but he would visit Anne. When Brenda moved there he visited both of them. I think that Pa sometimes slept there too. As he was leaving today, on this Christmas Day, you saw me running out to speak with him… I did so because when he will return is anyone's guess. There are things that I had to talk to Pa about. He was not interested this time. Before driving off he told me that we are going to sell this house. Pa wants to live closer to where he works, but there is no talk about my moving with him."

The discussion continued for a while. We finished the meal with sago pudding amid the customary bickering between Jane and me about who was going to enjoy the crusty bit with the cinnamon stick.

That afternoon Father Michael from the Catholic Church arrived to see how Ma was bearing up. Their roles were reversed: Ma played the part of Mrs Bonds while the very young priest gave counsel. When Father Michael left the three of us continued to talk and Ma, for once, spoke to us about how she felt:

"No person can be everything for themselves. There comes a time when we are reliant on others. I am always the wall-plug. People always take from me. When they leave, without fail, I yearn for a chance also to receive. There comes a time when each of us has to draw strength from another. I never thought about drawing from someone, let alone a young Catholic priest and particularly at a time when my loss is bigger than imagination."

For much of that Christmas afternoon Jane was not as vocal with her usual commentary; she probably felt bad that Pa had left after her challenge. Ma and I knew that it was not true, that it was not Jane's fault. Jane must have thought that this was a chance for us to be a normal family, had it not been ruined by her big mouth. I chose not to discuss Pa and their altercation.

Ma's pain was dominated by a need to be rational about that which was unfolding in her life. All I wished for was that Ma would be happy again. The thought was naïve, but I longed for my Ma of old. I did not know the extent of her pain. What had happened could not be reversed. The tragic events of that Christmas season changed our family forever.

When I asked if Ma would ever heal, her reply had a rehearsed ring to it, as though that question had already been put to her and answered.

"Change is permanent, yes, but it replaces a past with a future. No amount of future can ever make way for the pain when a mother loses her children. You know, it is true, somewhere between what is right and wrong there is a garden. I shall meet my girls there someday..."

I had a sense then that our Ma of old was gone; forever gone. But it was not acceptable then and could not be acceptable afterwards either. The reality is that Ma, as we knew her, would never return, probably because part of her soul had been amputated.

All the unfairness, prejudice, exploitation and the taking that never stopped had reached a zenith. Ma was saturated. She was broken. Her soul had been in an accident; an accident that made her tremble and feeble. Ma had let go of what had been a courageous and determined life.

I shall always remember our Ma of old. My Ma, who was driven by unwavering principles and a philosophy that strengthened her resolve to soldier on. She had an impact on others and made them strong. It was not as a result of what had been said, or achieved, but by the example that she set—my Ma, the one who patiently listened when I struggled with learning to think and reason.

§

I was on my board, bobbing behind the breakers at Muizenberg Corner. A passenger train had gone by. Jovial noises came from one of the carriages. The passengers seemed happy and it was infectious. I smiled knowingly and thought of all the fun experiences Mammy Cynthia, Jane and I had shared on trains; subject matter for another book.

The surf was flat that day. There was no wind to drive the swells. My thoughts turned to Ma, as they so often did when I straddled the board during that time of bereavement, all the while hoping that a big swell would roll in and take me to the beach on a crest of note. I thought of the young priest, he of the Catholic faith; of people who are human first and then choose to follow a form of worship. I remembered Ma always leading from the front; and how she had handed her proverbial baton to the young priest on that Christmas afternoon when he visited. When the priest left I was watching from the upstairs bedroom window as Ma walked him to the front gate. From there I saw how my Ma uncharacteristically had thrown her hands in the air while walking back to the front door. She stood on the porch for a moment and spoke as though to someone there: "What is said and done cannot be unsaid and undone."

I always thought that Ma used familiar sayings when other words failed her. As we were growing up, and at random times, Ma's words would become more meaningful. Both Jane and I realised that. Though it was easy to think and say what was on our minds, often it was much better to hold on to the opinion and forego the chance to say that which cannot be unsaid. When I think back then, as children our opinions were often far out, or better if they remained unsaid. "Sorry is not medicine," was another of Ma's refrains. The one that Khokho often reminded me of when I dared to be critical was: "Sammy, do not relieve yourself upstream because downstream you have to drink the same water," she'd say.

I understood things better as I grew older. At first it felt uncomfortable to admit, but Ma had been right all along.

What about how Jane and I came to be? We never finished that story. Jane probably knew, just like she knew the rest of Ma's story but never shared it with me, and I was too proud to ask. It was not the right time anyway; but was there ever going to be a right time, or would I have to find another way?

Sitting out on my board, bobbing was thinking time; and it would always end in a wonderful rush with arms swinging for balance and knees bent on a driven board.

Sympathisers continued to visit Ma during the two weeks after Christmas and before I left for school. They arrived from all over to offer condolences. Most of the people were new 'friends'. Jane and I had not met them previously and they, most of them, had not known that we existed.

Our home telephone had been ringing off the hook for weeks, but at six in the morning, on 29 December 1975, the telephone rang again. I woke up and stumbled down stairs to mumble a 'hello' into the mouthpiece.

"Sister St Claire! Is that you?"

Her voice was unmistakable and I was embarrassed, standing there talking to the head teacher—me, not being dressed appropriately! She asked to speak with Mrs Levy and without hesitation I rushed back upstairs. Ma was already tying her dressing gown and making her way downstairs to the telephone. She listened as Sister St Claire spoke. Listening more than speaking had become Ma's professional persona; one where she would only answer when a specific question was put to her.

"Thank you for informing me, Sister, bye-bye." That is how the telephone conversation ended and I could not deduce the detail.

I waited upstairs on the landing for Ma to return and share what our head teacher had said. My wait would be in vain. Instead Ma had poured tea and was sitting in the lounge room when I finally ran out of patience and checked on her. I could not contain my curiosity. It is not every day that the head teacher of a school calls a parent's home, particularly at six in the morning. Ma was in the lounge room, on the sofa. She had been crying again. Instead of telling me what Sister St Claire had to say, Ma instructed: "Go back upstairs, wake Jane and tell her to come here at once?"

When Jane came down she sat next to Ma, I hid behind the curtain, the one that divided our lounge room from the spiral staircase. My action was a remnant of having thought of myself as being invisible. I had to hear first-hand why Jane was in trouble. Ma had poured two cups of tea. One was for Jane:

"Well, Jane," was how Ma started the conversation. She looked at her for just that bit longer than usual: "I have always wished the best for you and Sam. Money and nice clothes were not always possible. A long time ago I decided to invest in your education. My intention was that you two children might learn and become proud adults. It was a pleasure to sacrifice personal effects in the knowledge that I was raising two people who would one day be independent thinkers. Many people have fancy academic qualifications, but whether they can think is often not consistent with how they behave. My dream is that you and Sam will be different. I dream that you and Sam shall use your learning opportunity and become assets to our world."

Jane was partly asleep. I sensed that she was trying very hard to focus on the heaviness in Ma's early morning speech.

"But why are you telling me all of this now, Ma, at six in the morning?" Jane was like that. Sometimes she spoke without first thinking.

"Well, Sister St Claire called me ten minutes ago." I peeped through the curtain and saw Ma lean over to hold Jane's hand as she said: "Sister called to tell me that you have achieved eight distinctions in the external school leaving examination. Look Jane, because you have made yourself proud, I too feel entitled to be proud of you, congratulations. Thank you for being my wonderful child."

Ma paused for a moment before saying: "You see, my girl, the God of Life does not only take from me."

When I peered around the staircase curtain, Jane, with all of her 1.79 metres was sitting on Ma's lap. They were in a tight embrace and I could not stop myself from joining in. The three of us hugged for what must have been twenty minutes. Jane made us the right to be proud that morning, as she has done on many other occasions.

Jane had to get ready for her part-time job at Grand Bazaars (a chain store in Wynberg) where she was a part-time cashier.

It was miserable to be home when Jane was away. Her job took her away from home for an entire day at a time.

I knew that she sought every opportunity to be away from home. I too took my chances to escape the sadness of being there and having to welcome a steady never-ending stream of strangers. They were all sympathisers.

Jane moved to the Medical Residence at the University of Cape Town during that first week of January 1976. It felt final and I was sad. My sister had grown up and we would never be together again, that was what I thought. We were no longer reliant on each other. It was an empty feeling, but for Jane's sake I feigned excitement and happiness so that she did not feel my pain.

The Groote Schuur Hospital is attached to the University of Cape Town's Medical School. It is a teaching hospital where all medical students practise the theory they learn. Groote Schuur Hospital is where the first human heart was transplanted from one person to another, back in 1967. It is also where Brenda and Anne died.

I helped Jane to move her clothes and a few books. We only had one suitcase, so I unpacked my clothes and filled the blue suitcase with Jane's. We travelled by bus from Busy Corner to Wynberg Station and then by train to Observatory. The entire journey is etched in my mind. I carried the suitcase from Observatory Station, first to Main Road and then up the hill on Anzio Road, past the Medical Library, and around the corner to the medical residence. Jane spoke non-stop all the way—she was always talking. It was like years earlier when Mammy Cynthia carried the same case on her head as we walked on that orange road to school. That time the walk with Jane did not feel good. Having to do the return journey with an empty suitcase and without Jane felt worse. Had it been possible, half the case should have stayed with her.

When I arrived home Ma was sitting on the sofa in the lounge room. Despite her change Ma sometimes resembled the woman I knew—like that day, when she sensed my sadness. Ma spoke to me without hesitating: "Being sentimental about life is too much like living in the past. You cannot have peace in the future if you do not settle with what happened in the past. Remember, Boy, the future is more important than the past. You have to embrace it because if you don't then you will be left behind. Change is permanent, remember that too. Get the mix between the past and the future right and spend more time planning tomorrow and less on thinking about yesterday."

Often times, when Ma spoke, it was as though she helped me to look at my life through the filter of her experiences.

Ma continued to make statements that, at first, I had to memorise and then think about when either bobbing my board or during other alone times. As time went by Ma became cynical about her own life. She began to question the value of her contribution.

§

There was a surf shop in Main Road, Muizenberg, and with Jane no longer at home I'd go window-shopping there. It was like watching an exciting football match. My fascination with the new surf paraphernalia was obsessive. I asked many questions. The surf shop owner was not to know that it was in my nature to be inquisitive. People who looked like me were not surfers back then, so it was not unreasonable for the shop owner to appear suspicious about the motive for my questions.

Other surfing people were greeted and treated a lot better. By then I had almost accepted how life was. The shop owner's manner was evidence enough. He did not believe that I could surf. He probably thought that I was up to no good. To protect him against the prejudice that had infested his mind and me from humiliation I stopped walking up and down the little aisles in his shop. Whenever the opportunity arose I'd stand outside on the pavement, out of sight, cup my hands against the window and peer in to feed my fascination, curiosity and to acquire ideas for my surfing dreams.

The stock inside that shop included easy-dry shorts in different colours; wet suits; flip-flops; waxes; boogie boards; woogie boards (a knee-board that never became popular); skateboards and surfboards (new and second-hand). I had no money to buy any of the boots, suits, boards, waxes, creams and magazines that were being displayed. Window-shopping was an alternative to being with all those strangers who visited our house and made Ma cry.

Most of the time in Muizenberg was spent leaning up against the station railings and staring out to sea. I stood there and watched surfers ride at the famous Surfers' Corner, the part of Muizenberg Beach closest to the railway station. Cars were parked there. Some had roof racks with the most modern boards and paddle skis tied to them. Windsurfing was becoming popular then. Strange music, the Muizenberg Surfers also listened to strange music, like Led Zeppelin's 'Stairway to Heaven' and a new favourite, 'Mammy Blue'.

While inspecting a few boards tied to the rack of an old VW camper van, I saw (for the first time) an original Rip Curl tri-skeg (three-fin) short-board. I was awestruck. While standing there, gawking, the owner arrived.

Without thinking I asked the man about the board. He was a very gentle man. Instead of dismissing me, like the surf shop owner did, Rusty explained how he had acquired the collectable board. Then he did the unimaginable: he offered that I ride his prized possession. Without hesitation I agreed, stripped down and walked across the white sand of Muizenberg Beach with what, to me, was the prettiest board in the world. With the leash tied to my leg, I entered the cold surf at another forbidden beach.

Short-boards are used by people who can surf. I knew that Rusty had called his mates to watch and I did not want to disappoint.

"There's a difference between surfing with skill and showing off," is what Mr Thompson yelled when he thought my style to be like a ballerina. "Don't forget that you are a boy, Sammy!" was how his bark would usually end, as if boys could not be ballet dancers. What he meant was not clear to me. Maybe Mr Thompson was referring to having respect for skill, dexterity and for the unpredictable might of the sea, but where being a boy fits in baffles me to this day.

From Muizenberg Corner, while waiting for the right swell, I watched commuter trains go by. The water was sometimes murky and the waves erratic, but the beach was always reserved. The swells seldom grew higher than six feet. Frequently, the south-easterly wind tore in and ruined the potential for a pleasant ride. The short-board and those swells were not always compatible. That was why the fancy board remained tied to the roof rack of Rusty's van. At first I had difficulty but it didn't last long. Not even a side swipe from a gust of wind could stop my ride from singing. The sound the board made when driven by the wave's energy was an experience to behold.

Rusty and his friends were surprised to see that I could ride, let alone the fast board. So surprised was he that on my return Rusty gave me a pair of leather sandals. They were handmade. He had made them from a piece of car tyre; cattle hide leather; two buckles; some stitching; and glue. We became beach friends, Rusty, some of his mates and I. Whenever he was not selling sandals, bags and belts, Rusty was on the beach and I got to ride his fancy board. Those sandals were one of the two pairs of shoes I owned and wore for more than ten years.

They continued life after being mine. I reconditioned them and they became a gift to a young surfer. I told him to pass it on when done.

The board with which I had competed at Scottburgh was also a short-board. I began to lug that board on the bus and train after Rusty's had been bitten by a sea animal. Fellow train and bus commuters were very unhappy, particularly those on the bus, but such is life.

Muizenberg is a Vaseline beach. Even those who had thick neoprene suits smeared their bodies with a layer of Vaseline petroleum jelly. It was supposed to increase the length of time that we surfers could spend in the very cold water. Some said that it is a myth to apply petroleum jelly or fat to keep the cold at bay. I agreed, but did it nonetheless because the water was achingly cold. Bobbing on a board in that cold water, wearing only a pair of grey school shorts and a T-shirt was no fun. I sought relief by smearing my body with Vaseline, or fat when there was no petroleum jelly. The wait for a good wave was determined by how strong the wind was on the day. The Vaseline made my surfing experience at Muizenberg Corner very slippery.

The average mid-summer water temperature was about eighteen degrees Celsius (64°f). During the winter months the sea there was reported at eleven degrees (51°f) actual, but in reality it felt much colder. This was due to the wind chill factor, so people said when it was very cold and felt colder. To make matters worse, there were hungry sharks lurking where the short-board swells began. I got away on the day a shark demonstrated its appetite on Rusty's board. Perhaps it was aiming for my skinny legs that dangled on either side. By that experience I was reminded of the story Mammy Cynthia told about the people who smeared fat on their bodies and had to run from the hyena. But it was not fair because I had nothing to hide.

The waves at Muizenberg Corner were different from beaches where I had surfed previously. The Muizenberg waves were short. Their speed would change midstream—then my board was at its most slippery. It was those erratic conditions at Muizenberg Corner that improved my dexterity—that and being forced to write with my right hand.

A City Tramways bus operated on the route between Muizenberg Station and Busy Corner, a five minute walk from where we lived. The cost of a bus ticket was slightly more than the train ride between Southfield (the nearest train station) and Muizenberg. The walk home from Southfield was thirty minutes longer than from Busy Corner. 'Slightly more expensive' on the bus was very expensive for me. The train was a good alternative, even though I always anticipated being robbed on that route. My survival technique was to adopt a non-defeatist posture when approached by a would-be robber. This response was usually in the form of a suitable and equally intimidating swagger. Knowing when to run often saved my life. The brutality of the streets where we lived was not to be underestimated. Gangsters were more dangerous than sharks. Their eyesight and aim were much better too and as a result I hold the unofficial record for running five kilometres with a surfboard tucked under one arm!

Occasionally Jane would give me bus fare to feed what had become an addictive need for the cold surf of Muizenberg Corner. When Jane was away I surfed every day. Sometimes the surf was up and other days it was down; the wind howled from time to time, but then there were times when surfing conditions were perfect. I was there throughout. It did not matter, even when waves rushed in at right angles to the beach I surfed—that is what surfers do. Nearer the end of my stay I surfed with greater intensity. The dreaded necessity of returning to school began to beckon louder at the passing of each day.

Maybe I was suffering from depression. I did not know that such an ailment existed, let alone its symptoms. All I knew was that to commune with the surfboard and the sea was the only okay alternative to being at home. Too complex, that's what I think about depression. Ma knew, but asking her to explain was out of the question then. Perhaps Ma was also depressed; perhaps Ma remained depressed throughout her life; perhaps Ma's surfboard was the young priest, her conduit to commune with the God of Life, the God of all faiths.

The droves of visitors never stopped. Every evening when I arrived home there would be different people commiserating with Ma. People (as if pre-programmed), all of them would make the same comments when they saw either Jane or me; and did so in that sing-song way in which many Capetonians speak: "Look how tall he is! My word! He's going to be very handsome, hey?"

Jane came home for the weekend on the Friday before my return to school. We had planned to meet at the Busy Corner bus stop and walk home together. I sat underneath the bus shelter, waiting. I sat there for a long time before the bus Jane was on arrived. It was better to sit and wait because the sympathisers were at our house. Jane wore a pair of Wrangler Jeans, a loose fitting white blouse and sandals when she got off the bus. Her light hair was tied back and bobbed like a tail when she walked. As predicted the sympathisers were there when we arrived home.

"H…i! She's a grown woman, tall and so pretty."

Jane seemed normal to me, nothing that vaguely justified the sing-a-long outburst of pretty: "Y…es, Mrs Levy, your daughter is beau-tiful, like a European girl! You can't tell the difference hey? …"

The guest was a Mrs Arendse. She had bright orange hair, like a mango, that colour. Her hair had been straightened and appeared uncompromising. One of her front teeth was lined with a gold strip in the shape of the letter 'L'. Mrs Loraine Arendse thought that her comment to Jane was the highest compliment. Jane was appalled, but smiled dutifully, so as not to embarrass Ma. She retreated to her bedroom and stayed there until the last guest left. When Jane emerged from the cocoon of that room to join Ma and me in our lounge her tone too was uncompromising: "Mamma!" was how Jane began the conversation. "Why did you not correct that woman when she said that I am beautiful like that; why can't I just be beautiful; why do I have to be compared to someone from Europe, as if those people are more special than any others?"

"Sometimes, my girl, you have to leave people be. Like when the man who worked with me on the farms came here to offer his condolence. He said that I should accept that which I cannot change. How can any mother accept the death of her children and not want it reversed? I accepted his gesture. You see, it is about knowing when to respond and when a response will add no value. Sometimes our silence allows us to rise above that with which we may not be in agreement. At times silence is a very loud response and other times it is a curse. If you respond to everything then people will stop having respect for your views. Then, when your contribution is most valid, it will be ignored. Here in Cape Town we have the strangest phenomenon: we suffer from the 'mule syndrome'. Do you know what a mule is, Jane?"

"Yes Mamma." There was a sarcastic lilt in her voice. "Is it not the offspring of a male donkey and a female horse?"

"Yes, that is how mules are conceived. Well, then you will understand the logic of the metaphor, mule-syndrome. Figuratively speaking, when the mule is asked about its parents, it is likely to refer to the champion horse and ignore the donkey. The donkey is often described as stupid and stubborn. By the way, a study that I read debunked as myth claims about donkeys being less intelligent than horses.

"So, how is this relevant, you may ask? Well, if you ask a person of 'mixed' origins who his parents are, then he will most likely tell you about the grandparent who was European and ignore the other who was Khoi. There are a number of reasons for this: the most popular being that people are embarrassed about their forefathers who were hunter-gatherers and herders who lived off the land. They wore nothing but loin cloths and we forget that it was so because of the heat here in Africa.

"You will have begun to realise that those who have light skins are automatically labelled beautiful. People create their norms from stereotypes and prejudices. We use these norms to make value judgments.

"It was not the right time to have that discussion with Mrs Arendse, so I let her comment be."

§

Sundays were together days. Pa worked—he always worked. Ma was up early to fry the *koesiesters*; and once fried they were dunked in syrup and then rolled in crumbed coconut. Like the Cape Doctor (the south easterly wind that blows the city smog out to sea), so *koesiesters* are synonymous with being Capetonian.

On Sunday mornings we ate *koesiesters* and drank *rooibos* tea before I went to sing with the Anglican Church Choir. That morning was no different other than it being the last Sunday that I would sing with the Church Choir before returning to school. Jane and Ma cooked a traditional lunch of roast chicken, rice and beetroot salad on Sundays.

After having had lunch, and when all the dishes were tidied, every one of us was occupied by our own respective interests. I used the time to pack while Jane and Ma read. At about four o'clock I bathed Lampo and we, Jane and I, took her for a walk. Lampo was always excited to be on a leash. She enjoyed the walkabout. To me the walk was tedious. There was always that wind and the sand it carried. Jane hid underneath a big cap and her windbreaker, a reversible Tiger Jacket, which she wore as if it were a blanket. Yet another car was parked in front of our house when we got back from walking Lampo. Again it was one that I did not recognise. Though they meant well, I was tired of all the visitors. We were not accustomed to so many different people visiting.

Jane was always the last to notice something: "Oh! Sammy! Look, more visitors!"

I just cringed. To walk more, until the visitors left, was out of the question; it was too windy, but I could not resist a mumble: "I don't like it when these people visit, because they make Ma sad."

Jane pulled her face in that sarcastic smiling way she sometimes did. "Yes, and they say stupid things."

That was a bit unusual of Jane to say. She was seldom critical of people.

As the front door opened we braced for the usual comments that were to follow. The lounge room, where the two visitors were seated was right there, across from the front door. We had been taught to be polite when greeting visitors. That time was no exception. Those visitors were different. I caught my breath and heard Jane do the same.

"You look like Ma."

I should not have spoken that thought, but sometimes I run ahead of myself. Eagerly I shook hands with the two women.

"Exactly like Ma."

Jane too could not help herself before speaking. While the two women looked at each other and laughed, Jane whispered: "The older woman looks like Ma in a pale skin." We laughed too.

The attempt at small talk with the guests was not finding fluency when Ma entered the room from the kitchen bearing a big serving-tray of tea, and with that she saved us from further discomfort. We had already exchanged pleasantries with the visitors and were preparing to leave them talking with one another when Ma intervened: "Have you met my sister?"

It was Auntie Agnes, the one about whom Ma wrote and we read; about whom Ma had told us; and for whom we had prayed each evening at bedtime over a period that was longer than Jane and I could remember.

Auntie Agnes stood there, in our lounge, wearing a big proud smile. "Hello, Jane." The two hugged. "You are very pretty ..."

Jane and I did not know whether to be happy, or sad. Auntie Agnes's voice, like that of Auntie Winnie, sounded almost exactly like Ma's.

"Thank you Auntie."

Jane was done and it was my turn: "You must be Samuel?" Auntie Agnes turned to hug me too. "Such a big boy ..."

Auntie Agnes also had cue cards! I smiled. It was my gesture of thanks.

Ma then introduced us to Auntie Agnes's daughter, Linda. She was an older cousin, but all our cousins were older. It was Linda's red car parked outside. On the rear bumper was a sticker that read: 'I brake for no reason'. Linda seemed scary. She had a very boisterous manner. But our Ma was happy, and that was enough.

Later, when we were upstairs in the bedroom, Jane volunteered her view of Linda: "She is a pleasant person, but cannot relate to us."

"Can you blame her? She grew up hearing talk about how dangerous and uncouth people who live on the Cape Flats are; and then she meets you and me who are unaffected by people who brake for no reason!"

"You are a fool, Samuel Levy."

I suppose this response was the best that Jane could manage! After all, she had been complaining of a terrible ache on the side of her head since we met at Busy Corner bus stop.

Later Ma told me that Auntie Agnes and Linda were members of the Salvation Army Church and that they wore uniforms.

"You think they have guns too, Ma?"

"Why are you being so stupid?"

Maybe that response was the best that Ma could manage! Did Ma's head ache too, I wondered?

We were called to say goodbye when Auntie Agnes and Linda were preparing to leave. I found it disturbing when old women insisted on kissing me on my lips. We stood at the front gate as Linda drove her red car up Fourth Avenue. At the top of the street she turned right onto Victoria Road. Linda headed back to University Estate. The roads there had no pot-holes, there were sidewalks for pedestrians and people used telephones instead of to scream across the divide.

Without missing a beat, as the car left Ma began to re-tell the story of her elder sister, Agnes; the significant role she played in her early development; her dress-making skills; that she had married Jesús and adopted a little baby, Linda.

Jane found it interesting that Ma could so easily forget how Auntie Agnes had denied their relationship as sisters. It was all because of what her neighbours might think. It seemed Ma had also forgotten about the talk she had with Jesús the day they met on the street. I remembered the story about Mommy Wilson's death. It did not stir in Auntie Agnes a need to step down from her perceived position of privilege and mourn together with the family where she was reared.

After the visit, Ma was in her element, uplifted. Without talking Jane and I listened to a story that we had heard many times before:

"When I was a young girl Auntie Agnes made all my clothes and people commented about my beauty whenever I wore a frock that my sister sewed. Yes, she made me feel very pretty.

"The night before I'd wear one of Agnes' creations the excitement would cause me to have difficulty sleeping ..."

Having to sit through Ma tell that old story, again, did not bother me. But Jane could not share my peace.

"Yes Mamma, you forget about all the other things ..."

"You know my child, Agnes is my sister. Sam is your brother and there comes a time when we have to let bygones be bygones. All people make mistakes. They live with their scars. It is usually their decisions that lead to the scars. Who are we to remind them of what they did thirty years ago, particularly if their actions prove that they have changed? Or, is it your view that people cannot have a change of heart and be forgiven?

"Maybe Agnes realises how she has denied herself and those dearest to her. I shall not remind her. Agnes is my sister; and as it is so much gets taken from me."

I sat there and sucked my thumb, wishing that Jane had indulged Ma, but instead she encouraged the boring repetition.

"After many years of being away, my sister took time and looked for me. She's found me and I can no longer let what happened in the past stand between us. That time is gone and there is nothing we can do about it. You can't fix stuff that happened in the past. This is a new time. I love my sister and I have lost enough."

Unlike in the past, Ma began to speak more about how she felt. Prior to that her talk was almost always about what she thought. That time she did too: "My sister experienced an epiphany; and I have to forgive her."

Without intending to, Ma could stir a deep emotion within a listener. At times like those I wondered whether it was due to her sincere manner, or her simplicity. Maybe it was because of her ability to forgive-without-judgment that the taking from Ma never stopped? I remembered the conversation with Jane when we returned home that December. The discussion was about Ma Khumalo who gave even though she had nothing. Jane asked me then, I remember, she said: 'How is it that those who have the least give the most?', or words to that effect.

Meanwhile Jane and Ma's discussion continued: "... I understand Mamma, but why do you always have to come second?"

I knew that Jane had Ma's interests at heart, but sometimes there was little to no subtlety beneath her honesty. Ma exposed herself to abuse, and afterwards she sought refuge in her familiar refrain: "The taking never stops."

Auntie Agnes and Linda were probably home by then. Their suburb looked down on the busy Port of Cape Town. The Safmarine ships docked there, in the shadow of our mountain. Across the bay they could see the maximum security prison on Robben Island. We were in our township house on the windswept Cape Flats, listening to Ma speak lovingly about her privileged sister.

As far as I can remember that was the first and last time Jane saw Auntie Agnes.

It was during the time when the purpose of Ma's life became one where she began merely to exist.

Chapter Eleven

Captain Subramani

"Oh! Look! Look! Here's my child!"

Jane and I leapt to our feet. Charles was struggling—he must have forgotten to lift the gate before the lock mechanism could shift. Ma was out there like a flash. So excited, it seemed that she would have lifted him over had he taken any longer to enter.

They stood in the driveway, and Ma could not stop touching Charles. Her speech was animated, her hands waving about as she dusted and berated him at the same time: "Look at you! You are as dark as midnight again!" As she spoke Ma rubbed his face and arms. "I told you to stay out of the sun, it is dangerous; you should wear a wide brimmed hat; and apply lotion to your face and arms."

Ma spoke with Charles as if he were a boy who had been found playing in a dusty road under the African sun. All the while Charles stood by making a dry giggly sound. Charles's giggle had a deep tone, unaffected but very brief. Jane and I were waiting for our turn to greet the 'stranger', our big brother.

It had taken three weeks. When he finally arrived we too were happy, but also sad. Charles was streetwise and accustomed to an on-the-edge dangerous township lifestyle. He was a man who should not have consumed alcohol, because when he drank then the gentle, caring and loving manner he exuded was replaced by hooligan behaviour.

He looked good that day, wearing a peak cap, a short sleeved green check shirt, blue jeans and Adidas sports shoes. Charles loved me almost as much as he did Jane. Everyone loved Jane more, including me. We hugged, exchanged pleasantries and, as was his norm, he gave Jane money for us. Looking at me Charles noticed that I had developed a soft hair growth on my cheeks. "Boy, before I go, let me shave that stuff off your face." Much later that night I had my Minora blade encounter, my first shave.

Jane cooked dinner while Ma and Charles spoke in private. That was when Ma informed him about Brenda and Anne. It was almost eight o'clock when we were invited to join the conversation. Charles went outside to smoke and stayed there until the summer sun had set. The miasmic cloud of cigarette smoke did not matter, because Charles too needed comfort more than he needed words.

Jane embraced him like Mammy Cynthia did when we needed comfort more than anything else.

We had the sausages that Jane had bought on her way home that afternoon for dinner. Together with baked potatoes, olive oil and salt, that was the entire meal. Jane had become a vegetarian and only ate what looked like weeds and seeds with, as she would say, "A drizzle of olive oil."

Not much was said over dinner that night, until Jane spoke about how difficult it had been for us to reach Charles. One of the people we spoke with had given him our message, but that person only remembered to do so a week after we sought her assistance. Charles explained that it was holiday time in the building industry and that he had a private bricklaying job to complete before returning to full-time work. We joked and said that Charles was like Pa, always working, but none of us knew where he worked!

Our walks from one public telephone to another, criss-crossing the pot-holed and dangerous gravel streets of the township had paid off. Ma was happy again. Ma was always happy to see Charles. She often told us of her guilt for having agreed that he could live with his father in Worcester. Her stories about Charles living with his father were usually accompanied by the one about having found a telegram in the inside pocket of Pa's jacket.

It was when Ma was helping Pa press a suit. Charles's father had died in a car accident. Pa received the telegram but he chose not to tell Ma. No-one who heard this story understood Pa's motive. The news was kept from Charles too. Pa did not tell Charles about his father's death even when visiting him in prison. It was almost a year after James de la Cruz had died that Ma found the telegram. Charles had not yet been released from prison when Ma informed him of his father's death. This issue was raised over many years whenever Ma and Pa quarrelled.

Meanwhile Jane seemed to settle into the routine of being a university student. I think that she had difficulty accepting being one of many first year students. Perhaps it was a diminishing experience. Jane worked hard, much more so than was required. Although her room in the medical residence was small it was not tiny. Jane settled in easily; on weekends, if she was not preparing for tests, home was only a bus and a short train ride away.

It was to be my second year of junior high school. I was a senior in my own right. The excitement about surfing the warm waters of the South Coast, and participating in competitions was, to me, the greatest advantage of being at school.

Saying goodbye to Ma was difficult. Jane studied at the University of Cape Town, about thirty kilometres away from where we lived. It was close by and also faraway—a different world when compared with the township where Ma lived.

The train ride to school was lonely, long and uneventful. I missed Jane but found solace in the routine of school.

The scroll of honour hung at the back of the hall. Jane's name was at the bottom, printed in gold leaf and in the same font as all the other names. I was proud of Jane, but to let the others know would not have been regarded as 'festive'. While I had no aspiration to equal or better Jane's accomplishments, her scholarly achievements remain legendary.

My relationship with the other boys at school was fine. By then I had spent more time with most of them than I had at home in Cape Town. They played football and other ball sports. I could too, but surfing was my thing.

Most of the free time I had was spent riding my locker-door-on-wheels, which by then I had shaped to look like a surfboard, complete with proper wheels. The days when I travelled to the coast were the best. Once there I surfed from sunrise to sunset. I thought that shark warnings were meant for other people. Surfing and more of that followed by geography, science and the study of two languages was what I existed for. The rest of my school life was mundane and unnecessary; that was what I thought.

Our meals were routine and predictable. Every day at school was characterised by a particular meal. Every one of the pupils had his or her favourite. I enjoyed the stews because they were big servings. The 'mac and cheese' on a Thursday evening was good and so was the fish on Fridays, while the roast chicken with vegetables was traditional Sunday lunch.

"He has the appetite of a horse" also featured frequently in the arguments between Ma and Pa whenever I was home. That comment usually followed Pa's refusal to leave money for food.

I was bored with much of the stuff we were taught at school. Ever since Jane had left, Mammy Cynthia spent an unusual amount of time with me. There was suspicion amongst the other pupils that someone had put her up to it. I also felt it unfair to get more of Mammy's attention than the others did. When I told her she giggled, like only Mammy could. It was a deep, growly giggle through closed lips. Then she pushed me away, held on to my arms and looked up at my face. When I was younger, Mammy Cynthia did the same but held me by my shoulders. When I grew taller, to 1.82 metres, and Mammy was only1.52, it had become nigh impossible for her to reach my shoulders, let alone hold me like she did in the past. The rest of her routine included hugging me tightly until everything felt okay. My Ma in Cape Town had a smile that healed, and Mammy Cynthia had a hug that did much the same.

We spoke for a while: "You know, Mammy, last week we had a class test. Until then I liked economics. The question, for ten marks, was to describe how a postal order is sent and cashed. Remember when Ma sent us money, and I was unable to read properly—you taught me how to cash postal orders?"

Mammy seemed a bit surprised that I remembered. "Yes, I remember that."

"Well, Mammy, Jane told me that you showed her too: just as soon as she was able to read, do you remember?"

"Yes, I can remember. It was when we walked, Jane was with me. It was a Saturday." Mammy became very animated when she remembered that incident.

"We walked the same route as if going for the bus. Yes, it was when Jane had to stand outside with the security man while you and I went in to learn about postal orders. I remember that day very clearly."

Mammy Cynthia loved to reminisce with me, probably because we had history, she and I. However, while some of the experiences were sore, most were very 'festive'.

Mammy giggled after remembering that day. It was not the usual happy and comforting giggle.

Retirement was just a few months away then. Mammy's work defined who she had become. The prospect of not having us pupils in her life and no longer playing the matriarch role for her colleagues weighed heavily on her mind. She reminisced more than usual that day and, like Ma, Mammy Cynthia also began to mutter to herself, but in Zulu: "Anyone can be replaced," I overheard her say that several times.

Everyone was aware that the end of her working life was approaching. Mammy Cynthia began to look like the older woman she had become. The reality of this retirement became even more evident when Sister St Claire asked the rest of the caregivers, cleaning staff and teachers to suggest the format for a retirement function.

Mammy always composed herself after a bout of reminiscences. In this instance she proceeded to explain how I was taught to cash a postal order: "You had to complete the little section with your name and address. The post office clerk then took the paper that you and I signed, checked your birth certificate and my pass book. He gave you the money. Your Ma in Cape Town always paid the commission so that you could get the exact money. Did you learn that in economics too?"

"Yes Mammy. We learned about that not too long ago. The problem was different. I wrote down all the steps we followed to buy and cash a postal order. Ms Najwa Parker, the economics teacher, she said that my explanation was totally wrong. The result was that I got no marks for my answer. No amount of explaining that postal orders were used to transact and pay for all our expenses and debts could make her accept that I knew the procedures. How was it possible that I got no marks? My explanation was exactly how I have bought and cashed postal orders over many years.

"Ms Parker had said that I would get marks only if the written answer was as it appeared in the textbook. In other words, I had to memorise and recite word for word that which is written in the textbook. What was more important: that I understood what a postal order was and how to send money that way; or was it more important for me to recite the ten points as detailed in the textbook?

I think that we waste a lot of time at school. Education would be a lot better if I could learn about our environment and speak in different languages. As for the rest, I can surf and those who want to do other things should be encouraged to do so. How does learning to recite ten points teach me to think?"

Mammy Cynthia listened attentively while I spoke. Moments later, the familiar laughter erupted and echoed down the hallway. She grabbed me close for a bosomy hug: "You are such a child, Sammy my boy, but look how tall you are!"

Mammy resorted to that refrain whenever she disagreed with me, or when she thought that my views were lacking in some way. That laughter and hug were Mammy Cynthia's method of criticism. It was one of the qualities that endeared her to the naughtiest of the naughty people. Her manner always made one think and sometimes it created a feeling of guilt for disappointing her. Thami and I had many such experiences over the years. On a day when I was bad, Mammy said to me: "Don't disappoint yourself Sammy my boy. When you disappoint yourself then I shall be disappointed too." Having to hear Mammy say that was one of the worst things I have had to digest, but it was my own fault.

I received a long letter from Jane. Her letters were filled with information about what it was like to be at university. My seat was the same spot where we always read our letters. Yes, there where Jane had always read Ma's letters aloud to me. I continued to enjoy receiving letters from Ma and from Jane. Ma's letters had become shorter, more about how she felt and less about what was happening in the world. It sounded as if Ma needed something more to do than hear people tell her about their problems. I wished that Ma would continue telling 'our' story, the one about how Jane and I came to be.

Jane's letters were fun and written to stimulate my interest in attending university when I finished school. In one of the letters she included a brochure about the University of Cape Town Surfing Club, but I did not know any of the featured names. Jane's letters always made reference to her headaches.

Mr Thompson had found a way that would get me invited to participate in a big surfing competition. It meant spending more time in the surf. There were several problems that preceded my entering the competition. Firstly, it was to be held at the main beach in Durban and secondly, I was not allowed to surf there. Yet, Mr Thompson told me that he had a plan. The third significant factor was that the competition was held during June. It was significant because that was when all schools in South Africa closed for an average of three weeks—the winter recess. I usually went home during that school holiday. The final and probably most important factor was that the Durban surf challenge formed part of a World Series and only the most competent surfers were invited to participate.

From the beginning of February Mr Thompson and I left school on a Friday afternoon. We'd return on a Monday morning. I did homework on the beach when it was low tide, and in the evenings too. Sleep came easily at Mr Thompson's house. There were always young people milling about, but at night we were exhausted and slept, like security guards!

The police presented a big problem for me. They arrived on the beach when least expected and would summon me, with a loudhailer, to come out of the water. Others were left to ride without interruption. In order to attract less of this embarrassing attention, Mr Thompson decided that I should surf on the rocky side of Scottburgh Beach, the non-reserved part. There, the swells were only good for surfing at high tide. Together Mr Thompson and I developed a series of hand signals. That was how we communicated after he watched every wave I rode. He watched through a pair of weathered binoculars.

"All for a good cause, Champ! Not to worry!" he'd shout, while I made the treacherous return journey across the rocks to where the van was parked.

Early one Saturday morning, at the end of high tide the reserved beach was deserted, save for Mr Thompson and me. The surf breaks and swells were beautiful that morning as I paddled out to practise a particular technique with which Mr Thompson was not happy. As was our norm, Mr Thompson remained on the beach from where he shouted instructions. That morning the police arrived. After making loud, siren-like noises with his loudhailer, Lieutenant Subramani again summoned me to return to the beach. I heard him with the first holler and was making my way back, but the Lieutenant did not stop shouting: "… return to the beach!" Another police vehicle, also with its siren blaring and blue lights flashing, drove onto the beach at high speed. Three similar vehicles sped to arrive on the same beach within minutes of one another. I was trying to paddle back as fast as possible. The tide was retreating and the water's push was not as intense as it had been when the tide grew. Meanwhile two officers, each wearing bullet-proof vests, drew their guns and took up positions about ten metres away, on either side of Lieutenant Subramani. Their car doors were left wide open when they rushed to take up position. The police radio was turned up so loud that I could almost follow the conversations while battling to get out of the surf. Lieutenant Subramani silenced his siren, but he continued to scream into the loudhailer: "Will the surfer wearing grey shorts return to shore! Return to the beach at once!" I was already on the beach, but Lieutenant Subramani continued to call. There were no other surfers or bathers in the water that morning.

As I walked out the two policemen on either side of Lieutenant Subramani had their guns trained on me. I proceeded to unleash my board. While one policeman kept his gun pointed at me, the other secured my hands behind my back with handcuffs. I heard Mr Thompson plead with Lieutenant Subramani. He begged that I be allowed to surf behind the rocks on the far side of the reserved beach, where we usually went. Mr Thompson promised to ensure that in future I would only surf on properly designated beaches and never again on Scottburgh Beach. Amidst Mr Thompson's pleas I was led away to a waiting police van. Once there I heard the Lieutenant assert: "Enough warnings were given. There is no adherence to the law. I have no alternative but to place the suspect under arrest."

Mr Thompson had my surfboard under his arm by then, but continued to plead with the Lieutenant. I sat dripping sea water on the floor, inside the wire mesh section of that police van. By then I had been involved with the police so many times that being placed under arrest was not traumatic. All I asked was that Mr Thompson would not inform Ma of my arrest. Ma had heard enough bad news.

Mr Thompson interjected by raising his free hand in a gesture for me to be quiet while he made a final attempt with Lieutenant Subramani: "Please Lieutenant, this boy is only fifteen years old, man. I'm teaching him to surf. He has a talent. The bloke comes from Cape Town and is a boarder at our school. He can surf, I promise you. When the tide comes in, then we'll move to the rocky beach."

By then the number of people on the beach had increased and included six policemen who arrived at high speed. Every one of the policemen, apart from Lieutenant Subramani, had his firearm drawn.

"Please Lieutenant, let him go? You won't be sorry. This boy is a winner. I give you my assurance that we will not use this beach again. Please Lieutenant?"

Mr Thompson was relentless in his attempts to convince Lieutenant Subramani that I should not be arrested.

"Look Mister, y'all, teachers, have a job! This here's my job! I don't stand in your way when you, when you do your job! Why you obstructing me and all?"

By then Lieutenant Subramani had his head close to Mr Thompson's chest while screaming in supposed anger.

"You know that obstructing an officer during the execution of his duty is a crime! I can arrest you! Please man, please, just go, go! I'm sure you have too much of plenty to do. So, let me take this man to the station and charge him for the violation one time."

An uncertainty began to dawn after hearing the Lieutenant speak like that. As the salt water dried my hair and skin felt sticky. I was locked into a cage attached to the police van. Mr Thompson had exhausted every possible plea with Lieutenant Subramani. He turned to me and said: "Don't worry, Champ; I'm not going to leave you." Lieutenant Subramani got into the passenger side of the arresting van and gave instructions to the driver. We drove to the charge office. It was very embarrassing to be held up in the back of a police van in full view of all the town-folk that Saturday morning. We raced to the charge office with sirens blaring and blue lights flashing. With my hands fastened behind my back I could hold onto the wire mesh for stability when the van moved, all the while watching to see if my coach was following.

Once in the charge office Mr Thompson asked to see the Station Commander. It was Captain van Deventer: Head of the Scottburgh Police Station. He had an imposing presence; I remembered from the time when the same police captain warned me against using that beach. Captain van Deventer had a reputation for being intolerant with people who continually disobeyed the law.

After the matter had been resolved Mr Thompson gave me a blow by blow account of his meeting with Captain van Deventer: "You know Champ," he began, "I sat out in the corridor for about thirty minutes before he would see me. He remembered me and extended his ample hand to greet.

"Without offering me a seat Captain van Deventer began speaking in that guttural tone. You know how he emphasises the letter 'r', as in: *'You see what happens when you insist on brreaking the law? You know that the main beach herre in Scottburrgh is not to be used by those people. Why do you keep brringing that man herre when you know that it is against the law for him to play with a surrfboard on Scottburrgh Beach? If you move furtherr down the coast therre is a perrfect area for them to play. That main beach is reserved and I do not carre what you say, because I cannot allow even one Indian to be therre. You know what they is like, if you allow one today, then tomorrow all of them will arrive. They will brring big pots of curry and swim in theirr saris. Then, Misterr, where arre we going to swim? As Station Commanderr, I have a responsibility. My responsibility is to look afterr the community herre in Scottburrgh. This is my prrecinct and I cannot neglect my responsibilities. I cannot fail the community that we is herre to serrve.*

"No, Misterr, I must teach this man a lesson. We will keep him forr the weekend and you can have him back on Monday morrning. Next time I shall instruct my men to lay charrges.

"Let this also be a warrning to you, because I know that you arre the instigatorr. I know yourr type. You play with these people, but watch out, therre will come a day, when you least expect it, when he will turn on you. Anyway, if this happens again, Misterr, then I shall instruct Subramani to arrest you too.

"You have to underrstand that not even Subramani, no matterr how good a man he is; and he is a good Indian, don't get me wrong; but no matterr how good a Indian he is, not even he is allowed to swim on that beach. So, how the devil then can I allow yourr Indian to swim therre, while my men, who are also Indians and Zulus too, arre not allowed?"'

"After this monologue Captain van Deventer stood up and answered his ringing telephone: "Van Deventer!" he barked into the mouthpiece while extending his arm and a giant hand, for the second time. Again my hand was dwarfed by his.

"A uniformed woman with fat ankles, very red glossy lips and pink cheeks entered the office to usher me back to the main charge office desk.

"Once there I spoke to the first officer who seemed likely to listen: 'Please help me, officer?' I pleaded, 'I cannot leave this child here to share a cell with thieves and other criminals. Please, can you arrest me too, so that I can be with him?

"The officer doing desk duty gestured for me to wait. He went to the back to consult colleagues. Their conversations were peppered with raucous laughter. People passing in the street turned to look, probably wondering why the police were so jovial.

"Lieutenant Subramani emerged from the noisy room about twenty minutes later. As you know, he is a tiny slim man with salt and pepper hair neatly parted on the left side of his head. I noticed his trademark extra-large moustache. Such a moustache can affect your breathing. Well, Lieutenant Subramani responded to my request after stepping onto a platform on the office side of the counter.

Together with artificially acquired height and speaking fast in a broad Indian accent, he said: 'You have one unreasonable request, so you will excuse our laughter. In fact, I find the request ridiculous, but the men back there in the office, they find it extremely funny.' He suppressed a barely noticeable wry smile beneath his ample moustache and then continued: 'Let me tell you one thing, err… Mister. No, let me explain first; and then, let me tell you a few things. Even if I arrest you the cell where you will be kept is at the Bisset Street Station in Umkomaas. You see, we don't have facilities to keep you people here, because this is not a multi-racial station, and… so in any case, you cannot stay in the same cell and all. We cannot keep you together with those people, it is against the law and very dangerous. It will cause too much of trouble. Need I say more?'

"I continued to plead: 'I understand Lieutenant, but please, Sir, this child could be your own son.'"

"He scowled at me: Yes, but I would not allow my son to break the law, repeatedly; do you follow? This boy deserves what he gets.'

"I didn't give up: 'Okay then, Lieutenant, but please can I see the boy to explain what is going to happen?' I asked."

"Once the person is booked then you cannot speak with him. Sorry. Come here on Monday morning and we will release the offender from about 7:00am, after the day shift get their standing orders and all."

"This is a very young boy, Lieutenant. Please can you ensure that he is not exposed to rough elements? His family is in Cape Town and he has no one here."

"I hear you and I have heard you before, Mister, but here we treat all offenders alike. We ensure the safety of all the men and I shall do my best to ensure that there is no monkey business in the cells. But, you should know better than to get this man in trouble. You should know better, I tell you now. You owe him, and before you go Mister, listen, we do not allow meals to be brought here for awaiting trial offenders, because that leads to fighting and this is not a 'otel. I hope I'm clear?"

"That was how it ended, Champ. I tried and failed."

I gathered that a dejected Mr Thompson then went home to consult his family. They called a lawyer friend, but, after going through all the possibilities, the result remained the same. I had to stay in the cells until the Monday morning. In a last act of what must have been desperation Mr Thompson called on Sister St Claire for help. On hearing the news she was distraught and immediately called Station Commander van Deventer, but also to no avail.

I spent almost the entire day in the cell, waiting for a policeman to open the grid gate and tell me that there had been a big misunderstanding. That was not to happen. The cell felt sticky and it became hotter as the afternoon grew toward evening. There was only one other person in the cell and he desperately needed a shower. That man had a rotten smell and his bare feet were crusty, cracked and very dirty. My cellmate did not say even one word. He just sat there, on his haunches, leaning up against the wall. I did the same, against the opposite wall. When I told him what my name was he cracked the tiniest mouth movement, followed by a slow continuous nod. Eventually he stood up, stretched and took up position on the lower of a double bunk bed that stood in one corner of the four by three metre cell.

During the course of that evening a policeman unlocked the steel gate on three occasions. Every time another man in handcuffs entered. Once the cuffs were removed, the new arrival spent the first few minutes rubbing his wrists. I had done the same. Strini was the last man in. By then we had not introduced ourselves. Strini Naidoo was neatly dressed, but his belt, laces and watch had been taken at 'check-in'. Only one of his hands was free, the other kept his pants from dropping. He was a skinny man and had a red thread tied around his right wrist—a kalava, he would later explain, along with: "I caught my 'cherry' with a woman, what you think of that? So I had to give her one quick hiding man, and look where she got me now ..." I shrugged my shoulders.

We were five by the time a container, the size of a big round cake tin, was positioned on a small table outside the cell bars. Speaking first in Zulu and then in English, the policeman summoned us to eat. I measured the cell again while three of the men stuck their arms through the grid to eat maize meal that they dunked in a brown sauce. The sauce was in a separate container, also inside the cake tin. The three men ate from the same dish.

It must have been about midnight when I realised that Mr Thompson was not going to get me released from police custody. None of the men wore a watch. I was not sure of the time, other than that it felt late.

My stomach was grumbling. The familiar hunger pangs were back. I did not eat, hoping instead that the policemen would set me free. The others, those who ate, were not going anywhere. They needed food more than me. Perhaps I was just not hungry when the food arrived ... nervous too, maybe. Not knowing how long I was going to stay in those cells felt very scary. I can't remember much of that first night, other than that it was late; that I was tired; and hungry. There were no leftovers in the cake tin. The hunger pangs were biting worse than before, but there was nothing for me to eat. Half of the dish, the empty cake tin, was by then crawling with the biggest, shiny, hard-shelled cockroaches. Every cockroach was at least the size of my little finger.

The last men to arrive were also positioned on their haunches, leaning up against the wall; one stared at the floor all the time; another looked up at the ceiling, just like Ma did while telling the story about Pa.

The smelly man continued to lie curled up in a foetal position on the bottom bunk bed. I noticed that there was a crust of blood caked on the side of his pants. The blood could not have been his because he had no visible wound. I remember thinking that it would be a matter of time, that evening, before his clothes became a meal for hungry roaches. Strini, the man who had arrived last, dangled his lace-less white shoes from the top bunk bed as he lay there.

Five of us were to share two single beds that were stacked one above the other. Only one toilet bucket was provided. It had no lid and stood in the corner, close to the cake tin. I spent the best part of that night trying to keep the cockroaches away from the bucket. Eventually their determination to migrate from the empty cake-tin to the bucket was successful. The lights were never turned off and the single dirty window up against the ceiling faced what seemed like another room. When the four men were asleep I too sat down, folded my hands under my ear and promptly dozed off on the cool sticky cement floor. I was not wearing shoes then, just my branded Student Prince grey school shorts and a white T-shirt.

In the morning the four with whom I shared a cell seemed much the worse for wear. Every one nursed scars, bumps and scratches. My hunger seemed to have gone. That much I expected, because of previous experience. If you sleep when hungry and wake up, then for the first number of hours the hunger pangs are gone; that's how it is.

None of us spoke. Strini sat on the top bed with his lace-less shoes hanging down while he leaned into his lap. Another man, one who had not said a word, sat there, shook his head and then cried softly for about ten minutes. He appeared calm after the bout of crying. And then, without warning, he began to shake his head followed by an almost uncontrolled involuntary sob. That man must have been between thirty five and forty years old. He was clearly the oldest. Later that Sunday morning the crying man had the most to say.

A long time ago I learned, mainly from talking to fellow players, after a football match in Cape Town that people like us, who were detained, always believed in our innocence. The football mates would laugh and then tell how people sat in police cells, like us, would stew over what had happened to get them there. They would invariably find themselves innocent. For that reason I did not ask why 'Scaly Feet', with the blood caked clothing was there. "Wait long enough and they'll tell" had been the advice given during the after-match discussion back home.

Meanwhile, the foul smell in that police cell had disappeared, or so I thought. It was probably because by Sunday morning we had become accustomed to the stench. The crying man sat with his bum flat on the cement, and his legs were drawn up almost to the same height as his shoulders. He was just a little bundle of a man. With arms resting on his knees he sat, nodding as if in agreement with something. All of a sudden he lifted his head and glared ferociously at me. He seemed very angry and looked at me as though no-one else existed, just he and I. My seat was the floor across from that angry man. He scrunched up his face. At first I thought that this was due to a very unpleasant whiff from the bucket latrine. But then he asked: "Why are your arms and legs so hairy?" I looked him in the eye and shrugged my shoulders. "Where do you come from?" was his next question.

"Cape Town."

"Nah! Originally?"

"Hey, he told you where he comes from."

Until then I had not known that 'Scurvy Feet' could speak. The two went off at each other in Zulu: "You! You mind your own business!" said the angry man.

165

With that 'Scurvy Feet' got up from his bed. They squared off right there, in the police cell.

"I want to know because he does not look like a man who comes from Cape Town, he's a spy and who are you to tell me?"

The two were posturing with an exchange of swear words. They threatened each other. The older man said: "I am older than you, and you have to respect me."

By then Strini had climbed down from his top bunk. He was standing by, holding up his pants, and ready to referee the imminent fight. I do not know whether Strini understood when people spoke in Zulu. It seemed as if he only spoke English. Meanwhile, the man who was not involved in the pending skirmish was preparing to be out of harm's way should a fight break out.

As the posturing continued Strini paced up, down and then around in our little cell.

'Scurvy Feet' was not done: "You can't tell what people in Cape Town should look like, who are you and when were you there?"

I could see that the two were venting other frustrations on each other. It was my turn to intervene, I just knew. "Gents, listen to me! There's no need to fight. I am hairy like this and I don't know why; maybe it is because my father is hairy; but why do you two men want to fight over it? No man, let's be all right?"

The older man had the last word—

My wish was that Mr Thompson would arrive so that I could leave that place. The issues that swept through my mind concerned Ma, surfing, homework, school and when I would be released.

The men spoke with one another for the rest of that Sunday. Strini was like the chairman, facilitating the various discussions. I noticed that the older man and the younger one were quite chatty. The two who had nearly fought kept their distance. Others spent the day smoking and daydreaming, probably about their respective innocence.

The older man, Khoza, was his name. He was very interested in the prison gangs of the Cape. Fortunately, I had listened when the topic was discussed after football matches. Those who had been to prison enjoyed talking about their experiences. It gave them status in the ghetto. We were football friends. The apparent knowledge I had of prison gangs and the way they operated was a great hit and seemed to earn me a lot of respect from Khoza. I always knew that prison logic was very different from the way in which other people reasoned. It was obviously not Khoza's first skirmish with the law. I was not going to ask, but he certainly pretended to be an old hand.

On Sunday night Khoza slept on the top bunk. He tried to depose 'Scurvy Feet' from the bottom bed, but was unsuccessful. Moodley was removed without any fuss. Khoza bullied him off the top bunk, like a big dog does to a little one. Moodley came to sit next to me and that was where we slept.

Early on Monday morning the remand vehicle reversed up against the back entrance to the police cells. No-one had told me why the noisy trucks were there.

A man who looked like the driver, clad in khaki, called out names that he read from a list. A policeman handcuffed each person before directing him to sit in the back of a big Ford Bedford truck, cream in colour. People in other cells were called first and then it was our turn. When I queried what was going on, Moodley said: "This lot, 'the alleged' offenders, are being transported to the Magistrates Court in Airth Street and all." The clanging metal on metal sounds ended when the trucks departed. Moodley was also taken away, but my name had not been called. The cell was empty, leaving just the cockroaches, the overused latrine bucket and me. I yelled out when a policeman passed in the passage: "… and what about me?"

"Your name is?" he barked in reply.

"Samuel Arthur Levy."

The policeman lifted his schedule to check.

"Levy! What-kine of Indian name is Levy; you come from Verulam?"

"I am not Indian, Constable." The term 'Constable' was written on his epaulets.

"Where you come from if you not Indian? You look like someone who comes from the north; or *you're* just a light-skin Chatsworth Bobby and all?"

Ma would have been disappointed had I succumbed to the mongrel label. Instead, my reply, following a slight pause, was: "I come from Cape Town, Constable."

"I see. You are the surfer on a reserved beach; here's your name."

The constable pointed to the second page of a schedule, which was attached to the clipboard he held, a paper that he must have thought I could see from behind the bars.

After unlocking me he pointed to the charge office: "Go man! Go to the front desk; go quickly! Don't keep that boss who is there waiting for you."

Mr Thompson was in the charge office. We hugged for the first time.

Lieutenant Subramani had just come on duty that morning. He administered a warning to both Mr Thompson and me as if he had special powers to do so: "If you are ever again found in violation of the beach regulations, then I shall ensure that we chuck you with the book and all. Next time…" He paused, looked down at a sheet of paper, as if to consult a script. "Next time, Samuel A. Levy, you will also go to court. Then you will be guaranteed a stint in the reformatory. Go man, go, and let this be a warning to you; and to you, Mister, this fine you've paid is just the beginning."

Mr Thompson was rushing so that I did not miss too much schoolwork. He must have been concerned about being late for work too. We moved fast on that winding R612 road from Scottburgh, travelling inland. Mr Thompson was a safe driver and I was relaxed.

I had many stories to tell and Mr Thompson did too: about his meeting with Captain van Deventer, the call to Sister St Claire and wrestles with lawyers. "But before you tell yours Champ, let me apologise for bringing this trouble to

167

you. We should have waited another hour and surfed behind the rocks; then the trouble we saw would have been avoided."

"Don't worry Mr Thompson. This was an interesting experience. Not one that I'd want to repeat, but interesting nonetheless. When is our next trip to the beach? I want to correct that error in my technique."

"We'll be back next week, Champ. We've got to catch up if you're going to be ready for North Beach. You have to do all those stretches I taught you, every day, you hear?"

"Yes, I shall do my stretches every day, Sir."

Mr Thompson parked the van in its usual spot and instructed me to shower before joining the class. Sister St Claire was there, waiting; she did not look pleased when Mr Thompson entered her office.

Afterwards it was my turn. Sister St Claire insisted that I stop surfing and use the time to concentrate on doing schoolwork. Ma was informed of what had happened.

Late that afternoon, Jane and Ma called Mammy Cynthia on the pay telephone. They spoke for a long time before I had a turn. Sister St Claire had told my Ma that I was more interested in being a good surfer than doing well at school, and that she had recommended to Mr Thompson that the surfing stop, or be limited to school holidays.

It had not taken much persuading, by Jane, for Ma to agree that I should continue surfing. I was later informed that Jane and Ma had held an extensive discussion about my surfing. Jane had argued that withdrawing my surfing privilege amounted to punishment, and that I did not deserve to be punished for entering a reserved beach. Of course, that statement found resonance with Ma who, on hearing that reasoning, immediately flicked into being her old feisty self, albeit briefly.

Jane wrote to me that evening and described how Ma had nodded in agreement when she explained: "… fighting injustice and unfairness is something that all of us should do; often the reward for resisting injustice is painful; but it is an honourable pain to bear." Jane said that it seemed as if her explanation had made Ma's heart sing and that for a brief moment the Ma whom we had known all our lives returned. Immediately, according to what Jane had said, Ma sat and wrote another respectful letter to Sister St Claire. I never got to read that letter. Ma must have written, in that upright lettering, which was her trademark handwriting, and outlined her views. She clarified by stating reasons and then concluded with granting Mr Thompson permission to continue his role as my surfing coach. After writing Ma must have said to Jane: "There, read my letter and see how you can catch more bees with honey than with vinegar." Ma always passed that refrain as a lesson in diplomacy.

News of the arrest had spread throughout the school. I did not disclose anything, but that didn't stop word from going around. My peers were all sneering, some made scathing comments. The older boys passed remarks, such as: "What's wrong with you, Levy?" and "You think yourself one of them now that you also ride a board. Let this be a lesson to you."

It was disappointing hearing those remarks, particularly given that the boys were like my 'brothers'—they were the people to whom I was closest. I always supported them, but given the slightest opportunity they tried to pull me down. There were three good friends during my school years: Thami, Mammy Cynthia's grandson, and two older boys who had been in Jane's year. By then the older boys had left and my only real friend was Thami—who lived and worked far from my school. I listened to all their negative comments and realised that the boys at school were just other people. No brotherhood existed between us. We were acquaintances by circumstance; that was all. So, what they said did not matter, that was my resolve. My decision that day was not to pursue relationships with any of them after school.

Jane's letter ended with her informing me of the various medical tests which she was to undergo. They would determine why her head was always aching.

When I got back to my room, after speaking with Jane and Ma on the telephone, Mammy Cynthia was there, sitting on my bed. As I entered the room through the little sliding door she stood up and hugged me as always when I needed to be healed. "You will always be my boy, Sammy. Let them say what they like, because sticks and stones can break your bones, but names can never decide who you are."

I explained my version of what had happened. Mammy Cynthia listened attentively, she always did. "All is okay, Sammy-my-boy, all is okay. You are a big boy now." Then, as if to reassure herself, Mammy repeated in a softer voice while she hugged me for a second time: "My wonderful Thami and my wonderful Sammy are big boys now. One of these days they will be men."

After Mammy left, Mr Thompson stopped by. He was en route to coach the football team. We spoke briefly about the coming weekend. For the rest of that evening I completed overdue homework that by then was very late. New homework had been added to the outstanding work. Yet, before bedtime I completed my weekly letter to Ma:

Monday, 26 April 1976

Dear Ma

... and then I was in the back of the van. It was as if the policemen drive badly on purpose, so that whoever sat at the back was flung around. It was unpleasant; the entire experience was unpleasant. The people who were held together with me were no different to those at home. These spoke English and Zulu, but they say and are interested in the same things as those at home. People are the same, it's like that.

Mr Thompson visited me this afternoon (after you and I spoke on the phone). He and I decided to no longer use the main beach, the surf beach. Instead we'd go beyond the rocks. I shall surf there. Don't worry Ma, it is okay, Mr Thompson will stand on the bigger rocks and watch over me. I shall never go out there and be completely alone, so all will be fine. Don't worry.

Jane's letter arrived this afternoon and I was very happy to read that she is doing well, but I agree, she must see the doctor about those headaches. The school misses her very much, but I miss her more. Not a day goes by without at least ten people asking me whether Jane is fine. It is very strange being here without her, but maybe this too shall pass.

The schoolwork is boring. I study in order to pass and not because of an interest in the subjects. The languages, science, geography and biology are the subjects that I enjoy. It makes studying exciting and I like the way Mr Hector teaches geography.

Economics is an important subject too, so I try and concentrate when I am in that class. I do not understand why teachers insist that we learn everything as if it is a long poem that needs recitation. It makes the subject boring. I am not interested in Mathematics.

Frequently I wonder how the passing of Anne and Brenda affects you, Ma. Forgive me for raising it again, but this repeats in my head. It is not possible for me to feel your pain, but Jane and I, we will continue to try and understand. Jane will make you very proud and maybe I shall too.

We did not have a chance to talk more about the story of how Jane and I came to be. You were going to write again, but then we wrote the Head Girl's Report and afterwards it was time to come home.

Will you write when you get a chance, Ma?

Someday you have to come and watch me surf, please?

I love you

Sam

Commentary

Almost thirty years later, when living in another province of South Africa, I took my car for its routine check. A courtesy multi-passenger vehicle was waiting to take other clients and me to our respective offices and homes. When we were all settled and ready to leave there was a call for me to collect a bottle of wine which I had left in my car. It had been a gift that had wedged beneath the front seat and I had not seen it when clearing the vehicle of personal belongings.

It was early morning, like the day when I had been arrested and held for the weekend.

But there I was, seated in a luxurious multi-passenger courtesy vehicle with an expensive bottle of Stellenbosch-produced wine on my lap. The other passengers were busying themselves with things that are usual for the circumstance. During a brief lull and while waiting for a green traffic light one of the 'client'-passengers commented on my wine. That comment was probably spurred by my clutching the bottle with both hands. "If you forget the wine it will be safe with me, don't worry, I am a whisky man." All of us laughed heartily, including the driver. For me it was too early to try my hand at being witty, so I just smiled.

When the others were dropped off at their workplaces the only two remaining passengers were the self-proclaimed whisky man, the driver and me.

"What business you're in?" asked Whisky Man.

"I am a labour lawyer."

He paused for a while, a long while, and then said: "Oh! Good! I want to send a man to you."

"Thank you, I need the business."

"He is having too much of trouble, that man, a police station commander. He can call you?"

"Yes, he can call me, here's my card." I handed the card to Whisky Man. Without looking at it he said: "I'm retired now and that man, he took over from me. Before, I was his commander. I'll tell him to give you a call when he feels better because he's got too much of pain and all, that man. I'll tell him of this conversation, to remind you. My name is Subramani."

"I know your name, Sir. My name is Sam Levy."

We did not speak again and I never heard from the station commander who was having 'too much of trouble'. I read about him in the newspaper—seems like the matter did not end well.

Chapter Twelve

Christmas in Mpophomeni

Mammy Cynthia had been asked to work for an extra year. I was happy and so were many others, but we did not know whether the decision was at Mammy's request or whether the school authority had decided. Mammy Cynthia was an institution at St Mary's, 'the faraway school'. It was hard to imagine being there without her. Every pupil who needed an older person, one whom they could trust, found in Mammy Cynthia a preparedness to listen. It was because Mammy instinctively became part of the solution they sought. The time of day or night never mattered, and whatever was said to Mammy in confidence was never disclosed.

Later it became clear that the school governing body had requested an extension of Mammy's employment contract. It was not often that the governing body enjoyed popular support. Cynics usually groaned about the inevitability of decisions taken, or not taken.

Fortunately, these vocal naysayers did not get any notice or commendation when the extension decision was communicated. Good too because it would have spurred more groans. According to the cynics everything at the school was always wrong. Why they did not move to another place of learning was one of the questions I posed to myself. Every community has to have its noisemakers, this is normal and it helps create balance.

The year progressed well. I continued to exchange letters with Ma and Jane. Their letters were a commentary which provided me with insight. Through those letters I kept abreast with what was happening in Cape Town.

Jane had ongoing tests to determine the cause of her chronic headaches. She wrote that the cause of her pain had not yet been determined. Jane was using medicine that helped her to concentrate on academic work, rather than suffer the debilitating effect of chronic head pain.

As Jane worked harder she achieved more. It was unusual to find a medical student in the community where Ma lived, and to find a woman who studied medicine was even rarer.

Ma reacted to my request, which was for her to continue with the story about how Jane and I came to be. Her response was predictable. Ma preferred to talk with me: 'When we have another face to face opportunity'. That day seemed a long way off; longer, given that it was not clear when my next trip to the Cape would be.

By then Ma was not earning a regular salary. Her financial resources to support Jane and me had dwindled substantially. Nothing was said, but I sensed that there was not enough money to keep me at a private school. Alternatives included finding a part-time job. By so doing I would be able to pay my own school fees. I could also transfer to a government school in Cape Town, but Ma did not want me to consider leaving school because of her inability to pay the fees. Finding work during my free time would signal the end of my surfing ambitions. Surfing is a sport that is completely reliant on how much practising is done. Not like a bicycle, where years later you can get on and ride as if there has been no break.

The sacrifices and lengths to which Ma went to so that I could live and learn at a private school had become very clear.

On the following Friday, Mr Thompson and I drove toward the coast. I shared suspicions about my family's dire financial situation with him: "You know, Coach, there is little reason why I cannot attend a school that is closer to my home. Imagine if I could get up in the morning, pack lunch and walk to school. In the afternoons I could do some chores and then homework. Weekends could be spent at Surfers Corner in Muizenberg. Imagine, I'd be there so often, they'd name a wave in my honour—a reserved wave! A policeman wearing a Subramani moustache will throw me off the beach there too, but I can live with that. Maybe, on occasion there'll be opportunities to surf Long Beach, Scarborough and off the Atlantic Seaboard. Surely Lieutenant Subramani and Captain van Deventer cannot reach that far? I did not share with you, but my last outing at Surfers Corner saw the police drop by. They instructed me to leave. At first I thought it was the end of me, but I've become accustomed to being chased, so it matters less every time. What do you think of my plan to go back home, Coach?"

Mr Thompson seemed to drive slower after hearing my views. He turned down the new reggae sounds that we listen to and mulled over what I had said. It took a good while before he replied: "Look Champ, you are near the top of your game. It would be wrong to change now. We have to raise the money, not only to assist your mother with school fees, but also so that you can show them how real surfing is done. I've never known someone to ride like you. Don't waste the opportunity, Champ. I want you to be in the final line-up and win; you can. You have to believe that you can." By then Mr Thompson had switched the *Wonder Dream Concert* recording off. He grabbed my right upper arm with his left hand and looked at me briefly. I had not seen my coach look like that in the past. There was a tremble in his grip and a tear on his cheek. "You can win; show them how to surf and set the bar, Champ!

"You know, the fees you pay to participate are high; in addition, you have to qualify before being invited; and you will only qualify through participating in recognised competitions." My coach paused for a moment: "Tell you what,

Champ; let me pay your fees for the rest of this year. I shall make an arrangement with the school to deduct it from my salary. No-one need know. The school will send your father the account and it will reflect that the fees have been paid—how's that?"

"Wow! You'll do that for me, Sir? Thank you Mr Thompson, thank you very much!"

My emotions were stirred by his unexpected generosity. I restrained myself. During quiet moments I often thought about helping people who did not have enough money. Never did I think that someone who had enough, like Mr Thompson, would want to help me.

"You can regard the payment as a loan, Coach; one that I shall settle in time, do we have a deal?"

"Deal!"

We shook hands while Mr Thompson was driving. It was the last time that we discussed money. Before accelerating Mr Thompson changed the eight track tape and turned the volume up to give Procol Harem a chance to do 'A Whiter Shade of Pale'. It was not in reference to me!

I became more focused and determined to improve my technique, but Mr Thompson was never satisfied, he always demanded more. Even when I felt that there was no more room for improvement, he would be on his rock perch barking about a manoeuvre that was too short, too slow, too fast, or he'd strike his hand downward and shout: "Champ!" Mr Thompson would then turn and pretend to walk away before hollering some more "You, you look like a *[expletive deliberately deleted]* ballerina!"

It was definite; Mr Thompson did not like ballerinas!

Lieutenant Subramani and the rest of the gang from Scottburgh Police Station were like groupies. They were frequently spotted on the roadside at the rocky beach, checking through a shared pair of binoculars to ensure that all beachgoers kept to their demarcated zones. It mattered not that all of us shared the same body of water. I would see when the police arrived, but Mr Thompson was not bothered; his back was always turned toward them anyway. Not only was his back to the road, but he had to be vigilant out there on the sharp slippery rocks from where he coached me, without a loudhailer.

It was during such a coaching session, and when the police were looking on, that I made a judgment error; one that would plague me for the rest of my life. I am unable to explain exactly what happened; perhaps because it happened so fast.

That morning began like most mornings. First, Mr Thompson had me doing stretch exercises in the car park. Once I was warmed up, we crossed the rocky outcrop. I entered the surf and paddled out, way out, to a spot that was best suited for reading the swell sequence. I did not see anything unusual and when the opportunity came my first ride of the day started right there at the wave-sequence-reading spot. The size and speed of the waves were somewhat unusual. It had something to do with the prevailing full-moon being in alignment with the sun. Apparently the earth rotates in the same direction as the moon's orbit and when the sun aligns then a spring tide results in higher high and lower low tides some days later. It has to do with gravitational pull influenced by the sun, the earth and the moon.

I was up and away when some of the wave's energy transferred to my board on that day. The board hissed like an angry snake. Soon the water barrelled and I was inside a water tube. It was a long, dark blue-green tube. As the wave continued to curl I could see the light at the far end moving further away. The sound of Mr Thompson's referee whistle, which he used to warn of danger, was faint. By then the board was singing its familiar tune, and being tubed added an echo to that sound. The rustling water was loud, louder than usual given the enclosure formed by rolling water. In addition I heard the sound of a wave crash up onto, or against, rocks. That was when reality dawned.

Immediately I turned my board to break out. The rest of the wave crashed. The cymbal sound that precedes sea foam was there, in my ears. I was riding closer to the board's nose than was my norm. It is only possible to achieve that when there is congruence between body weight, the board, and the energy transfer from an unfolding wave. Of course, surfers don't really think of it like that while riding. It was a perfect ride, but as I began to hold back in the tail of the board, the wall of water ahead of me disappeared. That was when it happened. One of my three skegs (fins) struck something; it must have been the top of a rock. I was flung off.

"Champ! Sam-my! Sam!" called a distant voice. That was all, nothing more.

I awoke in the George Stegmann Hospital. My face felt swollen, my mouth numb and stuffed with wadding (cotton wool). 'Sister E. de Wet', I read her name tag. She was the nurse who cared for me in the Intensive Care section of that hospital. Sister de Wet first saw me in the surgical theatre during the emergency operation. She and my coach were together at the bedside when I regained consciousness. Mr Thompson checked if I could hear before he explained: "It was an unusual wave, Champ. It drew water from the beach area to feed the rolling swell. I saw it shaping. You rode with abandon. No amount of my shouting mattered because you were unable to hear above the water's noise. I gave up calling your name and used my whistle when you entered the barrel. You were tubed for a while. I panicked. From where I stood what happened was expected. You emerged riding the nose of the board and then moved back to the tail. Within seconds you lay sprawled across a sharp-edged rock. Other waves were approaching. There was not much time, but I got there, picked you up and rushed to the van. Damn! Sixty five kilograms is heavy, especially when running across sharp slippery rocks! The police were there too, watching but they did nothing. I reclined the front seat and strapped you in before heading to the hospital. You had a bad mouth bleed. Your ears were bleeding too. I stopped to turn you on your side and then drove the van as fast as it would go. I think that the police must have called the hospital ahead of my arrival, because when I got there they had a stretcher ready. They wheeled you to the non-reserved section of the hospital and that was when the work began. Later a doctor emerged to inform me that they had to remove eight broken teeth from your top jaw. There were other injuries too. The entire procedure took four hours. I sat there all the while, waiting—in the reserved section of the hospital."

My coach's voice was faint and I could not hear or understand everything that he was explaining. The bandages were wrapped over my ears and around my head. Perhaps I lost consciousness intermittently while he was talking.

I remembered that Mr Thompson was preparing me to participate in the big competition on Durban Beach. It was nearly time for the mid-year vacation. Mr Thompson had developed an elaborate plan to ensure that I would compete. The plan involved a name change. I was to participate using a pseudonym. Everything was in place, but the accident brought the plans to a halt.

Sister de Wet was constantly there. This professional nurse reassured me that all would be fine. She was to care for me during the evenings and through the night until I was ready for high care, or a general ward.

Two days later, Mammy Cynthia and Thami arrived at the hospital. The doctors had performed extensive dental surgery and their report stated that my teeth would never be the same again. The good news was that I would not be without teeth for long! I was discharged on the third day. Mammy and Thami had stayed overnight, sitting in the non-reserved waiting room on that Saturday. I was discharged on the Sunday afternoon. Mr Thompson offered to drive us to Mammy Cynthia's house in Mpophomeni, a journey of over two hundred kilometres.

To talk was difficult; and I was only able to eat soft food. Sister de Wet recommended a tube be used through which I could suck finely mashed food. Khokho and Ma Khumalo cooked marrows, pumpkins, carrots, potatoes and spinach. They also cooked chicken soup which I had to suck up through a tube. I had soup at every mealtime. Khokho let me in on the reason why I had to drink so much chicken soup. She had worked for a family of Jews for many years. According to Khokho, whenever a family member was ill or feeling poorly, chicken soup was prepared and served. 'Jewish penicillin', that's what they called it. The vegetables were boiled and mashed and when a few spices had been added the meal became tasty. This routine, together with the 'Jewish penicillin', continued for seven days. Thereafter I was able to eat soft solid foods. Since then chicken soup is my least favourite. Perhaps I have become allergic to 'Jewish penicillin'.

Khokho spent every waking moment by my bedside. She read and told me traditional Zulu stories. I loved the way Khokho spoke. She would change her voice to mimic the characters in the story. The tales Khokho read were very entertaining, but those that she told from memory were the best. Khokho was fluent in English, as she was in Zulu and several other very different African languages. My right hand had also been injured and was wrapped in heavy bandages. Khokho was very concerned about the recovery of my hand, more so than she was about my mouth. "We eat too much as it is, so you can do without your teeth, but you cannot clap hands with only one hand; and you cannot live without clapping hands for other people, Sammy."

Mammy Cynthia's house was small but it was always tidy. It was fun to be there. The vegetable garden was well maintained and produced seasonal crops that fed the family and some of the neighbours. Marigolds were the only flowers that grew in Mammy Cynthia's garden. Mammy insisted that the house had to have a bed of flowers. Thami's opinion was that marigolds were a waste of space: "They stink, those flowers stink, Gogo," he'd say to Mammy when she scolded him about not caring for the flowers. "Marigolds are like weeds. They grow and serve no purpose—not even the bees here in Mpophomeni want to sit on them!" Mammy would giggle with her mouth closed and hug Thami like she did me and any other person whom there was a disagreement with. The stinky flowers added to welcome the flare of friendliness at Mammy's home. It was a happy place to be. Jane and I shaped much of how we would live our lives from the experiences we had in Mammy Cynthia's home.

Over the years all the neighbours had become our friends too. Playing in those streets was like being at a carnival for children. Whenever we visited Mammy's home it felt as if we belonged. My different appearance mattered less over time. The children got to know me, and I became a familiar presence.

On a Friday evening the sprawling township became a carnival for adults.

During weekdays the younger men and women worked. Most had jobs with the biggest employer in the area, BTR Sarmcol, a rubber factory. Come the weekend, those workers were hungry for a party. The women wore their platform shoes and some were in bell-bottomed jeans. Large women in colourful curve-defining spandex outfits; men in shiny shoes, trousers, shirts and jackets; they were all ready for the party on Friday nights. All were equally attracted to any nearby makeshift disco. The disco was beneath a crudely constructed canvas roof in the backyard of someone's house.

My mouth was nearly healed. It was the first Friday in June, 1976. Thami and I stacked empty square paraffin (kerosene) drums alongside one another. He arrived home early on Fridays. Each of us climbed onto a paraffin drum, to check if we could see where a tarpaulin was being erected. Later in the evening, that was from where the music would blare. I was too young and Mammy Cynthia did not allow Thami to go either. But we could look and see where the carnival for adults was to take place.

As people who live on the coast flock to the beach on a hot day, so too, at the strike of eight on a Friday night, spandex-clad women and men in natty dress poured out of their homes and filtered into the tent. The mobile disco lights were set up and sound checks had long been done. When the music began, so did the adult carnival. The sounds were magical and the repetitive rhythms hypnotic. That Friday night Thami and I crawled nearer to get a closer look. We peeped through cracks in the fence and saw how the full-bodied women became dancing queens. The excitement was palpable and the men—wow! They could dance the pantsula; women too. Both Thami and I, we were mesmerised. It was like all of them were successfully surfing choppy seas. The movement, mainly in their legs, turned their bodies into a mass of rhythm. Shiny shoes on fast moving feet that always ended in a spin became blinding from the reflected twirling mobile disco lights. With high energy and classy movements the women and men converted an otherwise dull existence into a space to forget about life's hardships, albeit for just a while.

The township went quiet, save for the sound of a repetitive bass drum from the adult carnival in the distance. The loudness was relative to how far the adult carnival was from Mammy Cynthia's house. Mammy insisted that Thami and I were bathed and in bed by 22:30 on a Friday night. I was sixteen years old and Thami was nearly nineteen.

"You are only sixteen, go to bed! You, Thami; set a good example, go to bed too!"

The older Precious hooted with laughter in the kitchen as Thami and I were sent to bed. We knew better than to argue. Anything remotely disobedient was seen as a crime. It left me feeling guilty, the kind of guilt that no apology could fix.

When school resumed, I was again the butt of much teasing, having lost eight teeth from my top jaw. It was only after undergoing several surgical procedures that my mouth appeared to be restored.

My surfboard suffered surface damage only. It was nothing that Thami and I could not fix. Due to the accident I missed that opportunity to participate in the surfing competition for which Mr Thompson and I had been preparing. "Next year you can have another go at it, Champ," was his take.

Ma's letters began to read as if they had been written by another person. The feisty, socially aware woman who was larger than life, and whom I adored unequivocally had become ordinary. That the taking had taken its toll was evident. Jane's letters too were becoming fewer. In every letter she wrote about her head that ached, about new tests to determine the cause, and that I should define my contribution to life.

I managed to downplay the extent of my injuries, because Ma had heard enough sad and bad news. It seemed that Ma had begun to believe the bad news; and she became it. Jane too, she was battling with various challenging situations. I could always depend on Mammy Cynthia.

By the end of August 1976 township schools in South Africa were experiencing internal social combustion. It all began when the state insisted that the medium of instruction move from one language to another, but for only a certain group of schools in the north of the country. The groundswell of student resistance highlighted other grievances too. Separate education systems for the different groups, the poor quality of school buildings, and inferior equipment for those with dark skins were high on the list of pupil grievances. Light-skinned people had easy access to the best equipped and serviced schools. This added fuel to protest actions. Schools in townships and certain universities across the country had also joined the protest. The state labelled student uprisings 'riots' and suppressed them by using force.

Trade unions were affected by the growing atmosphere of resistance. They also came to the fore with demands for better working conditions and protective rights. Around the same time civic organisations were formed to address issues of poor service delivery in townships. Our school, being a small church-owned boarding school, remained largely unaffected. The rest of the country rallied behind slogans that served to articulate the demand for social change. Government schools were set alight. Road demonstrations and protests that often turned violent were regular occurrences.

So-called troublemakers were arrested but not charged. The state had invoked its law to arrest suspected instigators and incarcerate them for 90 days without being charged. While in prison the people were tortured until some revealed the names of 'their accomplices'; a number of students died while in custody. Others were released and then re-arrested for a further 90 days. Police informers were planted at universities and within 'suspicious' structures of society. That was how the state gathered information with which to suppress the rising wave of national discontent. South Africa was becoming more and more of a police state. Every person who had a dark skin was a suspect or a terrorist. Being labelled a communist by the state was like being accused of being a police informer by members of township communities. The fate of such persons was often the same: death.

Years later, in 1985 when living back in Cape Town, I read a short article about Mpophomeni in a journal. The township had been transformed into a hotbed of trade union activity. The article described how nearly one thousand workers were dismissed from the rubber factory, BTR Sarmcol. The employer, it was reported, refused to recognise a trade union. That was despite the trade union membership being a clear majority of all persons in the employ of BTR Sarmcol. Whilst reading I remembered that Mr Khumalo was a night-watchman at that factory. I wondered whether he too was affected.

As I accumulated more information it became evident that the industrious and sometimes festive people of Mpophomeni had been plunged into poverty. Employees, many of them breadwinners, suddenly became 'the unemployed'.

While negotiating a settlement, workers eked out an existence by participating in a range of self-sustaining initiatives. Desperation was again the mother of invention. Co-operatives were formed to manufacture t-shirts and other apparel. Those who were talented dancers and actors staged industrial theatre pieces around the country, all in an attempt to replace lost income.

The BTR Sarmcol strike is the longest strike in the history of South African labour disputes and ranks as one of the longest in the world.

On 6 March 1998, the final judgment in the South African Supreme Court of Appeal was handed down. That final judgment declared the dismissal of workers from the BTR Sarmcol factory in Howick, thirteen years earlier, illegal. Each of the employees, including Mr Khumalo, had worked at the factory for an average of 25 years. Many had died during the time it took to resolve the matter. Mr Khumalo too, he died, and later I heard some say that it was of a broken heart because he was unable to support his family.

During the 1980s I followed developments in Howick. I read about the people of Mpophomeni in *The South African Labour Bulletin,* a journal that featured articles about the BTR Sarmcol Strike from time to time. Those repressive times prevented daily newspapers from publishing and reporting on matters that the state regarded as subversive. In one of the articles I read that Father Terry had been arrested for his involvement in bringing care to the destitute.

I was on a business trip from Johannesburg to Cape Town when the judgment was handed down. After reading it, that judgment, I walked to the Company Gardens and found a park bench at the back of St George's Anglican Cathedral. I sat there and recalled the memory of long ago. It was the end of lunch-time. Earlier, the noon gun boomed and then echoed in the city. I'd forgotten about that, about the noon gun, a cannon sound that boomed out from Signal Hill to mark midday every weekday. After recovering from the shock of that sudden explosive sound I settled to think about the events of that day, that judgment, and how it had impacted on the people of Mpophomeni.

Meanwhile the midday crowd before me rushed and dawdled by, every one bearing sandwiches or drinks in their hands. They were heading for offices at Syfrets, The Board of Executors, *The Argus* and *The Cape Times* newspapers, to Alexander Joles and many more businesses that were anchor tenants in the city. It seemed that those employees felt their lunch break was all too brief on that perfect day, in a city more beautiful than most.

I savoured my childhood memories for a brief moment after having read that judgment. My mind continued to be awash with recollections of that time. Some were sad, but the overwhelming majority of my memories made my heart sing out loud in a joyous and veritable descant. It was reminiscent of a time when I'd travel from our house on the Cape Flats to attend the Sunday morning service at the Cathedral. Barry Smith led a choir and they sang the entire liturgy. To me it was beautiful. None of my friends thought so. I snuck out by myself on a few Sundays and never disclosed my mission to anyone—going to church was not 'festive'.

Jane left her radio for me when she graduated from school in 1975. That radio was a gift from a pupil who graduated ahead of her. I used it to listen to surf reports, music and to get updates about the unrest that was sweeping across the country. All I got to hear was news reports about mayhem and marauding hooligans. Other reports were about looters; that the police and army had been forced to use tear gas, rubber bullets and buckshot. Other broadcasts carried news that a certain number of dark-skinned people were shot, had died and that others were arrested.

It was clear that the time had come for the country to change, or be changed. I was already imagining what the progression to a better alternative was going to feel like. Being able to surf on any beach was uppermost in my mind. That was the most 'festive' thought. I was ready to compete against anyone who dared to challenge. But did people really have to die, so that I could surf on any beach?

One of my many dreams was to repay Mr Thompson's money. I wished to buy him some nice new music. Maybe such a gesture would have made Mr Thompson think that his interest in me had been worthwhile.

When the change arrived our entire country would resemble Mpophomeni—where Jane and I had visited with Mammy Cynthia; where our different appearance did not matter and reference to it would be regarded as anti-social. We'd all be the same and we'd *belong*. The young would have respect for the old; and those who were good at something would get all the opportunities that they needed, to become better. Skin texture, colour and disability would not matter. The anticipated change held promise that ability, passion and interest would become the new passport to opportunities and encouragement. Just as Cape Town is the prettiest, so our country would become the best, the most sought after, revered and respected. South Africa would become a beacon for the world to emulate; a beacon that grew from shame to celebration; and a lesson about how humanity can overcome evil.

A changed country; a free country, I thought, would be similar to when we stayed with Mammy Cynthia during school holidays. There had been times when we were there over the Christmas period, because some years Ma did not have money to bring us home. Those experiences also swept through my mind while sitting on that park bench behind St George's Cathedral. I sat there, on the bench, like a bookend for a long time.

Ma reinforced what we had to be aware of when the inevitable change happened in South Africa: "Do not let the people who lead do what those before them have done."

§

Those Decembers in Mpophomeni also had a carnival atmosphere in the street when the children played in front of Mammy Cynthia's house. Jane was always with the older girls. They never played outside the front gate. That was one of Mammy's rules.

Decembers were the best; it rained and the orange-coloured clay roads had different sized pools scattered everywhere. Some pools formed in large dongas (ditches), while others were smaller pot-holes that became puddles. When cars drove through smaller holes the splashes had a further reach. Those who were not streetwise, or who moved too slowly, were sprayed with orange water. As children we could do a lot with nothing: we played a special game that the children of the Cape Flats played in the streets. This was the alternative option when our football became saturated and too mushy to kick about on an equally wet road. That's what happens when you make a football by stuffing newspaper into a plastic bag.

Kennetjie was a game of skill: two sticks, one long and the other short; the short stick had thinner parts on either end, like a cricket bail. We'd make a hole in the ground from which the long stick was used to scoop the little one up and away, often into a sea of opposing team members. The size of the team did not matter. Like football on the Cape Flats, it was a free-for-all. People chose their team and that was the side they played for; nothing else would matter. The more team members there were, the longer the game took to play—everyone had to have a turn. We named our game Mpophomeni Cricket. The rules were a combination drawn from baseball, cricket and golf. Golf, yes, when the *kennetjie* was flung with the longer stick by a less skilful player and landed in a mud bunker (a pool of water in the clay-orange street).

Sometimes there was a false start. It was usually when the player was affected by unsportsmanlike jeering from the opposition. As I competed in more surfing competitions I learned about 'big match temperament', a kind of stage fright. It was the same reason why certain *Kennetjie* players responded with 'butter fingers' when the crowd jeered for them to miss a crucial catch. The excitement was no different to a final in a premier football game. The umpire had the final word. His word was never disputed. After the match, which lasted an average of four days, the winning team shook hands with the losers. The losers would protest and insist that they be referred to as having placed second in the contest. The winners were always threatened with a re-match. At such an instant, it never actually materialised, but nonetheless, in the instance of a rematch, those 'who placed second' promised to field some or other highly skilled, sought after and feared player from a few streets away. They also threatened to ingest muti—"It's an African thing, man," Thami would whisper to me. After that ingestion a plethora of fantastical things would supposedly happen in their favour. Once all the jeering had settled every team member was called to climb onto a paraffin drum. There he, or she, shook hands with the umpire, whose role it was to award an imaginary medal; gold for the winners and silver for those who came 'second'—just so that all the players could be winners.

Midnight mass on Christmas Eve was held at St Anne's, a Catholic Church in the North West corner of Mpophomeni Township. The choir was different from the choir that sang at the Anglican Church near my home in the Cape, or, for that matter, at St George's Cathedral—where I would occasionally sneak go. At St Anne's the parish was the choir; and a usually cold wet night became joyous with the warm sound of song.

It was a Christmas Eve. That evening, after dinner, Mammy Cynthia, assisted by elderly Khokho, suggested to Thami and me that we rest before going to church. "Otherwise you will sleep during Mass..." I heard her say to Thami in Zulu, their native tongue. That was a lie and probably the first time that I had heard Mammy Cynthia tell a fib, for the singing in that church was so loud it could wake the dead, on another continent!

By half past eight that evening we were up, Thami and I, ready for Mass. Thami was an altar boy and had to be at the church ahead of everyone else, so he and I left together, ahead of the rest. The girls made their own plans to get to church. They would implement their own ideas and it was always a secret. Khokho was ready to leave too. She wore a thick woollen cap and a skirt down to her knees, stockings that looked like socks, broad-heeled black shoes and a three-quarter length overcoat. Khokho had dressed for winter.

"Sam! Come back. You have to wear a jacket. Do you not have one?"

"No, Mammy, only a blazer, but I left it at school."

Shouts and more calls in Zulu ensued. There were responses from across the road. Within five minutes two jackets appeared. Minutes later, a third jacket was delivered, also from across the road, in the direction of where Ma Khumalo lived. From no jacket to having a choice of three, all within five minutes! That must have been what Ma meant when she explained how life was in Woodstock. I felt dapper to walk down the street. It was because my clothes were similar to that worn by all the other young men on that Christmas Eve.

"Here, wear this hat, it belonged to Baba Sipho. You must wear it because, when you come home after church, it will be very cold," was Khokho's contribution.

Thami and I were on our way, sidestepping and skipping across puddles of water. On occasion I would misjudge and, dunk! I'd tread in a pool. There were no streetlights and the night was dark, but the atmosphere was festive. We were the first three people at the church on that Christmas Eve, Thami, Khokho and I. Thami knew where and how to switch on the lights. He had been an altar boy for many years. It was a small church, more like a very big room. The pews were benches without backrests; and the altar was a table, just a little bigger than the one at which I did my homework.

I wanted to help Thami with the hymn boards, because my reach was higher than his.

"What are hymn boards?"

"Boards that let the people know which number hymn to sing."

"No, there is no need for hymn numbers here, the people know everything, and in this church you can sit anywhere.

"The parishioners are on their way, I can hear them, listen carefully and you will hear too."

In the distance there was a humming sound which grew louder as it drew closer. I recognised the tune. The parishioners were really on their way, I too could hear. People joined the informal procession as it passed by their homes. Just as when we started a game of *kennetjie,* or football, people joined in. The procession to the church continued to grow from every direction. Everyone who came out to walk also joined in the singing of 'O Come All Ye Faithful'. The singing procession grew just as rivulets and tributaries flow together and make a big river. So too did the singing procession to St Anne's consistently swell as people joined in their numbers on that Christmas Eve.

The first people filed in, some of whom looked familiar. We exchanged knowing smiles. Of the people put out their hands and I stood up to greet, as did others when approached with the same gesture. The hands I touched felt soft and gentle. Everyone smiled; all the while they continued to sing a new carol, 'Silent

Night'. I missed being at home. But I was happy to be in Mphopomeni. It felt like I belonged.

Thami lit the candles. The simple altar was dressed in purple advent garb. To complete the scene, a crucifix consisting of two simple sticks was mounted on the wall behind the altar. I sat gazing, too afraid to blink, lest I missed the greatness embedded in that simplicity.

The next carol was also a favourite: 'While Shepherds Watched Their Flocks by Night'. It was an *experience*. I have never before, or after, heard it sung quite like that. The church was full and all the windows were wide open. The altar candles flickered and there were a small number of globes arranged throughout the church. They were attached to electric cords and suspended from the roof. As we sang, so the globes gently swayed as if in tune with the magical soul sound of African rhythm brought to familiar carols. There were more people at the church that Christmas Eve than were at the tarpaulin underneath which the disco lights revolved. The crowd swayed and every verse was performed in descant. How did they know when to sing what? There was no conductor, no hymn sheet, no choir practice and no accompanying instruments. Yet, the people sang like a well-rehearsed choir. Me too, I sang out loud until my throat hurt. I didn't know all the words, but it didn't matter, for it was Christmas and we belonged to one another that night.

Father Terry was there bearing a little baby doll which symbolised the Christ-child. Thami carried the crucifix and led the procession. Father Terry danced and held the baby Jesus up high as Thami slowly walked to the front of that church. As the procession moved forward, we, in the backless pews, remained standing. We sang 'Away in a Manger' at that time.

We sang and created a collective feeling of great joy that night. It was all we had with which to make that big room beautiful. Some raised their hands while all continued to sing as Father Terry placed the symbolic Jesus in a makeshift crib amidst the joyous sound. Thami was on hand to help Father light the incense. The jubilant sound continued when Father Terry blessed the crib as a symbolic birthplace of Jesus that advent season. With the burning incense Father gestured peace, hope, love and forgiveness to the congregants.

Incense had filled the room like a cloud when Father Terry began the celebratory Mass: "In the name of the Father, the Son and the Holy Spirit…"

On Christmas Day I called Ma. Jane had done well and was all set to do year two at the medical school. She continued to suffer from headaches and no amount of investigation by specialists could determine its cause. Pa was working—he was always working and Ma was dealing with life. "One day at a time," was Ma's new refrain.

The following year, Ma announced that she was to adopt a nearly six-month-old baby boy. After a lengthy process Ma and Pa were granted parental rights over little Eugene. Ma had found reason to live again as she learned to love the little left-handed Eugene.

1977 was my second year at school without Jane. Doing well was not a priority—I was only passionate about developing the best surfing technique.

"It is something that I have to do, Jane."

This was my standard reply when Jane's letters claimed that I was more interested in my surfboard than the future. She was concerned that I would not get a good school-leaving certificate. I was concerned that without spending enough time practising, my surfing technique would not improve.

As soon as school re-opened (early January, 1977), Mr Thompson and I resumed our coaching routine. On Friday afternoons I waited for him at the main gate. From there we drove, just the two of us and *Dire Straits*, Coach's new favourite band. He listened to the then unknown Mark Knopfler's wailing guitar at full volume, and in the process shared it with the expanse of sugar-cane plantations alongside the long winding road down which we drove to the coast. We were headed for the rocks off Scottburgh Beach, where we'd spend every daylight hour in the surf.

In about March of that year, 1977, Mr Thompson appeared to become preoccupied with another interest. Perhaps my surfing was no longer good enough, was what I thought. This became a big concern. In addition to no longer discussing surfing techniques, competitions and detail about the sport that usually occupied our time together, Mr Thompson began to do and say things that were completely out of character. He would stop during our car journeys to use almost every public telephone; and increasingly he seemed to care less than nothing for matters about which he had previously been obsessed. Until then I had not known that Mr Thompson knew how to use a public telephone. I continued to be in search of the perfect swell, but Mr Thompson had eyes only for public telephones. Instead of preparing me for the training session he'd sit on a stone, and I'd see him grin while staring out to sea. Being around people who behaved strangely was not new to me, but I held Mr Thompson in different regard, for he was my coach. It was not my place to ask so I pretended not to notice his changed behaviour. More concerning was that he stopped discussing what could be done to arrange invitations so that I would participate in surfing competitions. Long Beach in Cape Town, Jeffrey's Bay and North Beach, those competitions were all seemingly forgotten. I sensed that Friday afternoons were a strain for Mr Thompson. He would leave me standing at the gate with my board for two hours before we'd begin a journey to the next public telephone. Often we would stop three times before reaching the beach. One Friday he arrived while I had gone to the toilet and then left without me.

Our trips were filled with long empty bouts of silence, and that constant surveillance for public telephones dominated the journey. Not knowing the purpose, but wishing to please my coach, my looking out for previously undiscovered public telephones became the private game I played while Mr Thompson drove us to the sea. In the past we spoke about surfing and nothing else on our trips from school. By then even the music Mr Thompson listened to shifted from rock, jazz and reggae to Richard Clayderman, a Frenchman who played delicate contemporary piano music. Stories and explanations about the art of surfing belonged to the past. Prior to the invasion of Richard Clayderman's music I had to struggle to get my opinion considered. The passion with which Mr Thompson approached any discussion to do with surfing was a constant when we were in the van. After another extended silent spell, while he was driving and I was looking for public telephones, Mr Thompson began to talk to me:

"Well, Champ, I have something to share with you. We have been surfing together for four years. It's a long time. If things were different, here in South Africa, then you would have been world champion by now. Take it from me, I know. This is the reason why I have invested all my free time in you."

I knew that he was placating me, particularly given that he spoke in the past tense. It worried me. I was nervous and apprehensive about what was to follow. It was probably something dreadful that he was to reveal.

"Look," said Mr Thompson, "as every man, and for that matter every woman, matures, they tend to find a mate. More often than not, it is a mate of the opposite gender. In my case, I have found a girlfriend. By now you will understand these things, Champ, so I feel comfortable explaining it to you. Sister O'Connor, the Irish nun who teaches mathematics and I, we are in love." There, it was confirmed, Mr Thompson did not like ballerinas, no, he preferred nuns!

"There are many things that have to be considered, discussed and decided upon. For this reason, I am not able to focus on coaching you any longer. You need to understand this, Champ, so that you know why things have become the way they are. I shall be there for you wherever and whenever, but for now there are my own matters and they are difficult. People create religion because of their need to find forgiveness and salvation. It is part of the dilemma that Sister O'Connor and I have to work through. This could mean that she may leave the religious life. As for me, after 34 years in this world, it is time to get a mate, a life partner, a companion; call it what you want, Champ. So, I suggest that we spend this weekend in the surf and that we talk about how you are going to go on with less of my involvement."

I thought for a moment before responding. Much of what Mr Thompson had said was not clear. He had obviously given it a lot of thought, but all I worried about was surfing and why could he not have a girlfriend like other people did— why did she have to be a nun? There were often seemingly stray women lurking on the beach. Some of them surfed. Why did my coach and a nun have to choose each other? I just could not understand that. Perhaps my thoughts were naïve; I was not sure, so my response was cautious: "Okay Sir, thank you for explaining to me. Good luck. It must be a difficult time. Thank you for not leaving me without first explaining. I shall explore other ways to continue surfing. Thank you also for believing in me."

After our discussion both Mr Thompson and I behaved as we usually did, but it felt contrived. No matter how hard we tried our relationship was different to what it had been. We had reached the end. I no longer had a coach. In my short life at that time there had been many gentle beginnings, and far too many abrupt endings.

Throughout, I remained committed to surfing and less so to academia. When we parted on that Monday morning, Mr Thompson told me to take and read a few copies of the publication, *Surfer Magazine,* from his collection. The more recent copies were in his van. I was grateful and promised to return them when done.

My trips to the coast became less frequent. Problems with accommodation turned what formerly was a weekend trip into a day outing. At first I woke up before dawn on a Saturday morning and carried my board to the big road from where I'd hitch a ride to the coast. Most times I made my own luck and got to the sea in record time. It was usually on the back of a big sugar-cane truck or something equally open-ended. It was a sweet ride! Rickety, but to chew on the left-over cane gave some joy. Once at the coast I'd wait for other surfers to arrive. I surfed far away from those for whom the beach was reserved, but distant companions were better than no friends at all.

During the summer months when a lift back to school seemed improbable, I stayed out and slept in the bush next to the reserved beach. Staying away from school on a Saturday night created its own trouble. Sister St Claire sat up waiting for me to arrive, like Ma did when Pa was out. Pa never arrived and I too let Sister St Claire wait up in vain. It was not right, but it would have been a lot worse had Sister known where I had slept. She scolded me nonetheless: "To prevent further trouble, Samuel, my reasonable expectation is to be informed, in good time, when Mr Thompson offers you accommodation. Let this be a warning." Occasionally Mr Thompson was my alibi, but I was hesitant to use his name because he had his own issues.

There was an advert in one of the borrowed *Surfer Magazines*. It called on surfers to audition for the filming of an advertising commercial. After reading it, I called Mr Thompson and told him of my interesting find and that the advert did not specify what colour skin the respondents had to have. He sounded happy to hear from me that day.

"Champ, it's best to play it safe. You know what these people are like. This time you will go in without me. Who knows, they may see you as a well-tanned surfer, that's all. Change your name, use mine if you want."

Several formalities had to be complied with before auditions began. The first few demonstration rides were challenging. Other contenders only looked the part. I was offered the job and immediately accepted it. "We have to change your name, just in case," was the ironic and completely unsolicited view expressed by the shrill-voiced, chain-smoking advertising man, a real Adonis. He seemed more interested in me than was comfortable, but there was no reason to be firm. I was fetched from school on two successive Saturday mornings. One of the 'job requirements' stipulated that I had to have all my body hair removed before filming could start. The process was very painful!

Filming was arranged so that it did not interfere with my being at school. I was paid even though the product being advertised was never disclosed. All the advertising man said was: "It's for an aftershave commercial." I was sixteen and it was my first job and the detail did not matter. The money was enough to settle the debt I had with Mr Thompson. With the balance I settled outstanding school fees. The remainder of the money was kept for the trip back to Cape Town—on the proviso that nothing else happened.

Months later, again on a Saturday morning, when home in Cape Town, I went to see *Enter the Dragon*, a film starring Bruce Lee. The Eldorado Bioscope was diagonally across the road from our house. It was there where I saw the advert for the very first time. It seemed hazy, but then I realised that most of the people in the cinema were smoking!

Chapter Thirteen

Mammy Cynthia's Farewell

Ma's reaction to my earnings was unexpected. Her letters had become less frequent, but after being informed that I had earned, Ma reacted:

Wednesday, 20 April 1977

Dear Sam

You see, you too are no longer relying on me for anything. Don't worry my boy. My sorrow is about me, not you. My happiness and pride are because of you; you are my child. Jane and I do not expect anything from you, only magic. Like when you sing on the steps here at home, then all of us become happy; no matter how sad the day may be we become happy whenever you sing.

This means that you can come home this year—bring us magic. I am happy. You have not been home in two years. Come and bring us some happiness, come home Sammy.

What do you look like now? Two years is a long time. I last saw you when you were fourteen years old. Did Mammy cut your hair after that work you did on the surfboard? That bush of hair made you look like an old man. It must have been very sore when they removed the hair from your body before the filming? I did not know that they had to do that. A friend and I went to watch two films at the Luxurama Bioscope last week. Adverts were screened before and between both the films. That was when I saw it. At first I could not see your face very clearly. You could have changed a lot in the two years since we've seen each other. I recognised the way you swing your arms. That was how I knew it was you. So, you see Boy, I have watched you surf.

Eugene can walk and talk. I wonder if he will remember you. I show him pictures and all he says is: "You, you, you!" He prays for you every night, but I do not think that he understands yet. He will, once you've come home.

In your letter you asked about Jane. I do not see much of her at all. From school she wrote a letter each week. These days are different. She's fine, working hard, but fine.

Manage your money well. Ask Mammy Cynthia to help you and come home soon.

I love you
Ma

This letter also forms part of my collection; it is one of the last letters Ma wrote to me. Letter distribution time at school took on a different meaning when pay telephones were introduced into the hostels. I thought that telephones were for emergencies only and not for casual chat. However, there was always a big demand to use the school public telephones. A roster was created and time was set aside for when calls could be received and placed. Rules governed how long a call could last. It was to ensure that everyone had fair access to the public telephones.

When I received an unexpected letter the excitement of old returned, particularly given that the letter was from Jane. The other boys teased me when I stood up to collect my mail from the new accountancy teacher, Mr Jean Pretorius. Jane usually smeared lipstick on her mouth and placed lip imprints on the back of the envelope before mailing it to me. She had sprayed stuff on it too, *Je t'aime*, her favourite perfume. It was deliberate because she knew that I'd be teased by the other older boys. "Fan mail for Levy!" was the best that Mr Pretorius could do while breathing over the envelope, like a dragon as he inhaled the sealed-in fragrance.

That letter was, for some reason, attached to a traffic violation notice that Sister St Claire asked should be handed to Boet Sam. After a few days of sulking he, Boet Sam, said to me: "Why does my traffic fine smell like Jane, did she send it to me?" He then slyly tried to have me return it to her, but I was no longer as gullible.

Mr Pretorius became one of the more popular teachers at school, mainly because it became his job to hand out mail. He was a giant. Not fat, but big, like Captain Van Deventer. Mr Pretorius arrived at school each morning driving the littlest of cars, a bright yellow Datsun 1200 Deluxe. His music would be blaring. It was always The Mamas and The Papas that belted out about 'All the Leaves are Brown', 'California Dreaming', 'Dream a Little Dream of Me' and 'Monday Monday'. No prize for guessing why his nickname became Papa Pretorius.

He was an interesting man that Papa Pretorius, always in short-sleeved checked shirts with narrow knitted neckties of assorted colours. His shoes had thick soles, as if this man, who stood more than two metres in his socks, needed any additional height. The fashion conscious girls suffered fits of hysteria whenever Papa Pretorius was near. They claimed that, by wearing those shoes, Papa was ready to walk to Timbuktu, but I knew that they actually found him irresistible—he could not surf though!

That time I received an unusually short letter from Jane:

Monday, 28 February 1977

Hello, Howszit Goofy Sammy

I miss you, actually. Congratulations with the surfing thing. What does it feel like to earn money from having fun?

To study medicine is difficult. It is all about learning to regurgitate very complicated names. Pardon me, I am not trying to be funny, but medical terms are a pain! Maybe there's a reason why our curriculum is structured the way it is.

'You have to learn to think like doctors before you can be doctors,' is what one of our professors tells the class on most days.

For the past month my head has ached. My eyes were tested today and they appear fine.

I heard that Mammy Cynthia was to retire. It was at her request. There's a lovely article about her in the alumni newsletter. Ask the school secretary to give you a copy. I suppose that many people want to make sure that her send-off is the best that they can do. If you think that it is relevant and if the opportunity can be created, then I would like to be present on the day. Will you keep me informed of developments, please? The date of her retirement, in the middle of May, will suit me because I shall have a short study break then. I shall be doing practical work at the hospital, but with advance notice my schedule may be adapted. Let me know as soon as you know?

I miss you very much, even though you are most irritating to be with!

Let me know how the surfing is going? Have you decided about the Durban competition? Sounds risky to me, but I'm sure you'll do what you want and not what they tell you to do. "They're just people, Jane..." I miss hearing you say that. Good luck!

Mamma and I looked at your report card last weekend. You can do a whole lot better than that. Your English and Afrikaans grades are great. Geography and Science, even Biology, they're fine, but what's going on with the Mathematics and the Economics? You know what to do...

Okay my favourite brother.

Oh, wait, before I go, last Saturday night, my friend Leslie (he is a 400 metres athlete) arrived on a scooter and we went to the Luxurama Bioscope. The main feature was <u>Saturday Night Fever</u>, with John Travolta and Karren Gorney. Before the film started, there were the usual adverts: cigarettes, wine and then aftershave. Wow! I saw you clearly. I could not help myself and said out loud: "Look, it's my brother!"

Maybe I shouted, because afterwards Leslie seemed embarrassed and people craned to see who this mad woman was. Since then I have been playing the scene over and over in my mind; as though the advert was better than the movie. I don't understand the relationship between surfing and aftershave lotion, but there you go.

Imagine: all the cinemas everywhere, even overseas, they screen clips of you surfing and not any of them knows who you are, how cool is that; or as you would say: 'How festive is that!'

Oh, another thing: last weekend, when I was home, Pa was there, wearing false eye lashes! He found them at his secret workplace and thought it a good idea to wear. I often wonder what goes on in his head, or what he really gets up to when we are not around. The way he treats Ma is not right and the way she allows him to treat her is like self-inflicted pain. The talk about their selling the house continues, but I shall not comment unless my opinion is asked for. You may have a different approach?

Okay, little big one. Look after yourself.

Love

Jane

After reading Jane's letter I went to the school secretary and asked if there was a spare copy of the article about Mammy Cynthia's retirement:

The Alumni Newsletter

Mammy Cynthia to retire on 20 May 1977

"I was thirty three years old when I joined the staff at St Mary's School. It feels like yesterday even though I am about to celebrate my sixty seventh birthday."

This is how Mammy Cynthia responds to the question of how long she has enjoyed employment at our school. Nomzamo Cynthia Mbala, née Zwane, is fondly referred to as Mammy Cynthia.

"Thirty-one years ago I was put in charge of a small group of pupils. They came from faraway places and I had to fetch and care for them until they finished school. Next year the last of my children will finish. They are a girl from Cradock and a boy from Cape Town. It is sad that I will not be here when they go, but I am tired, and need to be with my family at my own home. My mother-in-law is very old and can no longer care for our home and my two grandchildren by herself.

"I have cared for many children over the years. They live in different countries across the entire world. I have more good memories than sad ones. The colleagues who have worked alongside me, because I am the eldest, they are like my adult children. Many of them are the same age as my own two, Sibusiso and Thokozane."

The Alumni Newsletter interviewed several of Mammy Cynthia's colleagues, teachers and past pupils. Here's what a small sample of them had to say:

Nomusa Sabata (General Worker): "Mammy Cynthia is like medicine for me."

Maggie Vanga (General Worker): "My friendship with Mammy Cynthia is like no other."

Jean (Papa) Pretorius (Accountancy Teacher): "It is very easy to talk with Mammy Cynthia. The other day I spoke with her about a concern and she sat listening as if nothing else mattered. I needed that then."

Bridgette Summers (Standard Nine pupil): "I come from Cradock in the Karoo where it is spectacularly beautiful in spring and bitterly cold in winter. When I arrived at the school, six years ago, Mammy Cynthia reminded me so much of my grandmother that I could not help but be her granddaughter. She continues to be my best friend and probably will be for life."

Sam Zama (Boet Sam) (Driver): "Once, I asked Mammy Cynthia why she was not irritated when people told her their troubles. She looked at me and giggled before responding: 'There is an old tradition in my family. It stems from when I was recently married. My husband and I lived with my mother-in-law who worked as a domestic worker. She arrived home one day and told me what her employer had said while speaking on the telephone. It had to do with having two ears and one mouth because we had to listen more than speak.' I have not forgotten what Mammy said and I practise it every day."

Grace Makhubane (Head Cook): "Late on Sunday afternoons we would sit outside the school gate and wait for the others to arrive. Mammy Cynthia was always the first one there. All would sit with their legs stretched out. It is better that way, because we stand all day. Mammy always sat quietly and only moved her head to face whoever was speaking. Mammy only answered when a question was put to her directly. One day I asked: Mammy, why are you always the first one to arrive; and why do you say so little? Her reply was: 'When people speak then they are teaching me to be better. When we teach, that is when we learn most. I arrive early to be taught and so that those who teach can learn. As my teachers talk I listen and watch them find solutions to whatever it is that may be bothering. I listen as a friend. You cannot have a good friend, unless you are a good friend first.' Mammy Cynthia spoke directly to our hearts when she spoke in that deep traditional Zulu way. Many of the things that Mammy has said over the years stay in my head and affect the way I live."

Several teachers celebrated Mammy by reflecting what she meant to them. They were generous with compliments, some more than others. A woman teacher, Mrs Trengrove-Smith, described how, without speaking, Mammy Cynthia taught her to pause and think before saying whatever may have been on her mind: "I have since learned that if we think ugly things then it will show in the way we behave."

I had been told that when Mrs Trengrove-Smith joined the staff she continually spoke down to Mammy Cynthia. In response, Mammy was always courteous and respectful, even though the treatment meted out to her was often humiliating and embarrassing. It was Mammy Cynthia's grace, gentle attitude and the respect she commanded that caused this teacher to examine her own manner.

After many years at the school, and as her experience of Mammy Cynthia grew, Mrs Trengrove-Smith realised the errors of her thoughts and subsequent actions. When the occasion was opportune, and without prior warning, Mrs Trengrove-Smith summoned courage and apologised to Mammy in the presence of all the other teachers. When asked about the matter with Mrs Trengrove-Smith, Mammy chose to respond in Zulu: "We are not born racists. We become racist because of the company we keep. People who live in townships and those who live in suburbs, together we suffer the same affliction. We discriminate against people because of their outer appearance, even though they may have the kindest hearts. All of us are born with kind hearts, but we seem to develop big clouds over our minds and hearts. When that cloud lifts it signals a new birth. That is when we become embarrassed about our thoughts and actions. It is because we understand what it feels like to live where there are clouds. I also have clouds; we all have clouds, so don't be embarrassed, instead, just try your best to treat everyone well and in time your clouds too will lift."

The retirement date coincided with a number of important events. Maggie had formed a farewell committee to steer the event. The serving members were all Mammy's immediate colleagues. They insisted on taking full responsibility for managing and arranging the entire farewell function. Sister St Claire agreed that the big meeting room was an ideal venue wherein to host the event. Maggie, a buxom woman with no apology in her tone, was large and definitely in charge. The first meeting was convened in the workers' mess room. Those in attendance were Mary, Nomusa, Grace, Thandiwe and Boet Sam. Every member was given a task. Once members reported about how they would do the task it was discussed and in certain instances verified before being accepted. Thereafter the meeting considered correspondence that had been received.

A letter from Mrs Trengrove-Smith was tabled. She had donated a gift voucher. It was for Mammy Cynthia to enjoy a beauty treatment. The voucher also made provision for Mammy to choose between having a bouquet of flowers or a massage.

While reading the accompanying letter aloud Maggie was visibly itching to comment: "This is not the way we do things. Mammy Cynthia is a Zulu woman!" When Maggie spoke in Zulu her deep contralto voice was more accentuated than usual. The others agreed, save for Thandiwe, who was older and less hot-headed than the others. Boet Sam sat at the back, smiling like the Cheshire cat. Everyone wondered what he was smiling about, but he would not say!

Just when Maggie thought that she had the majority on her side, Grace, the quiet one, cleared her throat and spoke out: "I think that Mammy should go. Why not—even if it will be her first time; why not let her try something new? Other women enjoy it and she might too. I say that Boet Sam should take Mammy Cynthia and on her return we will have the party ready as a surprise."

Because Grace was not a big talker, whenever she had an opinion to share the others listened more attentively. After a bit of paper shuffling and some throat clearing, the meeting agreed. Though Boet Sam thought it a joke he knew better than to disagree, particularly when Maggie had made up her mind.

When all the plans were agreed to, Mary, who was in charge of fund raising, set out to collect contributions from whomsoever she thought appropriate. Neighbours, friends of the school, surrounding businesses and people who knew Mammy Cynthia, all had donated very generously.

Mr Leon van Heerden, owner of the Chubby Chicken butcher shop, arranged a special gift. It was a fundraising initiative inside his butcher shop. He raffled a sheep. There was a collection point in the butcher and for those who preferred it an arrangement was made with the post master at the Ixopo Post Office where direct deposits would be received. With the proceeds Mr van Heerden planned to buy air tickets for Ma and Jane, so that they could attend Mammy Cynthia's farewell party. In addition, Mr van Heerden prepared a substantial meat hamper as a gift for Mammy.

This was the first time that Ma would leave the greater Cape Town area, and the first time that she and Jane would travel by air. Their planned attendance was the best kept secret. I too was not let into the surprise visit.

None of the workers, save for Maggie the organiser, knew of the plan to have Ma and Jane attend.

On the morning of the party, Boet Sam drove Mammy to the beautician's house. As expected, she did not want to go; this, even though the beautician had telephoned her the previous day to explain what the gift entailed.

"Buti, why can't one of the younger girls go?" she asked Boet Sam.

"… because it is not their present, Ma. It is for you."

Mammy thought for a while, as she often did before responding:

"Yes, I think that you are right Buti; and if I don't go, then the person who gave me this gift will feel disappointed."

"I agree, Ma," is how that brief exchange ended.

Prior to the treatment Mammy Cynthia continued to feel apprehensive and uncomfortable. But after the first part she began to enjoy the pampering.

Ma and Jane arrived at Durban's Louis Botha Airport at ten o' clock on the morning of Friday, 20th May 1977. Jane recognised Mr van Heerden when she and Ma entered the small terminal building at that south coast airport.

On the drive back to the Van Heerden home Ma was able to identify the different place names that we children had written about over the years. Jane was unusually subdued because the fluctuating air pressure during the flight from Cape Town had brought on another headache. They drove past Scottburgh and Mr van Heerden was kind enough to drive by the beach, so that Jane could show Ma where I did my surfing. Once they reached Ixopo, Ma and Jane freshened up at the Van Heerden home. Sister St Claire visited briefly, marking the first time that Ma met our Head Teacher.

There was lots of excitement in the air that day. The big meeting room had been decorated with many festive trimmings. There were enough hot water urns to make tea for a small army. Cakes, and Ma's traditional bobotie, koesiesters and a sago pudding that she had brought along from the Cape, were there too.

Mary did one last check to see that all the glasses, cakes, cups, napkins and the rest were in place. All was set and it was nearly party time.

Maggie had prepared a speech for the event. It consisted of more anecdotes and memories about Mammy Cynthia as told by teachers and workers who had known and worked with her over the years.

"What can I say, from you?" was the question Maggie asked of every potential contributor. When they took too long to reply, Maggie, who was frequently impatient, would ask a follow-up question: "So, what stands out about Mammy Cynthia for you?" She had spent days collecting the information; had read it to the English teacher on several occasions; and in turn Ms du Pont had burned the midnight oil in order to get the speech written in a way that best suited the style in which Maggie wanted to present it.

The final speech, the one with which Maggie was most comfortable, was simple, to the point and very honest. Many of the teachers, including the Head Teacher, Sister St Claire, had all contributed. Maggie was determined to include all their bits. It was a collective speech, one that Mammy Cynthia would take away along with other cherished memories and gifts.

The drama teacher, Ms Lis Koekemoer, offered to be Maggie's coach. This teacher gave instruction about breathing technique, voice projection and generally how best to deliver the speech. Little did Ms Koekemoer know that Maggie was the original drama queen! Direction was not required. With a voice that projected jaw-dropping resonance, Maggie was a natural. Her speech was set to better anything previously presented at the school. Maggie's planned oration contained surprise pauses and parts where she was to speak fast; soft gentle tones permeated various descriptions; comical stories from yesteryear were to be retold; and abundant praise was a big feature. The other women were preparing to ululate when Maggie praised Mammy during the prepared speech. It had all been planned to ensure maximum audience participation. The speech was set to end with an illustration of how a simple woman commanded respect and love from all for whom she had cared during her tenure at the school.

As the appointed time for the party drew near everything seemingly was arranged. Boet Sam was already in the school utility van, ready to fetch Mammy Cynthia from the beautician's house.

Meanwhile, Mr Thompson, Papa Pretorius and Mr van Wyk were on the edge of their seats in the big meeting room. They were surrounded by trimmings, cakes, savoury dishes and urns of boiling water. The deciding 'overs' in a cricket match between South Africa and a rebel touring team was unfolding at Newlands Cricket Oval and screened on their little portable television. Maggie, having been alerted by Grace, went to the men and requested that they move their television set to the adjacent room. Ten minutes later Maggie asked them to move for a second time: "Excuse me gentlemen," she said, "... please will you move the television to the small meeting room? We are going to start the farewell function in thirty minutes. I shall bring some eats there if you want?"

"Yes," said Mr van Wyk as he held a hand up to indicate that Maggie should stop. But he did not shift his eyes from the TV screen. "We will move, but the game is very exciting now. South Africa requires forty-three runs off just twenty-one balls... we can do it!"

"Thank you Mr van Wyk. Sorry, I do not understand the rules of cricket, but please move, because the guests are about to arrive."

The other two were equally engrossed by what was happening on that small television screen. Mr Thompson wore a naughty smile; he knew that they were being bad by not moving as requested. Fifteen minutes later the three men had made no attempt to move. They continued to watch the cricket match.

Maggie went in and pleaded for co-operation. Mr van Wyk, this time joined by Papa Pretorius, both raised their left hands in a gesture for Maggie to stop. They refused to move. Maggie stood in the room and waited, but there was no physical reaction from the three men, just an instruction from Mr van Wyk: "Get the workers to come and move the tables to the other room, Maggie, and have your little party there."

"Yes, van Wyk, that's a good idea. Do that Maggie," Mr Thompson and Papa Pretorius spoke in unison, again without moving their eyes from the game. Maggie noticed Mr Thompson's naughty grin.

Maggie, a tall athletic woman, visibly angered turned on her flat heels and rushed to report the unreasonable behaviour to Sister St Claire.

After listening, Sister St Claire tried to see how she could accommodate both parties. Maggie continued to assert: "It had taken days to decorate the room. 'Move everything in fifteen minutes,' Sister, that is what they want us to do. It is unreasonable, impractical and very unfair.

"All the gentlemen have to do, Sister, is move the TV and its little 'bunny-ear' aerial to the small meeting room. In this way everyone will be accommodated. I've offered to serve them refreshments too, but they are not moving. Please Sister, you must go down there and tell them to move. I'm sure that they will listen to you. We can't change the room now. Mammy Cynthia has a bad leg, that's one of the reasons why she is retiring. She can't walk down those steps to the small meeting room any longer. Please Sister, ask the men to move; they will listen if you talk to them?"

While Maggie tried to convince Sister St Claire to act, Nomusa was fuming, but thought it best to wait for Maggie to return before intervening with the men. Boet Sam had by then arrived with Mammy Cynthia. The surprise was about to be ruined.

Ma and Jane were hiding in the nuns' house on the school premises. Together with the Van Heerdens, they were waiting for a signal before entering the function room. The plan was to have Ma, the van Heerdens and then Jane arrive ahead of Mammy Cynthia.

Maggie left Sister St Claire while she reasoned about how to appease all the parties. She returned to the big meeting room accompanied by Nomusa. They entered the room and found that, while Maggie was away, Papa Pretorius and Mr van Wyk had each eaten a plate of cake. They had wrapped pieces of Christmas tinsel that had been pinned to the ceiling around their heads. Mr Thompson had tinsel wrapped around his neck and had poured a glass of fruit juice.

Maggie had had enough. She lunged at Mr van Wyk, grabbed the plate from Papa Pretorius. Mr Thompson hid the juice. The two men defended themselves. The ensuing commotion drew attention and within seconds Nomusa and Mary joined in the fracas.

Realising that matters were out of control Mr Thompson quickly removed the tinsel trimmings from his neck and left the room. The crowd on that little TV set were cheering as if in support. In anger Mr van Wyk toppled all the tables. Cake lay strewn across the room when the police arrived.

Mr van Wyk had scalded his arms when an urn containing boiling water fell forwards, towards him when he toppled a table.

Nomusa, Mary and Maggie were arrested. They were handcuffed and led into the back of a police van. Watching the three women reminded me of when Lieutenant Subramani put his hand on my head as I cowered when climbing into the back section of a police van on Scottburgh Beach. This time though, Mr Thompson just stood there, speaking only when spoken to. Papa Pretorius was in animated discussion with the arresting officer. He referred to Mary, Nomusa and Maggie as 'the girls' and reported that they were unreasonable. Mr van Wyk insisted that the three be arrested and charged with assault. The police took statements from the three men. Paramedics urgently tried to contain Mr van Wyk's pain from the burn wounds. The three women sat inside the mesh surround of the police van.

Sister St Claire pleaded with the police and later spoke with the paramedics too. During her official statement about what had transpired Sister St Claire stated: "It is my duty as the Head Teacher and as a Christian to demand that these women be released."

"Nun, listen to me," said the policeman when he addressed Sister St Claire, "We have to take these three 'gils' to the police station and charge them for assaulting the two European men. Assault is a serious charge, 'Nun'. I suggest that you speak with the gentlemen, 'Nun'. The gentlemen, only they can withdraw these charges. Bear in mind, 'Nun', the state may want to bring its own charges because it is unacceptable for these 'gils' to attack people while they arre enjoying the television."

In an attempt to save face Mr Thompson asked that the charges be withdrawn. The other two, nursing head wounds and serious burns, disagreed and insisted that the charges remain in place.

The entire party was ruined. Sister St Claire telephoned a past pupil, a practising attorney in Pietermaritzburg, and asked him to intervene. He spoke with the Station Commander and when that discussion failed, a nearby colleague was asked to represent the three arrested women. That afternoon, Nomusa, Mary and Maggie were released and warned to appear in court on Monday, 23rd May 1977.

They returned to the school. There was not much left of the party and Maggie was in no mood to give her prepared speech. Much as the festivities had been spoiled by events of the day, other surprises helped to balance the combined feelings of happiness and sadness.

Mammy Cynthia was ecstatic to see Ma, and when told how this was made possible she approached Mr van Heerden, kneeled on her sore knee and thanked him amidst his protestations. Mammy Cynthia and Ma held hands whenever they spoke. Near the end of that celebration Mammy insisted that Ma, Jane and I spend the night at her home in Mpophomeni. Having met all the teachers, toured the school, and thanked Mr and Mrs van Heerden, Ma was ready to rest. That was not to be though—until after the journey to Mpophomeni. Mary volunteered to travel ahead of the others, so that she could help Khokho prepare for the visitors.

That Friday evening Mammy Cynthia, Nomusa, Ma, Boet Sam, Jane and I all travelled by bus to Pietermaritzburg and then on to Mpophomeni. Mammy called Father Terry earlier during the day and explained to him what had happened. Father in turn arranged with a group of men to erect a tarpaulin in Mammy Cynthia's yard. Khokho and Ma Khumalo, together with other women from the neighbourhood, cooked for all the guests.

When the bus arrived at Pietermaritzburg Station Father Terry was there, waiting. He had fetched us in a mini-bus. After being introduced to Father and without further hesitation, Ma used the opportunity to thank him for his assistance and prayers at the time when Brenda and Anne died.

In Mpophomeni Ma was introduced to all the people Jane and I had mentioned in our letters and about whom we spoke when home in Cape Town. Jane was particularly happy to be back; it had been nearly two years since she had left. Ma seemed overwhelmed by the love people demonstrated when wishing Mammy Cynthia well for her retirement. Finally, Ma was able to put faces to the names and was able to thank those who assisted us when we had nothing.

Tea and cakes were served. Later in the evening trestle tables were decked outside underneath the tarpaulin structure. People arrived in droves. I did not know half of them. Everyone gathered to celebrate Mammy Cynthia's retirement and to greet the ever-popular Jane. A hearty stew was served with maize and sauce. Khokho had prepared rice because Jane and I had told her that in the Cape people do not know that cooked maize meal is eaten like rice, or like couscous. The evening was memorable and pleasant beyond expectation. When all the guests left we settled down to make sleeping arrangements. It was not easy to find a place for everyone to sleep, but we managed and by morning all had had a good rest.

Ma and Jane travelled back to Cape Town that Saturday night. I had not spent enough time with them but it was okay, my next trip to the Cape would be in less than a month, after the surfing competition in Durban. I was looking forward to meeting and spending time with my new little brother, Eugene.

Maggie, Nomusa and Mary appeared in court that Monday. I noticed that Sister St Claire was not in her office. She was in court too. Later I heard that Papa Pretorius and Mr van Wyk refused to withdraw the charges and that Mammy Cynthia had called Gudrun Alexandra to assist. Gudrun was an ex-pupil and had become a prominent criminal lawyer in Durban. Without hesitation and as a favour to Mammy Cynthia, who once had been her caregiver too, Gudrun appeared for the three women.

Through court process Mr van Wyk and Papa Pretorius described their version of the events that led to them having been assaulted.

Gudrun responded by seeking clarity. The men were asked:

1. Whether they noticed that the facility had been prepared for a function;
2. Whether they were aware that permission had been granted by the Head Teacher for the facility to be used;
3. Whether they knew Mammy Cynthia and had knowledge of her imminent retirement;
4. Whether they had helped themselves to items, including luxuries that were not theirs to have;
5. Whether they were watching TV during official working hours; and
6. Whether it was possible that they could, within minutes, have moved to an adjacent facility?

The men objected to Gudrun's questions, arguing instead that the charges were to do with assault and nothing else.

The magistrate overruled their objection.

In a surprise turn, after Gudrun had concluded her clarification of the Plaintiffs' allegations, she called her only witness. Mr van Wyk and Papa Pretorius were visibly shocked when Sister St Claire took to the stand as a witness for the Defendants. Gudrun's first question to Sister St Claire was whether the two Plaintiffs, Papa Pretorius and Mr van Wyk, reported to her. Other questions included whether she, meaning Sister St Claire, had given permission for the party to be held in the big meeting room; and whether Sister St Claire had asked the men to move to the smaller room.

On hearing Sister St Claire's version of the same event, the magistrate interjected and ruled the matter a waste of the court's time. The case was dismissed and the two men were severely reprimanded for being rude, childish and disrespectful; also, that their actions, and those of the policemen involved, had racist overtones.

That having been said the matter was dismissed with costs to the Defendants. Mr van Wyk and Papa Pretorius were ordered to pay Gudrun's court fee.

Several people lost credibility as a result of this outcome:

• Mr. Thompson, for not speaking out; probably for fear that he might become unpopular with his colleagues if he did not support them, and;

- Mr. van Wyk, Papa Pretorius and Mr. Thompson, for hooliganism.

The story had gone around school, as such stories do. Its spread gained momentum when Sister St Claire's white VW Beetle was driven up the long school driveway to her parking space. Maggie, the biggest of the three women, was in the passenger seat, while Nomusa and Mary filled the back.

Discussion about the incident raged on for weeks. General sentiments amongst the pupils were that Mr Thompson and Sister St Claire were not as innocent as they wished us to believe. It was argued that had Sister St Claire taken a decision, and had she communicated it clearly, then the fracas would have been averted. Mr Thompson's role drew no commendation in the court of public opinion. Most of the senior pupils felt that he had sold his soul for friendship from hooligans and that as a result had lost their respect.

Mammy Cynthia had retired and the atmosphere at school had changed forever. By then Jane had been away for a while and I coped 'on my own', but when Mammy Cynthia left …

Chapter Fourteen

Marilyn

I could not understand Mr Thompson's decision to align himself with Papa Pretorius and Mr van Wyk, instead of with the retirement function for Mammy Cynthia. I could not move past the poor choice he had made; a respected man who, through one senseless act, had ruined his relationship with so many people who, like me, had held him in high regard. I just couldn't understand it. Why did Mr Thompson not challenge the two men? He could have told Papa Pretorius and Mr van Wyk to move to the other room. Was he really that concerned about becoming unpopular with them? To move, clearly, would have been the right thing to do.

"Pa failed me, but more importantly, he failed himself," was Ma's view about the manner in which Pa treated us. In that context I wondered what happened to Mr Thompson's refrain: "No pain, no gain." On that day, when he had the opportunity to gain something by going through a minor amount of pain, he had just sat there with Christmas tinsel wrapped around his neck and a stolen drink in one hand. It might have been awkward to tell his colleagues to move, but Mammy Cynthia, a woman he respected, and whose home he once visited, she would have gained. Instead of making a difference by taking a stand, he sat there, in silence when he should have been vocal.

The other men, Papa Pretorius and Mr van Wyk, had lost whatever credibility they had. The atmosphere at school was stifling. It was horrible to be there. Pupils were forming cliques that took pride in being critical of others. The cynics were in their element. I was okay, protected by my size and the reputation for being able to defend myself. The time I spent at St Mary's was longer than everyone else. By then I had been there for thirteen years.

The teachers continued to teach; the workers did their jobs; and the bullies bullied. It slowly dawned on me that my personal happiness would be regained by leaving the school. I could not bear the thought of having to be there for almost two more years. The only attraction I had left was the prospect of participating in another international surfing competition. Again I set my hopes on competing in Durban during the June school holidays, 1977.

As promised, Mr Thompson made some of the arrangements for my invitation and participation. I was to use a pseudonym. It was another of those 'precautionary measures' to avoid embarrassment for illegally using a reserved beach.

Since my relationship with Mr Thompson was somewhat strained, the prospect of competing became less likely. I continued to prepare for the contest nonetheless. My transport to the beach was with the help of a weekly boarder. His parents fetched him for the weekend on Fridays and they'd stop for me to get off the back of their utility vehicle when passing through Scottburgh. Sleeping arrangements were a problem. Occasionally I found accommodation with fellow surfers who had become my friends. These young men and women often paddled out to where I was allowed to share the ocean with them. They'd paddle to ask for tips on how to execute some of the more complicated manoeuvres, which by then I had perfected. Whenever the weather was good I slept in a tunnel beneath the railway line. My wetsuit became a very effective blanket, and my surf-booties, when rolled together, became a comfortable pillow.

Not so on the night policemen shone their torches in my face while I slept in a tunnel underneath the railway line. That night I scuttled down the road with all my possessions in tow, but minus my booties. The following day promised big swells during an early high tide. It was full moon and that always meant bigger swells were to follow a few days later. I could not afford to spend the weekend in cells at the Scottburgh Police Station, listening to people fight over rubbish, when there were good surf-breaks to be enjoyed. That night though, the police were on the prowl. I had had enough of being chased and decided to ask for help from the petrol attendants on the forecourt of a nearby 24-hour fuel stop.

Before I could ask, one of the attendants said: "You are the surfer boy; we know about you." The other attendant chimed in: "And a surfer boy needs all the sleep he can get." They then spoke to each other in Zulu as if I were not there: "He's good, I heard the people talking. They sit on the rocks and watch him dance on the water."

Turning to me the older of the two men said: "Come boy, come sleep; sleep and one day you can teach my children to dance too. You sleep; I'll sit here and study."

Their animated conversation continued way past what I expected. The older man was particularly keen that I rest. "Yes! He must have as much sleep as possible. Put him right at the back and point the heater in that direction."

Both men hurried to prepare a space for me to sleep at the back of their service room. They flattened cardboard boxes and placed them on the ground alongside their own. The two men shared one flattened cardboard box because they took turns throughout the night to tend occasional customers on the forecourt.

When it was the turn of the younger man to rest he said to me: "You sleep, and don't worry when we jump up, this is our job. If you snore, we'll give you one tablespoon of diesel with a tot of brandy and then you'll also be 'Number One', like this service station!"

It was a good sleep. No diesel-with-brandy was required. At about six o'clock that morning the older man woke me: "You have to get up now because the shift change is at seven and we do not like the others to see when someone has slept here."

We were sharing coffee when the day shift arrived. The two men, my new guardians, left for home. The older man, Zuvarashe (Sun Chief), was an Honours student of English. He made his way to the university in Durban for additional tuition before catching up on sleep. His dress was like mine on that Christmas Eve in Mpophomeni: with his usual clothes he wore a jacket, a hat, a briefcase and carried a stick with a knob at one end, like Mr Khumalo. I was standing on the outskirts of the forecourt with my board and other belongings when the kind gentleman walked by and left me with the following parting words: "One day, when my son is in Cape Town, and got no family, and is lonely, then you will do for him what we did for you?"

I smiled and nodded respectfully, wondering if his partial quote was from the famous Steinbeck book, *Of Mice and Men*. Was it perhaps a manifestation of his studies, I wondered. Ma often told me: "Education is only successful if it positively enhances the way you behave." So, the way people speak must be a form of behaviour too, I thought.

Later that morning, while sitting out on the rocks, waiting for the top of the tide to turn, I thought about how ordinary people said simple things, and that small things were the most important.

Sharks were always a concern and that was the reason I surfed in a full wetsuit and boots. Mr Thompson had taught me that sharks feed at dawn and again at dusk. Early mornings and evenings were thought to be the most dangerous—clearly not for sharks, only surfers! September was considered a risky time, because sharks came closer to the shore when the seasons changed. It is always safer to surf in rocky areas and on an outgoing tide, particularly in the early morning.

I became a regular at a park-and-eat facility, a roadhouse, on Marine Terrace, Scottburgh. Sometimes I managed to save enough money for a chip roll. When I had it for dinner then some was kept for the next day. Soft drinks were a waste of money because the drinking water in Scottburgh was fine, and when I closed my eyes, that water could have been anything.

When times improved and there was spare money in my pocket, a Hawaiian burger was what I bought. It was the closest I'd ever get to surfing the famed 'Off the Wall' on Hawaii's North Shore, about which I read in Mr Thompson's magazines. That burger, half in the evening and the rest for lunch the next day was my favourite weekend meal. As a snack in between I'd pick raw mussels and the odd oyster. There was ice cream too, in the form of a round vanilla clump on a stick covered in a skin of dark brown chocolate. It cost fifteen cents and was called Surf-Joy. Once a month I skipped the burger and the chip roll and had a Surf-Joy instead. Afterwards, when hungry, I'd drink water and eat from the rocks whenever the hunger pangs visited.

In time the owner of the roadhouse offered me an evening job. I would spend the daytime hours surfing, but from six to ten on Fridays, and from six to eleven-thirty on Saturday evenings I became one of three waiters in the car park in front of that roadhouse. There was a very big menu above the roof. It slanted towards the cars and was very brightly lit at night. If it were not for its slant that menu would have been visible from outer space, it was so big. Working at the roadhouse was like being on the set of *Saturday Night at the Palace,* the Paul Slabolepzy play, which I read years later.

I wore a black and white side cap with matching apron. The rest of my outfit consisted of Rusty's tyre-sandals, my school shorts and a white shirt. The night manager said that my dress was not smart enough. I felt that it was okay, particularly when the night-watchman intervened: "No, no, his dress is fine! Better dress is for people who do not have a personality. This man's sense of humour is legendary, trust me."

Customers would choose meals and remain seated in their cars. My role was to take the order and place it with the kitchen. When ready I'd serve the meal. The tray clipped onto a partially raised car window. I could also affix it to the car with suction grips. The blokes with shiny cars, girlfriends and rings on their little fingers always gave the best tips. Often, when the man went to the bathroom, the woman would call me to ask: "Where do you come from?" When I answered, most would frown and ask one of two follow-up questions: "Where do you come from originally?" or: "Where do you really come from?" I wondered why they were so interested, only the women, those whose boyfriends had rings on their little fingers. The girlfriends often asked to feel my hair and afterwards they'd pepper me with a number of what also had become usual questions: "Is that your natural hair; why, the curls are so soft? How do you get your hair to be so light, with different colours of brown and even streaks of blonde? Where do you really come from, tell me, I won't tell anyone else? What are you doing here, in this place; and, you don't belong, hey?" Boyfriends returned from the toilets surrounded by clouds of sweet heavy cologne fragrances. It was as if their visit to that roadhouse bathroom was a mission to manufacture one of the Brut products. Others usually went to the bathroom to wave their tackle at porcelain, but not those boyfriends. When the men, wearing their little finger rings and updated Brut 'bouquet' returned the women would pretend that I did not exist. This even though, just a few moments earlier, of the women would have asked to cut a piece of my hair.

I earned a standard casual wage at that job. The fee was nothing when compared to my accumulated tips. 'The ring-men' left the best tips, probably in an attempt to impress their sly inquisitive girls. Usually the tip, a one rand note, would protrude from beneath an empty coke bottle on my silver window tray. Sometimes, when I removed the tray, my tip would threaten to be blown in the sea breeze. On occasion when the tip did get blown I'd pounce and capture it beneath the broad sole of my tyre-sandal. After 'capturing' the errant tip I'd store it together with my other one rand notes in the back pocket of my shorts. It was the pocket that closed with a tie-back button.

Tipsters were more generous late at night I became friendlier and even quick with a joke, or provided a light for the men's smokes. Some I'd wish luck. The men would thank me. There were those who needed more luck than others despite their elegant clothes, Brut fragrance, Chevrolet cars and little finger rings. With hindsight, I was just jealous!

After the job was done I'd check tide times in the latest publication of that *South Coast Herald* newspaper. My regular sleeping spot was inside the cabin where the night-watchman sat. In exchange for a steak roll with monkey gland sauce, which was Mahachi's favourite, I'd get to sleep inside, while he watched over me and the roadhouse where we both worked. This became our routine, every Friday and Saturday night for about three months.

Wearing a uniform that included epaulettes, boots and a cap, Mahachi was transformed into the weekend night-watchman. He was Rhodesian, the country that would later be renamed Zimbabwe. During the week he studied engineering in Durban and stayed with his mother. Mahachi's mother was a live-in domestic worker for a wealthy family. They resided in the upper-class suburb of Kloof. Come Friday, Saturday and Sunday nights, Mahachi became a no-nonsense security man complete with stick and torch. Unlike me, I am sure that Mahachi did not close his eyes in a stick fight. That would have pleased Mr Khumalo, who years earlier laughed when he taught me and I shut my eyes when striking and blocking with my shield. On the rare occasion when Mahachi invited me to his mother's quarters I would be astounded to see how wealthy people lived. Mahachi and his mother shared a backroom with normal furnishings, which included a desk and drawing board for his homework.

Years later Mahachi invited me to his graduation. By then I was working on a beach in Cape Town and could not attend. Someday we'll find each other. Then I shall remind him of the stick and torch. We'll have a good laugh, but hopefully not cry, like Uncle Flippie and Pa did when they reminisced. But more importantly, I shall thank Mahachi for watching over me and for being my friend when I had no-one.

I stayed with Mahachi in his night-watchman's cabin while preparing for a competition that was to be held in the second week of June, 1977. It was the beginning of our mid-year school vacation. I found a lift with a classmate whose parents fetched him for the June winter holidays. They lived in one of the suburbs near Durban. Sydenham, or Overport, I am no longer sure what the suburb was called. I never went to their home. No, when Mr Young reached Brickfield Road, an exit off the freeway from Pietermaritzburg, that was where he stopped for me to get off the back of his open van. It was early evening, but still warm, when I began the seven kilometre walk down to the sea from Brickfield Road. Progress was slow because no public bus would allow me to travel with a surfboard and what must have appeared to be a giant blue suitcase. The only option was to walk. The sun set around five o'clock that June evening. Seeing a young man walk in the dark carrying a suitcase and a surfboard must have been a peculiar sight. I crossed the busy Berea Road at about seven o'clock that night, en route to the beach, all so that I could check the sea and surf in the big competition. All seemed fine. I had become a seasoned resident with forecourt attendants and night-watchmen. That night though, I slept in what appeared to be a reasonably clean drainpipe underneath Berea Road.

I arrived in the north of Durban City at about eight o'clock on a Saturday morning. By then I was carrying the suitcase and surfboard with difficulty. The end was near though. On the north corner of Stanger Street was a dusty enclosed field with a building. I could see several long-haul trucks parked there. Some were probably staying for the weekend.

It seemed that I had picked a fine place from where to fix the last bit of administrative detail. The Stanger Street Truck Stop was a block up from the main surfing beach. The truck drivers were friendly enough; some were from Cape Town and many shared broad toothless grins when I responded by speaking in my home-town dialect. I stayed.

Every night brought different drivers but the atmosphere remained the same. Women who hung around the truck stop were mainly sex workers.

"What are you doing here? This is no place for you. Can I feel your hair … My name is Marilyn, hello." That woman, with her raspy voice, asked many more questions than the ones I cite. It did not sound as if she wanted to hear my reply.

I responded anyway: "My name is Sam. I am trying to surf in the competition down at the beach, but it is more difficult at night." She looked at me, pulled her face and produced a sarcastic smile; then laughed out loud and almost burned her face with a lit cigarette. "Can't surf at night you say!" Her laugh was phlegm-infused and ended with an unhealthy cough. It was evident that Marilyn had seen better days; days when she had been pretty, probably very pretty. Her silhouette in the night light bore testimony to my thoughts.

"Is Sam your real name? People who work here don't use their real names."

I tried to speak, but Marilyn was not listening; she was not really interested in what I had to say. I tried: "It is better sitting here, than out there, Addington way, near the hospital. The people seem restless there and funny men in fancy cars lurk to pick up women. I want to sleep here under this veranda until daybreak and then I can head down to the beach, is that okay?"

Marilyn lit another cigarette and nodded slowly while staring straight ahead at the entrance gate to that dustbowl truck stop at the top of Stanger Street. I assumed that she was in agreement with my intention to spend the night there.

Marilyn, without warning, let out a raspy holler. It sounded louder than the noise made by a huge Cape Town registered truck that slowly entered the yard through its dilapidated entrance gates. Marilyn's scream was directed at a woman who walked toward the incoming truck. That truck driver was Marilyn's client, the one whom she had been expecting.

Different ladies arrived as the evening matured. Some spoke with me; and to others, I did not exist. Throughout the night, singly or simultaneously, the women disappeared and then reappeared. After about her fourth reappearance one of the women noticed that I was sleeping on several pieces of cardboard, between four big used truck tyres.

"Surely you can do better than stay in this dive?"

I woke to the sight of a pair of red, chipped, high-heeled shoes at the bottom of long skinny legs ascending upwards into an extremely short dress. She wore no underwear and it did not bother her that I could see.

Hurriedly I sat up, thinking it best to answer the question: "I do not intend staying here for long," I mumbled in my posh boarding school accent. She spat on me and proceeded to solicit a more likely prospect, a man who had emerged from the toilet entrance, near where I was trying to sleep.

Every night there was a mood that was created mainly by the sweet smell of marijuana and women arguing about clients, money and alcohol. Some described a fight that had been won, or more likely lost, when a truck driver thought his companion a she, when the she was actually a he!

Lying there on my cardboard bed, listening to the description of a recent scrap, was reminiscent of a bad spaghetti western film. The person describing the fight was, according to her, always right, and she was always wronged, by, amongst others: "A fat and ugly, short, bald, toothless bastard who was married to his sister!" The animated scene was better than any a fiction writer could muster. It was marginally comparable to a Cape Flats gangster relating a court scene when he explained: "… my argument, when I spoke in mitigation of sentence, was so convincing that the judge had no option but to serve the scheduled jail time himself!" The raconteur always won. Reality never mattered. It was like going fishing. Those who never caught, they bought; while those who caught small described the whale that got away!

The activity usually calmed down after two in the morning. But at the glimmer of first light a truck would be cranked, followed by another, and then all the others. It was no different to when birds begin to chirp as daylight gradually replaces the darkness. The ground would tremble as cold and overworked diesel engines roared back into life.

I was awake then, often with what felt like grit in my eyes from too little sleep. The noises and activity made it difficult to remain asleep. Hopeful travellers arrived throughout the night. My bed was in the corner under the veranda and furthest away from the toilet entrance. On the inside of the wall, where I slept, was the most frequently used toilet. The sounds produced from inside were ominous. I am sure that if the toilet had not had a roof or a seat to double as hold-on handle, then those upset stomachs would have caused there to be 'lift-off'. Those sounds were a direct result of having eaten the cheapest bunny chow. The sugar-bean-bunny consists of a quarter, half or full loaf of white bread, the casing. The soft inside of the bread was replaced with a spicy bean curry and topped with a grated carrot and cucumber in vinegar salad. The full loaf was called a coffin, and the level of backfiring produced in that toilet would usually bear testimony to the quantity of 'bunny' consumed. The sounds I heard from there could result in a nightmare, no matter what the time of day! The stench, ooh no … it is to die from.

At night I was the only occupant on the veranda; but in the morning there were often as many as nine others sleeping alongside me. These were people whom I did not know and would probably never see again. We had shared a sleeping space, as on an overnight train. Their objective was to ask a truck driver for a lift, but only after the night-woman who kept him company had left. The truck driver would usually alight after the woman. He'd wash (use the toilet!), smoke, have coffee and debrief with fellow truck drivers. Meanwhile, the truck engine would idle in preparation for the day ahead.

As soon as the driver walked back to his truck, my veranda companions collectively leapt to their feet. Sleep or no sleep, they'd buzz around the drivers like bees at a honeysuckle bush. The lift seekers offered money; their posturing dramatized desperation as they competed with one another for the best hard-luck story. Sometimes the driver would give the nod for one or two of them to join the trailer crew.

Truck drivers who arrived to offload at Durban harbour, and those departing for destinations across Africa, all used the Stanger Street Truck Port to refuel. Often they spent the night, particularly if a night-woman of their desire lurked there. It had become a sub-culture and I was on the periphery, looking in, and trying to make sense of things that were way beyond my nearly seventeen years.

The engines fumed burning oil and grease. It was a smell that first mixed and then replaced the sweet aroma of weed. The industrial stench caused me to lie flat on my bed of cardboard and so duck away from rising smoke. The tremble, caused by running truck engines was quite soothing, I remember. Women seemed to re-appear as the smoke settled. They climbed down from those huge trucks, looking dishevelled after spending the night with what often times looked like an uncomfortably corpulent truck driver. Some headed for the bathrooms and others had no need. Later, the women congregated on the veranda while I lay hidden below the side ridges of fat used-truck-tyres that surrounded my cardboard bed. Most of the women held a cup of steaming hot coffee. They stood there, each telling the other what had happened during the night. The night-women spoke in whispered tones, deliberate, but 'carefully modulated' so that everyone, including me, could hear.

I knew that those drivers had families at home, and I suspected that the women did too. The fattest of the drivers apparently asked one to go with him. They would return later that same week. One of the night-women was pregnant. Every morning she'd hover close to my bed and seek the same advice but from a different so-called friend. There was a favoured friend, one who seemingly gave the best pregnancy advice. That one had a deep voice, a protruding Adam's apple and hairy legs. Though I did not know much, I knew that the hairy-legged-night-woman could not be sufficiently experienced to provide pre-natal advice.

It all seemed humorous then …

Sometimes I think about those women and children born from the liaisons at Stanger Street Truck Port.

The pregnant night-woman often spoke within earshot of my bed. I grew embarrassed, felt sorrow and even longed to give her a comfort hug after hearing the sordid details of her life and what she had endured. It was far too graphic and included stuff, yes, stuff which I thought only adults should know. My uncomfortable dilemma was that I had to straddle the divide between looking like a man while being just a boy—one who would sneak the odd thumb-suck when no-one was looking.

I tried not to listen; but not to hear was difficult. To lie between my tyres was a process, a waiting, for the morning sleepiness to pass and for the eye grit to settle. As the group of women on the veranda grew, their discussions became more animated. The stories were no different from tales of conquest which men told their mates.

Truck drivers were the subjects of these women's conversations. Meanwhile they, the drivers, appeared less keen on the same woman over whom they had swooned the previous evening. Was everything about which those women spoke true, or was it all just fabricated tales? I'll never know.

It was not unusual to be offered an early morning cup of coffee, usually by Marilyn. The coffee was sweet, as if they had dissolved an entire stick of sugar cane into the splodgy chipped enamel mug. It was my fourth night on that veranda. I felt settled. Perhaps it was because by then I knew what to expect. It was like being home, where I'd hang out with the Harmony Boys, on the corner in front of M.I. Bazaars. We gathered there and harmonised to old tunes, the boys from nearby surrounds and I. Each boy had a street name. Mine was Jes, short for Jester, apparently because I was funny. Punch, one of the older boys, had a perfect natural red afro, blue eyes and freckles. He was a revered star on the football pitch. Punch could sing like Frank Sinatra and always led the discussions about sojourns with women. I don't know whether that was also like Frank Sinatra because he, Frank, never arrived to harmonise at our corner! Then there was Suzie, he was a hairdresser, worked in a bank, or both. Suzie could sing, and I mean sing!

The Stanger Street night-women, save for their carnal stories and gender bending, - would have given Punch, Jakes, Snowy, Tubby and Bunny, with whom I harmonised, stiff competition! Suzie never got involved in storytelling and the Harmony Boys would not have been interested in corpulent truck drivers.

Living in a world where I was expected to be both a boy and a man left me feeling 'too big for my boots' at times. There is a set of norms for everything. I learned this quickly. The challenge remained which norm to apply when. To learn a norm is difficult: like the Cape dialect, it is not taught, but observed, internalised and then applied. Becoming streetwise was a lot more complex than I had initially thought. Over time my new experiences made me feel much older than my years and my peers; I had been exposed more so than others of my age, that must have been the reason.

My routine stretches were completed shortly after the early morning commotion. Afterwards I would become the borrowed name and prepared for a day out in the surf. Part of preparing for the day included planning for that night. My tyres were stowed together with the others in the hope that they would remain there until the evening. It was never a guarantee.

When my teeth were cleaned I'd carry the board and my suitcase down to the reserved beach where the competition continued. The blue suitcase stayed with an informal curio trader on the beachfront. He transformed it by placing a reed mat over; and that was how my suitcase became part of his trinket and souvenir display stand.

The South African Police Force had a visible presence on the beach. They were particularly vigilant about identifying suspicious people. Mainly dark-skinned people were targeted for random body searches. In addition, seemingly angry security police clad in combat gear would hang from the back of grey Land Rovers as they slowly drove by; all in an attempt to keep 'undesirable' elements away. The collective security forces held big guns and kept them close to their bodies. I saw R1 rifles; 12 bore shotguns that discharged fat stubby rubber bullets; and either a .32 or a 9mm Beretta Pistol in a holster strapped to every policeman's side; other guns too, but I didn't recognise those.

Slowly the competition organisers would arrive. The foreigners were more aware of the police presence. To us, South Africans, it had become normal. I managed to get to the water by walking on the pier, up to the furthest point. Once there, I checked to see who was looking and then leapt into 'the drink'.

That was the start of Day Four. The water was warm and I could not imagine it getting better. The swells were fine, not the best, but fine. There were competition days when the swells were slight. Getting through those days required more skill.

When back on the beach, after the practise rides, all competitors had access to fruit and energy drinks. I ate and drank with abandon—to walk off the beach and get food when hungry was too risky.

The first heats began. A siren marked each set of rides, flags were in position and the timer began its countdown. The riders came in, one after the other, and often many rode the same wave together. To avert collisions, the unwritten rule and correct etiquette was to follow behind the rider who was first to stand. Even so, accidents happened and friendships soured. There were no rewards for fighting with surfers. It was said by fellow surfers that I had an air of entitlement in the water; apparently it was evident in the liquidity of my style. I practised hard to achieve fluency but even so it felt contrived, a feeling which never resolved.

Spectators gathered on the beach every day, but they were nothing compared with the throng of people who arrived to watch the final surf-off on 'Final Sunday'. An imposing scaffold served as the stage on which the judges sat. The competition was supported by a famous radio station. That radio station and the sponsors' names were very visible. Their music was different from the music I listened to at the time. Apparently the girls who gathered to watch the final that Sunday afternoon were very pretty. None of it existed for me. My focus of the task at hand and other worries was more intense. I did not understand about adrenalin and other woo-woo stuff at the time, only that there was a job to do. My ability to be afraid seemed to have been replaced by something else during that competition. The anxiety and ever-present threat of being caught, identified, exposed and charged for trespassing consumed me throughout those seven days, but not when competing. Maybe that was the reason why I never noticed the girls! The threat and possibility of being arrested grew stronger every day as various surfers were eliminated and I stayed. I only realised that after the competition. There was a job to do and little else mattered. Conversations with other surfers didn't count for much, save for a short, dainty, agile Hawaiian athlete, my role model.

Capital Radio 604 featured men to whom I listened when they broadcast on Medium Wave (AM) from a transmission point in the Transkei. The Transkei was then a homeland for Xhosa people, the second biggest group in South Africa. The same two men were there, then working for a different radio station and broadcasting while we surfed. The rapport between the two was much better than their choice of music. Without them knowing, it was their banter that served to lift my spirits when moments weren't 'festive'.

I was again in the line-up and rode. It came naturally. Mr Thompson had prepared me well and I had become confident as a result. "You don't have to panic if you know your stuff Champ, just do it!" was what he would have said. It was as though I could hear him screaming at me. In the beginning, his screams had made me feel that I was doing something wrong. Later I learned that his screams were meant to teach me confidence. That day, the second to last day, Mr Thompson's words reverberated in my head more strongly than at any other time. I imagined him strutting across the beach with a whistle in his mouth, in his favourite pair of Bermuda Shorts and being ever ready to summon my attention before letting out an instructive scream. "There's no need to plan, Champ! Ride! Ride! Ride! Ride the wave Champ! Do what comes naturally, show them! Feel the thrust; then up on your feet; ride on the board's nose when you need the extra boost!" That voice, the sound of it, his sound, was so clear to me that day, right inside my head. It felt like he was there, on the beach. For that moment my imagination fuelled me. I longed for Mr Thompson to scream at me. My concern was always that he would have a heart attack while I was in the surf. He would become very excited when I did something right. So much, that I would doubt being able to repeat the manoeuvre, in case my coach became disappointed. Only Mr Thompson could ease the loneliness I felt that day. There were thousands of people. I was alone, just my surfboard, the blue suitcase and the memory of my wonderful coach.

The board went faster when the thrust of the wave was there. Immediately I was up on my feet, otherwise the board would run ahead of the wave, or I'd wash over, lose momentum and points. I heard the familiar rustling board-on-water sound and my instinct was to swing to the right. Most natural-footers swing to the left. Coach Thompson was in my head again, screaming: "Ride the crest when the wave is small and the thrust is low! C-u-s-p the wave; bounce once or twice, Champ; then cusp the wave again! Cusp the wave!"

212

That day I struggled to stay on the ridge. In two of the heats I fell over onto the back of the wave. Coach Thompson would have been angry. I'd hear him again and again with each heat that I surfed. His voice was clear, as though we were at the rocky surf spot near Scottburgh beach. I even felt the same disappointment when I failed to match his expectations.

Greater speed meant that a three hundred and sixty degree airborne turn was possible. When it all came together and the manoeuvre was perfect, I instinctively stood up straight on my board with the wave at my back. My arms would be up in the air in salute to the God of Life, a phenomenon that is beyond my ability to understand. At those times I wished that many more in the world were able to experience the exhilarating magic of surfing.

While the daytime norm was exhilaration, at night I tried to sleep amidst the constant discussion about people's intimate regions. That sweet smell was all over the veranda as the spliff was passed from one eager woman to another.

My life throughout the competition was different from that of the other contestants. Very different in fact, but in the water we were the same. Some of the invited participants were better than others on the day. I wondered where they lived. We didn't talk much, lest my cover be blown. Their boards were new, custom built with their own names calligraphed underneath the final resin coat. My board was handed down; it had been in many accidents and was rebuilt several times. I rode a patchwork board. The board was too small, I thought. Not having money for food, plus the stress of living at the Stanger Street Truck Port had caused me to lose weight. Who knows, maybe the board and I had grown into each other and we were a good match after all?

Well, the reality was that my name was not mine; my board was too small; and I had not eaten in days. The Saturday competition was okay, but I knew it was not my best. I didn't expect to be in the final line-up. When the pairs were listed on the leader board the last to appear included my fake name. I was using the name of an Australian surfer who was not competing in that leg of the World Series. So, my fake name, my too-small board and I we had made it to the line-up on 'Final Sunday'. Most of the others, who might have been living a better life in the reserved hotels across from the beach, did not qualify to ride in the final.

That night I went 'home', took up position on the side of my tyre-bed and stripped the caked-on wax from the patchwork board. For the rest of the evening I re-waxed in preparation for the final. My hunger pangs were back but my appetite for winning was greater. "No pain, no gain, Champ!" That voice would not leave me. I had to believe in myself. To have a shower that night was a must. The communal showers were full and I had to sit on the slatted wooden bench and wait my turn. Every one there had an old plastic onion bag with which they washed their bodies. I was fascinated and knew that someday I'd try that. I did and it felt great, like a good scrub against my skin.

"What is that stuff that you rub on the board? It smells good, like coconut, what is it?" asked Marilyn. She was waiting on the veranda to meet with a certain driver, or so she said when I returned from the shower and found her sitting there. The answer to her question embarrassed me, so I smiled and continued to sit on the tyre while rubbing my board across its width with the compound. Marilyn crouched against the step across from where I was working. Her delicate legs and defined calf muscles were evident. She clutched her legs with one arm, in an almost self-embrace while smoking a sweet smelling something. Marilyn was probably also trying to forget about life for a while.

Her outline resembled the figure in Van Gogh's lithograph etching, which he aptly names, *Sorrow*. It was a loose picture that had fallen from a book in Ms du Pont's class, one that I was copying as a present for Jane on our birthday that October. Marilyn's legs were far better than those in the etching; she must have danced or done work at a studio bar. Other women of forty-two were already showing fatty deposits around their ankles, but not Marilyn.

I sensed her concern for my lack of response to the question about that rubbing compound. Marilyn raised her head and turned to look at me: "You do not belong here Sammy. Man, what's wrong with you? What's that stuff you rub on the surfboard? Tell me; I would like to rub some of that on me too."

Something was bothering Marilyn. I smiled again; first at the board and then looked up: "Sex wax. Sex wax is what it's called. You can get it from a surf shop; any surf shop will stock it."

"You bet boy, I will. What's your name again?"

"Sa…" but before I could finish a delirious Marilyn interjected: "Yes. Sammy! That's it, Sammy the surfer boy… yeah?" She dragged hard on the sweet-smelling reefer, sucking in the air long after removing the substantially shortened joint from her mouth. Marilyn flicked the ash with the remaining three fingers while clumsily holding on to the crooked burning Rizla wrapped dagga cigarette. "Sex wax, hmm … I wonder, will it make my pain less, what do you think?"

I was just a boy. "Nah, this wax makes the grip better on the face of the board, that's all."

Only Marilyn knew what she was saying. I didn't understand. Her voice became softer and raspier, but her words remained slurred: "How's the surfing *gwoing*? You been busy a long time. When's it end?"

"The final is tomorrow afternoon. I'm in the line-up, in a surf-off against that famous bloke. That is why the old wax has to go; I need better grip, and putting new wax on top of old will make the board heavier."

I paused because it seemed as if Marilyn was not listening, or perhaps she was slow?

"You're in the final! Really?" Suddenly the slur was gone and Marilyn stood up from her crouching position. She yelled at the top of her raspy voice: "In the final! Really; what time? I want to watch!"

Then she screamed out to everyone who could hear: "Hey! Sammy here's in the surfing final on the beach tomorrow!" She turned to me: "I wanna watch you man!"

214

Upon hearing that, I looked at her briefly and then my gaze fell, but just for a moment, a moment to think. By the time I looked up again, Marilyn had stepped closer. She had the best legs but her hazel eyes were red and bloodshot. I longed to have someone there, someone of my own, for whom I could surf. The others did not matter because to them I was just another unknown surfer from Australia, the Cape Flats part of Australia!

"Would you really do that for me?" I asked.

"Yes, I'll be there."

"Do you promise?"

"Yes Sammy, I'll be there ..."

"Okay, about two o'clock Marilyn; after lunch, I'll look out for you."

Chapter Fifteen

On Family; Truckers; Spectres; and Jane

Marilyn's client arrived. The horse of his truck had no trailer attached. He parked it in front of the veranda where Marilyn and I were talking. The driver, without switching off the engine, climbed down from his controlling perch. He rubbed his hands together, kissed Marilyn on the cheek and asked: "Hop in; come with me?"

"No, wait."

Again she turned to me: "This is Sammy. He's surfing in the final tomorrow. Sammy, meet Jeffrey."

Jeffrey and I shook hands. He was a bit older than Marilyn, but looked good, like a not too ex-football player. I could hear the song in his tone when Jeffrey spoke—another Capetonian.

"Have you eaten, Sammy?" asked Marilyn.

"Yes, have you eaten?" echoed Jeffrey.

I looked away, a bit shy to answer. "I've not eaten in three days, only energy drinks on the beach and fruit."

"Okay, we're *gwoing* to change that. Can we go now, to Johnnie's, Jeff?"

They were away for a while. I was hungry and the thought of eating, together with the wait, nearly paralysed me.

When Marilyn and Jeffrey finally arrived with the food I stood up and, with a lump in my throat, I hugged her bony figure tightly. Jeffrey too, we hugged because I was just too emotional, or maybe I was too hungry, to talk.

"There my boy," said Marilyn as she handed me a parcel, "eat! It's chicken. I got some milk for you to drink; they say it's good, better than Super Moo milkshake. When done, then go for a walk and I'll watch your stuff; and then you can sleep, so that you can dance on that water tomorrow."

Ma often compared my appetite to that of a horse. That night I ate like a herd of horses: an entire roast chicken, a carrot salad and a litre of full cream milk. My stomach ululated in appreciation and I could not thank Marilyn enough. As sleep came to me in my tyre-and-cardboard bed that night, my only wish was for an ideal wave formation. I imagined a barrel ride but was worried that the wave quality would not be good enough to get tubed.

That sleep was better than the previous nights. The surfboard-leash was strapped to my right ankle and the blue suitcase to my right wrist. The next morning, immediately when I awoke, the adrenalin began to course through my body. That would be my diagnosis years later. On that day though, I forgot about the mundane. Marilyn watched over my stuff after she emerged from Jeffrey's truck. I went for a long run, stretched and worked my way to the beach. The morning dragged on and the afternoon's event felt ages away. I walked up to Sunkist, a popular sit-down or take-out eatery up yonder, past the snake park, down there where the Umgeni River flowed into the Indian Ocean. I must have completed the walk three times that day before I was called to surf.

After several rides, two of us qualified to compete in a final surf-off. We walked across the sand to paddle out. The other man, a popular man, was cheered by his fans. I heard a lone voice screaming my name from a corner near the pier. It was the loudest scream! That was all I heard. The scream went on until I turned back to acknowledge Marilyn with a slight wave of my right hand. The screaming became louder as I got closer to the pier. It felt good to be surfing for someone, but I was anxious that the noise was too loud and because it was sure to draw undue attention. It is difficult to be under-cover if you are on the front page. Had I explained to her then Marilyn would not have understood. It did not matter so much if I was arrested after competing, but not before the event. I desperately wanted to finish.

Despite my bravado other thoughts also churned through my mind while I paddled out alongside the pillars of that pier: "What if Lieutenant Subramani, Captain van Deventer or any of the others are patrolling; and what if any of them see me, particularly after that screaming? What if the police stop me from using the reserved beach before I can finish?" I did a quick turn to check and then paddled faster.

A buoy signalled the starting point. The beach crowd seemed daunting. It was like a wall of people where earlier there had been only caramel coloured beach sand. There was a small, very distinct looking noisy group of people with Marilyn. They had gathered in the outside corner near the entrance to the pier and continued to chant my name.

Each of us rode the first and second heats. Wave selection continued to be a problem. The tide was low and the swells were weak. I was not the only one suffering. Pairs who rode ahead of us had suffered the result of poor swells too.

Neither of us spoke to the other.

We paddled out for the last ride. My wave selection had improved, but the wave quality remained poor. Up on the crest was where the most points lived. We caught the same wave but turned in opposite directions. It felt as if the momentum was flagging. Realising this, I swung the board back to the crest. Not too much. I was facing down-wave and bounced for greater momentum. It was about 25 metres from the beach. The momentum was there. I could feel it. To face the wave and ride up to its crest was how I was taught. As though the board was stuck to my feet I crossed the cusp and did a perfect three hundred and sixty degree turn; a full revolution and time enough for another. I stood up and with the wave at my back and arms into the air ... everything else became a blur.

The judges deliberated for some time and then announced the winners. When my fake name was called and Marilyn saw me walk forward to collect the prize, there was a burst of screams followed by a throng of people surging forward. Marilyn grabbed my neck with both her skinny arms. She kissed me on my lips, something I do not enjoy. Before letting go, she pushed me away while holding on, just like Mammy Cynthia did. Tears were streaming down her face, yet she was composed. I stood there and looked at her, not knowing what to say or do ... my seventeen years had not yet provided me with insight. The judges were waiting, but they didn't matter. I was not there for the judges, but for me.

"You know Sammy," Marilyn wiped her nose with the back of her hand and sniffed loudly before she continued to speak, "I've not been this happy since Jessica was born. You are twenty one, right?"

Again she did not allow me to answer.

"Well, my Jessica would have been the same age as you. We lived up there in Sparks Road, Overport, in a flat across the road from Johnnie's, the take-out place where we got your meal from last night. Today is the first time that I stepped onto a reserved beach. You and the memory of Jessica made me do it."

So, like many others Marilyn thought I was older than my seventeen years. She looked into my eyes; the tears and the redness in hers hid something more. I could see it clearly on the beach that day and, though I did not know what to do or to say, I felt her sadness.

"It was all before I became a working girl you know, but it's all right...," she said in that hoarse raspy voice before pushing me: "Go now big boy, don't keep those people waiting on their reserved beach. Get your stuff, all the people from the truck place are here. There's another man here too, a security guard, who says that he is your friend. We are all waiting to celebrate. You showed them Sammy. Showed them how it should be done, so let's get off 'their beach', come?"

I walked up the scaffolding steps to the podium. My concern was more about the questions I had for Marilyn. As she instructed, I took my stuff, smiled when people pointed cameras, and left even though there were those who wanted to talk. My job was done and home was three days away.

A woman climbed down from the podium, probably a member of the organising team. She wore a bright, orange or yellow top, I was never very good with colours, but she had branding across her chest. The woman smiled and asked: "Those people who screamed when you were preparing to ride, do you know them?" She seemed confused when I told that they were my family from the Stanger Street Truck Port where I lived during the competition.

Ma always taught whoever wanted to learn: "Never deny those who are closest to you. That is what Agnes did to me and I know that it is the worst feeling."

My riding had not only been for Marilyn, but for all the other women and their clients too. After all, who was I to judge them?

Then there was Mahachi. He had left home early for the nightshift in Scottburgh and thought to come by: "Just in case you were in the final, Sammy." We hugged. Afterwards Mahachi gave me a *vetkoek* (a traditional Afrikaner pastry) that his mother had learned to make. I am sure that it was his meal for the night, but that Sunday it was mine. All those people came out for me that day. I wished to change my earlier thoughts of loneliness. What is said cannot be unsaid, but what about thinking, can we 'un-think' some stuff too?

That day I belonged to Marilyn, Jeffrey, Mahachi, the 'woman' who had a deep voice and hairy legs, the pregnant one and others from Stanger Street Truck Port. They took their own time and gave it to me. Being able to surf for them made me proud. I felt happy because I belonged to them.

My vendor friend returned the suitcase and I told him that it would be the last time. In response the jovial man, whose name I never knew, took one of his items, a leather strip with a few beads, and tied it around my right wrist. It was my farewell gift. I wore those beads for five years until the morning when they lay broken next to me in the bed. It was their time, and perhaps it's true, 'there's a season for everything in this life'.

Jeffrey, the man who had bought me dinner the previous evening was there too. In his sing-song and animated way he described my surfing: "You jived on the water; and it was like watching a false jazz at the Galaxy Nightclub ... and in the end the board was stuck to your feet." Marilyn and two other women carried my board and a different man, one who I had then not yet met, Fred, he carried the suitcase. Mahachi carried the trophy while I continued to eat his *vetkoek*.

As we walked back to the truck stop Jeff told how Marilyn, during the previous evening, had kept the noise levels down so that I could have a peaceful sleep.

"Oh! And I decided to postpone my trip. Cape Town had to be represented, and so that Fred and I could take you home afterwards."

My gratitude was huge. In fact, it was more, much more and evident too. I was going home.

When we reached the truck port I built my bed and sat on one of the tyres with Mahachi while the others lit their sweet smoke. Jeff and his offer to take me home was the best possible prize.

I was returning to school after the competition. It was three weeks to the start of the new school term. But then I was offered a lift home. I would probably have travelled with Mahachi that evening. Instead, I walked him to the train station for the trip to Scottburgh, so that he could do the night shift. It was the last time that we would see each other.

The money I saved had all been consumed by competition fees. Having used a pseudonym, there were certain requirements that needed to be met before I could receive the prize money. Jeff and his co-driver, Fred, were leaving early the next morning, Monday. Together we planned to travel in a truck drawing two trailers laden with new imported furniture. The detail was unimportant because I was going home!

We left just as soon as Fred arrived from wherever he had spent that night. Marilyn climbed down from way up high in the truck's horse. We had more sugar-cane sweetened coffee.

After a short cowboy splash I returned the tyres and cardboard to where they had been found. The others laughed but years of boarding school had instilled certain disciplines that were hard to break.

Ma had not known about the big competition. She would have worried about my possible arrest, and Ma had enough about which to worry.

Nearly twenty years later was when I went to that beach again—with my own son. He was just two years old and would not understand the significance. I have a picture though, of him standing there without a shirt, on a crowded North Beach. We were spectators then, at the same event. No one knew, just me. It is the only picture in my file of that place where I did a jive on water for my Stanger Street Truck Port family.

Before we drove off that Monday morning, I thanked Marilyn for being my friend and from the truck window, way up high I dropped the trophy down for her to keep as a memento. After all, what other purpose could it serve? Marilyn caught the trophy, kissed it, and waved at me. That was the last time I would see her.

I was happy to leave and excited about going home. Some of the competitors were en route to the airport that morning. I saw them drive past with designer surfboards strapped to the roof of hired cars. They were off to participate in other big wave competitions in far-flung places. My job was done, but without Mr Thompson having introduced me to the sport, his support and encouragement, none of what I had achieved would have been possible. There were many boys back home whose sporting ability was obvious, but they seldom came across a Mr Thompson and rarely realised their potential.

When Jeffrey drove past Pinetown and the truck began to climb the steep road there, I asked if he would drive so that we could go past Pietermaritzburg City Hall, where the public telephone booths were. All the while Jeffrey was talking, but I could not concentrate on what he was saying. He was telling me about Marilyn and I felt that it was not my place to know about their relationship.

"It's not what you think, hey, Sammy. Marilyn's not married. You know when something like that happens then marriages don't last hey?" I did not understand, or have knowledge about that which Jeffrey tried to discuss with me. At the time there were other more important things on my mind.

We stopped at the city hall. By then, necessity had taught me many things; things like how to manipulate public telephones so that I didn't have to pay for the call. I had no money, not even five cents for a local call, and asking Jeffrey for money was not the right thing to do. He had done more than enough already, but above all I was too proud to ask for more. In the past, I placed collect calls where the other party, usually Ma, had to pay. That day at the Pietermaritzburg City Hall was different.

It was early morning when I called. A woman, speaking with a familiar Irish lilt in her tone, answered the phone. I asked to speak with Mr Thompson. There was a pause on the other end before the woman exclaimed: "Is this Sam?" and before I could reply she said: "Sammy! You did so well! We were on the beach and watched you every day. Andrew sat there quietly. He was transfixed and spoke to himself all the time. I don't know why, but he didn't want you to know that we were there. Thank you for calling. I shall tell him later when he's home. Thank you Sam, you've made us proud. Thank you for calling. Andrew will be excited to know that you remembered him."

I could not speak after that, and just put the phone down, slowly; then I turned and walked back to where Jeff was revving the truck. After the call had ended it dawned on me that my only part in the conversation had been to ask for Mr Thompson. I should have demanded my money back from that telephone!

I think that Mr Thompson was embarrassed for having left me when he did; and about the incident at Mammy Cynthia's farewell. Having thought about it, my conclusion was that Sister St Claire and Mr Thompson both had been well placed on the day to prevent the nasty incident at Mammy Cynthia's farewell function. To me Mr Thompson was always the older more responsible person from whom I chose to take direction. It had been disappointing to think that the same person I so revered did not do what he must have known was right. I do not believe that Mr Thompson condoned his colleagues' behaviour on that day. He was present and did not do anything when he should have. I learned that when something is wrong and I do nothing, then it is worse than being unaware.

Mr Thompson and I stopped being in touch after Mammy Cynthia's retirement; that was my silent protest against his poor judgement. Making my own surfing arrangements was not easy, but I had had no alternative and to give up was not a 'festive' option. I had to explain the situation and request permission to use the name of another surfer, an Australian, one who was not going to participate in that leg of the world surfing championship. It was Mr Thompson's idea, but I did it on my own. All the techniques that he taught me, his advice and appetite for perfection, those were also followed diligently. Despite all that had happened between us, I remain indebted to Mr Thompson. The same applies to all those who helped me along the way. Incompetence breeds nastiness and my coach, Mr Thompson, was not incompetent.

We continued to drive. I sat quietly; deep in thought. My thoughts were so vivid it felt as if they were being spoken: how could I pass on the bit of experience that I had; and how could I demonstrate being thankful? Sometimes we forget about those who taught us. Without being taught by people who were good, I would never have become better. Mr Thompson had identified what he said was a talent, potential and what became my passion. Ma taught me to think and not what to think; Mr Thompson taught me about surfing and not how to surf; and Father Terry explained that there was a difference between who was right and what was right.

A deviation perhaps, but while we were driving those were the thoughts I used as tools to grasp, or perhaps understand, that which Jeffrey was explaining to me. Jeffrey was talking about Marilyn. He was also talking about Marilyn's Jessica. All the while I continued to wrestle with the difference between what I already knew and what Jeffrey was explaining. Nothing I knew and could reference had any bearing on what Jeffrey had to say, no matter how hard I tried. Perhaps my head was too young; my experience too limited; my obsession with self too great—because I failed to understand what Jeffrey explained, as he drove the truck from one hill to another.

When Jessica was four years old, her uncle, Marilyn's brother-in-law, raped and then murdered her. Since then Marilyn had been embracing those who reminded her of the child she once knew; the one she once had. Worse yet was that the brother-in-law was paroled for 'good behaviour' after serving only two-thirds of his sentence. Marilyn and Jessica could not be paroled, ever, that much I understood. These things were too big for me. In trying to understand I wondered whether the pain we humans inflict on one another will end someday. Who was taking responsibility for healing the rot that was strewn across our country and maybe even the world? While people like me were rabbiting on about surfing, the size of the swell, the potential of the barrel, cusp of the wave and reserved beaches, what was being done about those who held the power to act, yet abused it?

The behaviours of adults whom we trusted were at times the most despicable. Adults sat in silence, like Mr Thompson did while I was surfing. Mr Thompson had done the same when he should have spoken out to save Mammy Cynthia's party. Jeffrey too; he was driving home to a loving wife and children, but he probably loved Marilyn more. Why was it that adults so often inflict the harshest pain on children, even sending them to war where they, as young adults, are so frequently killed?

I sat quietly in the truck cabin with these thoughts swirling in my mind. The truck struggled up through the beautiful Valley of a Thousand Hills with Jeffrey rapidly changing gears as he bobbed up and down on his springy driver's seat. He went through the routine, all to get the heavy truck up the mountain pass. Jeffrey hummed along to a new tune playing on the truck radio. I'd not heard it before, but piano music, or any music that includes the piano, has always been and will always be the harp of my generation. The piece he hummed had a simple four beat to the bar piano introduction and then followed the lyrics, something to do with a crazy child that has to slow down, but throughout, the piano was there. I listened attentively to the story. Jeff had a good voice, could hold a tune and like few, Jeffrey's soul was there, I could hear. It was beautiful. I wished that we could rewind the piece. The lyrics made me think of Jane, of Ma and even of Pa. I was coming home and they did not know.

'Vienna Waits for You' became my favourite Billy Joel song. Like a painting, which with every viewing reveals more of itself, so each time I listened to that song a bit more was said. Jeff knew the music and was ever eager to tell the story of each piece I liked. We turned the radio off after a while, so that Jeff and I could harmonise to old tunes with the fluctuating drone of the truck on backing vocals.

When we finally got the heavy load to the top of the Van Reenen's Pass, Jeff put his left hand to the middle of his back, pushed his tummy out, and sighed: "My gosh, it must be an Oshkosh!", then he patted the dashboard, changed to an appropriate gear and worked the air-brakes for the descent into Harrismith. We were travelling in the Orange Free State en route to the Cape Province, towards Cape Town, our home town.

Jeff and I sat in silence for a while. The entire journey was punctuated with silent patches. It was time enough for my mind to wander back to where I had left those earlier thoughts of Marilyn, Mr Thompson, Mahachi, the vendor who cared for our blue suitcase and others; Jessica too by then. I wondered how many Mr Thompsons and Jeffreys were out there. Were they also encouraging the decay? Was it decay? Perhaps it was supposed to be like that?

Becoming a Mr Thompson was easy. The alternative was isolation. We place a lot of value on issues that are trivial and in the process we sell our souls. Sometimes to stand for what is right means to stand alone. I was only seventeen and these thoughts were too big for my head, so I kept them to myself.

After we had travelled over the Drakensberg Mountains the radio reception was restored. Jeffrey turned the radio slightly louder. We heard good music that afternoon. There was a mountain that resembled Table Mountain on the vista of that escarpment.

Jeff had been quiet for a long time. Later he spoke about people whom we both knew, musicians, athletes, gangsters and beautiful women. The truck continued its crawl toward Cape Town. Jeff spoke about the long hours on the road and the time spent away from home. He told me about the comfort he bought from women, but I had seen some of those women and very few looked like comfort. "What I do is wrong, Sam. I want to break the habit..." I thought he was referring to the women with whom he occupied himself whenever the truck stopped—

I listened, and heard, asked the odd question too, but bore in mind that Jeff was a man old enough to have been my father. I had certain questions but felt uncomfortable discussing them with him. Jeff volunteered most of what I was interested in. As for the rest, I just listened. Mammy Cynthia had taught me that to listen is also a form of communication.

We drove via Kimberley, a dusty small city surrounded by arid land and open spaces. The area became known when diamonds were found in the rock formations there. We drove along that route in order to drop one consignment and collect another. I was told to wait at the side of the road while the two drivers and their crew went to a warehouse in an Industrial Park. Before he left me I had a sandwich and a mug of the sweetest coffee ever made, Marilyn's coffee!

The rule was that bosses should not know when truck drivers carried passengers; that was why I had to wait at the side of the road until they returned.

Loud truck noises woke me about three hours later. I had been asleep in a ditch alongside the road. Flies caked around my mouth; they were after the sweetness in the residue that remained on my lips after drinking Jeffrey's syrup sweet coffee.

"H-E-Y! If not for that surfboard sticking up, then I would have missed you; and then you would have been in the dirty stuff, man!" said Jeffrey after having struggled to stop the truck within a reasonable distance from where I had been sleeping.

I apologised and put the suitcase and my board back in the trailer where the men were lounging, each on their own plastic wrapped Sealy Posturepedic factory guaranteed double bed. We were on our way, or that was what I thought.

Jeffrey parked the truck on the outskirts of Kimberley. Across the road was a motel. He checked the time and said that it was too early to drive; too early for my 'surprise':

"You will see the surprise after we've driven through Worcester. It is only visible if we arrive there at a certain time ..."

There was a woman standing outside the truck—there were always women, no matter where the truck stopped. Jeffrey and that woman disappeared. I stayed with the driver's assistants and the co-driver. They had created a very comfortable setting in the back trailer, and were playing dominoes and a card game on a plastic-clad coffee table.

Later, when we departed from Kimberley, I was asleep in the truck cabin. It was Jeffrey's turn to rest and Fred was the fresh driver. My sleep on that entire journey was intermittent. It was a tiring sleep. Something was not right. I was having doubts about Jeffrey's 'surprise' for me. What were they going to show me, or allow me to experience that was not to be discussed, explained, or disclosed?

Fred was a recent convert to a certain charismatic church; 'born again' was what he kept telling me. He was a big man and in a literal moment I could not understand how he could be born again!

"I also hammered away at those women, like Jeff; but then I found the Lord, and my life, the way we lived and thought, it all changed. If you think differently Sammy, then you will behave differently too. Muriel and I renewed our wedding vows on my birthday, 22nd May 1977. Now we are a happy family again."

I knew what he meant and nodded in agreement. Spiritual transformation and religious commitment were foreign to me, at the time. I had nothing else to say, but remembered that there were many fellow Protestant church 'brothers' and 'sisters' in the working class environs of where we lived, our township. Fred and Jeff were about the same age. Throughout the journey Brother Fred listened to recordings of people preaching; those preachers had no need for amplification! Even when they prayed, it was a shout. I could not help myself from wondering whether their God was like Pa, hard of hearing. The preaching was a perpetual scream. Maybe that was how they guaranteed that their Lord would hear them above others who also prayed. I had no alternative but to hear; after all hearing was compulsory. Fred randomly answered the hysterical preacher: "Amen!" I got a fright the first time Fred screamed back at the preacher, my initial thought being that something dreadful had happened. Throughout the recording Brother Fred would shout in response to the excitable preacher's statements: "Amen!" and "Praise the Lord!" to which, and after a brief pause, the recorded Pastor exclaimed. "Help yourself!"

Jeff had instructed Fred to show me the 'something' that they had found along the road. Both persisted in not discussing the detail. Whenever I asked, Fred would interject with: "Only at four o'clock in the morning, Brother Sam!"

It was close enough to home and I was filled with bittersweet memories about that part of the journey, but the familiar tinge of excitement at being close to home superseded everything else. Fred checked if I was awake. The National Road (N1) snaked past Worcester. The only sound in the cabin was a monotonous drone of the engine. It was early morning and winter again. The Cape was cold and wet. Earlier on, before I slept, the all-night radio host, Robin Alexander, had reported snowfalls on the higher peaks of Du Toit's Kloof Mountain Pass, and had warned that road users should heed all traffic rules and slow down. It was about a quarter to four when Fred called out again: "Brother Sam, are you awake?" I was barely awake, but the unusual strange feeling from before seemed more prominent. It had started before Jeffrey told me of the "surprise". I was familiar with the road and surrounds, so that was not the cause of my discomfort and apprehension that something was not the way it should be. Even the railway line, Jane's and my railway line, was visible as the truck went around in a wide bend. While the truck struggled up the steep gradient Fred engaged a lower gear. He switched the headlights to bright as we rounded the last corner before Du Toit's Kloof Tunnel. We could see the far end of that three hundred metre long tunnel. But there, before us, were four people, two in front and two behind. They wore light white clothes, sheets almost, and stood in the road, on the same side that we were driving, the left side. All four had their heads turned to the right. They were staring down the valley into darkness. The radio was off; Fred must have turned it off. He engaged an even lower gear. The truck was moving slowly; so slow that I could have kept pace by walking alongside it. I was wide awake. The people in the road were not going to move and the truck, it seemed, was not going to stop. Assuming that Fred had not seen the people, I shouted: "Brother Fred! Watch out for those people!"

"They're not people Brother Sammy," was his croaky reply. We drove through them as he said that. Brother Fred then made the sign of the cross and kissed his fingers.

"Look back Brother, look Sammy!"

"Yes, I see them. I see the sides of their faces; but there's another truck coming, Brother Fred; warn them!"

"If that driver does not know about them he'll give way."

There were no other cars on the road at that hour. The driver of the approaching truck sounded a horn, flashed his lights and swerved to avoid collision. As the oncoming truck swung wide the four figures resumed their mournful pose, gazing into the valley below.

"Wow! That was creepy! The truck behind us nearly tumbled down the cliff when it swerved. Is that what you wanted to show me, Brother Fred?"

"Yes. The story started about four years ago. Brother Jeff and I were doing a trip down from Alrode, near Johannesburg, to the port in Cape Town. Jeff was driving. We had to get a container onto a ship early that morning. The vessel was scheduled to depart between eight and eight-thirty. It was a Thursday morning, I remember. Those four people were driving recklessly on the same road throughout the night. They stopped and started. Every time their driving became more erratic. They overtook me several times, all the way from Jo'burg when I was driving, and also when Jeff drove. I remember them passing shortly after we refuelled at the Shell Service Station near Worcester and for some unexplained reason they passed again about five minutes before the Du Toit's Kloof Pass Tunnel. Maybe they had stopped, I don't know, but as Jeff straightened the truck in our approach to the tunnel, that was when we saw it. The car's driver had misjudged that long last bend. He had driven straight through the embankment and over the cliff edge, right there where you saw those people. All four of them died on impact. Since then, their images have been seen on the road, around the time of the accident. We were on time that day, but could not stop for too long. We left when others arrived, but not before determining that all four passengers had died. There was nothing else to do. The four young people were university students, I think. But that was the story. This has always been a very dangerous road."

"Why don't the authorities put traffic signs there to warn motorists who use the road, say between three and six in the morning?"

"And what would those signs say?"

Even after the Du Toit's Kloof Pass the unusual feeling I bore continued.

The huge truck struggled to fit into the narrow street where we lived, but Brother Fred insisted that he stop in front of our house. It was a little more than two hours after the ghostly incident. Six o'clock, Tuesday morning, that was about the time. Ma opened the door. She was beside herself with anxiety. Instinctively I knew that something bad had happened. Ma told me that she had been awake and up since an early phone-call. There had been no reply at the school phone when she called.

It was about Jane. She had been taken to the hospital from the Medical Residence at about one o'clock that morning. My Jane had suffered a brain haemorrhage and had lost consciousness. The doctors called Ma again at five o'clock and advised her and Pa to go to the hospital without further delay. Knowing the hospital procedure, Ma expected the worst.

Pa was working, because he was always working and we never knew where. I tried to reassure Ma that Jane would be fine: "Jane is a fighter, Ma, and won't give up. She is sleeping, but when we get there and once she's heard your voice then all will be fine. Don't worry."

I emptied the blue suitcase and filled it with clothes that Jane might need. Ma washed Eugene in the white plastic baby bathtub while I gathered nappies and liners, waterproofs, bibs and a change of clothing for him. Ma reminded me of the sterilised baby bottles and teats which I also hurriedly placed in the suitcase. Everything had been completed in record time and all the while I assured Ma that all would be fine. I carried Eugene and the suitcase to Busy Corner so that we could catch the first bus. Ma locked the house and later caught up with us. At Wynberg Station we boarded a very full train heading to the city. I pleaded with the commuters in that third class carriage to allow us room. Most were more than obliging. Young men assisted with the suitcase. Several of the women helped my distraught Ma with Eugene. He, Eugene, sensed our anxiety and cried intermittently throughout the journey. I held him a bit and then Ma did. Others offered to hold him too, but then he cried more. Eventually a tall man held him above the rest until we got to Observatory Station. From there we walked up Station Road, across Main and onto Anzio. It was the same road Ma used several decades earlier and where Jane and I walked when she moved into the Medical Residence.

We were at the hospital entrance within about an hour and fifteen minutes of my arriving home. A hospital orderly had been instructed to meet Ma. He escorted us to a private room where a doctor was waiting to tell us that Jane had died.

I felt severed, dislocated and dismembered. We embraced, Ma, little Eugene in her arms, and I. We just stood like that. I don't know for how long. Afterwards my T-shirt was damp; my face wet and Eugene, he just cried. For me nothing else mattered; nothing existed; Jane was my life in so many ways. I knew then that my impossible task was to try and live for two people. Ma straightened up from our embrace and looked me in the eye. Briefly I saw the Ma I knew. It was the one who had a healing smile. She was the strong decisive woman who would rescue me from the consequence of what I'd heard. That day no amount of healing in her smile could bring my Jane back to life. She looked at my face for that moment and I looked back seeking the comfort I knew she had. But instead her tears returned like blood to a deep wound: "Please tell Sammy; tell me it's not true?" I couldn't. The news that doctor gave us was not the truth—that was what I wanted to believe. To this day I do not believe that Jane is dead. They say that she is dead, yes. They tell me that Jane is dead, but to me she lives. Jane, my sister mommy, lives on, albeit in my head. Tell me that I am mad, for I now have the right to be mad. How could this possibly happen, how; why, oh why?

Both Ma and I have scant recollection of the funeral. All I recall is Ma saying that Pa bought Jane the most beautiful white coffin.

Jane was buried on the Cape Flats, in the Klip Cemetery. I have not been to the grave again. Why should I? Jane is alive in my head.

Chapter Sixteen

A New School; Singing in the Dark; Looking for Work

It was a difficult time; a replay of what had happened just a few short years earlier. Ma was even more broken than before. It was as though her life had come to naught. I too was disillusioned. There was no point in returning to the faraway school when my family was collapsing. Pa was gone most of the time— working, always working; or that's what he said.

In the past all my time at school had been about how far or near we were to the date upon which we would return home. The going home was always great, although being at home had become upsetting. There were always issues, unfairness mainly. It was obvious that Ma was being taken advantage of, and I could not understand why she allowed Pa to do that to her.

Pa stayed away from home for even longer periods after Jane's death. There was a huge void in all of our lives. I coped by refusing to discuss it with anyone. To me it felt as if something deep inside, something that no-one knew existed, had broken. I also knew that whatever had broken could not be fixed. I've had to learn to live with it like an amputation, because there continues to be no alternative. Time cannot heal when a soul is maimed.

Jane had sometimes called me an idiot, but I knew what she meant. That too I can't describe. Sometimes I think of the letters Jane wrote, letters that made me stand up and clap hands after reading. Jane's letters were always vivid. When in the mood my Jane was meticulous about describing detail. During our last telephone conversation I reminded her of how well she described the creamy white arum lilies, her favourite flowers that grew on the slopes of Devil's Peak: "... So well, that even though those flowers have no noticeable fragrance, after reading your description I could also smell their beauty." She giggled: "You are such an idiot, Sammy! Someday your daughter will also love those flowers, you hear?" Then there was a pause as Jane took a deep breath before continuing: "I want you to be next to me like we always were. That is the reason why I try to make my descriptions as accurate as possible." No matter how hard I try to do the same for Jane it never ...

After she had gone, my trying to describe how I felt was impossible. It must be because of that broken something inside of me, but who among us is perfect?

Ma had changed after Brenda and Anne died. After Jane's death, it was as if Ma had finished with being the person she once was. Ma changed into a completely different person in the years that followed Jane's death. Even her appearance changed. Ma lived almost exclusively for Eugene. Whenever appropriate she'd resort to what was her usual refrain: "The taking never stops." Then she'd wipe her face as if to brush away the pain.

Maybe it was my youth, or maybe it was my callousness, that sometimes boiled over into words: "You allow it to be like this, Ma. Others do not see that you are treated unfairly by Pa. They don't, because they do not expect you, of all people, to stand for it. You tolerate it, and that is why you get it. Remember, when I was a little boy, you told me that we teach people how to treat us by the way we behave; and that if we behave badly, then people will treat us so in return. Do you remember saying that, Ma?"

Ma's answer was in the form of a cursory affirmative nod. "Why does this not apply to you then? No, Ma, instead you tolerate Pa's rubbish treatment of us."

"Yes Boy, I hear you. One day, when you have children I wish that they live full lives and do not get taken from you like mine were from me."

"Ma, people take from you without taking any responsibility for the state in which they leave you. You are the most gifted and knowledgeable woman that I know, but you allow people to take from you." Ma paused for a while and looked at me before she replied: "Why are you blaming me for everything that is not going the way it should? I did not have a hand in my children being taken."

Perhaps my shallow, but painful 'go' at Ma was fuelled by frustration. The taking that Ma experienced also affected me. I had no explanation for it, other than that Ma allowed Pa to abuse her, and that I suspected that Anne and Brenda had paid with their lives as a result.

"Ma, you allow it to happen. You take daft decisions to please others, often at your peril. Your decisions suit Pa, but they often affect you negatively. Yet you take the same, obviously detrimental decisions, every time. It is not right, Ma. I am concerned about you, because you are my Ma."

I was overcome with emotion when speaking like that to Ma. Her only concern was the past and the far future, but to Ma, the present was not important. When I criticised Ma for allowing Pa to behave the way he did, her response was: "Don't worry Boy, he will have to answer before God someday."

"That God is in your imagination. Someday will be too late Ma, and in the meantime I worry about you. You do not seem to worry about yourself and I have to prepare for my own life too. That God you so often talk about …"

Three weeks after Jane was buried, I dragged myself back to school. I was no longer interested in being at a faraway school. During the last months of that year I focused on getting better grades in the final examination. I had decided that it would be my last examination at St Mary's School.

In any event, the atmosphere had become depressing. A Memorial Mass had been organised by the school for my Jane. Many teachers, including those who had left the school, but who had taught Jane, made the effort to attend the Mass.

With all those familiar people there it felt as if I were reliving our time at school. In many ways it was a farewell, both for Jane and for me. It was sore, very sore. Jane's Head Girl Report was read at the Mass for all to hear. Again I was reminded how much a part of our lives we were. I saw all the old people who mattered to us. It would be for the last time and again only I knew.

Mr Thompson was there with his wife (the former nun, Sister O'Connor). It was an opportunity for me to thank him in person. There was no need to say anything, so we just hugged each other. I could feel his tremble. Both of us knew what it meant that second time Mr Thompson and I hugged each other.

Mammy Cynthia arrived together with Khokho, Precious, Thami, Boet Sam and Ma Khumalo.

Papa Pretorius and Mr van Wyk were there too and so were Sis Maggie, Sis Mary, Sis Nomusa and Sis Thandiwe.

I saw many people whom I had not seen in ages, many of whom had travelled from Mpophomeni and other faraway places. All were there to commemorate Jane. They wore black clothes. Ma Khumalo whispered to me: "This hall is filled with love, because all these people here love your sister." She then wiped her tears.

We sang before Father Terry preached. We sang so beautifully that day that I didn't think there would be time for Father to preach. We sang and praised for a life that we all had known and loved. Only the good die young, was what I thought. It was a stupid thought; much like when the man said that Ma should accept that which she was unable to change. Yet, both her daughters had just died. Sometimes we talk rubbish to people when all we need is a hug.

Afterwards, when tea and biscuits were served the people formed little groups to talk among themselves, particularly those who had not seen one another in a long time. I stood quietly with Khokho, who by then was holding onto me for support, and Mammy Cynthia. I was feeling alone again, and those two iconic women did not only make me strong, but also belong.

First, Mr Thompson approached Mammy Cynthia; they spoke softly to each other, held hands and hugged afterwards. Just as when the umpire at the end of the *kennetjie* match handed out imaginary awards, so Mr Thompson went to Sis Maggie, Sis Mary, Sis Nomusa and Sis Thandiwe. They too first held hands, gently spoke and then hugged.

Papa Pretorius and Mr van Wyk followed Mr Thompson. Both these men were moved to tears after apologising to Mammy Cynthia and the three women who by then had moved closer to Mammy and Ma Khumalo. On seeing Pappa Pretorius' tears Mammy turned him aside to where the rest of the people could not see. She dug in her handbag, balanced on the balls of her feet and raised her heels as far off the ground as she could. With an outstretched arm Mammy wiped Papa Pretorius' wet face with her small light blue handkerchief. She then put it, her handkerchief, in his jacket pocket. Mammy then pushed him away, but did not let go of his arms; they hugged, and then I knew that everything was okay, because Mammy had a hug that healed. After the three men had apologised it felt as though the umpire had handed out real medals. This time all the players got gold, everyone won. Where there is no pain there is no gain. But what had I gained? My sister was gone, forever.

To have paid my own school fees was a major accomplishment, but there was nothing more that I found attractive about being at the faraway school. The objective of surfing in a premier competition had been achieved; there was nothing left, no reason to stay.

The situation at home continued to spiral out of control. It was disheartening and particularly bad. I was not in a state to discuss it with anyone. To complete my last year of school in Cape Town was the only alternative. I planned to find a job and study part time, or finish school and surf in every scheduled competition. But surfing for a living was not practical—not only were all competitions held on reserved beaches, but it cost a lot of money to enter and travel to those destinations. Professional surfing in South Africa was the domain of those with access to money and who could access surfing beaches without breaking the law. Sponsors could not support me, because the relevant beaches were reserved, but not for me. Also, earning an income from surfing would mean being away from Ma and Eugene for months at a time. It was a foregone conclusion that my surfing days were over. That Sunday in June at North Beach was the last time that I made magic with my board.

I travelled to Mpophomeni two weeks before the end of my final term at the faraway school. I went there to read and then give my goodbye letter to Mammy Cynthia. Upon arrival I asked her whether we could talk alone. Without saying a word she took me by the hand and we went into her bedroom. Mammy sat on the side of her bed while I read the letter out loud. As she sat there, Mammy looked like a schoolgirl waiting for a scolding from the teacher. I read the letter aloud. When I looked up from reading, Mammy was transfixed; although she was looking at me I sensed that Mammy was not seeing. My letter was meant to be heartfelt and I had filled it with sentiments of gratitude. After I had finished reading, Mammy wriggled off the bed until her feet touched the ground. She stepped to where I was standing in her simple bedroom. Her face was expressionless. Mammy looked up at me and smiled: "A man almost. Sammy is almost a man." She continued to look up at me as a tear spilled over and rolled down the flawless skin of her pretty face, the face that had brought comfort to so many when they had no one. We hugged, long enough for me to inspect every one of the photos on her dressing table. They were of Baba Sipho, Khokho, Precious, Thami, their parents, Jane, Ma, Mammy, and me. Behind the movable mirror on her dressing table I also saw the framed picture of Elvis. Mammy Cynthia always thought that Elvis was very 'festive'. There we all were, on Mammy's dressing table, like a family, one big family. I left Mammy with the letter and went out to greet Khokho, Thami and Precious.

Before leaving school that December, Sister St Claire gave me a letter that had arrived shortly after Jane's death. It bore her trademark lipstick kiss on the back of the envelope. I could see from the franking that the letter had been posted two days before Jane died, but my courage to read it was not there. Instead I tied the unread fragrant letter with the rest of our collection and stored it in the blue suitcase.

Before departing, I placed a note on my desk. It was addressed to Ms du Pont, who was first Jane's favourite teacher, and who had then become my English teacher. I was not going to return for the final year. My letter served to thank Ms du Pont for teaching me to communicate in this medium and to inform her of my plans not to return.

The Cape Town bound train departed on Friday, 2 December 1977. I have not been back to the faraway school since; too many memories and it is too sore.

Once home I learned that Ma had given up her consulting job. The people who visited were no longer her clients. They were friends who dropped by. Ma and her friends drank tea and exchanged pleasantries, just a few and only on rare occasions. When I asked why she was no longer working Ma's reply included many things, but each statement ended with: "One person can only endure so much taking."

Listening to and thinking about Ma's comments enabled me to develop an understanding of her resigned attitude. There were times when our conversations came close to addressing the questions in my mind about how Jane and I came to be. Each time that our discussion threatened to enter that elusive sphere, I held back from asking questions; always in the hope that Ma would volunteer more. She never did. Her comments broadened my understanding of the situation at home but never revealed the information about which I so dearly needed to know and understand. Aged only sixty my Ma was the child and I had become more of the adult in our relationship. It was obvious that my being far from home was no longer feasible. Yet all my abilities and interests would have taken me away from home for extended periods.

During the first week of January I approached a Catholic school near the city of Cape Town to see if they had room for me in the final year class. I was accepted, almost without question. The money I had won at the last surfing competition paid my fees, accommodation and travel. At first it had been difficult to get the prize money paid over. It had to do with my having used a pseudonym during the competition. Many telephone conversations and an equal number of letters later resulted in the competition organisers agreeing to make payment in parts. In the middle of January, six months after the competition was held, the last payment was credited to my post office savings account. Once the new school had been arranged, I wrote to notify Sister St Claire. It took two days to compose the letter:

Monday 16 January 1978

Dear Sister St Claire

It was a very difficult decision to take. Please try and understand my reasons for not returning to school?

The situation at home has been deteriorating over a number of years. My resolve is to move closer, so that my mother and I can have better access to each other. Since Jane's passing I want to be more available and accessible to our mother. The burdens of distance add to my concern and tamper with my concentration. It is important to do well this year, otherwise the universities and other places of higher learning will not consider me.

I have applied to a Catholic boarding school near the city of Cape Town. Please do not be alarmed should you receive a notice requesting references?

For as long as I shall live, the experience of being in your care will remain with me. My blessings include having three mothers and possibly four. I count you as one. The lessons drawn and experiences earned are worth much more than my physical presence at the school. Thank you for all that you have done, Sister; thank you for watching over me.

Nervousness and apprehension seem to define my decision, for I have only ever known one school. The thought of different people makes me wonder whether being at school will be the same as that to which I am accustomed. I want to fit in and not regret this decision.

Yes Sister, there are many questions that whirl through my mind at this time. I am afraid, resolute, sad but also happy. The decision to leave is mine and I shall bear the consequences. I have to live more for tomorrow than for yesterday. There's a time when every one of us has to leave. This is my time.

Should I have disappointed you then please consider forgiving me?

Yours faithfully

Samuel Levy

The letter was sent with the first mail on that Monday morning. The following Friday, 21 January 1978, was the day I received my first ever telegram. It read:

Dear Samuel

Thank you for your letter. I am saddened by the news that you are leaving us, but I understand and respect the reasons for your decision. You and Jane both live in my heart. God bless you.

Sister Carmel St Claire

The new school year started with the usual flair. Being at school in Cape Town was not as daunting as originally thought. The initial stress to do with distance, school and accommodation had been resolved. Settling in to a year of pure academic concentration was marred by my domestic circumstances. I had become very outspoken against the unfairness meted out to Ma. Whenever the opportunity arose I would address Pa on the subject of his exploitation and abusive behaviour toward us as a family. He, Pa, would dismiss me and say: "Ya! Find a job and pay for living here before you utter an opinion."

I had long suspected that Pa had set up home with another woman. In order to confirm this, I decided to find out where Pa 'worked'. With some effort, I did. My suspicion was confirmed. When I informed Ma about my discovery her quiet response was: "God will take care of the situation my boy, you need not worry."

Ma was always seated in the lounge room when I arrived home for the weekend on a Friday evening. The lights were usually switched off and little Eugene would be sleeping. As I approached the front door there would be a red glow moving in the darkness of our lounge—the burning coal from Ma's cigarette.

Yes, Ma smoked, but not many people knew because she never smoked in public. Smoking was Ma's crutch and she did not like reference being made to it. All my life I knew that Ma smoked cigarettes and it never dawned on me to deny her the pleasure she derived from the ever-present little box containing ten Cavalla Kings cigarettes.

After greeting each other, Ma and I sat down to discuss the week that was. At month end, when I got home, Ma always had fried meat and roast potatoes ready. On other occasions we sat in the lounge and I ate whatever there was amidst the sharing of relevant information. Invariably the discussion turned to Pa:

"Oh! What did he say, Ma?" Despite what he had done to us, I was always keen to get news about Pa.

"He collected paint here and complained about the expensive telephone account. You know, it is usually fourteen rand, but because of those calls you made to Durban, the account was twenty-seven rand. Well, Pa was very unhappy about it. He also removed the radio from our bedroom that night. Remember the old radio to which we listened; the one next to his side of the bed? When he left the telephone was also gone. I had many James Hadley Chase books to read, so not having a radio did not bother me much. You know Boy, during the war we would visit our neighbours to listen to their radio. You see, I am accustomed to living without. Yet, given the things he does I wonder what goes on in your Pa's mind."

Listening to the passive way Ma accepted what Pa had done to her was something I could not understand.

"The telephone is fine too, let him keep his telephone. Nobody phones me anyway. Pa popped in for five minutes on Wednesday afternoon. He said hello and then went into the garage. On his way out, I asked: 'Samuel, what did you do with the telephone and radio?'

'Ya! Robbers, they must have come into the house while you were watching TV.'

"I know at least one of those robbers. Someday, my boy, mark my words, God will take care of everything. The truth has its own inviolable logic and sometimes it does not seem apparent. Just because people are poor does not mean that their souls are not rich. Pa's hello always just ends in goodbye, nothing more and nothing less. I wonder where it will end."

"You should stop saying all those passive and up in the sky things wrapped in big words about Pa. He is nothing more than a crook who takes advantage of you and you allow it. Your situation is becoming worse and you should do something about it. You cannot rely on me to fix everything."

In my opinion, Ma was irrational about taking decisions, because she always considered others ahead of her own needs.

Pa drove around with the telephone in his car. Meanwhile, I collected bits from old radios. The big glass tubes I got from an old gram radio and plugged them into a rudimentary circuit board. Necessity remains the mother of invention. I switched on my creation, and after it had warmed up sufficiently the radio worked. Citizen Band (CB) Radio had by then become a fad. My radio reception was strong enough to receive several CB channels; in turn, I was entertained by the various conversations that took place across the different frequencies. At times reception on my handmade radio was better than the set 'robbers' had removed. But my creation would have other, less positive, consequences.

It was a Saturday evening in June, another winter in the Cape—cold and rainy outside. I added a new speaker to the handmade radio set. Ma and Eugene were to listen to my latest favourite song. That song formed part of a playlist for a weekly programme, *The Top Twenty*. It was broadcast on *Springbok Radio*, one of a few that transmitted across South Africa and one that was an institution in many homes. The song that I wanted them to hear was by Leo Sayer, 'When I Need You'.

Ma's favourite singer was Shirley Bassey. I thought that she might like Leo Sayer too. The countdown reached number three and the song for which I waited had not yet aired. I knew that it would be either number one, or number two. When the presenter, David Gresham, announced the number two song, 'Don't Cry for Me Argentina', I became very excited, because my favourite song had been the biggest seller in South Africa for that past week. It meant that other people, those who could buy records, agreed with me. In our lounge room that evening, the excitement to hear the number one song was a bit like riding that last wave in Durban. That was until the power supply to our house tripped. We had not yet heard the number one song when the house was swamped in darkness. One of my radio's valves caused the electricity supply's emergency switch to activate and trip.

The trip switch was inside the locked garage. Pa had previously locked everything away. In the garage, that was where Pa parked the car and kept his tools and anything else that he wished to hide from us. It was forbidden terrain. The door that provided access from the house to the garage was always locked, but I had found a key, an unusually long key, that could unlock that door. The electricity control board was in the garage. So, when the electricity tripped, I lit a candle and found my long key. It did not help much. Pa had anticipated and had taken precaution against my finding a way to access his garage. He had jammed the handle of a garden fork underneath one of the wooden horizontal beams at the back of the door. With the tines digging into the floor it became near impossible for me to pry that door open. The axe with which to break the door was also locked away in the same garage.

That night we did not hear my favourite song. Instead, we spent the evening pretending that radios, televisions and electricity had not yet been invented. I played with Eugene by candlelight and silently hoped that Pa would arrive. Unlike Ma, who had become accustomed to accepting things as they were, I was very disappointed. My favourite TV programme was a detective series, *Longstreet*, and it was broadcast on Saturday evenings. I could not watch it that week.

There was no place from which to call Pa; and there was no number to call him on either.

Public telephones were vandalised over weekends. What joy could people get from cutting the cable between the telephone receiver and the rest of the instrument? Or, they'd try to remove the money and leave the entire telephone in tatters! The same with people who cut the overhead hand straps on trains, why did they do it?

Finding a working telephone on a Saturday night was a trouble much greater than its worth. Only a miracle intervention would have brought Pa home that night. We had no choice, but to accept the situation.

There was one piece of candle. Ma had saved it from the last time when there was a similar problem with the electricity supply. We spent the evening around that piece of candle. For entertainment I sang the song, the number one song. I sang it over and over. I sang, and Ma did not tell me to stop, she never did. Ma knew that the joy, the only joy that Saturday evening held lived in the song that I was singing—*When I Need You*.

"Whenever you sing like that, Boy, then it is like happiness comes to visit." I just smiled in between the singing. "That is a beautiful song."

"It's by Leo Sayer, Ma. I saw a picture of him at the record shop."

"You sing it well, too. I like …"

"What is your favourite song, Ma?"

Without hesitation Ma spat out her reply: "It has to be *Grande Grande Grande*. Someday, when you get the chance, you should read the story of almost any Italian Opera. There is always a story told. Often it is the most heart wrenching tale, be it love, tragedy, or celebration. But it is always big and dare I say, extreme."

The way Ma described situations transported me there and that time was no exception.

"My favourite song was originally composed by two Italian men," said Ma, "Alberto Testa and Toni Renis. For me it captures all the emotions to do with love, sadness and disappointment."

Whenever Ma was interested in something then she was completely interested in it. When I asked she responded with much enthusiasm: "The English version is sung by that Welsh singer, Shirley Bassey. Her version is entitled, 'Never Never Never' and it tells the story of Pa and me."

I watched as Ma's expression changed, when she prepared to say: "Pa is such a naughty man."

I remembered that song, *Never Never Never*. There was a swearword embedded in the lyrics and to me it was a big issue. I could not wait to tell Jane, so that she too could listen out for it.

"It went like this, Jane: *'You stay away and all I do is wonder why the hell I wait for you ...'* was my excited rendition when I saw Jane. Her response was to look at me as if I wore a dirty smell. 'Hell' was an expletive back then! That was my only concern, which I simply had to share with Jane, but clearly she was not interested.

Well, that night, when we sat in the dark house, Ma tried to sing the same song for me. Ma had many talents, but to sing was never one of them. I knew the tune.

Ma stood up out of habit and walked to the kitchen for a cup of tea, but we had no electricity. We did not have paraffin for the little emergency heater either. It was only eight in the evening and M.I. Bazaars, the corner shop, continued to trade until after ten on a Saturday evening.

"Ma, let me run up the road to get a bottle of paraffin?" She agreed and while I searched for an appropriate container Ma counted the small change she kept in a glass jar. There was enough for the paraffin; a bit more too. My run to the shop was brief. The Harmony Boys were there, but I was in a hurry that evening, so I only harmonised to one tune. The emergency heater had a hot plate, so Ma could boil water for her tea. There was enough change to buy a *Weekend Argus (Late final edition)* and another candle.

Ma followed developments in Rhodesia. That country had made the newspaper headlines again and I thought that my mother would be interested; I was right!

Soon the house was warm from the oil fire. The smell of paraffin replaced that of mothballs. Clumps of mothballs were attached behind and beneath the oriental and Persian carpets in the house. Our clothes too smelled of paraffin after a while; like our friends who lived in informal housing where paraffin and wood were the only energy sources.

While Ma sipped her tea our conversation shifted to the tunes that I knew. That night I also spoke about Suzie, who joined in at the shop, to sing in the acapella genre with the Harmony Boys. Suzie was a hairdresser when he was not working in the bank. His salon was across the road from the corner shop. Suzie's vocal range was astounding. Equally explosive was his temper, which would flare into a rage with the minimum of provocation, or when an unsuspecting fool teased Suzie about his effeminate way. Not only did Suzie sing like a nightingale, but like Ma, he was an avid reader. When tired of playing football

I'd join Suzie. He often sat alongside the field and read either a magazine, or book. Suzie would be on his fold-up beach chair underneath an umbrella and wearing women's dark Polaroid 'reading' glasses. His big feet were always squashed into women's sandals. I could only take that much of running after a football before it became boring. Suzie read while the other Harmony Boys played their favourite game. Afterwards we'd sing and the other players were our audience. The discussions I had with Suzie were often very informative. All the other men on the field, from both soccer teams, were protective of Suzie. That was how it was. All he ever wanted to do was wash my abundant mop of hair. He did on a few occasions.

During one of those impromptu chats I asked about the magazine article he was reading. It was a review of the play *Torch Song Trilogy* by Harvey Fierstein. After hearing my question Suzie paused, slowly closed the magazine and removed the Polaroids. He looked around in his inimitable delicate and different way before whispering: "It is about being GAY. The article and the play this Harvey wrote is about being GAY and it being okay: GAY is an acronym after all, you know, hey Jes? It means, Good as You. I may be GAY, but I am as good as everyone else; that's what the acronym GAY represents. You see, GAY people are not freaks. We're people like everyone else. Women too, they're not freaks either. Women are also like everyone else. Men! Men are not like everyone else though. They think themselves different, better, unique, the top dogs. The reality is that we are all just people, we're all just people, Jes." By then Suzie was no longer whispering.

"I can sing, you know, Jes, my singing is okay ..." Suzie's singing was not just okay, it was way more than that. "Like the way Punch can play ball, I can sing. Pelé has big competition. If things were different in this country, imagine Eusébio, Punch and Pelé in the same team; football would be an official religion.

"We have feelings too, GAY people do. Sometimes I see and other times I feel the world laughing at me. It hurts. When I hurt and cry then it is because I am disappointed; and Jes, GAY people love life too, like everyone else. We want to live, just live ... and to be GAY is not revolutionary, or seditious; and it is not treason."

Suzie, otherwise known as Adrian, was a natural singer, much better than the rest of us. He had a turn of phrase that, like his singing, was memorable to all who experienced him. Maybe that was the reason the rest of the young men were protective toward Suzie. He belonged to us.

After sharing my stories with Ma, I put Eugene to bed and then re-joined her to read the newspaper. We elbowed each other to share the small circle created by our candle light. Each of us read a different section of the same newspaper.

Sundays were generally dreary, and because we had no electricity it was worse. By then I had grown out of singing in the Anglican choir the choir. All our neighbours were cooking, talking, laughing and listening to their radios. People live within close proximity to one another in a township. It was easy to hear what they were discussing and the contents of their arguments were never secret. I returned to school on a Sunday afternoon. That Sunday, due to the circumstances, I decided to stay with Ma and Eugene for as long as possible. My new school was within walking distance from Cape Town's city centre. It didn't matter when I left as long as it was in time for the last bus and train. The thought of leaving Ma and Eugene by themselves was unpleasant. Ma would manage on her own as she always has. That much I knew.

I was embarrassed when friends visited. We had no electricity and our fridge was always empty. We seemed okay but the reality was different; however, Ma never allowed our lack of food and other basic home ingredients to become an issue of concern. Back then, when we had only rice for dinner, Jane and I would sit at the table and pass empty bowls around: "Would you like some beetroot salad, Sammy?" and another: "Some fried chicken, Jane?" Ma sat at our oval table and wore a sullen expression while we played the pretend-to-have-lots-of-food game. As her expression grew more intense, we knew what was to follow: "Well, at least we do not miss that which we do not know." It was true; we were not accustomed to lavish meals.

Pa arrived for a short visit two Wednesdays later. It was only then that the electricity supply in our house was restored—by a flick of the trip switch in our otherwise locked garage.

I would remain at school during exam time. To get the best pass was my main aim, but the stuff at home also lived, like Jane, in my head.

It was tough: a new school environment, a new syllabus, having to learn a different standard of Afrikaans, all of it was daunting. I knew that it was not readily possible for me to study at university after school, so I sat out while the rest of the class completed their applications to tertiary institutions. There were those who were refused permits to study at reserved institutions of higher learning. Their options included the University of the Western Cape, technical, teacher training or nursing colleges. I had two options: (1) to find a job, and (2) to find a better job. Staying at home and doing nothing was not an option.

In December 1978, after the examinations had been written, my focus shifted from school to work. I became desperate to find a job.

My routine was to go to the city every morning. Once there I'd stand on the Grand Parade, one of four squares around which the city of Cape Town was built. Across the street, Darling Street, was the Cape Town City Hall, which also housed the public library, the same library that Ma had used many years earlier. They received the morning newspaper and I was often the first to borrow it. I searched for a job, any job. Paging through the classified section in search of suitable employment opportunities formed part of my routine. But every available job sought applicants who had work experience. There were never jobs for people with boarding school experience, who were streetwise and who could surf.

Many of my friends were accepted to study at universities, and others joined the South African Navy, entered apprenticeship programmes, or teacher and nursing training colleges. I was unable to find an employer who was willing to have me. Joining the South African Navy was equal to joining the army or the police force of the time. I feared that my tasks would include having to evict people from a perfectly swimmable beach—like Lieutenant Subramani, who sold his soul for approval from Captain van Deventer. I also feared having to shoot workers when they were on strike. When Ma was more lucid she would say: "We cannot inflict the same pain on others simply because it was done so to us. That is also not right."

It was March of 1979. I had been job searching for four months and was yet to spend a single day in the world of work. All I had to show for the effort was about one hundred 'regret' letters and a blistered pair of hands from having manually written all the applications. Being ambidextrous had its drawbacks— instead of only having one blistered hand I had two. An extra blessing would have been to write two letters at the same time, but I suppose wishing for that was greedy!

The owners of M.I. Bazaars knew me because it was at their shop that I exchanged empty soft drink bottles for money. I used the money to mail all my job applications. Meanwhile my pile of 'regret' letters continued to grow. One day, after 'enough' 'regret' letters had arrived I decided to shelve my pride and approached a township builder for a job. So began my first formal exposure to the world of work. I was a labourer for an owner builder on the Cape Flats. Often the inclement weather conditions made it impossible for people in the construction industry to work. There were times when the owner builder would run out of money. Those times, and on rainy days, I stayed home and waited for the postman to pass our house on his rounds. Even though I only ever received 'regret' letters there was always a measure of optimism, just in case luck would be enclosed in an envelope.

He was a jovial man, that postman, and it was often the only happy part of an otherwise gloomy day. After delivering the mail and banging the lid I would instinctively rush out to fetch the letters. The postman always looked to catch my eye as he swung a leg over the bicycle saddle. Most days, when I was home he'd see me, and shout: "You must be famous Mr Levy!"

"With the postman and in those 'regret' letters was the only experience I had of being referred to as Mr Levy. Some would-be employers could not be bothered to send a letter informing me that I had not been successful. Nevertheless my pile of 'regret' letters continued to show steady growth. In time the collection of letters became my trophy for having tried and never given up. The layout and wording of almost every 'regret' letter is emblazoned in my mind, forever.

The same applied to the way in which job advertisements were written and published in the newspaper. Job adverts were divided into different groups and genders too. I would laugh at the temerity contained in some of the adverts, but later, when the wording in those adverts indicated my exclusion too, it was no longer funny. That South African society was obsessed with labelling people remained and remains a constant reality. I got the impression that the label worn by a person was more important than his or her potential and ability. Skin colour determined worth. Dark-skinned people were always appointed against more menial jobs and paid less too. Females in the world of work earned less than males, often for doing the same job. It was unfair, but no one I knew was objecting out loud. Those afflicted by the negativity of being mere labels, they who were divided and then ruled, accepted the situation as normal. Voluntarily we became the second and third class citizens as defined by the prescribed labels the state allocated for us to wear. Those with light skins were encouraged to believe that they were superior no other criteria seemed to matter more, other than being male and having a light skin. But just having a light skin empowered people to act, be taken seriously and to command respect.

Soon it was winter, 1979, and the building work was consistently interrupted by the inclement weather. My wages as a labourer for an owner builder, my employer, were very low. There were weeks when I'd only work on one of the five days. The costs of travelling to work were more than I earned. When desperation peaked I again set aside my pride and asked the few people I knew to help me find a job. Meanwhile, on rainy days my routine at the city library continued. Every rainy morning I'd pack smart interview clothes. They were neatly press-folded and packed in a green canvas bag together with my suede Hush Puppy wedge heel shoes. I carried those clothes everywhere, just in case there was an opportunity to attend a job interview. When I found a job advert, or when there was an interview to attend, the neglected art deco style building that housed a public toilet on the Grand Parade became my dressing room. Several people on the Cape Flats often think aloud, or as Ma would say: "They think with their mouths." There was no exception when I entered the toilet carrying my seemingly suspicious looking bag. I would laugh silently at the comments made, so as not to encourage the loud, lewd thoughts of others who used the Grand Parade public toilet.

Some days the Grand Parade was a market and at other times it was a car park. Every lunch-time, without fail (as happens to this day) a charismatic lay preacher convened a church service underneath one of several palm trees on the Darling Street side of the Parade. Watching him preach was a priority second only to rushing home if *Sportsview*, a TV programme, promised clips and other news sound bites about world surfing events. Watching the man preach at lunch time was the highlight of my day when in the city. That preacher said the most bizarre things, and did so at the top of a croaky voice. Apart from their rasping tone, his words were long and drawn out: "W o m e n w h o w e a r t r o u s e r s a r e r e p r e s e n t a t i v e s o f t h e d e v i l ..." and in similar fashion he'd say: "If you do not give your heart, your life, your soul <u>and your money</u> to the Lord then you'll go to the place where there shall be weeping and gnashing of teeth." Then, after adjusting his fat tummy, he'd say: "Those of you who do not have teeth, 'HE!' will give you teeth—because a gnashing of teeth is guaranteed ... it says so in the good book, Matthew! Matthew! Matthew Chapter 8 verse 12, it says so there!" The preacher would then haul out a tambourine and soon he'd be in a trance-like state, nodding as a gesture of thanks to those who placed coins in the tidings hat while he sang:

He sent me to give the good news to the poor,

Tell prisoners that they are prisoners no more,
Tell blind people that they can see
And set the downtrodden free ...

Some days the preacher was moved by the spirit and then there were other times when he would be moved by the tempestuous south-easterly wind. There were other days where he would be moved by the wind. I'd sit watching as the preacher did battle with the infamous south easterly wind. He'd adjust his ample stomach and wave his hands almost as if to retain balance. His face wore the expression of anger, probably with the wind.

On good weather days those who stood in the front had their umbrellas out, even when it did not rain or shine too brightly. The interesting part was that the lunch-time preacher believed everything he said. There were times when his biblical interpretation was memorable, like the one about Judas Iscariot who died in a high speed car crash ... on the freeway between Gethsemane and Bethlehem. A Ford Zephyr Six was apparently the getaway car, according to the vicar of Cape Town's Grand Parade—of course, the Zephyr had a nodding dog doll in the back window.

While at school we had to attend Mass several times per week. I was familiar with most themes that informed the various sermons. Maybe I was not sufficiently attentive while attending, or perhaps the school priest lacked imagination.

I wondered why he had to draw out his words like that; perhaps he was buying time to think of what to say next!

Chapter Seventeen

Maundy Thursday

When I arrived home one day there was a message. It was handwritten. Ma said that a friend had left it for me. "... see Mr Izak de Kock at Bathing Amenities: Sea Point Pavilion Pool."

I was very excited that night, so much so that the following morning took too long to dawn. It was six thirty, winter, when I reported for duty at the Pool. The only people out were those who jogged along the promenade wearing satin-like shorts in the darkness. Some ran as if they were being chased, but I soon realised it was the wind at their backs that got them to run faster. Their return runs were usually not as enthusiastic. I smiled whenever someone noticed me standing in the corner formed by masonry steps. After all, I wore my best clothes: my interview uniform, the pair of crimplene trousers, shirt, a jacket and Hush Puppy shoes.

Mr de Kock arrived at nine o'clock. I knew that it was him when a big white Valiant Regal complete with brown vinyl roof slowly cruised by and parked in the shade of a nearby tree on Beach Road. There was no one to introduce me, so I did so myself.

"Oh! You arre the new admin guy?" Without a pause he continued: "Listen, firrst thing ..." he spoke with a very prominent Afrikaans accent. Mr de Kock needed help with English; the same help I needed when speaking in Afrikaans, "...you need to understand: here we either wearr a bearrd or we shave, but the shorrt hairr arround your face is not acceptable."

Mr de Kock demonstrated the same manner that I imagined Commander van Deventer had with Mr Thompson several years earlier. With piercing blue eyes trained on me and his mullet quivering at the back of his head Mr de Kock shifted a name plate on his desk so I could see. It read, 'MR IZAK de KOCK, Head: Bathing Amenities, Atlantic Seaboard'. While continuing to look at me Mr de Kock wrestled a cigarette from a big box containing 30 Lexingtons. He had, a moment earlier, opened the box. It was much bigger than his hands. Even when he was striking a match against the sulphur, his fixed glare remained trained on me. But I had no intention of running away on my lucky day! He puffed out palls of smoke in rapid succession. It hid his head, like when the clouds spilled over Table Mountain. Even as the smoke cleared his glare remained fixed. The experience in his ample office may have been eerie, but my joy at having a job made me oblivious to peripheral detail.

My observations included that Mr de Kock had a tummy, one better suited to a much bigger person. There were traces of his having been handsome, albeit a while ago, but the remnants remained. He wore a check short-sleeved shirt, similar to those that Papa Pretorius wore. De Kock's shirt was unbuttoned to reveal a heavy gold pendant dangling on a chain and molly coddled in a lonely clump of hair in middle of his chest. He hung his jacket, turned on the electric heater and began to clean his ashtray of the previous day's smoke-ends. All the while I stood in front of his desk awaiting further instructions. A man wearing a signature white all-in-one jumpsuit with the letters CCC embroidered in red on the back wafted in to offer tea or coffee. I remembered those suits. The men, only men as far as I can remember, who worked at municipal swimming pools, they wore those suits. Mr de Kock nodded in response to the greeting followed by an instruction: "Give Sam coffee." I had not yet been offered a seat when he, without having shifted his glare, said: "Am I clearr, do you understand; about the shaving?"

"Yes, Sir!" was my grateful reply.

I got the sense that Mr de Kock was a very strict man. This I judged from his tone, but I had a job and that was all about which I cared.

Finally he offered me a seat. My seat was at a desk in the far corner of his big office. The desk had not been in use for longer than a while, that much was obvious from its look. My mug of coffee was served. The server, Desmond, a tall man with several gold teeth in his face, addressed me as 'Mr Sam' when handing the coffee. I could add sugar myself, unlike with Marilyn's coffee on the veranda at the Stanger Street Truck Port.

Mr de Kock made a telephone call and spoke in Afrikaans while I prepared to have coffee. I understood much of what he was saying. The discussion was about me; my role and to whom I had to report. He spoke as if I was not there, as if I did not matter. When Mr de Kock hung up, he resumed with that fixating glare before slowly shaking his head from side to side as if watching a fast paced tennis match, or as if very disappointed. "These days you do not know to whom you is talking," he blurted.

I thought that Mr de Kock was talking to himself, like Ma sometimes did.

He stood up and dragged his high chair across the floor. In front of the cupboard on the other side of our office was where he placed the chair. Mr de Kock first opened the cupboard doors, followed by a clamber and awkward movements up onto the high chair. Once there he stretched with one arm in the air while the other balanced against the frame of that cupboard. Mr de Kock just about reached the top shelf. Perhaps he did not want to ask an unshaven tall boy for help.

"Herre, change into this. Afterwards you go and wait by the van, you will see it parked in the loading zone. Go now!"

I had not yet had a sip of the coffee Desmond brought. Within minutes I was also wearing a stiff starched white jumpsuit. The letters CCC were prominently embroidered with thick red darning cotton on the back of my white jumpsuit overalls. It was unmistakable; I was a member of the world of work and enjoyed employment with the Cape City Council. Well, moments later I was on the back of a municipal utility vehicle. We drove through the streets of Sea Point, heading for Clifton Beach. The mist lifted after about eleven o'clock that June morning. A different angle to my city blossomed before my very eyes. The Twelve Apostle Mountains were majestic. A section of Table Mountain where the cable car docked was visible after the mist had dissipated. I was one of three cleaners on the most picturesque beach, a *reserved* beach.

My colleagues were two older people, a man and a woman. They were both of the Muslim faith and quirky. I was introduced by the driver: "Sam," see, I was no longer Mister Sam, "… this is Boeta Shafiek Adams and here is Auntie Ghaliema Isaacs." Boeta, as used in this context, is a term of respect and is usually reserved for an older man. It means older brother.

Boeta Shafiek wore a faded version of the same overalls as mine. His fez was taller than the usual, as if he were a relatively senior chef, save for the discrete eastern type silk embroidery. Boeta Shafiek wore sun glasses, ones that were big enough for two people to see through. I was convinced that they were women's shades!

Our office adjoined the beach toilets. Boeta Shafiek was my reporting officer: "I am your boss Sammy. You work under me and only when I am not here can you take instruction from Ghaliema."

I was allocated a broom and a place to sit in the little 'toilet-aligned' office.

"Sit only during breaks!" said Auntie Ghaliema before mumbling something in a dialect of Afrikaans.

Both Boeta Shafiek and Auntie Ghaliema each had a broom, spade and a two wheel wagon that held a big silver dustbin. Their dustbin had CCC franked into the metal casing. Their names were written on the equipment like a car's number plate. Boeta Shafiek explained that we had to label everything. Apparently the Cape City Council did not replace brooms when they went missing. Mr de Kock had dismissed my predecessor after he lost a mop and as a result could not clean the men's toilet properly. The tidal pool had to be painted with lime during low tide.

After a thorough induction I was set to work. Auntie Ghaliema undertook to write my name on the new tools that had arrived. Our office was also our storeroom and our mess area. While writing Auntie Ghaliema and Boeta Shafiek were arguing about whether or not my surname had Jewish origins:

"… he's a Jew, I'm telling you, Shafiek."

"He's not Jewish!" said Boeta Shafiek.

"No, not Jew-ISH, that's for the people who live here in Camps Bay. This boy is a real Jew, nothing 'ish' about him. Imagine, Ghaliema, if I refer to you as Muslim-ish, what will you say in reply? Wait Ghaliema, don't respond to that … because if you say Muslim-ish then your false teeth will fall out!"

"Don't joke, Shafiek! What kind of Jew is he who lives on the Cape Flats? Only his hair is Jewish?"

"I don't know, Ghaliema; why don't you ask him; I've not seen all of him?"

Those two also spoke about me as if I were not there. Maybe that was what Cape Town people did; or perhaps it was true and I was invisible?

The light argument became heated when Boeta Shafiek said: "Yes, Ghaliema, and while you are asking him about the Jews also ask if they threw the right piece away, otherwise he may be here with that problem too!"

"Is there nothing better you can think of?"

I left them to argue and went to paint the tidal pool from where I continued to hear Auntie Ghaliema yelling at Boeta Shafiek. They were arguing about the circumcision of Jewish and Muslim men.

"But seriously, Ghaliema, they make suitcases of the foreskin. Yes, at Citation Leather in Chapini Street, that's where they make it." Boeta Shafiek was teasing Auntie Ghaliema, but she was not tolerating any of it.

Fuming, she responded: "You should be ashamed of yourself to speak like that in front of this child."

Auntie Ghaliema was definitely not amused. It was about time for us to end the day.

I was on the back of the van for a ride to the city. Both my colleagues were in the front and I got the sense that the bickering had not ended. It continued every day thereafter. Shafiek would bait Ghaliema, possibly because he had to find something to make an otherwise dreary day pass faster. When we got to the city one evening I overheard Boeta Shafiek say: "… when did you become Mother Mary, Ghaliema?"

I had no idea about the relevance of that parting comment save to know that the future days seemed bleak.

Zip it in the Zibi Can and *Keep the Cape in Shape* were the two slogans on posters stuck in strategic spots across the beach area. I ensured that the reserved beach was clean. With my first wage I bought a big sun hat and mirror sunglasses as an antidote against the summer sun and sea glare. In addition to my painting the tidal pool, my main job was to collect cigarette butts and any other dirt that beachgoers frequently left behind.

Often surfers descended upon the beach. I watched with interest. Sometimes the urge to give advice had to be suppressed when poor technique was evident. After all, cleaners on a beach do not usually give technical advice to surfers who are followed by friends with long camera lenses and more.

At times the work was okay, but more often dreary was a better description. I had a job and that counted for something.

My supervisors continued their daily mindless arguing. The next quarrel was about who should work on Christmas and New Year's Day.

Boeta Shafiek had three children and Auntie Ghaliema had many more. I did not have anyone other than Ma and Eugene. Pa was going to be working—he was always working, so I volunteered to watch over the beach so that my colleagues could spend the holidays with their families.

Days on the beach during the festive season, although very busy, were extremely mundane. I had a lot of time to think, dream, imagine and plan the rest of my life.

My search for a better job resumed in the early part of the following year, 1981. It was my second year in the world of work. Despite that, all the jobs for which I applied elicited only more regret letters. That I did not have sufficient work experience was the standard reason stated. My skills were never right, nor were they enough; that I might become magical in the workplace did not matter and would never be known, because the barrier to entry was pre-emptively closed.

It was April of 1981, the beginning of winter again; another quiet time for us on the beach. There were days when we three cleaners outnumbered the beachgoers. The only trash I collected was strewn from cars parked on the parking lot. Days were so miserable that even the seagulls went elsewhere.

It was one of those, a wet and windy day. The sea crashed against the rocks and the wind blew froth onto the parking area. It was the sea's derivative of tumbleweed and snow. With foam everywhere, that was the day, during the week, when I saw Pa there, parked, for a view of the angry sea. He was with a woman companion. She was not my Ma. They left after about an hour of talking, laughing and touching each other. I didn't know what to make of the experience. At least Pa did not leave dirt for me to collect … or maybe I was being easy on him. After all, he never swore and he never physically abused Ma; but what he did was, dare I say, as bad?

On the way home that very evening I wrestled with whether to tell Ma about having seen Pa, or to be quiet. While travelling home I thought about very long ago, to when Ma said: "Sometimes our silence allows us to rise above that with which we may not be in agreement. At times silence is a very loud response and other times it is a curse."

When I eventually got home there was a big tipper truck parked in front of our house that evening. I thought that Uncle Flippie was visiting; I'd not seen him in many years. He was the only truck driver my family knew. Uncle Flippie had the biggest ears; that much I keep remembering — how could I forget! When I was little, Pa and I, on occasion, visited Uncle Flippie at his home in Sir Lowry's Pass Village, out there near Gordon's Bay. When we drove and as we got closer to Uncle Flippie's house, Pa would switch off the cassette player and instruct me to stop asking so many questions. Naturally I asked: "Why, Pa?" I must have been about eight years old then.

"Ya! Because, Uncle Flippie will hear us approach and it will spoil the surprise of our visit. He has big ears and can hear very well." Pa's sense of humour was always a bit off colour.

Sir Lowry's Pass is nestled along the N2 national road and the mountain; just there where the road begins its ascent to cross the Hottentots-Holland range. At the top of that mountain pass is one of the big South African fresh water reservoirs, the Steenbras Dam, where I had learned to swim all those years ago. It always seemed odd to me that the inhabitants of Sir Lowry's Pass used ground water, hard water, with a brackish taste. Yet they lived less than seven kilometres from the best water resource in the region.

I noticed that a part of the sofa from our lounge was sticking out on top of that truck.

Our house had been sold and it was not Uncle Flippie who was visiting. Instinctively I walked faster. On entering I found Ma, Eugene and Lampo huddled against the naked nail-marked yellow wall of our near empty lounge room. Most of the furniture and wall hangings had been removed and placed on the back of that construction truck. Ma's eyes looked the way they did when Mr Abrahams brought her back from Groote Schuur Hospital on the day that Anne and Brenda died. Eugene, sensing the bewilderment, just stood at Ma's side. I joined them. There was nothing else to do. The three of us felt utterly helpless.

The swarm of workmen walked in empty handed and when they walked out it was with an item that sparked a memory of what I believed had been a happy childhood. Even though we don't miss what we don't know, I had known a time when those toys were most important in my life. They were important enough to have names; like Jonathan, my blue rocking horse, the one Charles had made for me from random planks. My toys were strewn on the back of that dirty construction vehicle. Those were the toys that had taken away my darkness when I was unaware of loneliness.

The house was empty. Carpets, furniture, toys, all had been tossed onto and the back of that truck. It was our stuff. They were discarded, like Ma, Eugene, Lampo and me. It felt as if I could hear my toys call out: "… climb up and rescue us!" I didn't, and my guilt lingers to this day. I let them go to 'nowhere' on the back of a dirty construction tipper truck. I know not where the truck took our stuff and my toys.

It meant nothing to those men, just another load. When the house was bare, the men clambered up and sat on the pieces that they had removed from our house.

The truck engine cranked once, but it was not enough to start. I was hopeful that our stuff would stay longer, but the fourth attempt brought a familiar shudder followed by a plume of black smoke. The incessant revving before the truck moved made the rowdy workmen seem silent.

All we had left was an empty house surrounded by a pall of dirty lingering smoke. That smoke lingered like a thought of nothing; when instead I should have done something, but what? I watched until the truck reached the top of Fourth Street. It turned right onto Victoria Road. There too, it left smoke; incense in exchange for my departing memories.

The South East wind had not yet blown all the smoke away by the time inquisitive neighbours flocked onto the property. Inside the dark house Ma, Eugene, Lampo and I were trying to reconcile with the emptiness. Outside, many neighbours were peering through the lounge window of an empty building that once had been our home. Where was Pa? You may wonder: he was working —Pa was always working.

I whispered: "Where are we going to stay tonight, Ma?", so that the gawking neighbours could not hear.

"Mitchell's Plain. Pa found us a house in Mitchell's Plain," answered little Eugene.

Ma was being moved from a township to a new sprawling dormitory development situated much further away from the city of Cape Town. Pa was moving to the exclusive suburb of Camps Bay.

Eugene would be transferred from one township school to another, one that was close to the house in Mitchell's Plain. I refused to move there; it was much further away from where I worked and moving to Mitchell's Plain felt like taking a step backwards. Ma was extremely unhappy about my decision. I packed some of the clothes that had been thrown about when the cupboards were moved. With my dusty surfboard tucked under my arm, I explained to Ma and Eugene that I would visit over weekends and stay from time to time.

Like the furniture on the truck did, I also left for an unknown destination. Together with the blue suitcase and my old surfboard, I was on the road again. It was a cold winter's evening, about eight o'clock when we left for nowhere. There was no rain in the sky though. I was sad to leave and sad to go. My walk was down Victoria Road. I had no idea where the walk was headed. There was a public telephone en route, between First and Second Streets, opposite Bona Café, a fast food outlet. Jane and I had tried to use the same phone when searching for Charles years earlier, at the time when Brenda and Anne were killed. It was broken then.

Surprisingly the phone was not broken that evening when, again, I set aside my pride and called a friend to ask for help. She agreed to speak with her parents and return the call. I read the telephone number to her and then waited outside the phone booth, listening for the return call. A stout, young woman wearing clothes that were several sizes too small, approached. She was intent on using the phone and did not care that that I was expecting an important call. In an attempt to buy time I told the woman that Bona Café would offer her a cup of coffee and a mutton *salomie*, without charge, if she told them to register it against Sam's account. To her the offer of more food was more tempting than making an urgent telephone call. My sense about that woman's healthy appetite was right. She grumbled profanities at me while struggling across the road in her tight clothes, headed for the fictitious windfall. Fortunately the shop was busy; I could see that it would take a while before she was served; long enough to take the call and get away. Many others arrived to use that public telephone while I waited. It was way too risky to send all of them for a free meal. Instead, I tried to appeal for goodwill. It was difficult to convince those call-hungry folk. Most objected to my request. A man, one of medium build and poor diction, threatened violence and when the others heard, they immediately suggested that more severe action be taken against me if I did not move away from the entrance to that telephone booth.

A group of young men approached. Their knives were drawn and slyly concealed. There was no doubt in my mind about their intentions. It was to kill. I knew better than to argue with a group of angry men who had weapons, for it would result in certain death. That was all too frequently a reality on the hard streets of Cape Flats townships where group think and gangsters defy commonly accepted logic. The woman whose meal I 'sponsored' re-appeared. She too was angry. Later I learned that her anger was also directed at the shopkeeper. The owner of Bona Café had threatened to shoot her after she had demanded food.

Using gangster lingo and speaking in dialect, the tight clothed woman instructed her group of young men: "Make him white bones!"

My translation is direct, but in that street language '… white bones…' is an instruction to kill. I tried to explain that the shopkeeper's reaction was brought on by her attitude, but she was in no mood to hear more stories.

The men instinctively went into attack formation. I've seen the manoeuvre many times, but never before had I been the target. The telephone rang. I hurried inside the cubicle, jammed the door with my foot and answered Mr Andreucci's voice was clipped: "Meet me in front of Bona Café." He was on his way.

By then, more would-be telephone users had arrived. Everyone wanted to be first in line. The bickering that ensued distracted my attackers. I got away, but only just. Crossing the road was swift, to the spot where Mr Andreucci and I had arranged to meet. People had surrounded the public telephone and were trading insults. A fight seemed imminent. The impending skirmish no longer had anything to do with me.

The buzz around that telephone booth continued, but by then I was watching from across the road. Sounds included screeching brakes, blaring hooters and swearing that would cause a sailor to blush.

Mr Andreucci and I did not know each other. We had met on a few occasions, but it had not been enough for us to be friends.

I was surprised at his preparedness to help me. It was also somewhat embarrassing that I had to ask for help. He made an immediate assessment, and realised my dire predicament, even my shame. Given my embarrassment, Mr Andreucci chose to discuss the audible cursing that continued around that public telephone instead of the reasons that left me wanting.

I laughed when he explained that there were rules for uttering profanities on the Cape Flats. Over the years I had witnessed many swearing bouts between folk in the area. It was true: fights often resulted from swearing that involved someone's mother's honour.

The police arrived as we were leaving. They were there to save the telephone booth and shoo away the mass of cursing people. Mr Andreucci had to drive up a curb and across a small field to avoid the jeering crowd. Onlookers too were cursing at one another. It became apparent that taller people were deliberately causing an obstruction. The shorter folk were craning to get a better view of the commotion, hence the internal combustion amongst the spectators.

Once at the Andreucci home, we made a bed for me on the parquet floor in their small dining room.

I slept well that night but the morning dawned too soon. Waking up was easy, even exciting, until I remembered the loss of my family. I realised that it would be forever. Meanwhile, down the road, an Imam's voice sounded from the minaret at the mosques as he called the faithful to prayer.

Mrs Andreucci found the biggest red lunchbox in which she packed half a loaf of bread every morning. I left home at six o'clock, in time for the usual train. My lunchbox attracted much attention from the other commuters. The interview clothes would have attracted similar attention had I been wearing them in that third class commuter train carriage. There were only two classes on those trains, first class and third class. I only ever got to see first class through the window when the train entered the station; it cost three times more to travel in those carriages.

In the morning people were quiet, save for the odd preacher who chose to share his religion with all the head-shaking commuters. They shook their heads, probably just to keep the peace. But on the evening train the same people were more vocal. On Fridays they were positively 'festive'. Most commuters were fascinated by my lunchbox as others were by my hair. Some would venture a comment, like the observant man who always sat across from me and frequently siphoned something, perhaps from a bottle which he had wrapped in newspaper. One Friday evening and speaking in reference to me he said out loud: "... been watching him all week; keeps that lunchbox on his lap as if it is a trophy."" The train people also spoke about me as if I was not there!

That Friday an older woman, also a usual commuter, was quick to defend: "Leave him! Construction workers eat a lot, hey?" She turned to look at me for approval before continuing: "Mister," said the older woman to newspaper drinker "why is it that you talk only when there is a bottle in your newspaper? You think that we do not know that there's a bottle of wine wrapped in that newspaper you keep on putting to your lips?" She again turned to me for a reply, but I just smiled politely. There was no point in doing anything else. The drinker wore a toothless grin, but stopped to take another deep swig before answering: "Yes *Mummy*, you will always protect him, hey?" I got a big wink, a toothless grin as he took a further swig from his liquid newspaper.

Every older woman got the title 'Mummy' and older men were addressed as Uncle, Mister or Boeta.

In time I learned to speak all the dialects spoken in the broader Cape Town area. The metaphors are mixed; words drawn from different languages take on new meanings, like the term 'festive' which I liked to use. It can mean a number of different things and often deflects from the traditional use, or meaning. There appears to be no one reason for this. Perhaps it has something to do with the high levels of mispronunciation, or misinterpretation prevalent in the region, I'm not sure. One of the dialects became the language I used most frequently during those years.

There are a smaller number of people living on the Cape Flats who do not speak any of the Afrikaans dialects. These are generally English speaking folk and *'sturvy'* is the term used to describe them; apparently because their behaviour presupposes 'a cut above the rest'.

There are forms of the Cape Afrikaans dialect that cannot be spoken without the accompanying posturing and hand gestures. It is in part like sign language.

§

My lunchbox and I continued to report for duty at the Sea Point Pavilion Pool. Mr de Kock persisted in not returning my morning salutations. Whenever there was a need to communicate with me he'd do so via the driver.

Boeta Shafiek and Auntie Ghaliema were always seated in the front when we drove to Clifton Beach. Given that I was the youngest, my place was to sit at the back of the utility vehicle; my lunchbox and I among the bags of lime, refuse containers, weed-killer, and whatever other equipment was needed to keep the beach and its surrounds clean.

If the tidal pool was not painted regularly with lime, then algae would grow. It remained a substantial mission to remove algae with a wire brush, so I painted the pool diligently every day during low tide. There was always a written message attached to the purchase order whenever I collected a requisition voucher from Mr de Kock. Despite my being right there, in his office, Mr de Kock preferred to write messages rather than speak directly with me. Mr de Kock's spelling, general writing and conduct were equally poor. He mixed languages when speaking, but my bother was that Mr de Kock refused to speak with me. After all, his speech was perhaps marginally better than how he wrote.

He, De Kock, was a Job Reservation appointee.

Mediocrity, self-importance and entitlement were the characteristics that became evident when people were appointed because of skin colour and not as a result of their ability. Management skill was measured by how confrontational the incumbent was. I realised that the City of Cape Town also favoured pigmentation above ability when it appointed people, but there was no facility or platform from which I could comment. In fact, if the truth be told then I had no money with which to buy shaving blades. That is why I did the close trim with a pair of paper scissors instead.

I sensed that Mr de Kock deemed himself entitled to treat me the way he did; all because he was the 'boss'. In many instances Boeta Shafiek tried to emulate Mr de Kock. Ma often said that people learned how to manage others from the experiences to which they have been exposed.

Mr de Kock was angry with me and I did not know why. Despite it being a 'one-way exercise' I continued to greet him every morning. I thought it the right thing to do, but Mr de Kock never responded.

One rainy morning I arranged the lime bags underneath a canvas cover on the utility vehicle so that I could shelter and the equipment could remain dry. The rain was torrential that morning, driven by a very angry wind. When I had finished packing, loading and had made myself comfortable the driver ran past. I did not know his name. All the people there referred to him as 'driver', so for all intents and purposes his name was 'Driver'. Mine was probably 'Cleaner' but Mr de Kock, his name was 'Boss'. That morning, as quickly as the driver ran past, that was how fast he returned, stuck his head in underneath my makeshift canopy and said, in that sing-song way: "I have been wondering about you; congratulations man, I think that you are very well bred!" My immediate thought was that it was an unwelcome comment, similar to when lascivious men made lewd overtures to unsuspecting women.

Only after analysing his broken English did I realise what he meant. His intention was to pay me a compliment, albeit for something over which I had no control. His comment was indicative of the flawed criteria we use to assess one another. It was a spillover from the applied job selection criteria; the criteria that had selected Mr de Kock. Sharp features, light skin and hair were an automatic qualification for being better. I heard others comment like that too, all of my life. Every time it happened I'd wonder how Jane and I had come to be. Whenever I asked her Jane had been non-committal. The way she answered had raised more questions in my mind—the most important being, what did Jane know that I didn't?

Well, there I was, near homeless, under a makeshift canvas canopy and on the back of a utility vehicle. We were driving so that I could collect trash on what was usually one of the most picturesque beaches in the world. Being supposedly well-bred did not count for anything. Although I was disturbed by the driver's comment my response was another respectful smile. That morning I remembered the sympathiser who had visited Ma after the deaths of Anne and Brenda; she had said that Jane was "beautiful, like a European girl." That woman also thought she was complimenting my Jane. Is it stupid to make a value judgment based on things that we have been conditioned to think are pretty?

As we drove along the Atlantic Seaboard, Robben Island was vaguely visible through the rain. I could see it peeping above the horizon behind the high seas that broke over Whale Rock. Usually the sun shone equally on the island of desolation as it did on the most beautiful city in the word. They were a mere 13 kilometres apart. The sun was not reserved and neither were the wind and rain; no, they belonged to every one equally.

The beach that I cleaned remained quiet that entire day. While Boeta Shafiek checked the newspaper for horse racing results and new tips, I stole a peek at the jobs section. *The Cape Times* had one that I could do: "Pack Fish for Irvin & Johnson," read the caption. "...a commercial fishing company ... men needed for casual work at Quay Four. Start at seven o' clock on Monday morning, 6th April" was the wording in that advert. Mr de Kock had given an instruction for us to have holiday leave when the beach was not busy. It was my turn to have a break. The advertised opportunity to pack fish as a casual worker during my annual leave was ideal. I had planned to use my holiday leave to find suitable accommodation and a better job.

Finding accommodation was easy. Across the road from the Andreucci home lived a retired teacher, Ms Maselele. I approached and asked to rent one of her rooms. Ms Maselele agreed. I continued to take meals with the Andreucci family. Mr and Mrs Andreucci had become my de facto parents. After all, Mr Andreucci, though he had not realised the significance, he also 'picked me up'. On occasion I overheard Ma say to Pa: "… that's what you get from 'pick-up children'." I did not understand at the time, but she was definitely referring to Jane and me. Ma was cross when she said that, cross with me. I had done something that stirred her anger, but that was what she said and it bothered me.

Maybe Ma did not know how Jane and I came to be. That was why she was not able to tell me.

My excursion into the fish packing industry was interesting. Inside the warehouse, the walls were adorned with posters warning about dangers. Protruding fish bones posed a particular danger. No protective gloves were issued. The job entailed stacking pre-packed fish from a conveyer belt onto a pallet. When a defined height was reached a man driving a forklift took the pallet into a refrigerated warehouse. Ten minutes for tea and twenty for lunch.

The days were long. It was already dusk when we, the casual workers, were instructed to form a queue outside the paymaster's office. A short balding man who tried to walk around his tummy arrived at about six o'clock that evening. He was introduced as the paymaster and without further ceremony proceeded to call our names. He had a peculiar loud and very high pitched voice. He should have auditioned for the Harmony Boys! On hearing my name I stepped forward to receive a brown pay envelope containing my day's wage. After taking receipt, each casual worker was directed to another man, the paymaster's assistant. That man had peculiarities too. Not only were his four front teeth missing, but they seemed to have been gone for a long time. So long, that the shape of his mouth had taken on a depressed contour and it changed his facial expression from happy to that of one who was experiencing a constant foul smell. His job that evening was to hand out 'gift' parcels to those who had received a day's wages.

The wage was ten South African Rand and the gift parcel contained two small fish. No, maybe the Grand Parade preacher would have been relieved to know that the gift did not include five loaves of bread too. Probably because there were no multitudes, or perhaps it was due to modern day inflation.

Nonetheless, the financial rewards amounted to exploitation wages. Not the fish: they were given at the right time.

A day in the life of a fish packer was very similar to that of a farmworker. Both worked from sunrise to sunset: one in the warehouse; and the other on the farms. All of us were workers, be it on a farm or packing fish. Every one received a reward after sunset: a stipend and two fish for the fish-packer; a stipend and bottom barrel wine for the farm worker. The wine contained near poisonous non-oxidised sediments. Before consuming that wine workers usually joked amongst one another about the after effects. It did not stop them from drinking though.

My fish packing experience strengthened a resolve to learn and challenge unfairness and the scourge of exploitation that people visit upon one another.

It was my third Easter in the Cape; a new experience. The culinary custom in my then surrounds was different. I had been told about the traditional cooking in preparation for Easter but had never experienced it. We were always away at boarding school at that time of the year. When I was home Ma did not eat fish because it activated the eczema at the bottom of her right leg. One week before Easter, Mrs Andreucci, like most women of her generation, prepared the traditional pickled fish. Pan-fried fish placed on a bed of onion rings, cardamom pods, cloves, cinnamon, pepper corns, curry powder, bay and lemon leaves. These were layered in an appropriate dish and soaked in white wine vinegar. A bit of sugar was added to break the acidic monotony of the vinegar and onions. Some women used raisins instead of sugar while others added Mrs Ball's chutney, a traditional South African product. The layered fish was placed in a concealed cool place where it pickled until Good Friday. Hot cross buns and pickled fish were the staple diet for the entire Easter weekend. It always rains in Cape Town over an Easter weekend, that's how it is.

Being able to contribute two fishes to this traditional fare gave me much joy. Small things matter, that's what Khokho would have said. Giving made me feel good, as opposed to always receiving. Weekends were fun too. Some Saturdays we'd walk down the road to a dance hall, the Five Two Four. But every Sunday I visited my Ma.

The dance hall was almost completely dark inside, save for the bar area and parts of the stage that had dimmed lights. Soft lights identified a small wood covered dance floor, which was surrounded by tables and chairs. The crowd that gathered there seemed a pretentious lot. They spoke English and became louder with every drink. Rum and coke as the mixer was the favourite. There were suave men from all hues and many very pretty women. All wore smart casual clothes and gathered in groups. Men in faded jeans were not allowed to enter, but women in tight fitting Wranglers were every man's favoured prospect.

Four musicians would arrive as the crowd mingled amid the sound of canned music. A very old man with his tweed jacket and 'comb-over' hairdo to hide his bald pate; he, with both hands in his trouser pockets, would mosey across the tiny dance floor. One delicate step up was the low, yet elevated stage. That man, it was said, could make a piano talk. He had apparently played for the Queen of England when only in shorts. No-one ever described what the Queen wore. As with the three wise men who came from the East; nowhere is it stated whether the three went back.

The other band members who arrived to replace the canned music were a drummer, a bass and lead guitarist.

I watched as the drummer created and then maintained the beat to every different piece they played. When the groove was on and the sound tight, his 'mobile' teeth came out. He'd put them in his shirt pocket and roll up his

255

sleeves, all without missing a beat. It was the level of his concentration and perhaps his shock of white hair that made any rhythm possible. He dribbled with sticks across several drums, like a consummate footballer in a demonstration game; and simultaneously he manipulated a foot cymbal and a big bass drum.

The bass player was a renowned drunk. He was a little man but that never bothered him. During the day he sold clothes at a man's shop. Come Saturday afternoons, with a double bass in his left hand and a deep drink in his belly, the rhythm and sound he produced were what legends could only dream about—it was like that.

A fourth old man appeared on the stage, having arrived there with the aid of a walking stick and with assistance from a younger man who carried his guitar. This musician sat on a chair and placed his left foot on a short stool before positioning an electric lead guitar to lean on his bad leg. He'd shift dark-rimmed spectacles up onto the bridge of his nose and then play. I watched, as older Latin music enthusiasts in the audience went silent in disbelief at the wail of that guitar in the Five Two Four on a Saturday afternoon.

The cantankerous old piano man reacted with less than a royal touch when mistakes were made by the other three musicians during any of the standard renditions. Piano Man's angry response to errors knew few boundaries. First he'd scowl and then he'd scold the players, for he had no care about who saw, and less about who heard. While scolding, Piano Man, like the drummer, would not miss a beat. It was obvious that those musicians were there to play music. The audience was incidental. Many were caught up in the musical moment.

That was, until Zelda Andreucci stepped up to sing. Those jazz standards shall forever ring in my ears. They are so much bigger than my all-important red lunchbox and listening to them was my chance to forget about life for a while. The crowd fell silent when Zelda sang. Afterwards, following a short pause, they erupted with applause on that particular Saturday afternoon. Shouts included: "…Sing 'Summertime!' followed by, "and 'Fly Me To The Moon'," another crowd favourite. In the lull that followed the clamour to have their song sung came a clear but gentle request. It came from about where the bar was. "No! No!" pleaded a man as he briefly paused to compose his request, "… please do Valentine, sing 'My Funny Valentine', please?" It was a dapper looking middle aged man who asked. He was sitting at the bar by himself, nursing a half-filled stubby glass. The patrons all giggled at his uncanny timing; for unwittingly he chose to use the break in noise to make a soft but distinct request of his own. Realising afterwards that fate had dealt him an audience with the masses, the solitary man seemed embarrassed.

The piano player never cared about what those who gathered wanted to hear. This was evident in the way he glanced, scoffed and then continued to play. He did not stop until the GIG was over. When all was done that piano player stood up, closed the lid, put his hands back in their pockets, and left the building. Until then he led the band into the next piece with the opening chords from a memorised playlist.

I saw how the vocalist stood in the nape of that grand piano. Her pose remained unassuming while the audience tried to recognise the new introduction. Mrs Andreucci slowly moved out of the dark and into a small spotlight that shone down onto the microphone on that smoky low stage. The four beats to a bar piano tempo filled out as the other musicians played their gentle parts. Then she sang:

My funny Valentine,

Sweet comic Valentine

You make me

Smile with my heart

Your looks are laughable

Unphotographable

Yet you're my favourite work of art ...

The spellbound crowd seemed afraid to clap when recognition dawned, lest they'd miss a nuance that was unfolding on that small, but seemingly vast stage. I watched as the man on the bar stool bowed his head to stare longingly into his glass. From my seat, in the corner, I wondered what he was thinking while the song slowly meandered along, from lyric contralto, through vocal peaks, and melodic valleys. The crescendo near the end left even more silence in its mesmerising wake.

When Zelda stepped back from the foam clad microphone, the resounding applause was gentle, yet it represented so much more. The music voyeurs returned attention to their drinks, all for different reasons, while the rest continued with their pretentiousness. A sort of quietness reigned and friends were more subdued. Mrs Andreucci was the conduit and with this writing I recognise her for bringing joy and emotional memory to so many over more than fifty years of song. It was the same woman who packed my lunch. There she was, just having sung the most beautiful rendition of an evergreen standard. I wondered if she was also moved like the many others who gathered there that afternoon.

The man and his stubby drink, for whom the song was sung, seemed immersed in solitude. I saw him. He dabbed his face and what appeared to be a lesion of sorts below his right ear with a neatly folded handkerchief; the initials J.G. were embroidered in one of the corners. It was Jeffrey. He mopped his eyes while sitting there, in the dim bar light. Jeffrey had lost weight and had several seemingly inflamed blotches visible in his face. It had been more than three years since I last saw him. A small world; indeed, a small world, I thought. Before saying hello I filled a glass with water. I did not want him to feel obliged and buy me a drink. Jeff seemed lost, just sitting there, looking down, probably sad too. I moved a chair closer and said: "I guess that you won't remember?"

"Sammy! Where have you been, Sammy; what happened to you? I have been searching for you all over." His eyes welled up and to calm the situation I asked the barman to get him another drink and more water for me.

"... for four months Sammy. Four months," he reiterated, "I've been searching for you for four months. It's about Marilyn." He mopped more with his J.G. handkerchief while I asked: "Where's Marilyn?"

"She was sick for a long time and always when I saw her, these last months, she would ask after you. That is why I was searching, but Marilyn died last week. In the end she lived to use and used to live. Heroin, it was heroin that killed her, that's what they say. She had a last spike with my money; I gave it to her ... do you know how that makes me feel, Sammy? On Valentine's night, that was when she did it, in the toilet at that junkyard in Stanger Street. That girl loved you. She never stopped talking about how you jived for her, on other people's sea water, and how you showed them even though they never knew that you did not belong. Does anyone know, Sammy?"

"No, it is not important to tell them ..."

"Well, for what it is worth, Marilyn never stopped talking about you. Whenever I saw her she looked worse, and every time she'd ask me to find you and have you call her, for just one last time."

I felt sad for Marilyn. She was a person too. Marilyn was my person when I had no one. Yet, when it was her turn to need me then I was cleaning a beach; again, other peoples' beach.

I sensed that Jeffrey wanted to talk, and I listened: "I loved that woman Sammy, you know, I loved her? If things were different; I would be with her, for that vibrancy, that raspy voice, her madness, it all rings in my head. Marilyn could cook a curry hey!

"But like I shall probably become, toward the end Marilyn was very sick. All she wanted was to say goodbye to you. Hell man; I couldn't find you, Sammy!"

Jeff and I hugged. We had some history; and who was I to cast aspersions? I had loved Marilyn too. She was after all the woman who fed me when I hadn't eaten in three days; she was the woman who trespassed on a reserved beach for me when I wore someone else's name—

"Marilyn's letter is in my suitcase, Jeff. I did not have her address and to find it always felt like too much trouble."

It lived in the blue suitcase, yes, together with my last letter from Jane, which also remained sealed.

"It bothers me, you know, Jeff; I even remember the date and the first line of that letter to Marilyn, it read:

Friday, 30 August 1981

Dearest Marilyn

It is a real pity that she never read the letter."

Jeff nodded, but he had not finished speaking either, so I let him talk: "Before she died, I took the trophy, your trophy. I promised to find you and give it back. My wish was to find you and return the trophy before it became my turn.

"Marilyn kissed that trophy and held it to her bosom before handing it to me. It lives in my lounge room, in the display cabinet. Fetch it anytime. I live at 146 Table Mountain Road, Bishop Lavis."

"Do you know where she is buried, Jeff?"

Jeffrey did not respond, save to say that the name, Marilyn, was a stage name. "In that business all of them have stage names, Sammy. At home they are one person and at work another. Marilyn did administrative work for a Catholic church organisation; that was her day job."

While some people were loud at the end of that afternoon others, like Jeffrey, settled into melancholy. It was not unusual to see members of the audience sit aside and appear far away. That's what good music does. As with Christmas carols, they take you back to a time of sweet memory, back to when the cost of a fridge meant no money for a month. It was because people did not own fridges that fish pickled fish became an enabler for the poor to observe a custom of eating fish from midnight on Maundy Thursday to Easter Sunday.

Chapter Eighteen

...We came to be

On Sundays I tried to arrive in Mitchell's Plain in time for lunch with Ma and Eugene. I rode my bicycle there and back. It was about 45 kilometres each way. In Cape Town cyclists develop close and personal relationships with every hill, but nothing can be more intimate than to cycle against that wind—tell me about it!

Our Sunday lunches were always the same, roast potatoes, chicken, rice and beetroot salad. While we enjoyed the togetherness and the meal, Ma would update me about family matters. Pa always featured prominently and his behaviour seemed more bizarre with every update. The latest news was that he had arranged that a coffin be delivered to the house. The instructions were that it should be stored in the roof cavity for use when he died. Ma always saw the humour in Pa's madness and that occurrence was no exception. I was livid and made my views known.

The routine was that in the late afternoon, before dusk, I would bid farewell to Ma and Eugene and then cycle back to my new home. It took me a long time to get there but I always did, every Sunday.

After spending my annual leave packing fish, and with about seven days in hand, I decided to hitch-hike to Johannesburg. My objective: to see the big city. The entire journey took about three days and the last bit was at the back of an open flatbed truck. For four hours I sat up against the spare wheel and a big folded rope net. It was late afternoon when I arrived in the city; going home time for working folk. The roads were teeming with people. I was near Johannesburg's Park Station and on my way to the Carlton Centre, the only landmark I knew about other than the tall Brixton Tower. Once the blue suitcase and I were away from the bustle of early evening commuters the city seemed like any other. It looked like Durban, like Cape Town, but it felt like Johannesburg. It felt cold, I remember, icy cold. Never before had I experienced a cold that ached like it did on the back of the truck and again while walking in the streets. I searched to find a public telephone in the Carlton Centre. The only person I knew in Johannesburg was Suzie. He had moved from Cape Town a short while earlier. His telephone number was not hard to locate:

"Hello, Adrian speaking," was how he answered the telephone.

"Hello Adrian, it is Sam, 'Jes'."

He paused before acknowledging me. "Hi Jes … how are you?"

"All right," I said. It was a lie, I was not all right. In fact, I was cold and hungry, tired and destitute. It was as a result of my own making though, that much was noted, but it did not make the situation any better.

"Oh! Good," said Adrian when he heard that I was okay. That was when I summoned courage:

"Adrian, Adrian..."

"Yes Jes, what is the matter? I am listening."

"Well, I am in the Carlton Centre."

"Oh, when did you arrive?"

"About three hours ago. It took three days from Cape Town. I did not expect it to take as long; and for it to be this cold."

"Yes, it is very cold."

"Usually I would stay over at a service station, or a truck stop, but I have not seen any in this city. It is bitterly cold. Is it possible for me to sleep at your house tonight, please? I'll make my way in the morning, early morning." As Adrian began to compose his response I added: "The security people in this building here, the Carlton Centre Security folk, they don't allow me to stand still, or sit and it is really cold outside."

"Sorry Jes, I know that you've come a long way, but my house is full tonight: I can't help you." I was about to plead with Suzie. He and I had a shared history, after all. But then it did not feel right, so I let what he had said be: "Thank you Adrian, it is okay, I'll make another plan, bye-bye." As I lowered the phone back onto its hanging cradle I heard Suzie's high pitched voice as he said:

"Bye Jes, sorry hey, but good luck …" Good luck is also not medicine, particularly if you have nowhere to go, let alone sit.

Yes, that was Suzie, the man who always asked to wash my hair with Earth Born, a popular shampoo; it was the self-same Suzie who explained the meaning of GIG (God is Great) and GAY (Good as You) to me.

Well, it was not okay to be out in the cold that night. Suzie had developed the courage to survive not fitting in. He knew what it felt like not to belong, but he could not find space for me on that cold night. There were other reasons, I knew. Reasons that Suzie was not prepared to show me, let alone discuss. I remembered Khokho saying 'We cannot condemn a person just because he did one thing that we thought to be wrong.' That night I did not agree with Khokho. I can only speculate why Suzie did not want to help me. Those with light skin tones often moved from the Cape to Johannesburg where they assumed an identity akin to the superior group. They lived in reserved areas, dined in restaurants and mingled with others who often unwittingly lived a very privileged life. I have not seen or heard from Adrian since that chilly night in September, 1981.

After speaking with Suzie I called an old football friend in Cape Town. He once mentioned his father's friend who lived near Johannesburg and I remembered. Perhaps that friend could assist me, I thought. Within minutes my call was returned and I was given a telephone number for one Devon Manichand.

I called, albeit with a measure of trepidation. One continues to have pride and dignity even when desperate. The telephone rang at Mr Manichand's house: "Hello, Manichand residence." It was the stern sound of a woman's voice. Somewhat unsure of myself I responded to the cross sounding voice on the other end: "Good evening, my name is Sam, I am from Cape Town. Can I speak with Mr Devon Manichand, please?" There was an impatient pause before she replied: "No, no he's not here. Devon works at night, you don't know?"

"Is this Mrs Manichand speaking?"

"Yes."

That was her curt reply. Mrs Manichand had no interest in the reason for my call. "Call him at work. You got a pen and paper?"

"Yes, I have a pen." Once I got the number and thanked Mrs Manichand, she hung up. I then called Mr Manichand: "Hello-Devon-speaking," he answered without a pause. I explained how I got to call him, my location and that his number was given me by Mrs Manichand. Finally, I explained my reason for calling. Throughout, Mr Manichand did not interrupt, other than to make the odd sound, 'mmm' and 'okay'. When I was done speaking Mr Manichand took a deep audible breath before he replied: "I am in the building diagonally across from where you are, the IBM Building, on the corner where Fox and Commissioner Streets meet. Tell you what. Wait there 'til the morning and come outside at seven o'clock. I'll be waiting at the front entrance on Commissioner Street. You come to my house then?" Mr Manichand spoke fast and his words were all clipped, as if it hurt to say them. I spent the rest of the night playing on an oversized chess board on the ground floor of the tallest building in Africa.

At seven that morning the sun was out, but it seemed as if someone had forgotten to put the cold away. Mr Manichand was there as promised: "Hello Sam, I am Devon, put your suitcase in the boot and get in the car." I did as instructed and soon we were on our way. "You must be tired?"

"Yes, I have not been able to sleep in four days. It is my own fault. All of this is self-inflicted. Thank you for helping me."

"No problem, I told my wife, Sathi, that I was bringing you home. We live in Lenasia. When we get home you can have a good bath, have breakfast and then sleep. What you doing here?"

"I hitched a ride from Cape Town to Johannesburg. Just to see what it was like." We spoke non-stop, like old friends, for the forty minutes it took before we reached Devon's house. Lenasia seemed empty. There were houses and brown veld, no trees. People drove expensive cars and some lived in houses that resembled hotels while other homes were quite normal. "This is where the Indian folk live Sammy; Lens, that's what we call it."

Sathi, Devon's wife, was home when we arrived. She had already taken their three children to school. Sathi was very different from what I had expected. After placing the blue suitcase in a bedroom I had the most welcome shower, breakfast and then slept.

Devon had arranged not to go to work that Thursday night. Instead, Sathi, Devon and I spent the evening eating crab curry and talking as if we were old friends. It was interesting to learn that we shared similar views about fairness and injustice.

I had to get back to Cape Town in order to report for duty on Monday morning. It was early in the morning on 11 September 1981, a Friday. That was when my journey began. This date would, twenty years later, become synonymous with the mass death of innocent people in retaliation to or defence of …

Devon left me at Uncle Charlie's, a big intersection south west of Johannesburg. From there I began to hitch hike back to Cape Town. Three hours later, and the sky had turned dark with black low hanging clouds. I wished that it would not rain. Many potential lifts rushed by as I became more desperate for a ride. So desperate, that I forgot about the cold. At first there was a gentle flutter of what seemed like tiny balls of fluffy cotton wool wafting to the ground. It seemed to appear from nowhere—up in the sky nowhere, like where the rain usually came from. Excited drivers hooted. Perhaps they thought that noise would make the fluff fall elsewhere. No, the hooting was an expression of excitement, for it was snowing. My first time and also that of many others who drove by Uncle Charlie's that day, it was our first experience of being in the snow. I often saw it at a distance but have never before experienced the flutter that other authors describe.

There was a slight breeze blowing. Eventually the breeze became a wind and the flutter of cotton balls turned into a blizzard. What was a brown veld had become awash with white. At first it was a misty, cloudy, almost dirty whiteness that replaced the brown end of winter look on the Highveld. It was a wonderland unfolding before our eyes—the snow was leading the transformation and it was unreserved. The falling snow was for all. I was begging for a lift while others rushed by in a haze of excitement. The snow looked the same for all of us. Yet, our experience of it was different. To me, it was like being stuck in one of those freezer warehouses at I&J where I had packed fish a few weeks earlier. The depth of driven snow had reached my knees. There was no prospect of a lift and I had no other option but to continue. I just stood there, with my naked, flat right thumb pointing at the driver of every potential lift that passed.

It was about four o'clock in the afternoon already and yet no prospect of a lift for me. I had been standing on the same spot for eight hours. By then I was wearing all the clothes that were in the blue suitcase and covered it with my two-piece-rain-suit to insulate against further loss of body heat. Passing drivers continued to gaze at the wonderland before them. There was no sign that the driven snow would stop falling.

It was shortly after, no, closer to five o'clock that afternoon, when I heard the familiar sound of air brakes. At first I saw bright yellow lights and seconds later a truck appeared out of the snow. The air brakes brought the truck to a halt some three hundred metres from where I was standing. With hazard lights flashing, almost like a big jet had landed, the truck driver leaned on a horn in quick succession. The boom sound I figured was a call for me to approach. I rushed while simultaneously dragging the empty suitcase along. Gratitude preceded my pace. The truck had a Cape Town registration and when I got to speak with the driver, it was Brother Fred. I was rescued and all he asked was that we pray together: "Let's give thanks to God, Brother Sam? We have found each other again and it feels like a miracle." I closed my eyes. For that moment it felt as if I too believed that religious doctrine. Brother Fred prayed for all the people who were cold, tired and hungry. We said 'Amen' in unison because that was also my wish.

I got back to Cape Town on Saturday night, 12th September. My thank you letter addressed to my new friends, Devon and Sathi was written that very night. Devon, Sathi and their two children subsequently emigrated from South Africa to the United States. I have not had contact with them since. It had not snowed in Johannesburg like it did on my own 'September Morn' of 1981.

Monday morning I returned to my beach job. The older people, my colleagues, had saved the more strenuous tasks for me.

In order to keep the peace I did as instructed. It was much better out on the beach than being cooped up in a room adjacent to a regularly flushing toilet. My colleagues continued to discuss their family feuds and quarrelled among themselves from early morning until the workday ended. Rainy days were the worst. I could not work outside. Instead, I had to endure the inane discussions and bickering. During these sessions Boeta Shafiek and Auntie Ghaliema consumed copious amounts of coffee made from water boiled in an old tin can; its label had been replaced with a name printed in black bold letters, MRS ISAACS.

Tuesday morning, Boeta Shafiek was checking the newspaper for horse race fixtures and reading what the tipsters had to say. I sat alongside him and paged through the relevant section of the jobs supplement. I applied for any job that seemed vaguely suitable. That morning there was an advert calling all suitably qualified and experienced people to apply for a job controller position. The work opportunity was at an electroplating plant in Salt River, a suburb close to the city. At the time I did not know what electroplating was. The advert referred to requirements that included much experience. Surfer, school leaver, labourer, cleaner on the beach, and fish packer did not count as sufficient experience.

All who were interested and qualified were invited to apply. My response was to carefully adjust my standard letter.

Weeks later Mr Andreucci took a telephone call on my behalf. It was Mr Manie Steyn. He requested to interview me on a Saturday morning.

The interview went well. The job was at a very drab looking factory in Voortrekker Road, diagonally across from SA Metal, one of the bigger scrap metal dealers of the time. My weekly wage would be more than I had earned as a beach cleaner. Salt River was also closer to where I lived. Despite not having any experience of metals and how different types are plated, I was offered the position. It was unbelievable, but the owner of that business was also called Manie Steyn! The man who owned a perfume factory, where Ma had worked, more than forty years earlier, had the same name.

This Manie Steyn was probably born around that time. Many similar coincidences happened and continue to happen in my life. When I tell of the stories they are sometimes regarded as fables. In fact, there are many stories that were omitted from this work because they are too unbelievable.

After resigning from the Cape City Council and serving seven days' notice, I greeted Auntie Ghaliema, Boeta Shafiek, Desmond, 'Driver' and Mr de Kock for the last time. As had become his norm, Mr de Kock did not reply to my greeting. He refused to shake my extended hand. I held it out to him for what felt like forever before he said: "You tried to fool me, just go." Those were the last words I heard Mr de Kock say.

§

A requirement of my new job was to draw all the pieces that were presented for plating. In addition, before the process could begin I had to engrave tracking numbers (usually the invoice number) on the back of every item.

Many years later while attending an auction I came across a brass plated and lacquered milk can. An old habit kicked in and I lifted the can to check beneath its base. Yes, it was there, my engraving of the invoice number!

After marking all the items, I had to monitor the plating process until the piece, or consignment was returned and ready for the customer to collect.

My work area was a dingy and windowless room in the middle of a very noisy factory. What I used, instead of a chair, was in reality a cyanide container upon which I had placed a plank, turning it into a high chair. The men who worked alongside me were very 'festive'. I remember, Shepstone, he was marginally older than me; and 'Driver'. Yes, there was also a 'Driver'. I never got to know his proper name either, just 'Driver'—ooh! But he was a very naughty man.

I've always been able to draw equally well with both hands. Early experience at school had served to sharpen my ambidextrous trait. It proved handy when trying to keep up with the fast pace of that workload. I enjoyed doing the drawings, and watching how rusty items were restored to a former glory, or how they became useful and pretty when plated in nickel, copper, brass, chrome, or silver. The men who did the plating, the 'festive' men, they

265

were like magicians and in time all of us became best friends at work. Before working at the plating plant the only drawings I had done were of multi-skeg surfboards, cars and faces. I loved to draw faces.

My faces always had ears attached to them. At first it was difficult to draw a good ear. Hands and feet are a little less complex. I often passed the time while using public transport by memorising the contours of the various ears, hands and feet that were on display. By the way, in addition to his cleft palate, Pa's little finger, the one on his left hand, was deformed. He could not straighten it; could not wear a ring there! But when I drew his hands the disabled finger was fixed. If I had been able to do the same with his palate; and if it were real, then perhaps Pa would have been a nice man.

Anyway, when done with those earlier drawings, I'd look at the work and imagine driving to the beach in my own car. My fancy surfboard would be strapped down and I'd be listening to a select choice of music.

Cyanide is used in the plating solutions. That is probably why cutlery and pots are never chrome plated—always stainless steel, cast iron or copper. But at Bona Café there are plastic forks!

One day curiosity, mixed with a big dollop of stupidity, got the better of me. I tasted a crumb of cyanide. Salty, that was what it tasted like. My hair began to fall out around that time, but maybe there were other reasons for that! Nothing else happened and I have no need to taste again. One day, when the factory ran low the contents of my high chair were used. The empty container, made from thick cardboard, could not support my weight. I was high-chair-less for a while. It happened when Manie Steyn's wife undertook a pilgrimage to Israel. Ruth had always been by his side, jabbering, much more than Jane ever did.

The job was fine, but it was not ideal for what I wanted to achieve, and part-time study was nearly impossible, given the long working hours. It was just an excuse though. I set myself the goal of working at the University of Cape Town. Many of my friends from school were studying there; some had already graduated by then. Working at the university held the potential for reduced academic fees.

The better part of each Sunday was spent with Ma and Eugene. Eugene was growing into a wonderful young boy. I had big dreams for him. His academic talent was way superior to mine. During one of those Sunday afternoon visits Ma told me of Pa's intention to sell her Mitchell's Plain house. It came as a shock; this had happened before. Not only did I know what it meant, but I was also familiar with what it felt like to suddenly become homeless. Ma was set to be homeless for a second time. Without first thinking I raised a number of questions. Many remained unanswered. That Sunday I left Ma and Eugene with a resolve to seek legal advice.

The next day, Monday, during my twenty minute lunch break, I left the factory to call various lawyers and other knowledgeable people from a public-phone at the nearby post office. My objective was to determine Ma's standing before the law. The upshot of my calls led to two possible solutions: first, Pa must agree not to sell the property, and; secondly, Ma could file for a divorce and retain the house as part of the settlement.

Ma's reaction was reserved when I informed her of the choices. At that stage my parents had been married for more than thirty-five years. After careful consideration Ma agreed to file an application for the annulment of their marriage. Pa had inflicted many bad experiences on Ma and our family. I was aware of several. There were more, but Ma did not disclose. We had no money to pay for an attorney and an advocate was completely out of the question. The only alternative to Ma remaining married and exploited was that I do the research into how divorces are processed. Once done I could manage the procedure of Ma's divorce from Pa myself.

I gleaned the format from past documents in libraries, archives, from people who showed me their divorce papers and from examples found in the clerk's office at the Supreme Court. After careful study of the relevant documents I helped Ma compose the summons:

SUMMONS

IN THE SUPREME COURT OF SOUTH AFRICA
[KEEROM STREET, CAPE TOWN]

Thelma Elizabeth Levy PLAINTIFF
[born Llewellyn] [ID: 230815 8585 086],

and

Samuel Arthur Levy DEFENDANT
[ID: 19190209 8967 080]

DATED at CAPE TOWN on this the 14th day of April 1985.

Plaintiff's Particulars of Claim

1.

The parties are domiciled within the jurisdiction of the above Honourable Court.

2.

The Parties were married to each other on 21 MARCH 1954 at CAPE TOWN, in Community of Property.

3.

The assets which comprise the joint estate of the parties consist of:

a. The immovable property situated at: 33 Holden Way, Beacon Valley,

Mitchell's Plain, the value whereof amounts to approximately THIRTY THREE THOUSAND RAND (R33, 000.00).

b. Furniture and household effects.

c. Mercedes Benz motor vehicle, the value whereof amounts to approximately SEVEN THOUSAND RAND (R7,000.00).

d. Property, businesses and other assets which the Defendant has concealed should for purpose of these proceedings be noted.

4.

The marriage relationship between the parties has broken down irretrievably and no reasonable prospect exists for its continuation.

5.

The Defendant stays away from home for extended periods. His irregular visits are characterised by quarrels, mainly about money.

6.

I, the Plaintiff, have decided to institute this action because the Defendant made it known that he is to sell the property in which

I, the Plaintiff, live. On a previous occasion the Defendant also sold the house in which I lived. As his spouse I contributed to the home, but did not receive my share of the proceeds derived from that sale. My fear is that the same will happen with this proposed transaction.

7.

It is known that the Defendant is frequently seen socialising with other women.

WHEREFORE THE PLAINTIFF CLAIMS:

1.   A decree of divorce;

2.   That the Defendant pays alimony in the amount of FOUR HUNDRED RAND (R400.00) per month. That such payments increase by TEN PERCENT(10%) on the 1st day of March following the divorce decree and;

3.   That the Defendant relinquishes all rights to the property in which the Plaintiff resides ...

After Ma had signed the document I sought further guidance before filing it at the honourable court.

The summons to appear was served on Pa at his house in Geneva Drive, Camps Bay. Pa's responding document was received a week later, several days before the required deadline. As per the required procedure, one copy had been handed in at the court for the file and another was hand delivered to Ma. The notice from Pa's attorneys, on their letterhead, informed us that the divorce action would be contested. Ma called me late in the afternoon after Pa's attorneys of record had served his responding document on her. I was at work and took the call there amidst the factory noise. Ma sounded stressed, I could hear.

"Come, you have to see me today, Boy. I have something very important to discuss with you. Come see me, Boy? I am waiting for you." That was all I could hear above the factory noise.

My day began at seven in the morning and ended at five thirty in the evening. There was no chance of leaving early, except on Fridays, when we closed at three.

As the hooter sounded on that day, and just as soon as my time-card was clocked, I tore up the road to the station. Once there I caught the train to Mitchell's Plain.

When I opened the front door Ma was there, seated on her new favourite lounge chair with Lampo on her lap. Friends had donated all the furniture in the house. That evening there was no expression on Ma's face, not even when she saw me. It was unusual. She had an ashen look. I asked for the document. Ma remained seated, staring at me while sipping from her cup. As she lifted the cup to sip I saw that her hands were shaking. That too was unusual. The Ma of my first memories was a confident woman, unflappable; one who had witnessed and stepped in to quell the most violent occurrences. I have seen her confront an agitator and within moments calm was restored. What about the others that Ma never mentioned and that happened when we were at school? Yet, there she was, the same woman sat before me, forlorn and trembling.

Again I asked to see the document, but Ma's response remained a stoic and very definite: "No. Let me put my child to bed first. Then there is something that we have to discuss before you read those papers," she said, pointing with a trembling hand to the document on her dining room table. I recognised the format and the big Department of Justice purple franking. By then, and due mainly to my research into the divorce procedure, I was familiar with the look of summonses and responding documents. That was a responding document and it caused Ma to tremble. I dared not read it while Ma put Eugene to bed. No, that would have been like stealing; a lesson we were taught at boarding school. There was an uncomfortable feeling in the house, more so for me, because I was unable to determine its cause.

I thought of Ma's tremble and likened it to a favourite anthem, the one I sang with the choir all those years ago:

"Were you there when they crucified my Lord?
Sometimes it causes me to tremble ..."

The bass, alto, contralto, soprano and treble parts of that inspired anthem merged to ring in my ears. I sat back to wait for Ma. She had gone to put Eugene to bed. Perhaps I was just seeking salvation from the devastating sight of my Ma appearing helpless. What could it be, I wondered; what was it that caused my Ma to tremble?

This was the same Ma who held Mrs Anthony's hand when her son, Cedric, was hanged by the neck until he was dead.

It was the same Ma who was always strong when others needed comfort.

Who was going to give Ma comfort? And what was of such magnitude to make her tremble?

Was it Pa; had he again threatened her with death like he did when she refused to marry him? Perhaps he threatened Ma with death after learning of her intent to divorce him? If that was the reason for Ma's tremble then I needed to plan for her safety.

Many similar thoughts passed through my mind while waiting for Ma.

Ma returned to her chair about an hour later. The tremble had been replaced by a wringing of hands followed by her wiping the dress she wore. Ma wiped with a small handkerchief. There was no mark, but Ma kept on wiping. The look of her worry was extreme. That look was exaggerated by the immediacy of her prominent dimples. She looked gaunt.

I heard a shudder as Ma inhaled before speaking. "What's the matter, Ma?" I interjected.

"I am sorry my boy. I should have told you a long time ago. I tried to tell you many times, but I needed you to know the entire story so that you could understand. Maybe it was not meant to be; maybe it was meant to be for you to find out like this. Every time when I prepared to tell you then something would happen. Something always prevented us from talking the way we should have. I wanted to explain how you and Jane came to be—why you and Jane are not my children."

It was my turn to hold Ma's hand, just as she had done for so many people when despair seemed to be their only reality. Ma dabbed her eyes with the same handkerchief that had previously wiped an invisible mark. Her trembling increased but her determination to continue was evident.

"There, look, it is written in those papers from Pa's lawyers. You see my boy, the taking from me just never stops."

"Don't worry Ma, we know; I have always known."

"How; how did you know … how do you know?" Ma asked, in a tone that sounded as though a horrible secret had unwittingly been leaked. "Did someone tell you?"

"No. No, Ma. My word for it is 'lateralism'. It is what comes from linking all the bits that I've heard over the years. I can remember all that was said. That is how I knew, but Ma, you never wanted me to know the truth.

"When I was about nine years old, you and Auntie Liza were speaking in the lounge room. I was having a slice of bread with mixed fruit jam in the kitchen. You told Auntie Liza about having had a hysterectomy after Brenda was born. I didn't know what the word meant then, but memorised it. Later I found its meaning in the *Webster Dictionary*, the one that lived on the shelf beneath our spiral staircase in the old house. That was when I first knew.

"I also remember a time when we walked in Heathfield, Chatham Road, and a woman, wearing thick eye glasses, I think her name was Nellie, she stopped to talk. Afterwards you said that Nellie had taken care of me when you had to work. I remember her inspecting my arm that day in Chatham Road. She spoke in Afrikaans, about me, as if I was not there. 'Yes. Yes, it is his child. I can see by the arms, they are the same hairy arms …' that was how I came to know that Pa was my father. Was he Jane's father too? Jane did not have hairy arms, but her nose is like his, while mine is like yours?

"You've never spoken about being pregnant with Jane and me. My friends' parents often refer to when they were pregnant, but never you.

"Then there was the time when you were cross with me, I can't remember why, but you were very cross; scolding and saying many things. You said: 'That is what you get from taking in pick-up children.' You said that several times, always when you were cross with me. I had been disrespectful toward you. Afterwards I always felt sorry. Of late I have been wishing that we could have

271

those times again, also with Jane, because my behaviour would be different. Sorry, Ma.

"Then there was the time when Charles had been drinking. He said that he was not my brother, but my uncle.

"Well, Ma, when all those incidents and what had been said over the years came together, that was when I knew you were not my biological mother. I never discussed it with Jane: was too afraid. I feared that Jane might have discovered that she was not my sister. Then I'd have no-one to belong to, no-one to call my very own. I want to belong to you, Ma.

"I think it must feel good to belong. I don't know but 'We do not miss that which we do not know', hey Ma?

"You are the only Ma that I know and want. Pa was naughty, bad, immoral and incestuous, that much I figured too. However, Ma, what brings you to make these revelations? What is written in that document; let me read and then we can decide what should be done?"

"It is written there, in that letter I received; that letter from Pa's lawyers. It states a number of things that you know are not true, but in the introduction they write that no children were born to us during our marriage."

Ma looked at me in the same way she had stared at the ceiling years earlier. Maybe she was expecting a reaction … when it was not forthcoming Ma continued: "I did not want you to read it without hearing my explanation. I have worried about how you would respond, and Boy, you must know that it has never been my intention to hurt you. I think and feel that you care deeply for me. That is exactly how I feel about you, about Jane, Brenda, Charles, Anne and Eugene."

"Well, Ma, you need no longer worry about me. I have my own life; I am making my own life. You will always be my Ma, because it is through you that I am and that is how it will be until I die."

Ma got up from her chair and we hugged each other. It was another embrace that lasted much longer than usual, probably because unsaid things speak the loudest, and because the God of Life is greater than understanding.

Before going to sleep on that 'revelation and confirmation evening' I reassured Ma that all would be well; that a settlement would be found at one of the pre-trial meetings with Pa's lawyers.

"If we fail in our attempt to negotiate an agreement, then you must not worry because I shall be by your side until the matter is settled. I shall be there, come hell or high water; above all, the taking from you will stop, be assured."

While lying in a bed at Ma's house, where the tiredness of the day was tinged with confirmation, I wondered about who my biological mother was. That mattered less, because Ma was my mother. I regurgitated the arguments between Ma and Pa, particularly those I overheard. The comments passers-by on the street had made over the years were also vivid in my mind on that 'confirmation evening'.

During the following day and as the secret of how I came to be matured in my mind the realisation dawned that it was time to read Jane's last letter. By then her letter had been sitting in the blue suitcase for five years. I kept the letter unread because it was soothing to know that there was something from Jane. It was like that present underneath the cypress tree waiting for Christmas Day. As with everything, there comes a time to change, and so it was with Jane's final letter. Perhaps the letter was kept because of my need for reassurance that I belonged to someone, even though she only lived in my head.

I opened the blue suitcase, and there it was, at the top of my pile. I sat on my bed with Jane's last letter in hand. The blue suitcase lay open on the linoleum covered floor, and next to the headboard of my single bed stood the patchwork surfboard wrapped in the blanket that Khokho had sewed. With its slight curve the board appeared to look down in anticipation of what Jane had to say. The board, my suitcase and I, we were a family and belonged to one another.

At first the letter felt thin, perhaps only one feather-light page from the Croxley pad on which we wrote our letters. The back of the airmail envelope held a faded imprint of Jane's lips. The faint fragrance of *Je t'aime* continued to linger even though I had sniffed it a thousand times. I opened the envelope quickly. It was time to read out loud, as we always did:

Sunday, 11 June 1978

My Dear Brother, Sammy

I am experiencing a lot of pain this evening. It is late and you are not near. The way it feels, I think, can only be eased by writing this letter.

There are things that bother me. It bothers me because I have not shared them with you. Brenda is your mother and Anne is mine. There it is, I said it.

Pa is our father. He is not a good man and it is time that you know. If anything should happen to me then let it be that, at least, I have shared this with you. I do not want you finding out and think that even your sister hid the truth from you. So, now you know and I have told you that I know too.

To tell a lie is like sleeping underneath a blanket that is too short. When your feet are covered with a too short blanket then you head will stick out. We live in a lie and it has to stop.

I love you,

Your big sister, forever, Jane

For the first time I fully understood the story of Jane and me, and how we had come to be.

We have the same father, Jane and I; our mothers were sisters; that is how we belong.

Chapter Nineteen

The Disabled are Able

Pre-trial meeting dates were set. I attended four on Ma's behalf. They were doomed to fail from the outset, mainly because of the false declarations, lies and inconsistencies contained in Pa's submissions. Pa didn't attend all the meetings, but those that he did were riddled with embarrassing and obvious untruths. At the final meeting I asked to speak with Pa in private. The request was granted. In that brief meeting I pleaded with him to spare Ma further embarrassment and not to contest their divorce. Pa refused and instead instructed his legal team to proceed with his version of events. My request was not agreed to but, given my promise of support to Ma, I pursued a toe-to-toe argument with Pa's people. I was not familiar with legal terms. My argument relied on the consistent repetition of facts that I understood. I lived that story after all. It did not take long before those lawyers found resonance with what I had said. Both seemed moved by my rendition of what we had lived through as a family. I turned to address Pa. He looked straight ahead—probably deaf as a post again, I thought. We were in the moment and it was my turn to speak: "Despite all that you have done to us Pa, we love you, and I can't help myself."

The point I left for last was that no children had been born to Ma and Pa during the tenure of their marriage, or words to that effect. It was a deliberate act to leave that point for last and instead of speaking to it I merely posed the question: "No children were born to my parents during the tenure of their marriage—how then did Jane and I come to be?"

I let the question be …, for, given earlier nuances, the lawyers appeared to have made up their minds. Their client's submission, Pa's rendition of the same story, was real, yes, just like rocking horse droppings are a most sought after fertiliser. In summation at that final pre-trial meeting I concluded by highlighting several deliberate lies contained in Pa's version. Yes, Pa's was just a 'version' of the story. My view was that it did not constitute sufficient truth and therefore should not be regarded as a submission before the honourable court. I had found that sentence in one of the documents used for purpose of research and thought it particularly fitting to repeat in that pre-trial meeting.

I was also deliberate about not raising Pa's unconventional behaviour patterns. This was so because I understood how and also why he protected himself from humiliation. It remains my opinion that in most every instance Pa's behaviour was always a step too far.

When I had said enough the two experienced legal people glanced at each other. The advocate, a certain Godlontone QC, then wrote and handed his colleague a note. After reading it, the note, Pa's attorney looked at me with what she probably meant to be an officious glare. That attorney, one Van der Merwe, she glared at me in the same way that De Kock had done. Izak de Kock, Head. Bathing Amenities, Atlantic Seaboard, his glare was similar to Van der Merwe's. I could feel my blood stir when she did that and it had a riling effect. By then I had not only learned, but had accepted that intimidation was a state of mind, one to which I refuse subscribe.

She took a while, that Van der Merwe did, but unlike the time I stuck my hand out for De Kock and he failed to do likewise, this time I was not going anywhere. My resolve was that Van der Merwe could glare until that frown she wore became a tattoo, for I was not interested. In her own time Van der Merwe blurted: "But … no children were born to the marriage?"

I accepted her point with a single nod. My acceptance was followed by a barrage of questions from the attorney; questions to which I responded by staring at her, like De Kock once did to me—

How Jane and I came to be had little bearing on the matter and the question, in a rhetorical format, was already left to be. I refused to dignify her inquisitive posturing with a response. By then it had become more than important that even the slightest remaining modicum of dignity for the memory of my Jane and Ma be protected and defended against further tarnish.

That two children had been born during the marriage was evident, yet I was mandated by Ma to accept the point as was stated in the responding document of reference. Pa's lawyers must have deduced the reality: that two children were born during the tenure of the marriage; that their client was the father; and that the 'mothers' were not his wife. I was not privy to the detail of subsequent discussions between Pa and his lawyers.

That these children, Jane and I, were conceived by Ma's daughters from a previous marriage, and that Pa, their client, was the common father had no material impact on Ma's pending divorce action. Self-preservation was ultimately the purpose of the action brought.

For his lawyers, the reality of logical deduction must have cast final aspersion on Pa's integrity. Although that was only my assumption, a week before the trial was set to begin Pa's legal team served notice to withdraw as the lawyers of record. These notices, according to court procedure, had been served by Pa's lawyers at the Registrar's Office with a copy for their client. Ma and I were not privy to exact reasons, but consequently the lawyers, Van der Merwe and Godlontone, had recused themselves from the proceedings. The only corroborated evidence in Pa's submission was the spurious claim that no children had been born during the marriage.

On the day of the trial Pa arrived without legal representation. The court understood that Pa was to contest the divorce and represent himself. I assisted

Ma as promised. Pa portrayed himself as destitute and disabled. The sorry picture was complete when a bailiff wheeled Pa into the courtroom. He clutched a walking stick between his feet while sitting in that wheelchair. It was a charade for effect. I imagined the expensive Mercedes Benz, Pa's latest motorcar, parked around the corner from the Cape Supreme Court in Keerom Street. When asked by the judge, Pa said that he was present and wished to make a statement. He wished, with permission from the court, to take the stand, not to defend, but to make a statement.

When Pa had finished his reply I stood up, identified myself and asked if it were possible to break from protocol and approach the bench before the judge responded. The judge was surprised when I stepped forward and quietly offered to interpret what Pa had said. Even though the judge was bemused, I continued to feel an uncanny loyalty to the man who had wronged my Ma. The judge was also just a person and his black and red robe was just that.

Ma took the stand. The judge listened as she spoke in her own defence. When Ma spoke people always listened. Ma spoke eloquently that day, beautifully in fact. It was a lesson in respectful communication without the usual 'curry favour', or grovel tone that I noticed many of the lawyers used when they addressed the judge. Ma dealt with each of the points in the served summons. The detail was a modest sufficiency. At the end of her verbal submission a succinct summary followed. In conclusion Ma turned to Pa and said: "I forgive you Samuel, but you have to mend your ways." Ma thanked the judge for granting her the freedom to say that which was in her heart. There were no questions posed. As Ma left the dock three employees of the court rushed to assist her with climbing down the two steps. It was more a gesture of pride than an act of assistance. Those two men and a woman, employees of the court, they were as proud of Ma as I was and continue to be. It was as if the Ma of old had come to visit again. I wished to be as confident someday. People in the court gallery applauded as my Ma took her seat. True to style she leaned over and asked: "Boy, why are they clapping their hands?"

When Pa rose to speak the judge gestured for me to approach the bench from where he was presiding. He told me to step forward and interpret once Pa had spoken: "It is a certainty that I shall not understand everything your father says," is what the judge whispered to me while Pa was being assisted into the dock by the two bailiffs.

Pa did not have a lot to say, as was his norm, but just for that moment, I saw that he had been stirred by Ma's plea to the court. He stood, looked from side to side, and then addressed the judge in a very loud voice: "Ya! My Lord, I am very sorry for the pain I inflicted on Thelma." He looked at Ma, nodded several times and then sat down, almost as if not to invite comment or reaction.

The judge looked at me to approach and translate. I stepped forward and whispered to him so that Pa could not hear. Afterwards, and for a second time, the judge asked Pa, the Defendant, whether he wished to reply and be subjected to cross examination. Pa declined. The judge took no notice of his posturing or the pretence at being ill.

The divorce decree was signed and it became an order of court, the Divorce Order.

I was pleased that Pa had not chosen to defend himself. Despite everything that had happened, there was no joy to be had in Pa being ridiculed and laughed at, as on the day in that Tokai cake shop.

After the proceedings the three of us had a short but cordial discussion in the court lobby. By then Pa's inability to walk had miraculously been cured. His hearing had improved substantially too.

During that brief foyer meeting Ma told Pa about his lack of respect for her and that it had been the reason why she sought protection via an order of court: "It was to protect me from your greed, Samuel!" That was Ma's last words on the subject of her divorce from Pa. We never discussed it again. To that last statement Pa barely managed a reply. He turned, mumbled something, and then walked via some steps leading from the court building in the direction of where I imagined his expensive car would be parked.

Ma and I walked the three kilometres from Keerom Street to the railway station. All the while she wore a pained expression. We walked on the pavement along Queen Victoria Street with the historic Dutch East India Company's Garden on our right. We were approaching St George's Cathedral. From there the walk was down Wale Street and around the corner where it converges with Adderley Street.

"Sam, my boy, at least this part of the exploitation is over." Those were the first words Ma spoke after making Pa turn and go.

"You spoke very well, Ma."

"Thank you," was all Ma said in reply. Ma always responded to direct compliments with a very brief 'thank you'.

We walked in silence again; to where the flower sellers displayed their blooms. If I could, then to purchase four stems of arum lilies would have been sufficient for my Ma on that day. Instead, as we passed, Ma paused to half cup a lily bloom with her right hand: "It's pretty, hey Boy?" she said.

Sometimes I had the urge to suck my thumb for just one last time. When Ma and I walked past the flower sellers and she reached for the lilies was one such time. As a younger child thumb sucking was a placebo which I employed to suppress emotions. That 'Men should not cry' was of the nonsense I learned at boarding school. Ma noticed that I had been stirred: because she was like that.

"Yes, Boy, I sought advice before speaking in that court." I knew that her talking then was Ma's way of changing my melancholic mood. "The advice I got was not to address the court. I chose not to take the advice. When you get advice then there are times when you do not follow what others say, particularly if it is self-limiting. That is the reason why I decided to speak rather than sit there and wring my hands as if my tongue was on holiday.

"After all these years and with what has happened, of which you know only a fraction, I can continue with my life. But it feels like too late, and I am too damn tired."

I just listened as we walked. We boarded a train at Cape Town Station for Mitchells Plain. Eugene came home from school while I was there. I showed him how to ride a skateboard that day. The two of us played a bit, until it was time for me to leave.

Chapter Twenty

Fate Remains an Uncanny Something

I secured a job interview at the University of Cape Town. My interview clothes came in handy once again and particularly when I started to work there, on 15 October 1984. It felt like the beginning of my life. In many ways it was.

My plan to work and study was on track. As the years passed that was all I did.

Pa continued to visit Ma. I developed an interest in Employment Law, and my ability to draw was nurtured by designing sets for stage and film. In time I would practise both professions.

The 'nondescript' surfboard was a dormant companion by then. Its role was redefined to watch over me when I slept at Ms Masele's house. The blue suitcase was there too, on the floor, next to my bed. That case and the board were my companions whenever I felt lonely. Eventually I sold the board. I should not have done that, but I did. It would have been wonderful to give the 'patchwork' board to my own son. He may have wanted the sandals too, but perhaps of greater importance: my son may have wished to finish the journey that Mr Thompson and I began all those years ago; who knows, he may have become the real 'Champ', the world champion.

Oh well, it was sad to see my board go, but that's life, or *'C'est la vie'* as the twin brothers frequently said to each other when they spoke while seated on tree stumps in our backyard. In this life we often take things to a certain undefined point. Others then come along and take it further. I don't know what happened to my surfboard, for I was not yet ready to tell this story when it was sold. Hopefully the board is not stored underneath a mound of dust in some forgotten spot. The blue suitcase continues to enjoy pride of place in my office along with Zaideh Levy's wall clock. Those two items mean nothing to others, but they form part of what connects me to Jane, Ma, Mammy Cynthia, Thami, Father Terry and others who celebrated life with us back then.

§

The years following my parents' divorce presented their own challenges. I had a job at the University. To study was easy. The workings of trade unions and other organs of society interested me. Exposure to that was an experience that would shape the rest of my life.

Via the flexibility of a university environment I created work opportunities in the most sophisticated theatres in many modern cities around the world. After all, my objective was to live two lives simultaneously. One life was for Jane, even though I was lacking and could never compensate for her talents. The other life was for me. If you wish to worship the God of Life then it is done through consistently striving to maximise your talent, ability or passion. It is not done by attending ceremonies of whatever order.

Many of my experiences were memorable, unique and sometimes even beyond belief, like designing a set for operatic performances at Teatro alla Scala (La Scala) in Milan, where the audience would hiss when anything on stage was not to their satisfaction.

But the last trip the blue suitcase and I did together was in 1990. We were called to work in the construct of the Oberammergau Passion Play, in Bavaria, Germany.

I retired the suitcase after that trip: it felt like the right thing to do. The cover of this book includes an image of the actual blue suitcase. These days it contains the letters, postcards, photographs and posters taken from lamppost after our first inclusive general elections of 1994.

§

It was a matter of time before the effect of democracy was experienced by all South Africans. Sometimes we forgot that to have freedom was a responsibility.

Millions of people, the world over, contributed to building our new country.

I married and we had the means to live in a suburb that previously had been reserved in terms of the Group Areas Act. This Act, a statute of the South African government, determined where people could live and was based primarily on skin colour. All opportunities were determined mainly by skin colour and gender. Everything continues to be based on skin colour, even to this day. It may be applied differently, but the basis remains skin colour.

Back then, people of the same skin colour had to live in defined areas. My young family and I lived in a reserved suburb. While most neighbours were unaffected by our darker skins living in their reserved area, the friendliness of our immediate neighbour felt condescending. Perhaps I was being too sensitive, I thought. For that reason she was given the benefit of my doubt. On occasion, our neighbour would breeze through the house like a landlord on a mission to check that all was how it should be. During one of those visits she proffered a comment, one that would linger: "I do not have a problem living next door to

280

people of colour, because not every one of you misbehaves and it is wrong to assume the worst."

Possibly realising her gaffe, our neighbour switched the topic to the demerits of having a television in the bedroom. We had the tiniest portable TV there, stuck in the bedroom cupboard.

From the main room in our house we could see the neighbour's yard. It had been paved with spoiled bathroom tiles. There was a creeping grapevine that grew extensively and trained over a metal frame. Grapevines in South Africa only grow from about September through to March. Whenever our neighbours entertained, then loudspeakers were hooked onto each corner of the grapevine frame. I kept the consciousness to myself, but whenever the speakers were out my thoughts chucked back to those earlier experiences in Mpophomeni—the adult carnival.

Sometimes it was as if the Gypsy Kings were rehearsing in our neighbour's yard. I enjoyed the music, it was okay, but I wondered how our inquisitive neighbour would have reacted had it been me sharing my music with all who lived within earshot. To this day my child, who was a new-born then, cannot tolerate loud music. However, the aroma of paella and other fish that were cooked on a barbeque (braai) facility in that backyard had a huge appetising effect in our home. To this day my child eats like a 'herd horses'!

Ma visited infrequently. We usually went to her, particularly when the Gypsy Kings were next door.

I remember a much older resigned Ma visiting us on a Sunday afternoon in about 1993. During her visits Ma would stroll through the house, as if on inspection duty. She'd stop in front of a window to look at the garden, comment about the flowers or about the obedience of our Labradors, Boris and Bess. Satisfied that all was in order Ma would settle in the lounge to drink tea, watch TV, or read a *Poldy* book to my then two-year-old boy child. My boy would doze off to sleep, probably from the familiar drone about book characters, Poldy, Wagtail, Signora Pita Pati and others. After I'd put him to bed Ma's 'inspection' duties would resume. With hands behind her back she'd inspect every room afresh.

It was a Saturday afternoon, that time, the time when Ma paused in front of our bedroom window. I was watching as she craned to look into the neighbour's yard. Probably to spot one or more of the Gypsy Kings, I thought; when suddenly she exclaimed: "That's my sister! That's my sister!" Ma said so in rapid succession. She turned, saw me and said again: "That's my sister, Sammy! Agnes! It's her, there in those people's yard!" Ma's excitement so overwhelmed me that I instinctively shook my right hand.

Ma kept one arm to her back while pointing with her crooked finger to Linda's paved backyard.

By then the Cape had liberalised substantially: though perhaps only on the face of it, but most people were no longer as staunch in their fatuous concern about who wore what shade of skin.

Ma walked a whole lot faster than usual when she went outside that Saturday afternoon. As she got close to the wall that divided our two homes I heard her call. Yes, Ma softly called out: "Cooee! Cooee!"

Within minutes the two were in conversation. They spoke at the low section of the wall that separated our two houses. We watched from behind a voile curtain in our bedroom. Auntie Agnes spoke in hushed tones and kept her sister, Ma, out of sight. Linda was entertaining friends from the Salvation Army Church and her husband, José, was busy at the cookout facility, or barbeque, but in South Africa we call it a 'braai'. All the people there were focused on the cookout, and of course, the Gypsy Kings. None spared a moment to notice the old Aunties who were talking across the divide. The air was thick with a bouquet of seafood spices. Perhaps José was preparing paella. The aroma wafted across the wall and felt as if it had preceded the rhythmic sounds.

Linda knew who I was after that fence meeting between our mothers. Her discovery marked the end of our neighbourly relationship; the end of the flamboyant superior chatter and accompanying house inspection. Not too long afterwards the entire family, and their Gypsy Kings, all of them, moved elsewhere.

I've not seen Linda since, but have heard that she died. It is said that Linda slipped in the bath and hit her head. I am not sure what happened. José was an older man. He and Linda had two daughters. That was the last time I saw Auntie Agnes. Ma stopped speaking about her too.

I have tried to tell this story exactly as it happened and I feel that to embroider would take away rather than add. The same with when Brother Fred who rescued me in the driven snow, in front of Uncle Charlie's, where I'd been hitch-hiking all day on 11th September 1981. Fate remains an uncanny something.

Chapter Twenty-One

Whispers

We arrived in Johannesburg on 17th June 1997.

The Gauteng Province is where Johannesburg, Sandton, and Pretoria are business centres.

There are a million trees in greater Johannesburg—maybe more. In that same year we experienced the splendour of those Highveld summers too. Winters on the other hand, at nearly two thousand meters above sea level, are dry and colder than my warm blood could tolerate.

People converged in Johannesburg from everywhere. But the underbelly of that sprawling metropolis could not help itself from reinforcing the divisive methods which separated people into different groups.

Johannesburg City Centre had evolved from an era where Khoi people hunted and gathered there to a tented town; a gold mining hubris; and eventually an African megacity. The expansive development happened soon after gold was discovered in 1886.

It was 1997/8 and head offices: those of churches, trade unions, mining companies and the Johannesburg Stock Exchange were dominant in the Johannesburg City Centre—some for more than a century.

After the launch of a new order previously excluded people began to gain prominence. Business owners came into their own as they claimed participation in the socio-political and economic practices of the big city.

Along with the positive came the negative: unemployment increased; poverty grew; Lawlessness and corruption became evident, particularly in the inner city.

Ongoing crimes on the streets of Johannesburg resulted in many formal businesses relocating. The exodus created a new business district, Sandton, a mere fifteen kilometres away. The Johannesburg Stock Exchange (JSE) was one of the last to relocate to Sandton—probably the most notable departure from the inner city.

Organised crime continued to increase and reports of police involvement were later confirmed by various law courts.

Meanwhile, several business and government partnerships were purpose driven to rid cities and society of divisive laws—but despite many efforts, negative discrimination continued to flourish. Laws had changed. The intention was to make society more inclusive.

In time only a small percentage of people, those with the right contacts, got to benefit from new opportunities. Categorising people continued with greater vigour than in the past.

People could not resist labelling one another. Ethnic identity and group allegiances became more important than ability.

§

It was mid-afternoon when I prepared to draft an Affirmative Action Implementation Manual for a client company. Sitting in my office and looking out over the vista from the 25th floor felt different that afternoon. I knew, but had never thought about it—the building across the road, that is; tallest in Africa, the Carlton Centre. It was there where years earlier I had loitered, destitute. Security guards would not let me sit to rest. I called Suzie from a public telephone inside that building. His answer was no, when he could have said yes.

Other memories, like unwelcome visitors, came back to remind me that afternoon.

The building in which I worked was on Commissioner Street. As I looked down from my office the cars seemed a lot smaller. They snaked past the entrance where Devan and I first met on that frosty 11th September morning back in 1981 ... it was nearly seventeen years later.

The country, since 1994, had been experiencing an administrative revolution. We had chucked the old order out and were vesting the new. That South Africa was *alive with possibilities* had become a popular media retort. My clients had requested that I interpret, make the new laws industry specific and write implementation manuals. To transcribe the new affirmative action legislation was my task for the afternoon.

I expected many more companies to request the same. After all, preventing trouble is better than to find a cure. My approach was to prepare with greater focus on the detail—where it is said the devil lives. In other words, more than just the usual background reading was required ...

Johannesburg is the richest city in Africa. New laws and commissions had been created, '... to redress imbalances of the past,' said the powerful politicians.

South Africa was midway through the Truth and Reconciliation Commission. The media revelled in reporting gory detail and brutal atrocities. Families and commissioners who were overcome with emotion had become camera fodder. Horrible crimes were confessed and many of the criminals who committed those atrocities were pardoned. It was said that their gruesome, callous and at time cowardice crimes were politically motivated. The heinous deeds they committed were acts of war ...

"An act of war is not so when it kills a daughter, son and little baby boy," read a poster held by one amongst the protesters at such hearing.

Despite power having shifted from a minority government to a plural representative state, the existing stereotypes remained in intact. In the workplace people who were previously advantaged were being replaced. Those who were not immediately replaced were tasked to train the new employees, many of whom would eventually take their jobs, or become their seniors.

I continued to read various documents and articles in preparation ...

Pieces I read all contained the same racist labels and rhetoric that were applied to divide South Africans when men wearing black homburg hats and dark suits owned the power to act.

We were divided into separate groups back then. Every group had its own territory in those days. The bigger groups were in tribal zones—homelands.

Every group had a label and a set of rules that were unique to that category of people. The homelands were self-governing states and given that they existed inside South Africa did not matter.

The leaders in self-governing states were, save for having dark skins, replicas of their bosses in the mother country, South Africa. They too wore homburg hats and dark suits.

During 1994, when a popularly elected government acquired the power to act, they also, perhaps unwittingly, legitimised the continued use of labels to define citizens.

Inside the cluster of newly liberated groups was a group set to become the advantaged, like the pigs did in *Animal Farm* when they assumed the power to act.

At first the world lauded our achievement. We had shaken hands with the men who wore homburg hats. South Africans had secured their own social freedom. The men, then without their homburgs, were pardoned by the Truth and Reconciliation Commission and several became part of our first truly democratic government, a government of national unity.

Social freedom was ceded to all who lived in South Africa. Famous American Senators toured the country, kissed the tarmac and spoke about South Africa as if they knew what they were talking about. People applauded and had endless dinners ...

Meanwhile, a very dominant part of the economy remained under the control and ownership of a few amongst those who previously enjoyed special privileges.

This was the main reason why South Africa had to have new job reservation legislation. Job Reservation had a brand new label too. It was called, affirmative action. The objective was to create employment, empowerment and ownership opportunities for groups which had been left out in the past. This was one of many reforms, but I was tasked to interpret affirmative action for people who paid for my services.

After reading job reservation rules and comparing it to affirmative action my mind was clear that the core principle of both these programmes were the same.

Affirmative action had become law. This was the reason why my clients requested of me, a specialist in employment law, to draft an implementation manual.

Much as the principles were the same, there were key differences between the two discriminations. The first was that Job Reservation ensured employment for a minority when they owned the power to act in South Africa. Affirmative action, on the other hand, was geared to create employment opportunities and empower the majority. Those who previously benefited were excluded because it is said that they were over-represented at senior levels and in ownership roles.

To further aid the affirmative action objective academic requirements were reduced. Entry requirements for many tertiary courses were reduced on a sliding scale.

The result was that many University graduates were often less than competent. Yet, the same person would, a few years after graduating, be appointed against a senior position.

It had become the turn of those who benefited from job reservation and their children to be left out. In my opinion, the country seemed poised to celebrate mediocrity.

That afternoon ominous dark clouds had gathered in the sky. Thunderstorms and hail during summer are a usual occurrence in Johannesburg. Rumbles inside the clouds usually signalled the beginning of a thunderstorm. The sounds of those rumbles were similar to when people shift big pieces of furniture in an empty hall. The piercing crack of lightning briefly lit the darkened sky.

That sequence repeated two, maybe three times. And then, after a final grumble and a flash of lightning the inevitable cloudburst spewed a torrent of rain. Within an instant the rain was replaced with hailstones. Like falling marbles it would bounce off everything.

Ten minutes later, when it was all over, the city was gridlocked. Drivers were hooting at one another and all cars in the streets had different degrees of damage.

Most traffic lights in Johannesburg flash red whenever it rains. Where were the technicians who previously ensured that traffic lights were thunderstorm-resistant?

Twenty minutes later the roads, which had briefly become canals, were cleared. All that remained of the storm were broken cars, piles of hail and damaged trees set against a beautiful rainbow backdrop.

It is not always that hail accompanied the afternoon thunderstorm—that day it did.

The sun returned and life on the Highveld continued.

My thoughts about the changes in South Africa were encouraged by my task afternoon. After all, we were building a just society and had to correct the inequalities that were visited upon us by various injustices.

For a moment my thoughts wandered to whether there is a difference between justice and fairness. It was not the purpose of my task, I cautioned. My pausing for thought happened intermittently throughout the afternoon.

Those who once enjoyed social advantages must have struggled with being denied. There's was a silent grapple, perhaps a fight. They whispered their fight. Had to, because to speak truth to power could result in further alienation …

Meanwhile, some of the changes, particularly the reinventing of job reservation, had me feeling less than comfortable.

The novella Ma bought at Cranford's Bookshop had grown in my mind. I was experiencing its relevance. In that story, farm animals are an extended metaphor. Initially the animals fought to set themselves free from a cruel farmer's oppressive yoke. I remembered, even though I did not understand much of it at the time, but I recalled how the oppression of those animals made me sad …

Again my mind wondered. Other changes in the country were also beginning to show. There were positives as well: tiny houses were being built to replace crudely constructed wood and iron shacks that many called home; and the poorest of the poor in several townships were given access to running water and electricity. Yet, unemployment increased because there was no stimulus for the growth in business confidence and it seemed that the state was not there.

After careful thought and comparing past laws with the present I realised the similarity between what was unfolding in South Africa and the story about animals, which I had to reread several times.

Perhaps it was just me being me and that I did not understand the difference between fairness and justice.

I thought more about the complexity of creating a non-discriminatory society, particularly given that the new government was insisting, through its practise, that we use those divisive labels.

'What about inspiring people to excel, live out their true potential and contribute to making South Africa great?' were of the questions I posed to myself?

I kept on trying to focus on drafting the document. Given that my work would result in an implementation manual for a policy that I believed to be unfair was beside the point.

How would we become a non-racist country if we discriminated against a minority of South Africans and base such discrimination on skin colour? That was one of my recurring concerns.

In the novella, *Animal Farm*, a dystopian allegory, animals wrestled to be free. The pigs, who had used their power to act, created a favoured group—all other pigs. They changed the rules. Soon the other animals realised that their lives had not improved. The pigs were mimicking the previous farm owner—

More people became unemployed.

News reports of business failures, restructuring and retrenchment increased. The song workers sang was an aching echo: "Senzeni na, senzeni na, 'What have we done, what have we done …'"

The sound of that melancholic song could only be heard by those who listened through the filters of their consciences.

Little else is more moving than the haunting dirge of ordinary South African people singing about their pain, their hunger, their disappointment—

Ma's question about where it will end began to have greater relevance.

I was no longer going to write that afternoon. No—

"You are being too emotional about these matters, Sam," said the recently appointed senior partner. She wore shoes with red-lacquered soles and stood at the window looking out over the city. I smiled. She tapped her newly braided hair. The day had ended and I was packed to go.

To identify with unsuspecting people who were being robbed of their dignity was very emotional, was what I thought when leaving the office that afternoon. Why was I so intent on transcribing a law that contributed to the reinforcement of racism and encouraged the growth in unemployment?

Elected leaders control the power to act in South Africa. Many were once workers—they resisted retrenchment, armed against it and had served long prison sentences because they chose to speak out against inequality.

Mr Jones, the cruel owner in *Animal Farm* was deposed … ***but the mark of a good teacher …***

The South African reality, as I experienced it, was that those who previously enjoyed privileges had become the denied. Again, skin colour was the reason. Unfairness, like labels, had also been legitimised. Many politicians and their tune dancing senior public servants, many of whom contributed to the social freedom, had become less than honourable. Those politicians and public servants who remained true to the ideal of creating a better life for all were few and far between. They remained invisible—for fear of being alienated, I thought. Others said nothing when they had to speak out—like Mr Thompson at Mammy Cynthia's farewell.

Our wonderful president had who had been inaugurated in 1994 gave credence to our constitutional democracy. In his first speech after becoming president of a free South Africa President Mandela said: *"Never, never and never again shall it be that this beautiful land will again experience the oppression of one by another and suffer the indignity of being the skunk of the world. Let freedom reign."*

After our president retired we continued to hope that South Africa would flourish. That was not to be. Unemployment increased regardless. People became polarised and cocooned in their respective group identities. Superior and inferior ethnic group classifications and class consciousness again became the pestilence that disallows non-racialism from vesting in South Africa: *"... that this beautiful land will again experience the oppression of one by another and suffer the indignity ..."* had become an idealistic dream.

We are a non-racist country. It says so in the statutes. Yet, not a single day goes by without there being public use and reiteration of the labels that take us back to our divided past. You see, South Africans have accepted the use of discriminatory labels. Those labels shape our attitude and make us racists and benign discriminators. It shall continue to be the bane between our understanding of racism, multi-racism and non-racism. In South Africa we are unable to speak about one another without adding a racial classification.

'What are you?' was the question that replaced: 'Where do you come from originally?' I knew the desired answer, but I'd feign ignorance and say: "I come from Cape Town." Thereafter I'd listen to the discussion, because they were not interested in where I came from, but to which apartheid group I belong. Those who spoke wrestled to categorise me. The content of their discussions always included my darker skin tone, hair, speech intonation and other physical traits. They never considered whether I could think, or not; whether I was good at my job, or not and whether I wanted to contribute to building a non-racist South Africa. None of that mattered, just the colour of my skin and what label I should wear. South Africa refuses to colour me human.

A new middle class was fast developing. Lucrative business opportunities became the exclusive domain of those who had the right political credentials and contacts. Others were enticed with big salaries. They were appointed against senior jobs for which they did not, in every instance, have the training and experience. The new law dictated that all businesses should appoint employees according to pre-determined race quotas. Failure to comply resulted in companies being penalised.

Instant wealth became reality for a tiny number of those who were excluded in the past; while unemployment increased and poverty worsened.

Sometimes politicians would arrive in convoys of shiny dark cars amidst blaring sirens and flashing blue lights. They were often late. After blaming apartheid for everything that is wrong the politician, before speeding off to another appointment, would assure those in attendance that 'Rome was not built in a day,' but that everything in his or her power was being done to bring relief.

In order to be representative and inclusive the business sector resorted to short cuts. In the workplace, fast tracking became the norm. Very talented dark-skinned people were not fully develop and not yet vested their ability before assuming senior responsibilities. As a result, many failed.

Those who had the ability to do an exceptional job fell foul to entitlement and opportunism. There was no incentive to excel. Highly paid dark skinned professional 'proxy' employees moved from one highly paid job to the next. Every time they would complain that their previous corporate position at a usually well-known multi-national company had the title and most perks, but no responsibility—

Those who failed dismally and who were the cause of many others losing their jobs would be sacked, but not without a severance package that amounted to millions. Ordinary workers earned one week for every year of service.

Many underlying tensions resulted and were whispered about by overlooked employees. These tensions were corroborated when 'Affirmative Appointees' began to fail. In the wake of their failure followed a further rise in unemployment, and a drop in business confidence.

It remains easy to be critical, but what is the constructive solution?

As people from other African countries began to migrate to this promised land of opportunity and fairness, xenophobic attacks began to occur with increasing frequency. "They are taking our jobs!" cried the unemployed.

Angry songs were sung in informal settlements by growing numbers of unemployed people. Their misdirected anger targeted people from other countries—Africans who had arrived to find their opportunity in the country that was *alive with possibilities.'*

The group to which the president and his inner circle belonged was favoured above the rest.

Restrictions against South Africa had been lifted some years earlier and our then retired iconic president continued to be revered wherever he went. He was a global president and we glowed in the wake of his stardom. The world agreed that South Africans had made a miraculous recovery from tyrannical rule by implementing constitutional democracy. South Africa had become the world's sweetheart—but our status was not to last.

Black economic empowerment replaced affirmative action. Later, through an act of parliament a 'new' law, the Broad Based Black Economic Empowerment Act, was promulgated. It was much bigger and much more complex that Job Reservation—the principles upon which it was constructed remained the same. Only special people could understand it and to be rated, by special agencies, companies had to pay a percentage of their income. Without being rated a companies would not be able to trade with one another and the state.

Ever increasing unemployment numbers had no ceiling. The plan to shift ownership from one group to another was supported by experiments to build capacity.

State owned institutions were the first to fail—well-fed politicians blamed apartheid.

My country had set itself a task to redress imbalances but in the process it was sabotaging itself.

Opportunism, entitlement, nepotism, corruption and retribution are all topics that ran rampant through every newspaper I read.

I know about quantitative democracy, but explain that to a family in their one bedroom house with a bed on stones because water swirls around on the floor whenever it rains. The family sits on the bed then—five people. There was no money to buy food, let alone a plug to stop a leak when it rains. Theories are good only when they support reality. In South Africa the reality is that unemployment continues to soar and it corrupts people's dignity.

I remembered how Ma would repeat the same speech every time Jane and I left for school: "We cannot embrace the future properly if we do not make peace with what we did to one another in the past and; that which is done cannot be undone."

Ma nodded her head when she spoke, as if to encourage our agreement. She'd conclude with a lilt in her tone: "When fairness is achieved, then we will have to pool all our talents in order to make South Africa great, all of us." Like a soothsayer Ma would let go of our hands and say: "Go to school and learn so that you are ready to contribute when we are free."

I was working in Johannesburg, and on that afternoon, while looking down onto the City of Gold, my new home, only then did Ma's words finally find resonance and true meaning.

Ma's 'send-off speech', when we left for the faraway school, grew more vivid in my mind.

The past was harrowing and if we did not mind ourselves then the future could be worse.

We were learning to live in Johannesburg. I continued to compare the present with the past.

Job reservation was wrong. My understanding of that wrong dated back to when I was very young—Ma explaining how, as a social worker, she could not find a job. Even though she was experienced, Ma was not appointed against the position of her choice. People who were appointed often had lesser qualifications—the advantage they had was that their skins were not dark like that of my Ma.

I had heard that story too many times. Always in reference to job reservation and how wrong it was. Ma held that it was unfair to reserve jobs for people based on criteria other than ability.

I understood my role to be small in comparison with the bigger need. But that did not deflect from the reality, which was that if businesses grew then more jobs would be created. For people to have dignity must surely be more important to count how many people from different groups are appointed against which position?

Questions I have about job reservation and affirmative action persistently nagged at my conscience.

My past was the only filter through which I could view what was transpiring: that time when Jane was dragged away by the train conductor to travel in another carriage and; what about Ma who had to speak with Mrs Akkerman through a mesh covered window while Jane shopped inside, with Ma's money—all because Jane had a light skin. I was just a boy then.

"There's a difference between non-racism and multi-racism." That is written on the one rand note I keep, for just in case it is forgotten.

Non-racism is when all people are human; and multi racism is when all humans are identified by the colour of their skin and a something that people like to refer to as ethnicity—

One of the most soul destroying experiences occurred when, after offering one unemployed man sitting amongst others on the corner a few hours of work, six men physically fought and argued about whose turn it was to have an opportunity. For those men, some of whom were older than me, desperation had stripped them of dignity.

Is constitutional democracy supposed to create unemployment, prevent business growth and cause people to forgo their dignity?

South Africa was a Police State when I was growing up. We were afraid of the police then; but when I became a man there was more reason to be afraid of those who protect and serve. My experiences with police had never been pleasant. They always sought to 'correct' with force. There seldom was room for logical reasoning. When the country changed most police officers were replaced. Dark skins replaced the light skins. The brutality was never replaced. Corruption and brutality persists. It has become more pronounced and blatant than in the past.

It had become time for me to go home that afternoon. My children were waiting at the aftercare centre.

I refused to draft the manual. It resulted in me being asked to resign.

Chapter Twenty-Two

Conversations in the Renault 4

Ma also came to Johannesburg, but she missed 'our mountain' too much and returned to live on the Cape Flats. Eugene became a man. We love him, more than he will ever know, or realise. He lives in Durban and regularly swims at North Beach, because he may and there is no need for a false name any longer.

Over the years Pa would visit Ma. When he arrived, she said: "Yes, Boy, he comes here and sits on the lounge chair for a while; then leaves again. Often he goes on his way without having said much. It seems that nothing noteworthy changes in the way Pa lives his life, earns his money and does his business. His work remains a secret—but Pa is always working."

Ma acknowledged that though it was difficult, she had forgiven him. Those were not empty words, but evident in the way she treated my Pa. Despite the pejorative memories and much criticism from all who knew, Ma chose to remember the more interesting times, rather than the pain that Pa inflicted on our lives. I always knew that Ma loved Pa beyond the person; that is how it is, and I do not understand why. Perhaps it is not my place. There remains a lot that I do not understand.

Whilst on a short business trip to Cape Town, I found a car. It was one that I always wanted to own. The gear leaver was in the dashboard and that appealed to me when I was a boy. Surfers would arrive on the beach in their Renault 4 cars. Surfboards tied to the roof seemed like an extension of that vehicle. I had to have one someday. That day had arrived.

It was in excellent condition. People laugh and tell me that I have odd taste! I wonder why? Maybe eccentricity is hereditary!

While watching TV in the hotel that night I thought about how to get the old-new car to Johannesburg. The car was to be delivered the following afternoon at the Pinelands City Lodge Hotel, where I had become a regular guest. It was a Thursday. Perhaps it was a good idea to find Pa, was what I thought. He and I could drive my new car to Johannesburg. Both of us were useless at fixing cars when they broke, but we'd be good company while waiting for help!

Pa was at his house. When I got there he would not let me enter, instead he chose for us to speak outside in the street. When I asked him to accompany me, Pa agreed without hesitation to do the 1,400 kilometre trip from Cape Town to Johannesburg. At first I thought that his quick agreement was so that I could leave. We shook hands and then I turned to drive away in my hired car. I heard him say: "Ya! It's exciting!" as he walked back to disappear behind a substantial wooden gate, the entrance to his ample house. Pa seldom showed emotion; even that statement was bland.

He insisted that we meet on the main road, another Victoria Road, this time in Camps Bay and about a kilometre down the slope from his house, next to the sea.

It was five o'clock on the Saturday morning, two days after I had asked Pa to accompany me. The reason not to meet at his house became apparent, but only much later …

At five that morning, Saturday, as the light of day wrestled to replace the darkness, Pa stood in the street as promised. He wore a hat, shirt, jacket, and a pair of formal trousers with matching brown suede shoes. It was not unusual for Pa to wear odd shoes, but that day his shoes matched—the shoelaces were a bit mad but perfect is sometimes boring. At his side was a briefcase and apart from his light complexion, Pa looked like the petrol attendant in Scottburgh, the one who studied English—Zuvarashe—the gentle man who gave me shelter when I had no place to sleep all those years ago. Pa and I greeted each other warmly. That is how we began the fourteen hour journey to my house in the northern suburbs of Johannesburg.

The drive was uneventful, but much more meaningful than I knew at the time. Pa realised the significance of our being together, but he had no intention of discussing or disclosing his thoughts with me. Perhaps it was too private. It had been at least twenty years since we last spent real time together, Pa and I. He was just the same, eccentric as ever. As was usual, from what I remembered, Pa again said the most bizarre things.

At one stage I laughed so much that my stomach ached. Pa kept a straight face, which made what he said funnier. At one stage I briefly left the road and nearly drove into the Karoo veld after one of his quips. It was my Pa again—but that was only what I wished for. His observations continued to be insane. He was mad, my Pa. He noticed the most unnoticeable, pointed and then told a story about it. From time to time he would laugh at his own stories. Speaking to me was easy for Pa because he did not have to repeat before being understood.

The laughter, social, political and economic discussions were all punctuated by news bulletins on the car radio and telephone calls to a mobile phone from my two impatient children. They had then not yet met their grandfather. My favourite girl child, then only four years old, would call and ask: "What does Pa look like, Daddy; and, how many sleeps before you are home?"

"I look like Pa, but he is old, very stupid and his shoelaces do not match!" was my teasing reply.

My favourite boy child, then about eight years old, was concerned only about the car and whether we would arrive home before dark.

After hearing my replies whenever the children called, Pa eventually grumbled: "Ya! What's wrong with those children?"

He never had much time for children, my Pa; probably because he associated children with being teased about his speech defect. The only child towards whom I can remember Pa gravitating was Uncle Flippie's youngest son, Paul. Pa loved him—probably because Paul too had a speech defect.

I knew Pa's politics. My understanding of the political situation in South Africa is derived from having listened to his discussions with Ma and other men. In Pa's life there was only one thing more important than politics: money. He instinctively followed the money. The experience of driving all that way together revealed nothing new about my Pa, nothing that I did not already know. He was just older and more eccentric, but the same man that I had known all those years ago.

There was never a pause between our discussions; it was as if we were intent on cramming all the lost time into those fourteen hours we shared.

"So, what do you think of South Africa today, Pa?" I was baiting him.

It was my turn to drive. He thought for a while before responding with a story that I'd heard being discussed before, but one that in those days had become popular with armchair politicians and only in certain academic circles.

"Ya! Well, a long time ago, Khoi people lived across the whole of Southern Africa. You will find their drawings on rocks in the most far flung parts. Those drawings are the only remnants of the original inhabitants. People have always moved from one part of the world to another, that is how we are. The simple explanation is that the climate shapes what we look like. The first Africans arrived in Europe and on other continents over the past 70,000 years. While there, the generations that followed evolved to suit the climate. Physical changes, like colour pigmentation, slowly started to change. The sun in Europe is not like it is in Africa. Dark skins were no longer a requirement."

"So people who are light-skinned originated in Africa too?"

"Ya! Yes, and because there was greater need they developed tools and other aids—they had to, in order to survive in the colder climate.

"Other Africans moved elsewhere around the continent and the world. It is said that all human beings have strong traits that reflect a common origin in Africa."

"I have heard of that place, Pa. Apparently it is not far from Johannesburg, or is it in East Africa?"

"Ya! And if that is true and if we go back far enough, then everyone was an African at some point in their evolution.

"My question is about 'long ago', how long ago is long ago and how is it justified?"

"Well, I don't know how long 'long ago' is. What do you think, Pa?"

"Ya! I do not know either. There are many factors to take into account before making that determination. What I do know is that the majority groups in South Africa are wrong to claim that they should have more rights to this land than others.

"It is said that 'long ago' the Khoi were the majority group in this part of Africa. And that forefathers of those who today claim to be the majority or land owners killed the Khoi in order to occupy the land they lived off. If there is truth in what is said then my question is: whose ancestral land is this Southern Africa really?"

Pa paused as if to contemplate whether he had to say more.

"Ya! Can you see the relevance of my earlier question about a need to define 'how long, long ago' is? Does the land belong, I mean, does it really belong to the groups who today say that it is their ancestral home?"

Pa's argument was drawn from a particular insight. I knew that he had paraphrased a lot of the detail. That was his way, and to the unsuspecting it sometimes appeared rude. We discussed many things on that journey. Much of what he said was informative, but many of Pa's ideas had stagnated, even expired.

At times I sensed that Pa was posturing, like a snob with no substance. The picture I had created of my father was not there for some of the time. Pa was different from what I had imagined. The reality, while driving in my little old-new car, was different from what I had envisaged. I felt a bit sorry for Pa. The only person who would understand that feeling was Jane, but even though she lives in my head there was never an answer when I required her opinion.

Yes, I felt sorry for that man because he had become little more than a figment of my imagination. The Pa with whom I was driving was a different man from the one that I remembered. For the first time in my life, perhaps because of the disappointment that had become my reality, but for the first time ever, I also felt sorry for me, for I did not belong, not even to my own father. We had the same look, shared some of the same madness, and when my wife took pictures I saw that it was true, we even had the same body postures, but yet we were so very different. That feeling nagged at me for many years following its realisation. The recurring feeling of being too alone for comfort frequently knocks on the door to my soul.

I recall how a younger Pa told me not to do something only because others did it. And, it was the same man whom I overheard speaking in French to his brother when he said: "Revenge is best-served-cold ..." and "I think that we are popping the cork before the champagne has chilled ..." I had no idea what they were discussing, but that someone was going to get hurt was guaranteed. I have seen enough bloodstains. All was not as it seemed.

But there he was. It was his turn to drive. Pa did too, while continuing to share his insights about the country.

I disagreed with Pa about much of what he said. Often what he said would end with who was going to make the most money. There was seldom fairness reflected in his sentiments.

"… but what about building a capacity so that those who do the work can share in what they achieve? Why do the industrialists always take more and give less to those who produce?"

"Ya! That is a different discussion. It has to do with risk and invested capital. That is how capitalism works; the more risk you take determines how much you stand to lose, or gain."

"Yes, that may be so, Pa, but it is also the reason why we will never win the war against poverty. The rich getting richer on the back of impoverished people is just another form of slavery. Money, greed and opportunism knows no colour."

"Ya! That may also be true, but reality will always dictate, so stop swimming against the tide," said the man who once told me not to do things only because others did so.

I could see unfairness in our constitutional democratic society. We were all free. That is what we achieved, social freedom, but none of us worked so that some could be freer than others.

"Yes Pa, reality does dictate," said I, in response to Pa who seemingly swims with the tide while wearing odd laces in his shoes and two shirts because his briefcase was full. "But whose reality is it, Pa? We in South Africa insist on correcting the past. Is that what freedom should do; does freedom have to focus on retribution, and in the process spawn unemployment, or should it create a better life for all? What do you think of the unemployment in South Africa, Pa?"

"Ya! Most of the people do not have skills. How can you employ people who do not have skills?"

Unemployment reached embarrassing highs and our currency tumbled to record lows. Pa tried to justify it all, but he was out of touch with reality, that was my opinion.

When I was little Ma insisted that Jane and I understand that our success would not be inevitable: "You may have talents, everyone has talents, but you have to work hard otherwise you will be average, and average is never good enough."

"But Pa, people do not acquire skills by breathing, they have to be taught. Many of the people who had the skills were forced to retire. Their sin being that they were privileged in the past and therefore had to make way for those who were denied. The unfortunate part is that those once privileged people retired together with their skills, experience and without having taught anyone. How do you teach experience anyway?"

"Ya! Punishing those who had advantages in the past is also not right. Two wrongs do not make one right."

297

I was surprised at Pa's response. It was only the second time that I witnessed Pa being in agreement, the first being when he agreed to drive with me.

It was March of 2002 when Pa and I made that trip together, from Cape Town to Johannesburg.

To be a beneficiary of special favour because of my darker skin felt the same as having to compete using another person's name. It was akin to the sale of my soul. I sold my soul by surfing in a competition that did not want me. I did not belong. My ability did not matter because I did not belong. Although embarrassed, like a prisoner who professes innocence I too justified: "... but I can surf, so why should I not have competed?" That was dumb. It was dumb to have participated. My integrity should have been more important than to surf among those who 'belong' and then, afterwards, having to retire on a junkyard veranda and sleep between tyres, like a dog. What has changed?

§

I resolved, after that surf contest, never again to wear a label and never again to seek appointment unless it was on merit.

That which people did to one another in the past cannot be fixed by special favour or act of retribution; it is also not possible to unsay something, because what is said cannot be unsaid. We can, however, pool our resources, skills, experience and ability to create a better tomorrow. Our social freedom allows us that choice. It is also not possible to build a wonderful country if it is on the back of laws that cause pain to the children and grandchildren of those who earlier inflicted cruelty. As long as group identity continues to be legislated there shall always be a barrier to us being one nation. It is not right to hold the young prisoner because of what a number of their parents and grandparents did and supported.

Our country will grow if we stimulate competition and harvest the best talent. Instead, of our talented people are forced to make their mark on the world from other countries. It is often not by choice. How are we ever going to win if there is legislation that limits the strength of our potential? Meanwhile, we live with at least the same levels of discrimination and racism as before. However, racism is but one form of discrimination. Our reality is that we continue to divide people by the labels we enforce and encourage. It starts with the labels from our ugly past that we have legitimised in the new order—as we did when policies of racial discrimination determined how and where we lived.

There is a new upwardly mobile middle class. Their now privileged children are chauffer driven in security enhanced cars to private schools. On the other side, where the same sun heats, the squalor that results from poverty is also increasing. Dignity is lost *en masse* in my South Africa, where it has become dangerous to speak the truth, particularly about those who now have the power to act.

Unemployment causes desperation and the reality is that it is escalating. We persistently conflate sustainable job creation with temporary jobs and claim that it alleviates unemployment. The Broad Based Black Economic Empowerment Act is consistently amended to favour the 'majority'. Yet, there are now more ordinary persons who are unemployed because business growth, one of the natural creators of more jobs, is fast declining. Where is it all going to end?

I remember what it felt like, being chased off the reserved beach. The man who chased me off Scottburgh Beach did not belong there either. I was just a young boy then, but the taste of humiliation had already become a familiar flavour. Why would I want to be part of inflicting the same pain on others? It was inflicted on me when my complexion mattered more than my ability to become a world champion surfer. Why would I want to deny others merely because I had been denied; or now, because the roles have been reversed and people with dark skins have the power to act? It was not right then, how can it be right now?

He was probably right, my Pa: two wrongs do not make a right. Maybe my mathematics is not so bad, after all!

The debate between Pa and me ensued for some time throughout that journey. I tried to stop, but it just boiled over, there in my little old-new car.

"Ya! I think that your head is filled with hot air—rubbish! You are obsessive about your own experiences," said Pa. Yet, all I did was to assess the reality through the filter of what I knew.

We drove past towns that Pa recognised: "Ya! Look, it's Philoppolis! The pigeons were released there, in that town, for Federation races."

I remembered that too, the time when the yardmen gazed in admiration at the flock of birds that flew across the mountain.

Throughout the rest of that journey he cracked the odd joke, my Pa did. We laughed heartily. Pa's sense of humour was crazy but I appreciated it. I understood it and continued to laugh out loud all the time. "They are a pack of lies, every single one of his stories." That was Ma's response to his humour. It was always a situational story that he created. I laughed again until my belly ached: his stories were farcical, and all the characters were always stupid. But then there was a knight in shining armour to rescue them from self-destruction.

We finally arrived at my home. It was dark by then. My boy child was withdrawn when he met Pa. My girl was exuberant. She clambered all over Pa as if he were a new toy. All Pa said was: "Ya! Don't do that." Even my young child knew not to refer to Pa's different sound. I felt almost whole that evening.

We took Pa to Pretoria, the capital city of South Africa, to government buildings and to good restaurants.

On the fourth day Pa announced that he wished to return to the Cape. He had to work. Pa always had to work.

At Johannesburg Airport we shook hands and I thanked him for the time we had together.

"Ya! I'll see you shortly."

He walked away and I watched until Pa disappeared around the corner to board for Cape Town—he did not turn to wave one last time.

On my birthday that year, several months after Pa's visit, he called. I was in the same office, on the 25th floor, when we spoke briefly.

Weeks later an envelope arrived in the mail. It contained photos that Pa had taken of my children. In an accompanying letter he informed me of a new marriage—his. I knew then why Pa did not invite me into his house. He had married the woman I saw him with at the beach the day our house was emptied.

It was another first for me: the first time I received a letter from Pa. I did not want to have any part in Pa's new union. That was why our fresh contact reverted to indirect communication, via Ma, who told me when she saw him, and Eugene did the same. That was enough.

"When last did you hear from, or see Pa, Ma?"

"Oh heavens, I don't know. He visits frequently. Sits here, but never says anything about his life, just the same old story about working, always working. He does not look happy and he says less than before. Pa arrives unannounced, on a motorbike, and before long he goes off again. He seems troubled, your Pa does, but continues not to speak much. Eugene visits Pa; ask him to tell more?"

I accessed Pa's file in the registry office at the high court when doing research about what procedure to follow in order to process a divorce. Therein I found a copy of his previous divorce order, notice of his marriage to Ma and the police report after an investigation had been conducted into Brenda and Anne's death.

I paused to read that police report:

It stated that Pa had been a frequent visitor at the house where Anne and Brenda lived. The report also revealed that Pa visited the girls several times per week. It stated that he had done electrical repairs to the cooker a few days before the explosion. Among the debris was a handwritten receipt from a shop in Camps Bay. It was there where the gas cylinder which caused the explosion was refilled. Pa was the only one who would have brought a gas cylinder from Camps Bay to Woodstock when there were several gas suppliers within walking distance from where Brenda and Anne lived.

They used that gas cylinder for cooking—it exploded and caused their deaths on the Friday night before Jane and I arrived back from school. Strange too, was that Pa did not visit Anne and Brenda on the Friday of the explosion. Ma, Brenda and Anne spent the evening cooking.

The police report detailed steps taken by investigators who compiled the evidence that sought to link an alleged perpetrator to a crime. There was insufficient proof for the construct of a case against Pa, the only suspect. The investigation process revealed evidence linking Pa to what could have been the basis for criminal charges. It was not enough to charge him. The police dossier featured a concluding piece that served to cite the cause as an accident and/or due to negligence. The matter could not be tested. The evidence was too circumstantial. It would have been a waste of time to try and find guilt beyond reasonable doubt. Poor evidence was what the reports stated in conclusion.

The police investigation included a report of when Pa was questioned about the incident. Other pieces of evidence that further implicated Pa were also included in the police report. I do not know whether he was subsequently arrested or charged. What I do know is that the matter never went to trial, or if it did then the case was dismissed because of the circumstantial evidence.

That is how the investigation was concluded. Pa had been exonerated.

Despite having had several opportunities to reopen the investigation into the deaths of Anne and Brenda I decided to have the matter rest. My decision is unsubstantiated too, but is probably so because what is done cannot be undone.

Brenda had always been withdrawn and seldom participated in conversations. She preferred to write in her diary, which Ma read after her death.

Chapter Twenty-Three

Another Funeral

It was a Saturday morning, 2003. I was in a northern suburb of Johannesburg, where we had been living since 1997. My morning started with a long run and afterwards I set out to plant my tomato seedlings. The rest of the family were out, probably shopping. The home telephone rang. Boris and Bess were blocking the doorway. By the time I reached there the ringing had stopped. *Oh well, whoever it was will call back,* was what I thought. I clapped my hands and shouted at the dogs to get out of the way. As I got back to planting my seedlings the home telephone rang for a second time. With soil between my fingers I tore inside to answer. The path was unobstructed:

"Hello?"

Following a brief pause the person at the other end said: "… is that you Sam?"

"Yes, Melinda?" I would recognise that voice anywhere.

"Yes, it's me."

She sounded concerned.

"How are you; why are you calling me, is everything okay; how's your mother; and your brothers?"

Melinda was a stage manager when I worked in the Performing Arts industry. To my barrage of questions she responded: "My mother eventually died from 'that thing' she always complained about—breast cancer. My brothers are the same and the younger one, whom I raised, he is doing very well. How are you?"

"I am sorry to hear about your mother. Sorry is so empty …"

"But how are you Sam?"

"You keep asking Melinda, I am fine; I am fine, thank you for asking, but how are you?"

I heard an unusual sound to her tone.

"Why, what is the matter? Why are you sounding so worried, Melinda? Why are you calling my home line and not my mobile phone? What's the matter?"

"Your mobile phone seems to be turned off, but are you sure that all's well with you, Sam?"

I was becoming anxious, suspecting that something ghastly had happened, something about which I should have known.

"Yes, I'm really fine, Melinda. But what is the matter? Please tell me?"

"It is, Sam, I've just seen a notice in the *Weekend Argus* newspaper announcing the death of Samuel Arthur Levy of Camps Bay. It is the same name as yours, isn't it?"

"Oh, it must be my father … Eugene, my brother, said that my Pa was ill. Let me check with my mother. I'll call you later."

"Okay, good luck."

I paced up and down the little passage alongside our home telephone, to get the news I had received about Pa's death to settle. I instinctively knew that it was true, that Pa had died.

It took me twenty minutes to gather my thoughts, myself and then only could I call Ma. She was always happy to hear from me. I was always happy to hear Ma's voice. She has a distinctive voice. We didn't speak all that often but there was no need because we knew each other like that and we have a long history of being together, even though we are apart. I was never one to call Ma without good reason. That Saturday morning, after greeting, I asked Ma whether she knew anything about the death notice.

"What death notice, Boy?"

"Samuel Arthur Levy, Ma. My friend, Melinda called to say that there's a death notice in the *Weekend Argus*."

"Oh! No, Boy! Say it is not true!" Ma paused and then said: "Let me see what I can find out. I shall call the number he gave me and let you know. Oh please—say it is not true!"

After speaking to Ma I did not know what to do with myself. My family were not yet home so I returned to the garden, where I had been before Melinda's call.

"Oh please, say it is not true," was ringing in my ears. I sat on the low garden wall and looked down at the wilting seedlings. The telephone remained silent for a long time. Enough time for me to think through the meaning of my father and his death, and whether it was my place to be critical about how he chose to live his life.

About an hour later, the telephone rang again. It was Ma, her voice quivering as she confirmed that my Pa had died. I recognised her weep. It was the same as when Anne, Brenda and then again when Jane had died. Why should we be less sad when a naughty man dies? We cry because we are people and that is what we do when the hurt is bigger than us.

I called Melinda to thank her for the effort and for being my friend. I like to thank people for being my friend. Sometimes I am not the best friend. My family returned home. At first I did not tell them about my father's passing; I needed more time. There was apprehension. I was afraid; I feared that Pa's selfishness would haunt me even after he had died.

"He is not their father," was what I told myself. "He is my father. I did not choose him, but he is my father."

I anticipated talk about Pa having been a poor father, but he was *my father*! I could not find conviction in the accusation that my father was bad. To practise an injustice against an unjust action is also unfair.

I had taken nothing and expected nothing from my father. He occasionally apologised to Ma when he had wronged her. It was never a remedy or salve, for the hurt he caused was too big. "Sorry, you say! Sorry is not medicine" was what Ma said when Pa apologised.

It is strange, but the flawed example set by Pa had taught me that being a father is an honour, one that I try hard to wear with pride.

I spent the better part of that Saturday out in the garden. The times when Pa had been absent remained a vivid memory. Often his eccentric manner would cause me to be embarrassed, I remembered that too.

As my thoughts wandered back from that time to the present I continued the drive through Johannesburg's peak hour traffic to fetch my children at their aftercare class.

The continuing thoughts were of when I was very young. My yearning was to fill the days spent at home with my father. After all, we lived at the faraway school much longer than most other children did. I must have been about nine or ten years of age when the obsession to be with my father began to wane. That he was not interested was probably what I realised. I remembered being in the garden playing with our dog when Pa got into his car to drive somewhere. I ran alongside the moving car, begging: "Please Pa, I want to go with you, Pa, please!" All the while I hoped that he would stop for me to get in. Instead, Pa slowly increased speed until my little-boy legs could no longer keep up. My thumb became a substitute for Pa that day—everything always was a substitute for Pa. I trudged back home that afternoon, on a dusty untarred road and in a world misted over by my tears.

That was one of the many vivid memories I carry in my head and which was regurgitated on the day he died. It felt as if Pa had just driven away from me again. The consolation then was that Pa returned at night, back when I was just seven or eight and home on holiday from the faraway school. He was not going to be returning any longer, but the reality was: Pa had stopped returning home a long time ago.t

What else could I do, but slowly arrange those tomato seedlings in the soft, fertile soil of the Highveld? My concluding thoughts were that Pa was a cold and callous man, who did not really care for Jane, or me; who never showed any emotion, or affection; and who was ever only interested in himself. He had been hurt in life; and lived without care for those whom he harmed in return. Pa was selfish and greedy. Like those who support and benefit from injustice, unfairness, opportunism and the inhumane policies that infest a land with such beauty, my South Africa. He was my father though, and I too am not above reproach. How then could I judge my Pa? He was dead and I had to continue. I felt a need to ensure that others did not experience that which had been done to me.

The funeral service was held in Cape Town on the Monday morning. I arrived on the Sunday evening.

I called Mrs Andreucci because there was no-one else who cared to listen without judging my dead father. Most people did not know that I had a father. Many had errant fathers. People who did not know thought that my father too was long gone. Mrs Andreucci and I spoke for a long time that Sunday evening. She reminded me that there were many who face similar circumstances. It was true, but it was not right, neither did it make me feel better. It is unacceptable that parents, particularly men, are allowed to misbehave and take from their spouses without care and responsibility. They know, those men know that it is not right what they do, but yet …

On the Monday morning I rented a multi-passenger vehicle and fetched many of the remaining people who featured in this story. Those friends who were alive and living in Cape Town all attended Pa's funeral. The service was held in a Methodist Church on Main Road, Sea Point, just a block away from the Sea Point Pavilion Pool, where Mr Izak de Kock had been replaced by Mrs Mfufu Siyoli.

The church was filled with people whom I did not know. We took random seats; Ma sat with Eugene. Charles was there too. The body Pa had inhabited lay in a coffin at the front of the church. People filed past, making it a gesture of goodbye, possibly an inquisitive gesture too, but who am I to judge their motives?

Pa had died from colon cancer, a condition that had plagued him for more than a decade. He knew about the ailment when we travelled together to Johannesburg. True to character he had elected not to discuss his condition with me. Pa had received extensive treatment and had been hospitalised on more than one occasion. The medical staff and he were the only people who knew that his cancer was terminal. Even when he visited Ma for what, with hindsight, might have been in order to find solace, Pa had failed to disclose his illness.

I looked to see where Ma was seated inside that stone church. She was in a middle pew, on the right side of the church, near the windows. Old friends sat closer while other people continued to file by and gawk at my Pa's face as he lay in the coffin. It was not the same coffin that was delivered to Ma's house in Mitchell's Plain.

We were at the funeral of Samuel Arthur Levy, my father, who shared his name with me.

When everyone was seated and as the undertaker was preparing to close the coffin, I saw Ma slowly walk up the outside aisle. I joined, to support her. Perhaps that was what a son should do, I thought. While the congregation were singing the familiar 'Abide with Me', Ma was at the coffin fixing Pa's eccentric beard for one last time. It was her last, almost private moment with him. My heart ached as I stood next to Ma who looked in and saw the body of a man. He had lost so much weight that he resembled me in photos taken during a surfing competition, save for his grey beard.

In a near whisper, Ma leaned over and spoke to the corpse: "Ai, Samuel. That it has to end like this. Look at you now. Look at how much weight you've lost." Ma paused to observe the dignity of that moment. The other people did not matter. I continued to stand quietly next to her as she straightened more of Pa's beard. "Why were you so naughty, Samuel? Why? You were such a naughty man ... you were such a naughty father, but I can't help myself for loving you. Bye-bye." Ma then threw her hands up in the air. It was her symbolic act of rent as drawn from the old custom when Jews, at the news of death, would tear their garment, usually a shirt. I remembered the story Ma told about when Zaideh Levy died: on being informed of their Father's death how she watched while Uncle Pierre and Pa were rending their shirts in the custom of Keriah. Pa had lost much of who he was all because he chose to be a naughty man.

The Methodist Minister stood in silence before starting the funeral service. Some truths were told, other accounts were tales created by Pa. People there believed both. I recognised two stories from everything that was said that day:

1. That Pa had led many separate lives; and
2. That he always wore a flower in his lapel, usually a carnation backed by a small branch from a fine-leafed fern.

In the eulogy it was explained that Pa's previous wife had died. Pa's other sons, grown men, were there with their respective families. I had met them many years earlier, before they had families of their own. We do not have a relationship.

Not only did Pa and I share the same names, but also the same look. The cousin who spoke at the funeral did not acknowledge me. I did not belong.

The burial ended at a lonely grave near a big tree in the sandy soil of the Wolraad Woltemade cemetery, in Maitland, Cape Town. As tradition would have it, the men used spades to fill the hole once the coffin had been lowered into the ground. There were a few uncomfortable greetings among the cousins and half-brothers and slight smiles between those who did not know one another. I speak for a living, but never spoke at my own father's funeral and it bothers me to this day.

Charles, Eugene and I have not been back to visit Pa's grave. Ma and Auntie Liza have: "... but there's not even a mark where he lays, Boy, it's just flat ..."

The End

Epilogue

Many of the stories contained in this book are factually correct and a few are embellished. Names, places, detail and some of the sequences have been altered. All the characters are based on actual people. In every instance I have defined the featured personae as close as possible to the individual upon whom the role is based.

Ma celebrated her 92nd birthday on 15 August 2014. Fifteen guests gathered to have lunch on one of the more progressive wine estates in the Stellenbosch region of Cape Town. The farm owner presented Ma with a bottle of their finest wine while the guests, who included Auntie Liza, Charles and Sam, looked on. Mr and Mrs Andreucci and others who feature in the story were there too.

Mrs Andreucci sang as she has done since the annual celebration of this birthday started, back when Ma turned 80. This time there was a special request —she sang 'Funny Valentine'.

When it became Ma's turn to speak Sam helped her to stand up, for her knees are no longer as good as they once were. Her speech was articulate, but brief. After thanking every one for the effort they made to be present, Ma concluded by saying: "I no longer belong to you; I belong to the God of Life."

She's okay, Ma is okay.

Her memory is no longer what it used to be. Sam calls her from time to time, but sometimes Ma gives her mobile telephone away: "… to someone who needed it more than I do, Boy," she'd say.

During telephone conversations something Ma says sends Sam's memory back to long ago. He would become silent and Ma would say: "What's the matter, Boy, why are you not talking? Are you there? Don't put the phone down … because I have not yet finished…" She'd try to talk the hurt away.

Mammy Cynthia and Khokho died some years ago.

Sam has lost contact with Thami, Precious and Mr Thompson. He has not returned to visit the faraway school.

Father Terry and Sam talk from time to time.

Sam is a specialist in employment law. He persistently argues that to promote persons on the basis of skin colour and not ability is counter-productive; an unfair law, because it denies South Africa the opportunity to benefit from all its talent: "We cannot fix the wrong which was committed in the past by doing the same ...

"I want to be part of an enabling society, one that serves to encourage all people. The proliferation of entitlement, shameless opportunism without merit and blatant corruption holds back the growth potential of my country.

"I shudder at the thought of where it will end."

Thank you for reading *The Blue Suitcase*.